Designing for the 21st Century

Designing for the 21ˢᵗ Century
Interdisciplinary Question and Insights

Edited by Prof. Tom Inns

GOWER

© Tom Inns, December 2007

First published: December 2007

Published by
Gower Publishing Limited
Gower House
Croft Road
Aldershot
Hampshire GU11 3HR
England

Ashgate Publishing Company
Suite 420
101 Cherry Street
Burlington, VT 05401-4405
USA

Tom Inns has asserted his moral right under the Copyright, Designs and Patents Act, 1988, to be identified as the author of this work.

British Library Cataloguing in Publication Data
Designing for the 21st Century : Interdisciplinary Questions and Insights
    1. Design
    I. Inns, Tom
    745.4
    ISBN-13: 9780566087370

Library of Congress Control Number: 2007936938

Design and Layout
Victoria Hale, Gary Gowans, Dave Herbert

Printed and bound in Great Britain by MPG Books Ltd, Bodmin, Cornwall.

Overleaf
Image courtsey of Gus Colvin

Dedication

This book is dedicated to my Dad, Prof. Frank Inns, whose designs have improved the lives of so many throughout the Third world.

Contents

Contents *continued*

Acknowledgements

The Designing for the 21st Century Research Initiative is the result of an energetic contribution of time, mind and activity from many individuals and organisations. Thank you to everybody who has made an input to the work, in particular:

The AHRC and EPSRC for their vision in committing to the Initiative and to the staff in both organisations who have nurtured the Initiatives activities, in particular: Tony McEnery, Alicia Greated, Alison Henry, Gail Lambourne, Anne Sofield and Simon Glasser from the AHRC and Elizabeth Hylton, Andrew Clark, Jason Green, Stan Fowler, Paula Duxberry from the EPSRC.

The Advisory Group who have helped direct the Initiative through Phase 1 and Phase 2. In particular Rachel Cooper (Chair) who was instrumental in actually creating the Initiative, Stuart Walker, Bill Gaver, Alan Short, Stuart MacDonald, Fiona Lettice, Stephen Scrivener, David Humphries, Geoff Kirk and Andrea Siodmok.

Lesley Morris and the Design Council for advice and generous support of Initiative events.

All those who have contributed to the extensive peer review process associated with the Initiative and to those who made a considerable time commitment in sitting on commissioning panels for Phase 1 and Phase 2 projects, namely: Rachel Cooper, Stephen Scrivener, Chris Luebkeman, Rose Luckin, Sebastian Macmillan, Alex Duffy, Brian McClelland, Penny Sparkle, David Harrison, Colin Burns, Felicity Goodey, Alison Starr, Elizabeth Burton and Stephen Cage.

The Principal Investigators and researchers who bought the concept of the Phase 1 research clusters alive during 2005 and contributed to all the events organised through the Initiative Directors office.

Those that have authored chapter contributions for this book, taking the time to reflect on their activities and capture their thoughts in writing.

I would also like to thank: Suzie Duke, Fiona Martin, Gillian Steadman and their team at Gower Publishing Ltd for guiding us through the book writing process.

Dave Herbert and Gary Gowans, from the School of Design at Duncan of Jordanstone College of Art and Design, for both their design expertise and their generous guidance on the intricacies of typography.

All my colleagues at Duncan of Jordanstone College of Art and Design who have given me the mental space and support to undertake the role of Initiative Director, particularly Jeanette Paul, Seaton Baxter, Mike Press, Caroline Peters, Cathy Brown and Georgina Follett.

The biggest thank you has to be reserved for Initiative Co-ordinator, Vicky Hale, who over many hours, days, weeks and months has wrestled contributions from 60 authors into a meaningful format (whilst maintaining good humour, a considerable feat!)

And finally, both Vicky and I would like to say thank you to our loved ones for their support throughout this Initiative and book writing journey. Big hugs for Gavin from Vicky, and for Justine, Archie, Fergus and Ruby from me.

Prof. Tom Inns
Initiative Director
Designing for the 21st Centuy

Preface

Once you enter its world Design becomes a passion. For me it began
in 1973 as an undergraduate on a new and very innovative
Multidisciplinary Design course. I discovered I had the skill and
imagination to create something not only visually interesting but also
functional and useful, and had a way to improve aspects of the world
around me. As so many (young and possibly naïve) designers had done
before me, I wondered why so few people understood the power of
design. Ever since I have been on a mission to illustrate the value of design
and designers as professionals, as educators and as researchers. Indeed
I realised there was very little design (other than engineering design)
research undertaken in universities and very little funding to do it.

When I began my research career it was the Engineering and Physical
Sciences Council (EPSRC), I turned to (well actually its predecessor
Science and Engineering Research Council in 1993). Gradually EPSRC
funded more design research, especially as it funded sector related work in
manufacturing and construction. With the welcome formation of the Arts
and Humanities Research Board (later Council) another opportunity arose
to fund design research, especially when related to the creative industries.
Having been closely connected through my own research and roles on
EPSRC and AHRC panels and committees, I used every opportunity to
promote design research. I was convinced there was value in funding
research that addressed design research from every angle. I was therefore
thrilled when AHRC and EPSRC joined forces to fund 'Designing for
the 21ˢᵗ Century' as a research initiative, and very happy to promote
and support its development, through the appointment of Tom Inns as
Programme Director, the creation of an Advisory Group to the launch
of the call for proposals.

Tom has led the programme with enthusiasm, energy and professionalism, whilst we have been guided by an Advisory Group championing the programme and advising Tom and the Research Councils. As Tom says in his introduction we did not have a clue what might emerge, yet this book is evidence of the startlingly rich picture, with the emergence of new directions and new roles for designers, researchers and others working in the field of design.

Change is ever present, as the challenges of technology, environment and society demand our continuous attention and we struggle with issues of complexity, we see that the science, social science and humanities need a means of working together. Design research provides the orchestration, the systemisation and visualisation to bring together the disciplines to build bridges to the future. Such research will provide the evidence and insights upon which professional designers, industry and society can create solutions and contribute to global wellbeing.

This book is just the beginning. The programme continues and we look forward to a continuous flow of papers and books illustrating the value of design and design research.

Prof. Rachel Cooper
Chair
Designing for the 21st Century Advisory Group

what will the design disciplines look like in 2020?

Introduction
Prof. Tom Inns (Duncan of Jordanstone College of Art and Design, University of Dundee)

The Designing for the 21st Century Initiative journey began for me on a sunny day in July 2004. I had been invited to London for an interview for the role of Initiative Director. I was asked to make a presentation outlining my vision for design in the 21st century. Having originally trained as an engineer, worked in design practice, studied at an art college, directed a design research centre and with recent experience of teaching design in a business school I felt I might have some sense of the future of design. For the interview I cranked my mind and tried to broaden and then broaden again my view on where design might be heading in the 21st century. Staring at my presentation now, exactly 3 years on all I can say is nothing could have prepared for me how broad and interconnected the future opportunities for design might be. This book will hopefully communicate some sense of this territory through the words of a large team of researchers who spent time during the 2005 calendar year exploring future issues and research questions that might confront design in a 21st century setting. In total 21 projects were supported in Phase 1 of the Initiative, each one of these projects has contributed a chapter to this book.

In order to make sense of this work this chapter starts with an overview of what the Designing for the 21st Century Research Initiative is and how it is structured. The chapter then explores some of the lessons and insights that can be harvested from Phase 1 of this 5-year programme of research. Firstly, the generic journey taken by the researchers within each chapter is examined, this is useful as every project represents an interdisciplinary discourse over a 12-month period. There is a lot to be learned from the way the projects have engaged audiences, explored knowledge domains and harvested insights. The chapter then suggests a number of ways in which we can make sense of where design might be going. Many of the authors suggest ways of extending the knowledge domains of existing design disciplines, others report on the development of new design

[1] GREAT BRITAIN. Research Councils UK. Available at: http://www.rcuk.ac.uk/research/multidis/default.htm

[2] GREAT BRITAIN. Treasury, 2005. *Cox Review of Creativity in Business*. London: Stationary Office.

strands and the need for bridging or metadesign disciplines, throughout the book new interests in design beyond the traditional of existing design disciplines are also frequently mentioned. The role of the designer in 21st century settings is also explored. Six roles for the 21st century designer are described, each linked to insights from the collective work of the Initiative's Phase 1 cluster projects.

The chapters have been loosely ordered according to their topic of enquiry. Although each chapter covers similar territory, namely; background, activities and insights, the style of writing varies considerably. This reflects the many academic conventions associated with the broad range of disciplines represented in the book. Some of the contributions embody the style of an academic paper, others report in an essay form. In all chapters authors have been encouraged to reference carefully, a key value of a text like this being to quickly navigate through the literature associated with a specific topic or zone of enquiry.

What is the Designing for the 21st Century Research Initiative?

Academic research in the UK is supported by a number of research councils, each covering their own respective portfolio of disciplines and subject interests. The councils provide funding for research through a broad portfolio of project grants and studentships. Increasingly there is recognition that many of the problems, issues and opportunities that confront society can only be explored through an interdisciplinary research approach. As a result there are an increasing number of collaborative research programmes being supported jointly by these research bodies. In the words of Research Councils UK,[1] the body that represents all of the UK research councils: '. . . *novel interdisciplinary research is needed to solve many, if not all, of the next decade's major research challenges.*'

This approach is clearly highly relevant to current developments in the discipline of design. In the UK the Cox Review[2] has recently reported on the role design and creativity have to play in building the UK's national competitiveness. Like many reports before, the review concludes creativity and design have an important role to play, but only when integrated with technology and business, that is, driven by an interdisciplinary approach.

If we examine design in the 21st century we can quickly see why this might be the case, all around us what we are designing is changing. New technologies support the creation and embodiment of new forms of product and service; new pressures on business and society demand the design of solutions to increasingly complex problems, sometimes local often global in nature; customers, users and stakeholders are no longer passive recipients of design, expectations are higher, increased participation is often demanded.

Design practice needs to be highly adaptive and innovative to meet the needs of this rapidly changing operating environment. Generating the new knowledge and understanding needed to support these developments requires a collaboration of minds and provides some clear challenges for those engaged in design research.

The Designing for the 21st Century Research Initiative was conceived in response to these demands for new understanding in the design domain. The Initiative is jointly supported by the Engineering and Physical Sciences Research Council (EPSRC), who have an established track record for funding design research, mainly within engineering and technological contexts, and the Arts and Humanities Research Council (AHRC), who have a responsibility for supporting design research within an art and design context.

The AHRC and the EPSRC both started considering a programme directed towards interdisciplinary design research in 2002. Following consultation with representatives from the UK design research community the Designing for the 21st Century Initiative was formally announced in March 2004 with a call for Phase 1 research cluster project proposals.

The AHRC and EPSRC have each committed £3.25 million to fund the Initiative activities between January 2005 and December 2009. The total budget of £6.5 million has been split between two phases of research. £1 million has been used to support the Phase 1 research cluster projects; £5.5 million is being used to fund Phase 2 research projects. Across both phases the Initiative has the following aims:

- To help build a new diverse research community with a common interest in 21st century design.
- To help stimulate new ways of design thinking to meet the challenges of designing for 21st century society.
- To help support leading edge design research that is self-reflective, socially aware, economically enterprising and internationally significant.

The chapters in this book describe both the journey and insights generated through the 21 Phase 1 cluster projects supported by the Initiative.

The Phase 1 research cluster call, announced in March 2004, was launched to support cross-sector and cross-disciplinary networking activities through the formation of research clusters. In doing this, the aim was to build new relationships within the design research community, particularly between design disciplines and groups sharing common ground but with limited previous opportunity for collaboration.

In June 2004, 129 proposals for Phase 1 research clusters were submitted. 21 of these proposals were selected for support by a commissioning panel in September 2004. Between January and December 2005 each of these funded research clusters organised a series of workshops, seminars and meetings to support the development of design understanding. Table 1 provides an overview of each of the Phase 1 research cluster projects; more detailed information on each is available at www.design21.dundee.ac.uk or by accessing the relevant url in column 4 of Table 1.

During the second half of 2005 the Phase 2 research call was drafted and the Phase 2 research call was announced in January 2006. This was launched to support more substantive interdisciplinary research projects of between 12–24 month duration. Funding of up to £400, 000 was available for each project. In April 2006, 65 proposals for Phase 2 research funding were submitted. Following a detailed process of peer review over the summer of 2006, a commissioning panel met in September 2006 to consider project applications. 20 projects were selected for Phase 2 funding. Table 2 provides a very brief overview of each of the 20 Phase 2 research projects, more detailed information on each is also available at the Initiative website. Many of the Phase 1 projects described in this book have developed ideas that have resulted in successful Phase 2 project bids. Some of the authors describe these ideas within their chapters. It is hoped that a second book will be published in 2009 describing the territory covered by this second cohort of projects.

Cluster title	PI	Institution	URL
Design and Performance	Dr Calvin Taylor	University of Leeds	www.emergentobjects.co.uk
Technology & Social Action	Dr Andy Dearden	Sheffield Hallam University	www.technologyandsocialaction.org
Non-Place	Prof. Richard Coyne	University of Edinburgh	http://ace.caad.ed.ac.uk/NonPlace
Group Creativity in Design	Dr Hilary Johnson	University of Bath	www.creativityindesign.org.uk
The Healing Environment	Dr Jacques Mizan	King's College London	www.the-space-works.org
Spatial Imagination in Design	Dr Jane Rendell	UCL	www.spatialimagination.org
Nature Inspired Creative Design	Thorsten Schnier	University of Birmingham	www.nature-inspired.org
The Emotional Wardrobe	Prof. Martin Woolley	University of the Arts	www.emotionalwardrobe.com
Spatiality in Design	Dr John Stell	University of Leeds	www.leeds.ac.uk/SiD
Discovery in Design	Prof. Ian Parmee	UWE	http://www.ip-cc.org.uk/did/
Design Imaging	Gordon Mair	University of Strathclyde	www.dmem.strath.ac.uk/designimaging/index.htm
Design Performance	Dr Jillian MacBryde	University of Strathclyde	www.dmem.strath.ac.uk/desperf
Synergy Tools	Prof. John Wood	Goldsmiths College	www.attainable-utopias.org/ds21
Screens and Social Landscape	Prof. Gunther Kress	Institute of Education	http://www.lkl.ac.uk/research/design.html
Outdoor Spaces for Young People	Prof. Lamine Mahdjoubi	UWE	http://environment.uwe.ac.uk./publicspaces/
The View of the Child	Judy Torrington	University of Sheffield	http://vkp.leeds.ac.uk/Drive/gotobuilding.jsp?building=416559
Interrogating Fashion	Prof. Sandy Black	University of the Arts	www.interrogatingfashion.org
Sensory Design	Brent Richards	University of the Arts	www.designlaboratory.co.uk
Designing Physical Artefacts	Prof. Mark d'Inverno	University of Westminster	www.interdisciplinary.co.uk
Ideal States	Prof. Alastair Macdonald	Glasgow School of Art	www.idealstates.co.uk
Complexity in Design	Prof. Jeffrey Johnson	Open University	www.complexityanddesign.net

Table 1, Summary of Phase 1 research cluster projects

Project title	PI	Institution
Personalised Fashion Products	Prof. Sandy Black	University of the Arts
Branded Meeting Places	Prof. Richard Coyne	University of Edinburgh
Practical Design for Social Action	Dr Andrew Dearden	Sheffield Hallam University
DEPtH: Designing for Physicality	Prof. Alan Dix	Lancaster University
Embracing Complexity in Design	Prof. Jeffrey Johnson	The Open University
Inclusive New Media Design	Dr Helen Kennedy	University of East London
Services in Science and Technology-based Enterprises	Lucy Kimbell	University of Oxford
Stress Computation Visualisation, and Measurement	Dr Wanda Lewis	University of Warwick
Design Synthesis and Shape Generation	Dr Alison McKay	University of Leeds
Design Performance: ScoreBOARD	Dr James Moultrie	University of Cambridge
The Welcoming Workplace	Prof. Jeremy Myerson	Royal College of Art
People-centred Computational Environments	Prof. Ian Parmee	University of the West of England
Affective Communication, Personalisation and Social Experience	Prof. Chris Rust	Sheffield Hallam University
Bike Off 2	Adam Thorpe	University of the Arts
Emergent Objects	Prof. Mick Wallis	University of Leeds
Democratising Technology	Lois Weaver	Queen Mary, University of London
2020 Vision – The UK Design Industry in 2020	Prof. Alex Williams	University of Salford
Sustainability for Metadesign	Prof. John Wood	Goldsmiths College
Multimodal Representation of Urban Space	Gordon Mair	University of Strathclyde
The Design and Refurbishment in Schools	Dr Andree Woodcock	Coventry University

Table 2, Summary of Phase 2 research projects

Phase 1 Research Clusters: The Interdisciplinary Journey

Each of the 21 research clusters supported during Phase 1 of the Designing for the 21st Century Initiative and described in this book has explored a predefined theme. Each of these explorations represents a journey in building interdisciplinary understanding. Outlined below are some observations on the different approaches that have been taken.

These insights are useful at three levels. Firstly, they hopefully provide a way of navigating and comparing the material within each chapter of the book. Secondly, they tell us something about the challenges associated with building an interdisciplinary understanding of design and its knowledge needs. Thirdly, they also provide useful insights into the role design based approaches can play in facilitating interdisciplinary discourse. As researchers this knowledge is useful as we will all probably find ourselves working increasingly in collaboration through different forms of network projects in the future.

The original project proposals for each of the Phase 1 research clusters provided a plan outlining the process and methods that would be followed in establishing an interdisciplinary discourse into the topic under investigation. During 2005, the clusters held 126 events. 70 of these events were different forms of workshops, 8 involved exhibitions, 18 were symposia or conferences and 30 were meetings focused on planning cluster debate.

Although not made explicit within a majority of the research cluster proposals these activities were designed to guide members of the cluster through a journey of interdisciplinary enquiry. Reflection on the collective activity of all 21 research projects during 2005 suggests five generic stages within this iterative journey. An overview of this process is shown in Figure 1.

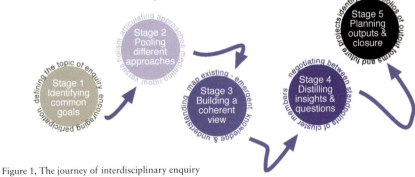

Figure 1, The journey of interdisciplinary enquiry

Stage 1: Identifying common goals

Each of the research clusters began operating in early 2005 with a set of goals that had been developed and laid out in the original proposal documentation. An early challenge for each of the cluster leaders was defining the topic of enquiry in an open way that stimulated interest from a wide range of disciplines. Different strategies were used for achieving this. The *Emotional Wardrobe* cluster very carefully chose a very charismatic title to describe their work. Some of the clusters sought to build a very large network of collaborators beyond the originating project team, using the cluster to build new connections. This was exemplified by the *Interrogating Fashion* cluster whose early events saw cluster membership grow substantially to 38 members, all united by an interest in the paradoxes of fashion. Others mindfully kept cluster membership more focused. The *Ideal States* team realised that by focusing their enquiry on the health-related issues of western Scotland, their exploration could be bounded and interaction between collaborators could be made focused, but with a clear intention to gain generic insights for broader application in other situations.

Stage 2: Pooling different approaches

Most of the clusters enjoyed the involvement of technology orientated disciplines such as computing and engineering alongside those homed within an Art and Design environment and areas such as Management, Psychology, Dance, Medicine, Language and Bioscience. All participants shared a passion for the topic under review but had to build respect for the diverse qualitative and quantitative research approaches taken by different cluster members in exploring territory. In most of the research clusters this was marked by an early conflict between rigour and holism. Many of the cluster members represented disciplines grounded in qualitative research methods and practice based modes of enquiry, others developed new knowledge and understanding through quantitative methods. It proved important to spend sufficient time to explain these approaches amongst cluster members. The *Embracing Complexity* cluster used a programme of 'Complexity Master Classes' to build understanding. Others chose to explore different standpoints by engaging in practical tasks, the *Emergent Objects* cluster for example used a series of workshop activities throughout the 12 months of the cluster operations.

3 DEARDEN, A., 2006. Technology and Social Action. *In:* T. G. INNS & V. HALE, (eds.) *Design Dialogues: Proceedings of Design Dialogues Symposium, London, 7ᵗʰ March 2006.* Dundee: Duncan of Jordanstone College of Art & Design, pp. 11: ISBN 1 899 837 493.

4 PARMEE, I., 2006. Discovery in Design: People-Centred Computational Environments. *In:* T.G. INNS & V. HALE, (eds.) *Design Dialogues: Proceedings of Design Dialogues Symposium, London, 7ᵗʰ March 2006.* Dundee: Duncan of Jordanstone College of Art & Design, pp. 19: ISBN 1 899 837 493.

A key observation from this stage is the importance of individuals actually being able to communicate their methods and practices to others, to work in an interdisciplinary manner we must first of all understand our own disciplines. This is an interesting challenge for those engaged in design research where so many methods and approaches are still emergent and poorly articulated.

Stage 3: Building a coherent view

Mapping existing knowledge and understanding within each zone of enquiry was a challenge for each research cluster. As Andy Dearden leader of the *Technology and Social Action* cluster commented:[3]

'The early workshops were open-ended struggles to establish coherent clusters of issues from a diverse group that extended from Indymedia activists, through trade-unions to open-source software developers.'

Much knowledge and understanding could be extracted from published sources, and a number of the clusters have collated very useful lists of relevant past research material. For example, the *Design Imaging* cluster who have built a profile of the role of the different human senses in design. For most participants the large body of existing knowledge came as a surprise, as Prof. Ian Parmee leader of the *Discovery in Design* cluster noted:[4]

'Most [participants] were largely unaware of the extensive body of existing design research although being active in their particular areas. The workshops therefore represented an opportunity to position and understand their design activities within a more global context in terms of associated research.'

In some areas of design practice where knowledge is emergent or highly tacit and consequently not codified in a written form researchers organised task orientated activities to help participants build an integrated view of territory.

Stage 4: Distilling key insights and questions

One of the core aims of the research cluster activity from the Research Council's perspective was to help identify the project ambitions of the design research community to help frame the Designing for the 21ˢᵗ Century's Phase 2 project call. Within the workshops and events being organised by each cluster this became a key area of focus in the latter part of 2005. Obviously this was a complicated area to navigate as distilling key insights and questions inevitably meant mediating between the interests and aspirations of individual cluster members. To assist in this process the Initiative Director organised a 2.5 day workshop in Glasgow in November 2006 for representatives from each of the 21 research clusters. At this event presentations were made by investigators from all 21 of the research clusters. Delegates also participated in workshop activities designed to help develop an overview of future research ambitions. One of these activities involved mapping potential future research projects from each cluster onto a large floor-based 3x3 matrix with axis representing project risk and project priority. Use of this method allowed over 120 future design research projects to be profiled and explored. Figure 2 shows the outcomes from this mapping process.

Figure 2, Images showing how a map of future project possibilities was built by cluster representatives during the November 2005 Reflection and Projection Workshop. (Images courtesy of Gus Colvin).

Stage 5: *Planning outputs and cluster closure or continuity*

Each of the clusters was given funding to operate for a 12-month period. A majority of the clusters used this support to pay for a cluster coordinator, to develop a web presence and to pay for organising events and the associated travel costs of delegates. Having demonstrated the potential for research in the topic of enquiry a majority of the clusters used the latter part of their period of operation planning future endeavours. For most this has meant identifying and applying for a portfolio of future grants to support further research. 15 out of the 21 clusters developed bids for the Phase 2 funding round, of which eight were successful. Interestingly of the 78 Principal and Co-Investigators associated with successful Phase 2 projects, 37 were involved in Phase 1 cluster project activity. Many identified opportunities for funding through other sources, one of the legacies of interdisciplinary discussion being the opportunity to see a broader range of funding sources for supporting research. It will be interesting to map how the interests of the Designing for the 21st Century cluster members manifest themselves in future research bids to councils beyond the AHRC and EPSRC over the next 5-year period.

Insights for Design

Each Phase 1 research cluster has had its own zone of enquiry and has helped build new knowledge about the act of designing in the 21st century. When examined at an Initiative level a number of common themes emerge. It is useful to summarise these as four new emergent positions for design and six new roles for the designer.

Emergent positions for design disciplines in the 21st century

Close inspection of Table 1 shows the wide variety of topics covered by the discourse within the Phase 1 research clusters. Some of these clusters were located in the context of a particular design discipline, for example *Interrogating Fashion*, others explored generic issues shared by all design disciplines, for example *Nature Inspired Design*. Others examined design's role in resolving issues confronting society, exemplified by the *Healing Environment*. Review of work within all 21 clusters suggests four emergent positions or scenarios for design disciplines. These are described in the following four figures.

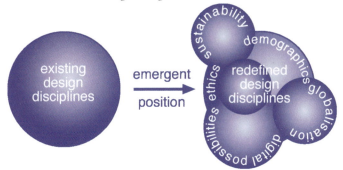

Figure 3, Emergent position 1 – Redefinition of existing design disciplines

One of the research clusters, *Interrogating Fashion* explored the emergent contexts within which fashion design is now operating and the strategies that the discipline of fashion design might follow to make the most valid future contribution. Such a research discourse could be happening within every design discipline, for example, product design, graphic design, engineering design and so on. We have a lot to learn from *Interrogating*

Fashion about how to conduct such a debate. Outlined in Figure 3 is a graphical representation of how the boundaries of a design discipline might expand in response to the demands of new contexts associated with 21ˢᵗ century society. Many of the new contexts for every design discipline could be common, a lot could be learnt from comparing the strategies that each might adopt to deal with changing operating contexts.

The next emergent position for design, development of new design disciplines is shown in Figure 4. This position embodies some of the debate generated within clusters like *Design Imaging* and *Sensory Design* clusters. Both these clusters (and others) suggested the emergence of new design disciplines based on the observation that we are designing new types of object, product and system in the 21ˢᵗ century, in the case of *Sensory Design*, potentially the design of the gastronomic experience. These new approaches find their routes in existing design disciplines but roadmaps for future discipline development needs to be identified.

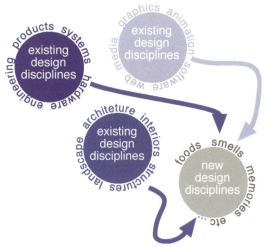

Figure 4, Emergent position 2 – Development of new design disciplines

Figure 5 suggests the development of metadesign disciplines that act as a bridge between existing approaches to design. This development captures the spirit of discourse within clusters like *Synergy Tools* and *Screens and the Social Landscape*. Here we see 21ˢᵗ century design being dependent on the evolution of new metadesign disciplines that help navigate between existing discipline silos. Again driven by the need for new design approaches to address 21ˢᵗ century issues like sustainability, heath and security.

Figure 5, Emergent position 3 – Development of meta design disciplines

Finally, Figure 6, explores the development of design outwith design
(outwith being a quaint Medieval term associated with being beyond
the city walls). Many of the research clusters found themselves with at
least one foot in this camp. Clusters like *Ideal States, Technology and
Social Action, Embracing Complexity in Design* all explored how design
knowledge might be exported and imported across the traditional
borders of design. How might design inform healthcare and vice versa,
in the *Ideal States* cluster Prof. Alastair Macdonald explicitly explored
design's contribution to healthcare beyond the design of product,
environment and communication material. He suggests that design tends
to person-centric, healthcare he suggests is not person-centric as we might
think but pathology-centric, if we want to understand the export market
for design we need to understand the currencies, concepts and values
beyond the walls.

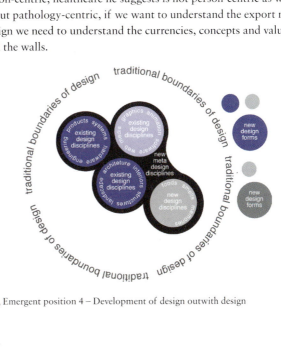

Figure 6, Emergent position 4 – Development of design outwith design

Emergent roles for the designer

Alongside these emergent positions for design disciplines the clusters also suggest many new emergent roles for the designer in the 21st century. These are probably best thought of as additional roles not displacement activities for the widely recognised skills of creativity and synthesis and the core technical skills associated with each design discipline. The six roles described below give a flavour of where the designer might be heading. The emergence of these roles is shown in Figure 7.

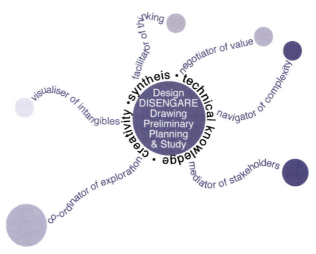

Figure 7, Emergent roles for the 21st century Designer

Designer as negotiator of value

We are now beginning to understand and articulate the financial value effective design can bring to a commercial situation, for example, how design can increase margins by reducing costs or enhancing price points. We also understand that this often calls for up-front investment and that value management involves a careful process of design trade-offs. The *Design Performance* cluster have carefully charted literature in this subject area. Value is however increasingly multi-dimensional, for example we must now consider ecological and ethical dimensions. The designer has an important role in negotiating decisions within these increasingly complex situations. The *Interrogating Fashion* cluster provides useful insights into the paradoxes associated with decision making in 21st century fashion design. Designers in all disciplines face similar challenges.

Designer as facilitator of thinking

Enhanced facilitation skills are another addition to the designers growing portfolio of skills in a 21st century context. We can see from the clusters that others are being empowered to design. The *View of the Child* captures a child's perspective in the design process. How do we design, design to allow extended participation? The 21st century designer will need to know how to mobilise and energise the thinking of others.

Designer as visualiser of the intangible

Perhaps more of an extension of existing roles than an entirely new one, the contemporary designer already visualises and synthesises future possibilities but still this role is mainly associated with physical entities. In the emergent positions for design, so many of the challenges might be associated with the visualisation of the abstract and intangible, perhaps the visualisation of systems, relationships, emotions, experiences and networks. The work of the *Designing Physical Artefacts* cluster and others centred on translating concepts from one form to another, particularly the physical to the digital and back again. *Spatial Imagination in Design* explored the translations of the intangible in the mind. Visualising, modelling and prototyping in this zone demands new skills from the designer. How do you communicate intangible concepts to others, how do you prototype them, test them and implement them?

Designer as navigator of complexity

We now no longer live in a world of linear systems and mechanistic processes. The interdisciplinary world is a world of complexity and ambiguity, work from clusters like *Embracing Complexity in Design*, demonstrated the role design could play in helping us understand complexity, but also the role an understanding of complexity theory might play in helping designers understand their own roles.

Designer as mediator of stakeholders

The designer often no longer designs solely for a customer, the user or a client, increasingly design solutions are for multiple stakeholders, often with different perspectives, needs and expectations. The designer must act as mediator to resolve multiple requirements within a design solution. The *metadesign* cluster have paid close attention to these issues, carefully unpacking the multiple relationships that are associated with contemporary design projects and suggesting tools that might help manage the mediation process. Likewise the *Designing Healthy and Inclusive Spaces* cluster have demonstrated how design can act as an organising concept to allow multiple stakeholders debate a complex issue such as obesity in young people.

Designer as coordinator of exploration

The designer has always played a lead role in planning future outputs. During the design process ideas are synthesised into concepts, developed into prototypes and realised as plans for future implementation and production. With technologies evolving quickly, the cultural context for design becoming a critical component within competitiveness and the boundaries of design steadily migrating a growing number of territories must be considered during the upfront exploration of ideas. Clusters such as *Nature Inspired Creative Design* explain the rich possibilities within the natural world, the 21st century designer must able to coordinate the exploration of relevant technical and contextual sources to maximise creativity in early stages of design.

Conclusion

These thoughts on developments within design disciplines and emergent roles for the 21st century designer are my interpretation of the work that has been conducted during Phase 1 of the Designing for the 21st Century Research Initiative. They are based on the mental models of design that I carry in my mind. These models have evolved in the last 3 years as I have observed the ongoing discourse within the cluster projects. As you read this book you will interrogate the work from your own perspective and perhaps draw different conclusions and suggest different frameworks that capture the generic picture. Certainly there is clearly a great deal that needs to be researched within the design domain. We will need a great deal of new knowledge and understanding to help the discipline of design fulfil its potential in 21st century society. The 20 Phase 2 projects are exploring some of these issues in more detail.

Within the UK the Initiative has tapped into an appetite for design research within many parts of the academic and design practice community, it is likely that future initiatives will build on this portfolio of activity as the century progresses.

Ideal States: Engaging Patients in Healthcare Pathways Through Design Methodologies

Prof. Alastair S Macdonald, (The Glasgow School of Art)

Overview

The age shift

Ageing of populations is a phenomenon occurring throughout much of the developed world. The 20th century saw life expectancy rise by 30 years. By 2020, half the adults in the UK and Europe will be older than 50.[1] By 2030, there will be more people in Scotland of retirement age than there will be children, and one in four people will be aged 65+ and one in 12 aged over 80.[2] As populations age, the numbers affected by associated impairments increase, there is an accompanying shift from a predominance of infectious to chronic diseases, and pathologies tend to be complex in the geriatric domain.[3] Global businesses responding to the demographic challenges of an ageing population have not only a vested interested but a moral responsibility in providing products and services that meet the needs of their clients[4] and governmental foresight healthcare and ageing population panels have scoped trends, future scenarios and actions required.[5] How can design respond to the challenges brought by an ageing population?

Healthcare delivery

Current healthcare tends to be organised for the convenience of the organisation and the clinical staff and most solutions are geared to the needs of these two stakeholders. The consumer of healthcare has traditionally been seen as the passive recipient; however, more recently through policy documents and the introduction of the 'Expert Patient' there has been a move to acknowledging the patient perspective.[6] Although patients and professionals may share the same goals, that is, the successful management and treatment of the patient, they do not necessarily agree on the important routes to those goals. While clinical models are

[1] ROYAL SOCIETY OF ARTS. Inclusive Design resource. Available at: http://www.inclusivedesign. org.uk/index.php?filters=f5 [accessed 28/4/06]

[2] GREAT BRITAIN. NHS Scotland, 2005. *Building a Health Service Fit for the Future: A National Framework for Service Change in the NHS in Scotland*. Edinburgh, Scottish Executive.

[3] ISAACS, B., 1965. *An Introduction to Geriatrics*. London: Balliere, Tindall and Cassell.

[4] COOPER, R., 2005. Ethics and altruism: what constitutes socially responsible design? *Design Management Review*, 16 (3), pp.10-18.

[5] GREAT BRITAIN. Department for Innovation, Universities and Skills. Available at: http://www. foresight.gov.uk/index.html

[6] GREAT BRITAIN. NHS. Available at: http://www. expertpatients.co.uk/public/ default.aspx [accessed 07/06/06].

[7] GREAT BRITAIN. Health and Community Care, 2003. *Partnership for Care, Scotland's Health White Paper*. Edinburgh: Scottish Executive.

[8] GREAT BRITAIN. NHS Scotland, 2005. *Delivering for Health*. Edinburgh: Scottish Executive.

[9] GREAT BRITAIN. NHS Scotland, 2005. *Building a Health Service Fit for the Future: A National Framework for Service Change in the NHS in Scotland*. Edinburgh: Scottish Executive.

[10] HANLON, P., 2005. Foreword. In: F. CRAWFORD, *Doing it Differently: An Asset-based Approach to Well-being*. Edinburgh: NHS Scotland, ISBN 1 901835 43 X.

evolving significantly, the tools to engage healthcare consumers are still rudimentary: very often the individual is disenfranchised from decisions about their care and not empowered to assist more effectively in their own recovery. However, the NHS is committed to change:[7] NHS Scotland has stated that its vision is to reapply its founding principles to meet the needs of the people and that this requires a fundamental shift in how healthcare is delivered.[8,9] Could design methods, particularly in the area of user-centred design, provide a way of engaging patients in this sector more effectively to obtain a better understanding of their needs and goals, and indeed, by increased empowerment, offer them a more proactive role?

Common purpose

The 'Ideal States' cluster was formed between individuals in the two fields of design and clinical healthcare, both concerned with people-centric practices and in how to respond to healthcare and quality of life issues associated with an ageing population. The cluster's title, 'Ideal States' refers to the aspiration for the two fields to be able to collaborate more effectively to the benefit of a healthier community. Joint preparation of the initial cluster research proposal had been an essential stage in clarifying its common purpose and agenda. The cluster's aims were 1) to identify ways to better understand one another's fields, and by so doing, 2) to explore how and in what ways the two fields could effectively collaborate to bring mutual benefit, through design thinking, to those individuals experiencing ageing, change in health, illness and disability, and 3) from the outset to engage clinicians, healthcare professionals and patients in this discussion.

Social context

Scotland has a problem: it faces the same spectrum of health and social issues as the rest of the world's post-industrial economies, but in a more virulent form.[10] This formed the backcloth for our study: the cluster was to later focus on the ageing population, associated chronic disease, in particular stroke. Grounding its discussions and activities within the west of Scotland context, to use this as a 'test-bed', was vital in avoiding the cluster engaging in a purely academic exercise. One intention of the cluster from the outset was to gain generic insights that might be valuable for broader application in real situations nationally and internationally.

Anticipating future design practice

A pressing question underpinning discussion was how design as a field could begin to shape its perceptions, practice, its paradigms, to anticipate tomorrow's problems and challenges today, to understand, and provide for future needs and goals. Not only will tomorrow's populations be older, but they will be more demanding in how they choose to live and accommodate age, disability and illness. This will require not only effective healthcare including strategies for adapting to limitations and rehabilitation, but also flexibility in the means to enable active, healthy ageing, socialisation and independence.[11]

[11] GREAT BRITAIN. Department for Innovation, Universities and Skills. Available at: http://www.foresight.gov. uk/index.html

Activities

Cluster members

The 'Ideal States' cluster held a number of meetings and workshops over a 12-month period to bring together practitioners and academics in the fields of healthcare, human factors and design, and to involve users (patients and carers), as well as attending Designing for the 21st Century events. Those substantially involved in shaping and driving the discussions forward were: Prof. Alastair Macdonald, Head of Department, Product Design Engineering, The Glasgow School of Art (GSA), as Principal Investigator; Prof. James McKillop, Head of Department, and Prof. David Stott, David Cargill Prof. of Geriatric Medicine, both in the Department of Medicine, Prof. Margaret Reid, Prof. of Women's Health, Department of Public Health, all at the University of Glasgow (GU); Lynn Legg, Project Manager, Stroke Therapy Evaluation Programme, Glasgow Royal Infirmary; Eleanor Forrest, Senior Consultant in Human Factors, HFE Solutions, Dunfermline; Gordon Hush, sociologist, Lecturer, Historical & Critical Studies, and Sally Stewart, Head of Undergraduate Studies at the Mackintosh School of Architecture, both at GSA. Cluster coordinator was Maggie MacRitchie and technical support was provided by David Loudon, both based at GSA.

Deeper understanding

An early decision was taken by the cluster to remain relatively small, to stay intensely focused, to concentrate initially on developing deeper insights into the two fields and cultures of design and healthcare, a choice of depth rather than breadth. The cluster was not so concerned with producing ideas for research or projects early on, but instead with listening to, and in beginning to really understand, how each field perceived its world, and how as a consequence these perceptions shaped

12 COTTAM, H. &
LEADBETTER, C., 2004. RED
Paper 01, *Health: Co-creating
Services*. London: Design
Council. Available at:
http://www.designcouncil.
org.uk/en/Design-Council/3/
Publications/Red-Paper-01-
Health/ [accessed 08/05/06]

13 GREAT BRITAIN. NHS
Scotland, 2005. *Building a
Health Service Fit for the Future:
A National Framework for
Service Change in the NHS in
Scotland*. Edinburgh: Scottish
Executive.

its respective world through how it acted and practiced. The first activities, then, were concerned with defining the respective fields, the areas of knowledge, normal practices and how subjects were engaged. As a result, perceptions changed and understanding deepened. When the cluster came to focus its enquiry and activity on the area of healthcare pathways, after we had developed a clearer understanding of our respective fields, the cluster began to make some real headway in how to begin to think its way forwards to meet these challenges.

Our subjects

Context was essential: the cluster was keen to continually reference the discussion back to the specific context of healthcare in its community. It was important to the cluster that the voice of the subjects, that is, older and disabled people, was introduced early on. Interestingly, a technique which is now commonplace in design research and which was used as a discussion activity (not research *per se*) in our March workshop generated a sustained interest in the healthcare professionals for the duration of the project that is, providing subjects with a disposable camera and questionnaire and asking them to document what enhanced or provided an obstacle to quality-of-life during a day of their lives and then to discuss the findings at a subsequent group session. Carers were also asked to participate in the same activity, which provided a complementary perspective. The cluster also ensured that advocates for its subjects, such as carers, public health and human factors professionals, were involved in some of the activities [Figures 1 and 2].

Emergent thinking, policy and practice

Having begun to develop a better mutual understanding of the nature of each other's field, the cluster then explored, in its June workshop, the changing contexts and practices of both design and healthcare through contributions from a series of invited speakers. For example, a member of the Design Council's Red team, whose stated purpose was to challenge accepted thinking on current social and economic problems by exploring new solutions through innovative design practice, provided an example of their approach to engaging people in the way that services were designed, through a process of co-creating.[12] From the healthcare side, a key briefing by a healthcare consultant provided a summary of the Kerr report. This outlined the Scottish Executive's new strategy for building a health service for the future through changing the nature of the way healthcare is delivered within the NHS in Scotland.[13] This latter presentation, in retrospect, became a key reference-point in understanding what was

Figures 1 and 2,
top and bottom

User research session involving older subjects discussing quality of life
issues that were self-documented with the aid of disposable cameras

actually already taking place at a national policy level in healthcare and, as discovered later, how this change was beginning to benefit patients. The cluster's questions would then evolve into one asking what role could design have in facilitating or influencing the changing healthcare delivery model.

Defining the focus

Given that, from the outset, the cluster's aim was to find ways to work together to address the healthcare issues arising from an ageing population, it required a real and tangible focus. There then followed two intense workshops, in August and October, to try to establish this. Because of the enthusiasm of, and suggestion from its geriatrician, the cluster agreed to explore patients' pathways through stroke. Stroke's pathology is complex, and the west of Scotland has a high incidence of this chronic disease. Early attempts to describe a patient's pathway through onset, the acute and the rehabilitation phases of stroke revealed how inadequately this could be described in a visual format that could be shared between the different fields and with non-specialists. This lack of useful mappings proved an incentive, particularly on the design side, to really understand what happened to a patient as they progressed through healthcare from one stage to the next.

The rudimentary mappings that were produced in these two workshops later proved highly significant, as they could begin to allow the cluster to think about a number of issues [Figures 3 – 5]. One was, for example, that by providing designers with an overview through means of a pathway, one could begin to think about how design interventions, in the broadest sense, could be mapped into that pathway. Secondly, this could begin to enable designers to think about how the responses to what are normally seen as separate and unconnected design problems could be thought about more coherently, as part of a system of products and services. Thirdly, one could begin to analyse different parts of the pathway and begin to understand how and to what extent patients could be engaged. Ultimately one also asked the question how would the patient design the pathway, not just taking a user-centred design approach, but one in which the patient was seen as one of the design team, a process of the 'democratisation of design'?[14] If a mapping were seen as a tool and understandable by all the parties involved, how and to what extent would the dialogue change? Other important factors driving our agenda were the need to report on progress, relatively publicly, at the November 2005 and March 2006 Designing for the 21ˢᵗ Century events, and the cluster's desire to define clear research questions as the basis for a further funding application.

[14] RUST, C., 2006. Discussion. Design Dialogues: Designing for the 21ˢᵗ Century, 7ᵗʰ March 2006. London.

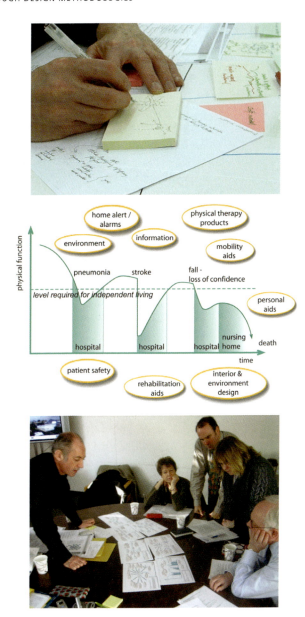

Figures 3 to 5,
top to bottom

Figure 3, Brainstorming session during patient pathway mapping workshop
Figure 4, Mapping design interventions into patient pathways
Figure 5, Ideal States cluster core members discussing design interventions in patient
pathway models

[15] GREAT BRITAIN. Centre for Change and Innovation, 2005. *Patient Pathways of Care: Outpatients' Programme.* Edinburgh: Scottish Executive.

[16] CLARKSON, J., BUCKLE. P., et al., 2004. *Design for Patient Safety.* Cambridge: Engineering Design Centre.

[17] HAWTHORNE, C., 2002. IDEO's Design cure: can it fix our sick health-care system? *Metropolis*, October.

[18] COTTAM, H. & LEADBETTER, C., 2004. RED Paper 01, *Health: Co-creating Services.* London: Design Council. Available at: http://www.designcouncil. org.uk/en/Design-Council/3/ Publications/Red-Paper-01-Health/ [accessed 08/05/06]

[19] RAMECKERS, L. & UN, S., 2005. People Insights at the Fuzzy Front of Innovation. *In: Proceedings of the Qualitative 2005 Conference, Barcelona.* Amsterdam: ESOMAR. ISBN: 9283113861.

[20] BUENO, M. & RAMECKERS, L., 2003. Understanding People in New Ways: Personas in Context: Forging a Stronger Link Between Research and its Application in Design. *In: Proceedings of the ESOMAR Research Conference, Venice.* Amsterdam: ESOMAR, pp. 1–15.

[21] GAVER, W., Dunne, T. & Pacenti, E., 1999. Design: Cultural Probes. *Interactions*, 6 (1): pp. 21–29.

Prior research

As a result of a scoping exercise, subsequent research revealed some previous work in this general area. For example, the Scottish Executive had carried out work on patient pathways.[15] In a scoping study on design issues for patient safety, maps of medication and information flow had been created.[16] In 2002, design consultancy IDEO redesigned the DePaul Health Centre USA, and developed a Patient Journey Framework, primarily concerned with the physical orientation of ambulatory patients making a journey through a health centre.[17] The Design Council's Red Project 'Health: co-creating services' concentrated on health in the community and explored two areas, diabetes and encouraging activity and exercise, and two key processes, co-design and co-creation, engaging individuals to help provide the key to solutions that might work.[18] Philips Design, in developing healthcare technologies and products, used insights obtained from people at the early stages and throughout its innovation process collecting data by 'multiple encounter' 'people research' techniques.[19,20] 'Cultural probes'[21] widely adopted by the design community, had been adapted, in some cases, for healthcare settings.[22] However, there was little available evidence that substantial research had been carried out in clinical settings, to the extent the cluster was proposing, to gain insights into healthcare pathways as experienced by patients themselves, and to establish what patients' own goals were, as distinct from clinicians' or healthcare managers' views and goals.

Insights

Preparatory work

The importance of the early discussions at the time of preparing the rationale and case for support for the initial research bid should not be under-estimated. It is worth quoting from the cluster's original Case for Support:

'*The disciplines of design, assisted by the healthcare professions, tend to provide characteristic types of responses and solutions for medically identified and conceptualised problems associated with ageing and reactions to illness or disability. However, within the field of healthcare there are currently many unresolved tensions between, for instance, concepts of illness and well-being, medical and social models of illness, and the influence of social and ethnic backgrounds and environmental conditions on one's health. These different paradigms of healthcare practice obviously influence the efficacy of design solutions. This proposed research cluster provides an opportunity to collaborate outside*

[22] CRABTREE, A. et al., 2003. Designing with Care: Adapting Cultural Probes to Inform Design in Sensitive Settings. In: VILLER & WYETH, (eds.) Proceedings of Australasian Computer Human Interaction Conference OzCHI2003: New Directions of Interaction, Information Environments, Media and Technology, Brisbane, 26-28th November 2003. New South Wales, Computer-Human Interaction Special Interest Group.

[23] How people survive chronic illness and disability has received some thoughtful attention within the social sciences, most notably from Strauss in the mid 1970s and more recently by BURY (1982, 1988), CHARMEZ (1983, 1990), WILLIAMS (1984) and RADLEY (1989). In: SIDELL, M., 1995. Health in Old Age. Buckingham: Open University Press.

[24] GREAT BRITAIN. Centre for Change and Innovation, 2005. Patient Pathways of Care: Outpatients' Programme. Edinburgh: Scottish Executive.

[25] GREAT BRITAIN. Health and Community Care, 2003. Partnership for Care, Scotland's Health White Paper. Edinburgh: Scottish Executive.

our usual immediate frames of reference and modes of response, and seeks to look at problems and challenges in new ways by discovering the areas of commonality between the design and healthcare professions, their creative differences, and the differences and misunderstandings that create obstacles to providing effective design solutions for healthcare needs and goals.'

One original aim was that the funding would provide the opportunity to explore ideas without resorting to 'default' thinking modes and responses in either camp.

Key opportunity

At the outset, the cluster did not anticipate that its focus would rest on patient pathways, but once this was established, the cluster quickly recognised what a key opportunity this concept could offer in how best to understand and map the complexity of the experience of receiving healthcare at all its stages. It also realised, given the limitations of time and budget for this phase, that it could not undertake a comprehensive survey of patient journeys or pathway mappings – there is much work on patient pathways it was unable to capture – but it could try to become aware of some of the work done in this area, and to gauge from whose perspectives these were mapped, and what opportunities this could offer for further research.

Patient pathways

Social scientists have investigated the patient's perspective in healthcare for some years, primarily using qualitative methods[23] but the concept of patient pathways, as a tool for facilitating improved healthcare delivery as a vital part of healthcare reform, appears to be a relatively recent one. The Scottish Executive (SE's) Centre for Change and Innovation (CCI) had recently developed Patient Pathways of Care models.[24] There is encouragement by the SE to utilise these new pathway models, where it is expected that GPs discuss with their patients where they fit on a pathway, what they can expect to happen next and discuss available options. Patient-centric views are beginning to emerge:

'We now require a major programme of service redesign across Scotland. This means looking at the pathway of care from a patient's point of view and making it smoother, more accessible, less complicated and less subject to delays.'[25]

The cluster's preparations for the October workshop revealed there were many ways in which patients' pathways could be mapped through chronic disease, rehabilitation and recovery. A fundamental, perceptual shift in understanding occurred within the cluster when what had been assumed to be person- or patient-centric pathways were in fact described from a clinician's perspective – pathogenically, that is, focused on the disease pathway. Subsequent work revealed another prevalent mapping – that of healthcare managers who were principally concerned with efficiency flow through the healthcare system, largely concerned with reducing the number of elements in the chain of events and patients' waiting time.

Mapping pathways

This recent pathway approach by the SE appears to have produced some very profound changes[26] by mapping out the whole process, and for example, reducing the number of elements in the process, resulting in a significant reduction in patient waiting times. Early pathway mappings tended to describe somewhat simple and linear pathways and did not reflect the complexities of pathology, need and expectation, or the full context. In reality pathways are much more akin to complex nets, and now one is beginning to find these represented in a more comprehensive way. The cluster thought it might be useful if these pathways could also embrace the earlier pre-onset phase of the prevention and tackling of the causes of ill-health. Of interest is how the patient's point of view is engaged. In one discussion about stroke, for example, it was revealed that the stroke team's contact with a patient in a rehabilitation ward apparently accounts for only 45 minutes of a patient's 24 hour day, that the patient may be in their bed for 60% of the time, and spend most of their time alone. It was recognised that this non-contact time was not 'designed' in any effective way to actively engage the patient in purposeful activity and as a means of hopefully assisting recovery. It was also recognised that the patient's voice would become increasingly important to listen to as the patient moved out of the acute phase, through rehabilitation, into the community and back home: could existing pathway models facilitate this and how could design methodology and practice assist?

Discovering that the patient pathway concept, as a tool for improved service delivery was relatively new, a question arose about what a design mindset could bring to this that was perhaps not currently considered or appreciated. This question was partly answered by clinical healthcare colleagues in the cluster.

26 GALLAGHER, S., 2006. Stirling Conference, 4ᵗʰ May 2006. Cited significant reductions in patient waiting and referral times.

Appreciating the design viewpoint

[27] STOTT, D., (d.j.stott@
clinmed.gla.ac.uk) 2006. 15th
February. Email to: Alastair
Macdonald
(a.macdonald@gsa.ac.uk).

[28] REID, M., (M.E.Reid@
clinmed.gla.ac.uk) 2006. 14th
February. Email to: Alastair
Macdonald
(a.macdonald@gsa.ac.uk).

It was interesting to note how our colleagues' perceptions changed over the duration of the project. This evolved from *'but what is design. . . ?'* to – and here it is worth quoting directly – one view that:

'design thinking seems to be 'boundary-less' or at least to cut across traditional boundaries in medicine, that is one of its strengths, and this approach can assist the patient or the staff perspective with more ease than someone who works in the medical world. The design perspective therefore brings clarity to medical problems.'

They also felt that:

'design places a strong emphasis on obtaining and acting on the consumer or user perspective. While this is widely recognised within healthcare as a critical component in planning, it has not yet been fully assimilated.'[27] *'Design has a number of approaches and methods that could assist the changing requirement for healthcare delivery through an improved earlier and ongoing engagement with the recipients of healthcare. Designers are also used to working with the users in a collaborative manner far more closely than medics with patients (the experiential approach). The design perspective tends to approach the user and ascertain what they would like out of the situation, which may be better health, but the route map may be different.'*[28]

Understanding the clinical perspective

Thought provoking, from a design perspective, were discussions centring on the robustness of clinical research methodologies to obtain an evidence-base for any change to be introduced in practice or procedure. En route, the cluster attempted to work up a proposal for a small amount of research funding but the cumbersome procedures around medical research – the necessity for ethics consent, organisational administrative structures – were a real deterrent for the size and timescale of this project. Understanding the robustness of the process for obtaining ethical approval for user-centred design research in clinical settings also proved an opportunity for reflection.

As a designer, it has been useful to understand just how empirically clinical healthcare specialists think and act. Often they may have to act in an area where clear evidence is lacking but they will not – understandably, given life-or-death scenarios – introduce a significant change in practice without the evidence and proof that this change will provide better

[29] HUSH, G., (g.hush@gsa.
ac.uk) 2006. 9 May. Email
to: Alastair Macdonald
(a.macdonald@gsa.ac.uk).

[30] PIRKL, J.J. & BABIC, A.L.,
1988. *Guidelines and Strategies
for Designing Transgenerational
Products.* Acton, MA: Copley
Publishing Group.

[31] The University of Toronto has
established a mixed discipline
group linking design to
healthcare and, in one project,
developing design ideas to help
people in winter time.

treatment, or recovery, or prolong life, or improve the quality of life.
However, our sociologist made a valuable comment that rather than
understanding medicine as a 'hands-on' activity, he now viewed it as an
organisational entity and a set of discourses.[29]

Bridging design and healthcare

Discovering the concept of the patient pathway was serendipitous,
resulting in an appreciation of the potential value of pathway maps.
The health service is a very complex system and without an understanding
of its complexity, design cannot begin to properly address the issues.
The rudimentary maps created began to function as a 'translation'
or 'bridging' tool that enabled the mix of disciplines in the cluster to
compare perceptions and to converse. With their demographic charts Pirkl
and Babic[30] had provided a bridge between the physiological change in
the senses which accompany age on the one side and design on the other
by providing the designer with guidelines and strategies for products and
systems. The opportunity to develop this and other translation or bridging
tools will be a fundamental requirement for design to be able to converse
with other disciplines.

Progress, achievements, and value

The cluster activity demonstrated to our clincial and healthcare partners,
through the two pilot workshops of user engagement and pathway
mapping, how qualitative design-based co-research and co-creation
methods could give potential end-users of healthcare services a much
more prominent role in the research and development process by gaining
insights into the complexity and uniqueness of their personal experiences
during illness and recovery. The common reference-point for this cluster
became the patient pathway model, one that facilitated discussion,
provided tangible context and one that enabled a better understanding of
how design might collaborate from an early stage in healthcare design and
delivery.

In addition to, and as a result of this Phase 1 opportunity, the cluster was
able to establish contact with a number of organisations and institutions
to explore further opportunities for research in parallel to the proposed
Phase 2 activity. These included for example, an international design
and technology company developing products and services for consumer
health and wellness, a Japanese university researching into healthcare
systems and a Canadian university linking design to healthcare.[31]

Afterlife: Questions for Further Research

The consensus view that emerged from the cluster was that the combination of design (ethnographic) methods, action research and an evidence-based (empirical) clinical approach carries great promise in advancing healthcare. Research questions that arose towards the end of this Phase 1 stage formed the basis for the Phase 2 bid. Although not exhaustive, these included the following. At a time when healthcare service delivery requires fundamental change, can it utilise design approaches, thinking, processes and methods to help it tackle some of the pressing challenges associated particularly with an ageing population and increased incidence of chronic disease? Can design's 'people research' methods enable patient needs, priorities and perspectives within healthcare pathways to be more clearly understood? If these were better understood, how would this change clinicians', carers' and healthcare managers' understanding, and in turn, the pathway models of healthcare delivery? Would this assist in a better understanding of where and how clinical and design interventions would bring best benefit? Would this help build a more productive relationship between clinician, carer and patient? Would this enable a more active engagement with recovery and healthcare processes, and more purposeful activity on behalf of the patient? How would this change the perception and role of design research and practice in the field of healthcare?

In conclusion, it would be fair to say that the cluster members unanimously found the 12-month experience a very positive one and hoped to be able to continue the collaboration through some substantial in-depth research.

Acknowledgement

This chapter is the result of the many stimulating discussions between the cluster members and reflects their various voices and views. Deep thanks for their commitment and contributions.

The Healing Environment
Dr Jacques Mizan, (King's College London)

Background/Context

[1] GREAT BRITAIN. NHS, 2004. *The NHS Plan*. Norwich: The Stationery Office.

[2] 'Primary care' in the UK context refers to any healthcare provision outside of the hospital setting.

[3] BARKER, R. G., 1968. *Ecological Psychology*. Stanford: Stanford University Press.

The concept of a 'healing environment' is not a new one. Indeed it dates back to the Crimean War and the work of Florence Nightingale who needed little convincing as to the benefits of light, fresh air and access to nature on recovery from illness and trauma. It seems to have taken an interminably long time for the built environment in healthcare to embrace these simple and seemingly common sense notions. Upon closer scrutiny it seems community healthcare facilities (GP surgeries, community clinics and so on) are amongst the worst offenders. Given that 90% of healthcare provision is delivered in the community,[1] it seems appropriate, if not critically important, to address the built environment in primary care.[2]

Why is the status quo of primary healthcare design so desperate? The reasons are complex and multi-factorial. I suggest that at the heart of it, certainly in the NHS, lie politics and organisational psychology, set against a cultural mind-set that revels in stoicism. And so we find that to this day patients in the NHS are remarkably accepting of dismal healthcare facilities. Such is 'their lot'. Without governmental support – perhaps borne out of this mind-set and coupled with a lack of supporting research – the modernisation of healthcare facilities, especially primary care facilities, simply stagnated in its post war comfort zone. Converted houses seemed adequate back then – why change? Even new primary care buildings simply repeated what had gone before based on unquestioned and rarely challenged templates. This last point can be understood from a human ecology perspective with consideration to Barker's postulate[3] on behavioural settings. Barker would suggest that we have become used to

[4] GREAT BRITAIN. Department of Health, 1996. *The Patients Charter*. London: The Stationery Office.

[5] GREAT BRITAIN. NHS, 2000. *NHS Plan*. London: The Stationery Office.

[6] GLANVILLE, R. & FRANCIS, S., 2001. *Building a 2020 Vision: Future Healthcare Environments*. London: The Stationery Office.

[7] WANLESS, D., 2002. *Securing Our Future Health: Taking a Long Term View*. London: The Treasury.

[8] GREAT BRITAIN. Department of Health, 2006. *Our Health, Our Care, Our Say*. London: The Stationery Office.

[9] KANTROWITZ, M., 1993. *Design Evaluation of Six Primary Care Facilities for the Purpose of Informing Future Design Decisions*. California: The Centre for Health Design.

[10] MACRAE, R. N., 1998. *Consumer Perceptions of the Healthcare Environment: An Investigation into What Matters*. California: The Centre for Healthcare Design.

[11] LAWSON, B. & PHIRL, M., 2000. *The Architectural Healthcare Environment and its Effects on Patient Health Outcomes*. University of Sheffield: School of Architecture.

[12] GULRAJANI, R.P., 1995. Physical environmentaal factors affecting patients' stress in the accident and emergency department. *Accident and Emergency Nursing*, 3, pp. 22-27.

[13] STARICOFF, R. L., (ed.), 2004. *The Impact of the Arts: Some Research Evidence*. London: Arts Council England.

behaving in a certain way in healthcare buildings – waiting in the waiting room and so on – to such an extent that the buildings housing these activities have become frozen in time and purpose – 'a way' of building healthcare facilities has become '*the* way', and there is comfort in such predictability and control. Change will not be easy.

That being said, change is indeed amongst us. From the early 1980s, it became fashionable to support the consumer, in health as in all aspects of life. With consumerism came rights, choice and the need to serve. The Patient Charter[4] was symbolic of this shift in attitude, to be further consolidated by the NHS plan.[5] Crucially, the importance of the built environment was meaningfully acknowledged for the first time. Compared to a fleeting mention in the Patient Charter, the NHS Plan outlined a massive redevelopment of the NHS Estates, with £1bn investment into primary care buildings and a commitment to 3000 refurbished/new GP surgeries by 2004. A number of reports were commissioned to explore the shape of future healthcare provision. 'Building a 2020 vision'[6] and the Wanless report[7] specifically pointed to a shift of healthcare provision into the community and urged policy makers to focus research and development on these areas. In January 2006 the Wanless vision came one step closer to reality. In its clearest statement yet, the government laid down a clear path channeling care away from hospitals and into the community.[8] Where and how these services were to be housed had not been clarified. However the answer to this question could never be more critical and needs to be informed by robust research – research which is at once innovative, challenges current design paradigms and most importantly involves the users who have been conspicuously absent till now.

A review of the literature shows precious little research has been done on the effects of the built environment in primary care. In the late 1990s Kantrowitz[9] and MacRae[10] produced some interesting work exploring user perspectives on primary care facilities in the US. The generalisability of this work to encompass different cultures and very different models of healthcare delivery is clearly limited, though there were some important take home points, such as the desire for smaller, more homely environments close to home. Interestingly, current planning in the UK is focused on large polyclinics and one stop shops, running counter to Kantrowitz' findings. Some research has been done in the UK, though its hospital setting limits its applicability to primary care. Lawson[11] explored the effects of the built environment on healthcare outcomes, Gulrajani[12] the effect on stress in Accident and Emergency and Staricoff[13] documented the effects on physiological markers important in recovery.

[14] ZIMMRING, C. & ULRICH, R., 2004. *The Role of the Physical Environment in the Hospital of the 21st Century: A Once-in-a-lifetime Opportunity.* Concord, CA: The Center for Health Design.

[15] YOTHER, F., 2005. Keeping patients happy in your waiting room. *Pa Dent J* (Harrisb) 72(1), pp. 15-16.

[16] RICHARDS, D., 2002. Calming ambience is latest trend in office design. *J Calif Dent Assoc,* 30(3), pp. 203-204.

[17] RISHI, P., SINHA, S.P. & DUBEY, R., 2000. A Correlational study of workspace characteristics and work satisfaction among Indian Bank employees. *Psychologia,* 43(3), pp. 155-164.

[18] MIZAN, J., 2003. MSc dissertation, King's College London.

[19] WILLIAMS, E.S., KONRAD, T.R., LINZER, M., MCMURRAY, J. & PATHMAN, D.E., 2002. Physician, practice and patient characteristics related to primary care physicians' physical and mental healtth: results from the Physician Worklife Study. *Health Services Research,* 37(1), pp. 121-127.

Staricoff,[13] Ulrich and Zimring[14] have all conducted systematic reviews of available knowledge on healthcare design: primary care based research is conspicuous by its absence. There is also a vast body of literature from the dental[15,16] and commercial sectors[17] which could be extrapolated to the healthcare setting. In 2002 Mizan[18] conducted a simple, single site interventional study looking closely at the effect of the environment on doctor-patient interaction in primary care – the first study of its kind. Important effects were noted – a reduction in patient anxiety, a more constructive and shared dialogue, a more satisfying consultation for the clinician. This last point – the effect of the environment on the clinician – echoed findings from the important Physician Worklife study[19] which suggested the environment as being one of the most important determinants of job satisfaction amongst physicians.

In summary, what little research exists not only points to a need to further understand the effect of the built environment but also a need to consider that there might be alternatives to the current design paradigm.

The 'Healing Environment' cluster was therefore created with these tasks in mind:

• To start thinking again about community healthcare facilities in the light of the new shape of the NHS.
• To forget what has gone before – to offer up a blank slate upon which novel designs can be generated.
• To create forums for discussion – different forums which work across disciplines and which, crucially, engage with service users and front line healthcare professionals.

Activities

The primary objective of the cluster was to generate a series of research questions for further interrogation in subsequent phases of the Designing for the 21st Century call. The methodology by which these questions were to be arrived at was purposefully left open, so as to encourage novel approaches and inter-disciplinary working. In the end, a number of approaches were adopted though the common theme was user engagement, be they professional or otherwise, as users were and are – in our opinion – the true experts.

This being the case the form of enquiry had to be shaped to fit the group under question. The first 3 think tanks followed a conventional approach, bringing together key stakeholders for a round-table discussion. Whilst there were some important outcomes, they were not as robust as outcomes from subsequent activities.

Cross-disciplinary think tanks I, II & III

These meetings engaged with key stakeholders (GP's, nurses, health authority representatives, medical educationalists, town planners, expert patient representatives) bringing them together in an open forum. Discussions focused primarily on identifying current trends and patterns of healthcare delivery in the NHS. A significant amount of time was spent questioning contemporary healthcare design in terms of both process and outcome and how/whether it dovetailed with design trends. This led on to an exploration of future design options and how an evidence base might be generated to inform future design.

Key outcomes

- Principles of – and trends in – current healthcare design were discussed in such a way as to engage and inform key stakeholders.
- A need for novel design and new built environments for health was identified, set against identifiable weaknesses in the current database, specifically the lack of user informed design guidance.

By contrast, the future search workshop stretched participants, forcing them to make decisions and resulting in more tangible and meaningful outcomes. Importantly, this format allowed the issue to be discussed as a whole – 'the whole elephant' as described by Weisbord – rather than in disjointed pieces gathered from separate meetings, a pattern which plagues so many initiatives. Encouragingly, the outputs were more in line with the aim of the cluster in that they did generate some options for future enquiry. Expanding this single session to a longer 2-day residential workshop, to include an even wider audience, is the ideal proposed by Weisbord et al.[20] and, given the output from this short session, I would strongly support this approach for future projects.

Future search workshop

Drawing on the methodology of Weisbord & Janoff, a Future Search workshop was conducted with a similar group of stakeholders as mentioned above. Delegates were invited to generate a novel concept healthcare facility set within the context of historical trends, political

[20] WEISBORD, M.R. & JANOFF, S., 1995. *Future Search: An Action Guide to Finding Common Ground in Organisations and Communities.* San Francisco: Berret Koehler.

and sociological perspectives. This was a refinement of the earlier think tanks, requiring more detailed work by the delegates, focused on a single build project, and which was to be realistic and presentable in a format acceptable to architects.

Key outcomes:

- A range of design options were generated and worked up in some detail. Most of these reflected current research findings and design of healing environments in hospitals, suggesting the same principles might be transferable to community facilities. This would need to be researched through action research projects.
- The trend toward co-localisation of services with shared facilities between health and social services, housed in a single large facility, was strongly challenged and perceived as a default option rather than an informed one, running counter to patient preferences calling for smaller units closer to home.[10]
- Wellness and health promotion will become priorities for a financially stretched NHS, and might need to be accommodated in existing illness/diagnostic dominated buildings. Options for this need to be developed and researched.

Described below are a series of workshops, loosely based upon the principle of 'thinking through doing'. Magnani suggests that, 'action provides otherwise unavailable information that enables an agent to solve problems by starting and performing a suitable abductive process of generation or selection of hypotheses.'[21] This approach was also felt to be a particularly suitable way to capture concepts, ideas and opinions from typically 'hard to reach' groups. Such groups were also likely to be unfamiliar with the language of healthcare design and architecture and the creative process would cut across this. It also served to enforce the inter-disciplinary nature of the enquiry, in that artists and designers played key roles in facilitating these groups.

[21] MAGNANI, L., 2001. *Creative abduction as active shaping of knowledge: Epistemic and ethical mediators.* New York: Brauch College, City University of New York.

Creating Healing Environments I – questioning feasibility and sustainability

A series of six creative workshops questioned the very process of how sustainable healing spaces might be created which at once empower the community and reflect its cultural values. Through engagement with Southwark Arts Forum and a group of older black women involved in an arts group at a local day centre, a pilot study was developed to test the process, the findings of which could then inform a wider research study. Facilitated by artists from Goldsmiths College, the art group created a piece of artwork which in turn was displayed in the waiting room of a local General Practice [Figure 1].

Key outcomes

- Community engagement in projects spanning the arts and health is fertile ground. Tapping into such enthusiastic resources would not compromise NHS resource, offering a sustainable way forward.
- The process of engaging with and creating artwork in the community needs to be carefully considered. Relationships need to be established and a detailed appreciation of the level of skill available in the group is essential. This takes time and needs to be factored into similar projects.
- Engagement with primary health care teams remains challenging – the reasons for this need to be better understood.
- A longer term, wider ranging pilot is called for, with more formal evaluation of user satisfaction, and evaluation of the cost/benefit of this approach.

Creating Healing Environments II – a younger perspective

As part of the process of wide ranging user involvement, a group of young people were invited to a series of four facilitated (thinkpublic.com) creative workshops and focus group discussions. It was felt that optimal engagement would be delivered through the process of design, in this case designing items related to healthcare and talking around these topics during the creative process. In the event, T-shirts were screen printed [Figure 2] with novel logos and strap lines for the NHS as viewed from the younger persons' perspective. Story boards were created reflecting idealised visions of accessing healthcare as a young person.

Key outcomes

- Engaging with this difficult to reach population needs to begin at a very basic level with no assumptions made as to level of understanding of the healthcare system.
- Trust, established over time, and close communication through respected peers is vital to the success of any project with such groups.
- For this population – and perhaps for others – the use of simple design tools to facilitate discussion offers an engaging alternative to routine methods of enquiry and needs to be developed and evaluated.
- Especially amongst youth, the perceived image of an organisation critically influences how it is accessed. This study suggests that the image of the NHS is sterile, dated and authoritarian. Suggestions were

made as to how to change this, with recommendations for youth friendly logos as well as design suggestions for healthcare facilities. In common with other groups, this group felt smaller units blended into local facilities were infinitely preferable to large polyclinics.

• Other design suggestions pointed to the removal or significant modification of waiting rooms, this has been supported by other research (personal communication).

• Options generated by this project could be applied to the provision of sexual healthcare facilities, currently an area of significant concern.

Figures 1 and 2,
left to right

Figure 1, Creating Healing Environments – section of tapestry created by Older Women's Art Group, Southwark
Figure 2, Creative output: Young People's Group

Creating Healing Environments III – the waiting game

This project engaged with a single family practice. Once again, process and outcome were explored in terms of addressing whether a primary health team, with facilitation, could engage and contribute to the process of designing a space and what the outcome might be? Thinkpublic.com designed a project pack which encouraged participants to identify items in their home/work life which were 'healing' in the sense that they relieved anxiety, and so on. Images of these environments were captured photographically and accompanied by a written narrative which also explored issues around accessing health facilities and services. A workshop then used the collected data to discuss and generate real options for the design of their waiting room.

Key outcomes

- Once again engagement with the primary healthcare team proved difficult despite initial enthusiasm. An alternative practice did engage readily, however, suggesting variability in response.
- Thinking imaginatively – and virtually – can be difficult for a team used to working and thinking within conservative and narrow boundaries. It can be done, though needs skilful facilitation and the use of imaginative prompts which actively engage with participants.
- Implementing environmental change seemed difficult for this team. They worked very well to generate new ideas for their waiting space, the majority of them in line with healthcare design theory, but stopped short of actually doing it, without good reason. Further projects should explore barriers to implementation of design concepts.
- Generation and implementation of healing spaces in healthcare needs firm and assertive leadership, ideally from within and without the team.

Out of the Box – an adventure in healthcare design

This workshop engaged with primary school children, artists from Goldsmiths College and architecture graduates from the Royal College of Art. As with the young people's project, this drew on a creative process – the construction of health facilities within shoeboxes – to elicit the child's perspectives and priorities in healthcare design. The completed buildings were displayed at The Prince's Foundation in London and served as the prompt for a focus group held on site [Figures 3 and 4].

Key outcomes

- Giving children ownership of some of the process yielded extremely valuable outputs. In this case a participant took on the role of filmmaker and interviewed fellow participants with startling results. This could be further tested in future projects.
- Children have very clear and remarkably detailed opinions on healthcare facilities. There has been very little consultation previously – this project suggests there should be more.
- A novel finding was the relative importance children gave to smell – preferring a fresh, clean and natural/floral smell – and cleanliness.
- Children expressed concern for staff and carers/guardians, suggesting that there should be provision of supportive spaces – tea/coffee facilities, comfortable seating were mentioned – whilst waiting and for doctors so they could perform at their best.

Figures 3 to 4b,
top to bottom

Figure 3: Out of the Box – An Adventure in Healthcare Design
Figure 4a and b: Waiting Room and Healing Garden – a child's perspective

The Mixed Media project described below was perhaps one of the most ambitious projects undertaken by the cluster, in that it brought together 3 disciplines – media, fine art, and medicine – as well as bridging commercial, not for profit and academic institutions that is CMP publishing, National Portrait Gallery and Kings College London.

Mixed Media – a collaborative project with PULSE, National Portrait Gallery (NPG) and fine arts photographers

This project reflected a truly innovative approach to inter-disciplinary collaboration as well as offering a novel approach to stakeholder engagement. Pulse is a weekly newspaper circulated to healthcare professionals – the NPG needs little introduction. The aim of the project was to engage with fine arts photographers to capture the practice of healing in primary care. Images were displayed weekly in Pulse and readers were invited to comment on the images and their place in enhancing their working environments. These comments were captured in a questionnaire which has been formally analysed. The project ended with a seminar hosted by the NPG during which the outputs were further discussed. The images [Figure 5] are soon to be placed in participating health centres as a means of enhancing the environments and user feedback is to be collected.

Key outcomes

- Questionnaire analysis: generated valuable insights into the place of the arts in healthcare from the GP perspective.
- Uniquely, the project offered support and learning to the arts whilst at the same time making a bridge between a commercial media operation, practicing clinicians and academic research.
- There is strong interest in a wider rollout of the project from all the key participants and this is currently being explored.

Figure 5, Mixed Media Project. The practice of healing: a photographer's perspective

The final work undertaken by the cluster was aimed at future planning, essentially through involvement in a high calibre leadership forum known as the Caritas Project.

The CARITAS project

[22] THE CARITAS PROJECT. Available at: www.thecaritasproject.info

Founded by Dr Wayne Ruga,[22] this Initiative offers a supportive network bringing together leaders in healthcare design. In May 2006 Dr. Mizan attended the first learning collaborative of the project. The work of the cluster was presented followed by an in-depth discussion on how to further develop its early work.

Key outcomes

- International links were established with leaders in healthcare design.
- The cross disciplinary and highly influential nature of this network will be invaluable in shaping future projects and supporting national and international dissemination
- The Caritas Project seeks to expand the definition of 'healing environments' to embrace not only physical change but also social and cultural change, placing it at the vanguard of current thinking. Involvement of the cluster at this early stage of Caritas will move its current and future work to a higher and more holistic level so that it can become a force for systemic and sustainable change.

Insights

General

- Projects delivered through this grant will have raised awareness amongst principal stakeholders, not only of the theory and importance of healthcare design, but also the complex nature of researching this field. This might lead to a more informed involvement in the generation of design briefs and, ideally, the creation of novel healthcare facilities that go beyond the functional and offer support to users and healthcare professionals. This could fundamentally alter the space of healthcare provision across the UK.
- New networks/collaborations have been described, bridging unlikely partners to good effect. Insights into how to create and work these complex networks have been described. Such exemplars might help reform the current approach to healthcare design research which seems to suffer from an isolationist approach, not helped by RAE (Research Assessment Exercise). The cluster concept itself is an excellent approach. Central to its success, however, are the cluster members and one is cautioned against exclusively approaching leaders in the field, as

[23] STARICOFF, R. L., 2004. *Arts in Health: A Review of Medical Literature*. London: Arts Council England.

[24] BELL, P., GREENE, T.C., FISHER, J.D. & BAUM, A., 2001. *Environmental Psychology*. Belmont, USA: Wadsworth Group.

work of this nature is time consuming and one might struggle to get real hands on commitment from such individuals. Academic institutions offer huge resources with eager graduates and PhD students who, unencumbered by other responsibilities, would readily input into such activities, as was the case in the *Out of the Box* project.

- It is hoped that this work will open up a discourse about healthcare research which is currently dominated by quantitative and qualitative methodologies. Other methods can be just as rewarding, if not more so in certain disciplines such as environmental psychology and healthcare design.
- From a societal perspective, the emphasis on user empowerment – a theme running through all the projects – is noteworthy. Initiatives developed in this way will be more sustainable, likely to reflect community needs and values more closely, and likely to lead to systemic change and meaningful progress.

Specific

Research questions stemming from this work and ideas for further study include:

- What is a healing environment in primary care?
- Does it matter and to whom?
  - Effects on recruitment, retention, job satisfaction, patient satisfaction.
  - Effects on healthcare outcomes.
- What are the barriers to implementing change in healthcare design at primary care level? Is change needed?
- Who should be the designer? Can design generated by users be translated into reality or is it just wishful thinking?
- In an evidence-based world, will softer outputs such as those described above have any impact on key decision makers? If not, what will? This is an issue that has dogged healthcare design since its inception. Other researchers have tried to harness the subtle effect of the built environment into scientific outcomes[23] though, despite admirable efforts, such studies will always be criticised for the confounding factors inevitably associated with built environments. It would seem therefore that perhaps the only way to explore a new environment is to create one, on best available principles, and to test its effects. In other words, action research. There is an opportunity through the LIFT (Local Improvement Finance Trust) program to do this. Researchers might need to look to simulation studies to test design concepts. Other research tools might include behaviour mapping and task performance.[24]

- How sustainable are healing environments in the primary care NHS? Economic modeling and cost-benefit analyses are needed – though will be complex if indeed possible at all.
- Different models of creating and sustaining ideal environments, such as artists in residence and so on, need to be evaluated, as it seems that neither front line healthcare staff nor managerial healthcare staff are able to take on this significant workload. The Space Works is currently exploring this option.
- Beyond the fabric of the built environment, people are the major determinants of whether an environment is truly supportive. Reports from experienced workers in the field (Wayne Ruga – personal communication), suggest that soon after a project is completed there is more often than not a return to the somewhat hostile environment that preceded the change, and this is bedded in the attitudes of staff within the facility. There is a need to determine the behavioural elements of healing environments, and how to create and sustain them, as it seems that without this understanding, other efforts might be of limited value beyond the immediate short term.

Conclusion

The value of this work depends on how you look at it. For the evidence-based scientist it will perhaps hold little value. For designers and architects it might offer tempting insights into the groups they work with. For researchers it might offer some intrigue, with lots of questions needing answers and clues as to where the process difficulties in such research might lie.

For the physician, it might suggest new ways of problem solving, introducing new networks, new ways of thinking and novel methods of enquiry. But perhaps the most value will come if, through it, all these groups can come together and work in the spirit from which the project was forged – holistically.

Additional Reading

GALLAGHER, W., 1994. *The Power of Place*. New York: Harper Perennial.

DE BOTTON, A., 2006. *The Architecture of Happiness*. London: Hamish Hamilton.

COOPER MARCUS., C. & BARNES, M., 1999. *Healing Gardens – Therapeutic Benefits and Design Recommendations*. New York: Wiley & Sons.

MARBERRY, S., 1997. *Healthcare Design*. New York: Wiley & Sons.

ZEISEL, J., 2006. *Inquiry by Design*. Revised edition. New York: Norton & Co.

ULRICH, R. & ZIMRING, C., 2004. *The Role of the Physical Environment in the Hospital of the 21st Century*. The Robert Wood Johnson Foundation and The Center for Health Design. Available at: www.rwjf.org and www.healthdesign.org

Center for Health Design. Available at: www.healthdesign.org
Environmental Design Research Association. Available at: www.edra.org

Coalition for Health Environments Research (CHER). Available at: www.CHEResearch.org

Designing Healthy and Inclusive Public Outdoor Spaces for Young People

Prof. Lamine Mahdjoubi, (University of the West of England)

Research Context

[1] CHINN, S. & RONA, R., 2001. Prevalence and trends in overweight and obesity in three cross sectional studies of British children, 1974-94. *British Medical Journal* 322, pp. 24-26.

[2] BURNIAT, W., COLE, T., LISSAU, I. & POSKITT, E., 2002. *Child and Adolescent Obesity*. Cambridge University Press.

[3] Health Third Report HC 10 May 2005. Available at: http://www.parliament.the-stationery-office.co.uk/pa/cm200304/cmselect/cmhealth/23/2302.htm (accessed on 12th June 2004).

[4] WANG, Y., 2004. Diet, physical activity, childhood obesity and risk of cardiovascular disease. *International Congress Series*, 1262 (May), pp. 176-179.

[5] REILLY, J.J. et al., 2004. Total energy expenditure and physical activity in young Scottish children: Mixed longitudinal study. *The Lancet*, 363 9404 (17), pp. 211-212.

[6] BIDDLE, S. & ARMSTRONG, N., 1992. Children's physical activity: An exploratory study of psychological correlates. *Social Science Medicine*, 34, pp. 321-331.

In recent years, new public health challenges have brought the issue of the decline of young people's physical activities to the forefront. It has been highlighted that one of the biggest epidemics facing the World in the 21st century is the growing obesity of children. Although being overweight showed little change between 1974 and 1984, between 1984 and 1994 being overweight increased from 5.4 per cent to 9 per cent in English boys and from 9.3 per cent to 13.5 per cent in girls; the prevalence of obesity reached 1.7 per cent in boys and 2.6 per cent in girls. About one in 20 boys (5.5 per cent) and about one in 15 girls (7.2 per cent) aged 2 – 15 were obese in 2002.[1]

Obesity can have severe emotional and psychological consequences for young people, ranging from lowered self-esteem to clinical depression.[2] It has also significant detrimental effects on their health. The recent UK Parliamen Committee on Health Third Report stressed:

'A generation is growing up in an obesogenic environment in which the forces behind sedentary behaviour are growing, not declining. Most overweight or obese children become overweight or obese adults; overweight and obese adults are more likely to bring up overweight or obese children. There is little encouraging evidence to suggest that overweight people generally lose weight; there is ample clear evidence that being overweight greatly increases the risks of a huge range of diseases, and that the more overweight people are, the greater the risks'.[3]

This report concluded that, so far, very little has been done to reverse the rising trend in children's obesity.

[7] MCARDLE, W. D., KATCH, F. I. & KATCH, V. L., 2000. *Essentials of Exercise Physiology*. 2nd ed. Philadelphia: Lippincott Williams & Wilkins.

[8] VANDEWATER, E. A. et al., 2001. Linking obesity and activity level with children's television and video game use. *Journal of Adolescence*, 27, pp. 71-85.

[9] JAGO, R. & BARANOWSKI, T., 2004. Non-curricular approaches for increasing physical activity in youth: a review, *Preventive Medicine*, 39, pp. 157-163.

[10] HAAPANEN, N. et al., 1997. Association between leisure time physical activity and 10 year body mass change among working-aged men and women. *Int J Obes Relat Metab Disord*, 21, pp. 288-96.

[11] BOREHAM, C. & RIDDOCH, C., 2001. The physical activity, fitness and health of children. *J Sports Sci*, 19, pp. 915-929.

[12] BARNETT, T. A., O'LOUGHLIN, J. & PARADIS, G., 2002. One- and two-year predictors of decline in physical activity among inner-city schoolchildren. *Am J Prev Med*, 23(2), pp.121-128.

[13] ASHLEY, R. et al., 2003. Commuting to school: are children who walk more physically active? *Am J Prev Med*, 25(4), pp. 273-276.

[14] RUDOLF, C. J. et al., 2001. Increasing prevalence of obesity in primary school children: cohort study. *BMJ*, 322, pp. 1094-5.

[15] SPEEDNET, 1999. Primary school physical education – Speednet survey makes depressing reading. *Br J Phys Educ*, 30, pp. 19-20.

[16] PANGRAZI, R. P., 2000. Promoting physical activity for youth. *J Sci Med Sport*, 3, pp. 280-6.

Although the causes of obesity are diverse and complex, it is generally agreed that too little exercise and too much energy dense food are the main causes of being overweight.[4] The epidemic of childhood obesity in modern Britain has been largely attributed to a decline in total energy expenditure (TEE).[5] Lack of physical activity is associated with the development of obesity, type 2 diabetes mellitus, and cardiovascular morbidity and mortality. TEE has often been associated with growing sedentary lifestyles amongst children and adolescents. Indeed, many aspects of social life have changed to encourage a more sedentary lifestyle. Sedentary pursuits that can lure children away from physical activities are becoming more available.[6] Some children between the ages of 6 and 11 years spend as much time watching TV as they do attending school (average 26 hours per week).[7] Recent research into children's activity levels and obesity confirmed that children with higher weight status spent more time in sedentary activities than those with lower weight status. Studies have shown that the time spent playing electronic games was associated with high weight status.[8]

Consequently, every effort should be made to help young people to develop healthy lifestyles, including increasing physical activity (PA). PA was defined as 'any bodily movement produced by skeletal muscles that result in caloric expenditure'.[9] Indeed, there is evidence to infer that increases in energy expenditure can help prevent obesity.[10] The risk of developing cardiovascular risk factors is lower for physically active young people.[11] In addition, reduced TV viewing among girls and increased participation in team sports in boys and girls may prevent declines in physical activities among pre-adolescents.[12] It was reported that walking to school was associated with higher physical activity after school and during the evening.[13]

Recognising the role schools play in achieving children's PA levels, recent efforts were directed at encouraging school-based interventions in physical education (PE).[14] The UK Government's Green Paper '14 – 19: extending opportunities, raising standards' recommends that there should be an emphasis on physical fitness, health and well-being during the 14 – 19 years stage in PE. However, there has been strong criticism that the current 2 hour target of PE per week puts 'England below the EU average in terms of physical activity in school, despite the fact that childhood obesity is accelerating more quickly here than elsewhere.'[3] Emerging evidence suggests that the recommendation for schools to increase PE is not being met.[5] The pressure on schools to improve their academic ranking in the performance tables has contributed to the reduction of school sport and PE.[15]

[17] PATE, R. et al., 1995. Physical activity and public health: a recommendation from the Centers for Disease Control and Prevention and the American College of Sports Medicine. *JAMA* 273, pp. 402-7.

[18] STRATTON, G. A., 1999. Preliminary study of children's physical activity in one urban primary school playground; differences by sex and season. J *Sport Pedagog*, 5, pp. 71-81.

[19] STRATTON, G. A., 2000. Promoting children's physical activity in primary schools: an intervention study using playgrounds markings. *Ergonomics*, 43, pp. 1538-46.

[20] RIVKIN, M., 2000. *Outdoor Experiences for Young Children*. Charleston: ERIC/CRESS. Available at: http://www. ericdigests.org/2001-3/children. htm (accessed 26 May 2004).

[21] WILKINSON, P.F., (ed.), 1980. *Innovation in Play Environments*. London: Croom Helm.

[22] MOORE, R. & YOUNG, D., 1978. Childhood Outdoors: Toward a Social Ecology of the Landscape. *In*: I. ALTMAN & J. WOHLWILL, (eds.) *Children and the Environment*. New York: Plenum Press.

[23] SALLIS, J. et al., 2003. Environmental interventions for eating and physical activity: a randomized controlled trial in middle schools. *American Journal of Preventive Medicines*, 24(3), pp. 209-17.

[24] INGUNN FJÙTOFT, I. & SAGELE, J., 2000. The natural environment as a playground for children: Landscape description and analyses of a natural playscape. *Landscape and Urban Planning*, 48, pp. 83-97.

Recent recommendations have advocated 30 – 60 minutes of daily PA, as a minimum requirement for children due to their tendency for intermittent style of PA engagement.[16] As these requirements cannot be met by school-based interventions, more attention is increasingly been diverted to informal PE. For example, school break periods or travel to and from school are seen as ideal opportunities to increase young people's PA.[17] Recent surveys found that British children spent only 15 per cent of their school break periods engaged in moderate to vigorous physical activity (MVPA).[18] Targeted interventions, such as painting school playgrounds, led to a significant increase (approximately 18 min/day) in the amount of time that 5 to 7 year-old children spent engaged in MVPA during school lunch periods.[19]

Other empirical research findings reported that a powerful strategy to counteract the deficiencies in the fitness of young people would be to create outdoor environments that can encourage children to spend longer periods of time outside, engaged in higher levels of PA.[20] It is believed that the most important and dramatic changes to young people's health and lifestyles will have to take place outside the schools playgrounds, in outdoor environment in which children live their daily lives. Outdoor play opportunities can exist for young people around the home (for example, gardens), the school and public park (that is, playgrounds), the city qua city (that is, streets, shopping centres, open areas and places,[21] and all manner of spaces 'left over' during the urbanisation process.[22]

The virtues of outdoor playing have been widely endorsed. Very strong relationship was found between the amounts of time spent outdoors and increased physical activity and fitness in children.[23] All-round playing and exploring the natural playscape improved children's motor fitness.[24] A recent study found a significant relationship between outdoor temperature and health in children attending day-care centres, which confirmed that outdoor activities are beneficial.[25] Similarly, it was demonstrated that children who increased their outdoor activities for 5 hours per week were healthier than those who spent that time indoors.[26]

However, it is emerging that over the last three decades, fundamental changes appear to have occurred in patterns of young people's outdoor play, which is now primarily centred on the home rather than the street.[27] There has been widespread popular concern about the future young people's outdoor play, indicating that children are being denied the outdoor play opportunities afforded to previous generations.[28] 'Streets used to be places for people. Today they are through routes and places for cars. The children have vanished.[29]'

[25] SENNERSTAM, R. B.
& MOBERG, K., 2004.
Relationship between
illness-associated absence in
day-care children and weather
parameters. *Public Health*,
118(5), pp. 349-353.

[26] BONDESTAM, M. &
RASMUSSEN, F., 1994.
Preschool children's absenteeism
from Swedish municipal day-
care centres because of illness
in 1977 and 1990. Geographical
variations and characteristics
of day-care centres. *Scand J Soc
Med*, 22, pp. 20-6.

[27] VALENTINE, G. &
MCKENDRICK, J., 1997.
Children's outdoor play:
exploring parental concerns
about children's safety and the
changing nature of childhood.
Geoforum, 28(2), pp. 219-235.

[28] CLEMENT, R., 2003.
Research Finds Decline In
Outdoor Play. *Education
update*, June. Available at:
http://www.educationupdate.
com/archives/2003/june03/issue/
child_outdoor.html (accessed 18
March 2004).

[29] UDAL, 2000. *Returning
Roads to Residents: A Practical
Guide to Improving Your Street*.
London: UDAL. Available at:
http://udal.org.uk/returning.
html (accessed on 2 June 2004).

[30] CAHILL, S., 1990. Childhood
and public life: reaffirming
biographical divisions. *Social
Problems*, 37, pp. 390-402.

[31] BALL, D. J., 2004. Policy issues
and risk-benefit trade-offs of
'safer surfacing' for children's
playgrounds. *Accident Analysis
& Prevention*, 36(4), pp. 661-670.

[32] MOORE, R. & WONG,
H., 1997. *Natural Learning:
Rediscovering Nature's Way of
Teaching*. Berkeley, CA: MIG
Communications.

[33] MOORE, R., 1997. The need
for nature: a childhood right.
Social Justice 24(3), pp. 203-220.

Several factors have paved the way for the decline of outdoor play, and thus contributed to the growing young people's sedentary lifestyle. Young people's reduced access to these outdoor spaces is often related to parents' fears of traffic and criminality, as well as the inadequacy of the physical environment. Common reasons given by parents of young children for not allowing them to walk to school includes long walking distance, traffic safety and fear of attack or abduction. Indeed, concerns about children's play are centred on debates about the provision of adequate play facilities (in terms of quality and quantity) and on the ability of children to play safely free from the risk of accidents, and traffic 'killer car', and/or 'stranger dangers'.[30] Parents are also often concerned about children's vulnerability to violence and drugs and therefore seek to control their play in order to minimise their exposure to danger.[31] As a result, many parents no longer allow their children to play outdoors unsupervised.[32]

Planning and designing outdoor environments has also contributed to the decline of play. Public parks, within walking or biking distance from home, are no longer being provided because they are more expensive to maintain.[33] Playgrounds and schoolyards consist of standardised commercial equipment where safety rather than play value is the dominant criterion.[34] The increasing fear of litigation is leading to the creation of unattractive public spaces for young people. The universal application of 'safer surfacing' in playgrounds is assessed in terms of absolute risk, cost-benefit and qualitative factors.[31] Consequently, many playgrounds are now so dull [Figure 1] that children reject them in favour of more exciting and potentially dangerous places.[35] Research established that parents considered play facilities to be generally poor (the older the child, the more likely a parent will consider that there is inadequate provision).[36] Child welfare and play communities are increasingly of the view that playgrounds are losing their appeal for children, which in turn has its own health, safety and developmental consequences.[31] Public and Local Government attitudes can also hinder play. For instance, some youth activities, such as skateboarding are increasingly under threat (a £20 on-the-spot fine has been introduced if you are found skating anywhere in the Square Mile of the City of London).[37] For these and other reasons the focus of children's everyday life has dramatically shifted from outdoors to indoors,[27] and fewer youth are playing outdoors.[38]

In the face of such challenges, young people's access to attractive and accessible outdoor areas is seen as potentially playing a key role in their health and well-being. Access to outdoor environments has potential to enhance levels of physical activity, both formal and informal, encourage

34 MOORE, R., 1989. Playgrounds at the Crossroads: Policy and Action Research Needed to Ensure a Viable Future for Public Playgrounds in the US. *In*: I. ALTMAN & E. ZUBE, (eds.) *Public Spaces and Places*. New York: Plenum.

35 CABESPACE, 2004. *Manifesto for Better Public Spaces*. Available at: http://www.itsyourspace.org.uk/manifesto.asp [Accessed 11 June 2006].

36 MCNEISH, D. & ROBERTS, H., 1995. *Playing It Safe: Today's Children at Play*. Essex: Barnardo's.

37 CABESPACE, 18 May 2004. *Don't design skating out of the city*, urges CABE (press release). [Accessed 11 June 2004].

38 JUTRAS, S., 2003. Allez jouer dehors! Contributions de l'environnment urbain au développement et au bien-être des enfants. *Canadian Psychology*, 44(3), pp. 257-266.

39 MORRIS, N., 2003. *Health, Well-being And Open Space*. Edinburgh: OPENspace Research Centre.

40 HARTIG, T. et al., 2003. Tracking restoration in natural and urban field settings. *JEP* 23, pp. 109-123.

41 NICHOLSON, S., 1971. How NOT to cheat children: The theory of loose parts. *Landscape Architecture*, 62, pp. 30-34.

42 COSCO, N. & MOORE, R., 1999. Playing in Place: Why the Physical Environment is Important. *In: Playwork14, the Playeducation Annual Play and Human Development Meeting: Theoretical Playwork, Ely, January 1999*. pp. 26 - 27.

43 RAPOPORT, A., 1977. *Human Aspects of Urban Form: Towards a Man-Environment Approach to Urban Form and Design*. Oxford: Pergamon Press.

independence and social interaction, as well as contribute to better mental health and relief from depression and stress.[39] Exercise outdoors can help maintain circadian rhythms and prevent sleep disorders and vitamin D deficiency. Physical exercise and other activities in natural surroundings have been shown to be particularly effective in reducing blood pressure, stress, and mental fatigue and improving cognitive functioning.[40] Access outdoors and use of public open space can also increase social networks and build social capital in a community [Figure 2].

It is increasingly recognised that the design of the built environment – the man-made physical structures and communities – has an impact on regular physical activities through outdoor play. Children prefer to interact with physical environmental features, such as materials and shapes, gravity, smell and other things, which they can discover, explore, and experiment with.[41] The physical design of the space can have a strong impact on the type and diversity of play and playwork possible in the space[42] [Figure 3]. Diversity is often related to multiple uses, choice and diversity of activities at one time and over time, spatial variety, many physical elements, varied surfaces, shapes, textures, heights, colours, light and shade, smells, sounds and materials.[43] In addition, good networks of streets and parks encourage people of all ages to be physically active.[35]

In order to promote young people's outdoor play, it is important to reflect on the opportunities offered by creative design of outdoor spaces to stimulate outdoor PA. It is also critical to identify the barriers and potentially effective strategies for surmounting the problems that hinder outdoor play.

Aims of the Cluster

The cluster sought to determine what should be expected from public outdoor spaces in the 21ˢᵗ century to encourage outdoor play and promote regular physical activities. Its aim is to explore the role of inclusive design of outdoor spaces as a vehicle to promote play and to overcome some barriers that inhibit outdoor PA. It built a multidisciplinary and inter-professional forum that identified critical research issues and priority actions, through the exchange of knowledge, experiences and case studies. It also stimulated further research through debate and collaboration between the participants. The cluster generated activities that identified the barriers and effective strategies to counteract young people's increasing sedentary lifestyles, address the issue of obesity, and above all, support their social, psychological, physical and cognitive development.

Figures 1 to 3,
top to bottom

Figure 1, Declining play provision in urban settings
Figure 2, Designing outdoor play environments that are socially inclusive
Figure 3, Designing flexible and varied outdoor play environments

The Committee on Health[3] recommended an urgent long term, integrated and wide-ranging programme of solutions, which constitute a consistent, effective and defined strategy to tackle the epidemic of obesity. So far, the issues related to young people's play were examined in the light of particular disciplines or areas of expertise, including psychology, sociology, geography, education, architecture, landscape architecture and so on.[21]

There is an emerging consensus that new multi-discipline/professional perspectives and scientific collaboration are essential to bring together the concerns, views and knowledge of the various researchers and practitioners in this complex field. Moore[44] advised that to succeed in this task, urban designers, landscape architects and architects will need to collaborate with professionals from other fields (public health; parks, recreation and leisure; education; traffic engineering, and so on), who share a deep commitment to systemic change. To date there has been no formal dedicated forum for exploring the role of outdoor public spaces in counteracting children and adolescents increasing sedentary lifestyle. The proposed cluster provided the ideal forum where the relationship between the design of outdoor public spaces, and the complex and interrelated pattern of factors contributing to obesity in children and adolescents are examined, shared, exchanged and debated.

[44] MOORE, R., 2003. *Counteracting children's sedentary lifestyles by design.* Available at: http://www.naturalearning.org/aboutus/countersedentary.htm [Accessed 12ᵗʰ January 2003].

Participants

The mission of the cluster was to bring together researchers, practitioners and professionals from several disciplines and occupations to shed light on important issues and research priorities, relating to the role of design in the promotion of young people's outdoor PA. Although it was envisaged that the cluster membership is set to grow, at the initial stage, several key disciplines and professions were represented. Participants included architects, landscape architects, urban designers, public health professionals, educators, community safety experts, and other individuals and organisations interested in creating environments for young people that can counteract sedentary lifestyles and stimulate PA [Figure 4]:

- design (architectural, urban and landscape design);
- Commission for Architecture and the Built Environment;
- Children Play Council;
- physical activity and public health;
- child and adolescent health;
- Learning through Landscapes Trust;
- community safety and crime prevention;

- Crime Prevention Design Advisory;
- Safe Neighbourhoods Unit;
- child psychology;
- education;
- transport and society;
- manufacturers and suppliers of play equipment and landscape construction and maintenance.

Figure 4, Multidisciplinary and
interprofessional research seminars

Objectives and Methodology

The overall objectives of the proposed cluster were to stimulate and sustain the exchange of ideas, nurture research proposals between its members and develop mutual understanding of needs and potential innovation of designing outdoor public spaces that can counteract young people's sedentary lifestyle, by inclusive design. Inclusive design offers better mainstream solutions for everyone, supported by new design research techniques to make the development process more user-centred.[45]

The cluster also sought to report and disseminate outputs/progress of national and international research activities in this field, and formulate the priorities for action and strategies for research and innovation to stimulate outdoor PA, by design. The specific objectives and the methods to achieve the objectives are given in Table 1.

[45] COLEMAN, R., 2004. *About: Inclusive Design*. London: Design Council. Available at: http://www.design-council.org.uk/en/About-Design/Design-Techniques/Inclusive-design [Accessed 12th June 2004].

Objectives	Methodology to deliver objectives
To establish a multidisciplinary and inter-professional forum that leads to innovative collaboration between (1) researchers in human aspects of urban design; (2) designers, including architects, landscape architects, urban designers; (3) child and adolescent health experts; (4) community safety and crime prevention advisors; (5) child psychologists; (6) teachers; (7) organisations involved in child and adolescent play and development; (8) play equipment manufacturers and suppliers; (9) landscape companies.	By the start of the cluster, a steering committee was in place along with a programme of meetings and events. The target is for 3 workshops, several coordination/management meetings and an international conference. These events involved international experts and participants to compare and exchange experiences and examine research issues related to this field of study.
To generate new ideas and debates on which factors have the greatest potential for stimulating outdoor play and promoting physical activities, by inclusive design.	Report on the impact of designing creative outdoors public spaces on young people's play behaviour and physical activities.
To formulate the priorities for action and, integrated strategies for research and innovation, on the role of creative design of outdoor public spaces in counteracting young people's increasing sedentary lifestyles.	Report on the effective approaches and strategies for stimulating child and adolescent outdoor play and physical activities, through design.
To report and disseminate outputs/ progress of innovative national and international research activities in this field.	State-of-the-art reviews on research activities and good practice in this field, taking place both in the UK and overseas.
To create a focus for information exchange and dissemination of ideas and activities of the cluster.	Advertise the cluster activities using high profile events and conferences. Dissemination through a dynamic web site, and an international conference, as well as brochures and other printed material.
To inform and advise, where appropriate, those involved in allocating UK public sector research funding.	Invite the Director of the Initiative, as well as AHRC and EPSRC representatives to attend workshops and cluster conference, and to provide keynote presentations.

Table 1, Objectives and methodologies of the cluster

Activities and Deliverables of the Cluster

The cluster's objectives were achieved through the following parallel streams of activities:

- focused workshops and a cluster conference to engage in debates and discussions of key research issues;
- regular discussions and exchange of ideas using electronic media; such as emails and video conferencing. It is also envisaged that the cluster website provides an information focal point, as well as a support for collaboration and virtual discussions. It was populated with reports, publications, and case studies.
- restrained network coordination and management meetings.

These activities converged into several key milestones. The following themes were examined:

Workshop 1 – March 2005:
Counteracting young people's sedentary lifestyles, by design.

- Examine the effects of outdoor physical activities on young people's health and social, emotional, physical and cognitive development.
- Explore how to promote children's physical activities through outdoor design interventions.
- Identify the opportunities and barriers for children's outdoor activities.

Workshop 2 – June 2005:
Safety and attitudes in children and adolescents outdoor play environments.

- Examine the role of creative planning and design solutions of public outdoor environments, which allow young people to play and move free from the risk of accidents, traffic 'killer car', and/or 'stranger dangers'.
- Discuss the effects of disruptive and violent behaviour on young people's use of outdoor public spaces.
- Analyse the effects of play equipment and playground injury risk.
- Examine public, local government and police's attitudes to young people's outdoor play in public places.

Workshop 3 – September 2005:
Designing inclusive and innovative outdoor environments with
young people in mind.

- Examine the planning, design and management of outdoor play settings for children and adolescents.
- Assess the role of inclusive design to address young people's needs, irrespective of age or ability.
- Explore the role of landscapes 'natural and man-made' in promoting outdoor play and PA.

International Conference – 5–7 July 2006:
Young people outdoor physical activities – A future research
agenda.

The international conference was used as a forum to synthesise the salient research issues and priority action strategies, identified during the cluster events and activities. The conference supported the dissemination of the research outputs and activities.

Outcomes

The first exploratory workshop stimulated a lively debate between disciplines which rarely sit together to explore the relationship between the decline of young people's physical activities and the design of outdoor public spaces. It highlighted some of the health, social, emotional and cognitive development dimensions and their implications on physical activities. It emerged that there has been a drastic decline in young people's outdoor activity, which included both unsupervised and supervised play. It was also stressed that outdoor play has gradually been replaced by adult-led activities. Cluster members focused on two areas that were identified as critical to overcome the barriers to play and offer better opportunities for young people to engage in outdoor physical activities. These key areas encompassed social and institutional issues; and physical environments. The debate raised the need to engage a wider audience on the fundamental question of, what are young people? It was proposed that it is necessary to challenge adult's misconceptions about young people's needs, requirements and capabilities. Powerful strategies to counteract the deficiencies in the fitness of young people, such as the use of an incremental design approach and playful landscapes were recommended.

The second workshop focused on safety and risk and how it affects young people's everyday lives and restricts their outdoor play activities. The discussions raised the concern that growing anxieties about youngster's

safety from strangers, road traffic and 'unsafe' outdoor environments
have impaired their outdoor play opportunities and encouraged sedentary
lifestyles. Parents are also often concerned about children's vulnerability
to violence and drugs and therefore seek to control their play in order to
minimise their exposure to danger. Consequently, many parents no longer
allow their children to play outdoors unsupervised. It was highlighted that
there is a tendency to regard any risk as unacceptable and a firm belief
that most accidents are preventable. This attitude is having detrimental
effects on young people's welfare, creative potential and health. Cluster
members stressed the need to accept the importance and positive value
of risk in young people's play and development. It was suggested that the
public debate should shift away from risk to challenge. It was recognised
that risk and challenge should be integrated in the design of outdoor
public spaces to promote stimulating and healthy outdoor environments.

The presentations explored ways of utilising careful design of outdoor
environments, including urban design facilitates; school playgrounds, play
areas; open spaces and neighbourhood play facilities to foster active play.
The speakers argued that outdoor design can play a significant role in
encouraging play and PA. Using real-life examples and findings of several
studies, the presentations demonstrated how innovative design can affect
children and adolescent outdoor physical activities. A future research
agenda was also formulated, which included priorities for action on the
role of creative design of outdoor public spaces. For the afternoon session,
three themes were tabled for discussion:

- link between play provision in the neighbourhood and youngsters' level
  of activity;
- relationships between community involvements in the safety of the
  neighbourhood and youngsters' level of activity;
- relationship between design of outdoor environments and children's
  changing needs, ability and age requirements.

Participants highlighted the need to cater for young people's key
developmental requirements particularly for social interaction and retreat,
by creating supportive and mutually acceptable physical environments.
The role of design in supporting informal supervision for mutual lookout
for children's safety was also explored. The concepts of shared spaces as
well as diversity, adaptability and flexibility of outdoor environments in
order to encourage multiple uses, choice and diversity of activities at one
time and over time were also explored.

Deliverables

The cluster deliverables included the following:

- interim reports that were disseminated widely, including work;
- newsletter to be disseminated widely through mailing list and the cluster website;
- refereed publications, which includes two special issues;
- cluster website, which was used for the dissemination of the cluster activities and outputs, as well as a discussion forum;
- practical case studies;
- Proposals for grants application.
- an international conference, 'Planning and designing healthy public outdoor spaces for young people in the 21st century', which took place at the Watershed, Bristol from 5th to 7th July 2006.

Sustainability of the cluster

It was planned to create a sustainable cluster, which continues its activities beyond the period of funding. To achieve this objective, the group linked with networks and individuals, in the UK and/or overseas, who are currently studying the role of outdoor built environments in promoting healthy lifestyles for young people through active play.

Most members of the core team attended the workshops and the conference. The attendance of the workshops varied according to the focus of the workshop. Most of the participants had a long term interest in the research issues addressed by the cluster. This was reflected in a high level of motivation. As most of the participants were geographically close, frequent meetings were possible to arrange, which contributed to the sustainability of the cluster.

Management structure

A flat management structure was adopted. The Principal Investigator was responsible for the smooth running of the cluster and interfacing with AHRC-EPSRC. The cluster was managed by a steering committee, which consisted of the investigators, the cluster coordinator, a representative from the academic partners and a representative of other organisations. The steering committee was responsible for the approval of the programmes of the cluster events and identifying suitable speakers and case studies. It also sought to develop a working strategy and ensure that the activities of the cluster are widely disseminated. Its remits also involve encouraging the participants to apply for funding to support specific projects and sustain the cluster activities, beyond its funding period.

Relevance to the outputs to beneficiaries

The direct beneficiaries of these outputs/activities of this forum
were practitioners, researchers, associations and other organisations
involved in the cluster. The conference disseminated the outputs to an
international audience and helped to foster a far-reaching debate. The
participants benefited from the development of a novel and integrated
approach, which deals more effectively with the study of the relationship
between the design of outdoor public spaces and young people's PA. The
cluster endeavours and the conference have delivered innovative ideas
and provided strategic directions to research and development in this
field. This led to substantial benefits to a wide range of professions and
disciplines; including architecture, urban design, planning, transport,
health, psychology, sociology and education. The ultimate beneficiaries
of the activities and outputs of this cluster are young people, as their
health, development and well-being were the main reasons for building
this cluster.

Additional Reading

HOLLOWAY, S. D. et al., 1995. What is 'appropriate practice' at home
and in child care?: Low-income mothers' views on preparing their children
for school. *Early Childhood Research Quarterly*, 10(4), pp. 451-473.

INTERNATIONAL OBESITY TASKFORCE, 2004. Obesity in Europe:
The Case for Action [online]. Available at:
http://www.iotf.org/media/euobesity.pdf (Accessed 12 May 2004).

PANTAZIS, C., 2000. Fear of crime, vulnerability and poverty: Evidence
from the British crime survey. *British Journal of Criminology*, 40,
pp. 414-436.

SALLIS, J. F. et al., 1997. The effects of a 2 year physical education
program (SPARK) on physical activity and fitness in elementary school
students. Sports, play and active recreation for kids. *Am J Public Health*,
87, pp. 132–134.

SEATON, J. and WALL, S., 2001. A summary of walking and walking in
the Perth metropolitan region. *Presented at Australia: walking in the 21st
century, Perth, Australia, 20-22nd February 2001*. Government of Western
Australia.

The View of the Child: Explorations of the Visual Culture of the Made Environment

Dr Catherine Burke,[1] Dr Claire Gallagher,[2] Dr Jon Prosser[1] and Judy Torrington[3] ([1]University of Leeds, [2]Georgian Court University, USA, [3]University of Sheffield)

Overview

The impact of visual culture on the current generation of children has implications for their future and the futures of us all, as all children are consumers of design and some may even become designers themselves. Children occupy and respond to designed spaces, but are rarely involved in decision making about the visual and material environment that surrounds them. Engaging with pupil voice has, however, become part of the agenda of developing citizenship and democracy in children's lives following the ground breaking 1989 United Nations Convention on the Rights of the Child. One of the central designed environments in the lives of children are schools yet these institutions are usually designed and reshaped over time by adults with little or no opportunity given to children to voice their views. Key research initiatives in recent years have revealed how children from a very early age can be experts in their own experience of such environments and given suitable and relevant means, are able to articulate their view and their needs.

The 'View of the Child' research cluster brought together a network of international scholars from across academic disciplines. Included were those with cutting edge knowledge of research methodologies involving children; authorities in the sociology and history of the material and visual culture of schools; international experts in architectural history and those directly engaged today across the world in developing creative design processes for engaging children, teachers and communities in new school design. This group was brought together with designers, stakeholders and users, to shape research that focuses on the relationship between the developing child, educational practice, and design.

[1] We used the term exchanges to recognise the interdisciplinarity of the overall project and the interactivity of the meetings.

[2] Six speakers presented papers. These included Bruce A. Jilk, the keynote speaker (Architect, School Designer and Education Planner), Prof. Ian Grosvenor (University of Birmingham), Bob Banks (Senior Analyst, Tribal Technology), Dominic Cullinan (Architect, Cullinan and Buck Architects Ltd.), Judith Sixsmith (Senior Lecturer in Psychology and Speech Pathology, Manchester Metropolitan University) and Alison Clark (Visual Artist and Researcher, The Thomas Corum Research Unit, The Institute of Education, University of London). Each had been asked to respond to images of drawings of children from 'The School I'd Like' project and to provide some analysis in the form of questions eliciting further research.

The cluster met at a series of 'exchanges'[1] to explore and develop research agendas for the future design of learning environments. Everybody in the group recognised that schools and classrooms need to reinvent or redefine themselves but appear to be trapped in formats designed for an earlier age. The current remedy to this issue is rebuild and the entire replacement of past answers to pedagogical problems. However, the View of the Child research cluster was keen to reveal new ways of seeing current designed learning environments and help formulate research agendas for envisaging the design answer to future pedagogical challenges.

The term 'visual culture' was used to reflect the cluster's intention to explore the cumulative, tacit and specific effects of the visual foci. The overarching aim was to identify a research agenda that would provide policy makers and practitioners with a basis for determining design strategies aimed at increasing the well being of all who occupy school spaces.

Key questions that were considered included:

- What is the visual culture of the made educational environment of children?
- How can designers, teachers, children and parents optimise the possibilities of the visual environment in educational contexts to enhance growth of visual awareness for future designers and consumers of design?
- How can designers be encouraged to recognise a view of visual culture in educational environments that incorporates values, beliefs and practices?
- What are the implications of major cultural shifts in communications and technology for the visual environments of children and young people?
- How do children 'read' their environment, visually?
- What would children recognise as an environment which recognises and respects them?
- Are visual methodologies, such as using photography, drawing and art an essential element of future strategies?

Activities

Five 'exchanges' were held during the year. The first meeting was intended to open up the way that the different academic disciplines and professions interpret the view of the child as evidenced in images produced by children and young people across the UK in the 2001: 'The School I'd Like' archive.[2] The second event focused on developing innovative methodologies to engage children's perspective in the planning process for building schools for the future. The third and fourth exchanges involved young children; the first designing a city, the second recording the visual culture of their school environment. The final meeting allowed reflection and planning for the future.

In this chapter, the exchanges involving young people will be presented and discussed. These both involved groups of children between the ages 7 and 12 years. The first worked with children to design and model a city environment. The second gave children the opportunity to reveal to us what mattered to them and affected them in the everyday visual and material environment of their school building and grounds. The involvement of children in the research process was serious and not simply tokenistic. We were committed to illustrate the potential for innovative methodologies that could be employed in generating data highly relevant to the educational sectors as western governments reconfigure and redesign learning environments for the 21ˢᵗ century.

The city building exchange was held at an inner-city Sheffield primary school in July 2005, and aimed to provide a supportive framework to enable a group of children to 'build a city' in a large space in their school. We were interested to observe not only what happened, but also to record how it happened. Presenting children with a challenge like this is very different from the kind of goal-driven projects that normally characterise the curriculum and much educational research. Here, children were put in a position to develop the answer to our question, not to give us the answer we wanted to hear.

Twenty-one children, together with their teaching assistant and eight students of architecture from Sheffield University, worked with members of the research cluster over 2 days. The children had been selected by their teachers to represent a full range of aptitudes, perceived abilities and levels of disaffection or engagement in school. Twenty children made the journey through the 2 days, one child being withdrawn by the teaching assistant as punishment for 'bad behaviour'. The group included boys and girls from very diverse cultural backgrounds. Not all children spoke English as their first language and a few spoke no English at all. The inner-city school they attended and which hosted the exchange workshop had been built in 1877, a classic design answer to the pedagogical problem posed at the end of the 19ᵗʰ century when mass compulsory education was introduced.

Figures 1 to 3,
top to bottom

Figure 1, From *The School I'd Like, Sweet School* by Rebecca, aged 8
Figure 2, *Building a City*, Sheffield, July 2005
Figure 3, *Building a City*, Sheffield, July 2005

The children were asked to design a city and to build a three-dimensional model of their idea from scrap materials. The adults present created an informal atmosphere whereby the children were encouraged to think of themselves as experts and as equals to other members of the team – all adults and children present were introduced by their first names and wore the same kind of labels. We talked about how we were going to work together over the following 2 days to make a city. The atmosphere was engaged and friendly. The large group divided into seven smaller groups with three children and an adult helper in each. The task was to brainstorm everything you might find or want to find in a city. Many ideas were generated and a helper recorded each one on a sheet of paper. In the initial brainstorming session personalised issues emerged: the need of an Iranian boy for security checkpoints along the 'seaside'; equality or 'money for everyone'; accessibility; the possibility of 'holidays for people who clean up the city'; and a concern for 'people with sticks'. Further discussions resulted in more elaborate and creative suggestions: a school and an 'unschool'; a hotel in the shape of a fish with a turf roof for football; churches; mosques; a language school; a space/time machine complete with a key to operate it; 'places for fun' in the form of sweet shops and adventure parks, farms and zoos; transportation on mermaid taxis and water flume monorails. Residential areas were peripheral to the city, with larger houses farthest away from the city centre. Public, civic and commercial buildings were included as well: hospitals, universal signage, trams, pubs and clubs, restaurants, car parks, limousine repair shop and toy shops. Open space was a primary concern, as were connections between and among elements of the children's design which were accomplished through physical connections such as infrastructure and psychologically through more abstract design responses such as visual accessibility from one city feature to another.

Some ideas were everyday and familiar such as hotels, houses and flats. Some were more like ideas for something new such as, 'a place where everyone can go and learn music and not ever fail and it is free and it takes as long as you want.' There were also concrete examples of the children's attention to more practical concerns. In consideration of context and deciding on the sites for their individual urban elements, a child remarked, 'the important things should be in the centre, the rest around the edges.' Another that, 'school should go next to the park in case school has no playground'

In the world of children's design there is not only the 'What?' but the
'How?' of their work. It has been demonstrated that the view of the urban
child is unique. Studies have shown that urban children exhibit strong
visual and spatial thinking skills and that their interaction with the built
environment may be one reason why this is so.[3] A child living in an urban
environment experiences pedestrian movement and has the opportunity
to explore their surroundings on a regular basis, thus establishing a
visceral connection to the built environment. It would then follow that a
child's development would be influenced by this mode of learning and,
in keeping with the premise, that the appropriate mode of expression
and problem solving for urban children would be by imagining, drawing
and building representations of visual and spatial concepts. In the case
of urban design this should be even more pronounced in that, in order to
address such a problem the children are appropriating space around them,
psychologically and virtually, and occupying it both in their minds' eyes as
well as in a physical representation.

The process of design in this exercise was democratic and inclusive.
Boys tended to work together, as did girls, but there was no evidence of
animosity in their interaction and there was no evidence of discord or
disagreement in the city plan or in the resultant physical model of their
'city.' In planning and building their city, the children began to occupy
their models and role-play. One boy, who was working alone, found a
'voice' and a reason to communicate with others when he began to offer
electricity from his power plant to his classmates. A team of Chinese girls,
who spoke virtually no English, designed a language school that was to be
worn on one's head in order to learn 'all languages.' A team of boys and a
team of girls designed their own respective mosques and then negotiated,
without argument, in what location each should go relative to the other.
The collective observations from the View of the Child Exchange in
Sheffield provide evidence that the process of design served as a vehicle
for these children to knit a fabric among themselves. It is clear that the
members of the group were designing for each other; they had formed a
community.

Having demonstrated how children bring with them to school a visual
and spatial literacy, a further exchange involving children directly took
place over 2 days in a Victorian-designed middle school in Norwich. The
intention was to define what we mean by the visual culture of school and
to explore methodologies to enable children's views to be revealed. In
defining what we meant by the visual culture of the school, we had in

[3] GALLAGHER, C., 2004. Our
town: children as advocates for
change in the city. *Childhood,
Special Issue: Children
and Youth in Public Places,
Geographies, and Cultural
Landscapes*, 11(2).

[4] Field notes from the research, CB.

[5] CLARK, A.,2005. Talking
and listening to children. *In:*
M. DUDEK, (ed.) *Landscapes
of Childhood.* London:
Architecture Press.
CLARK, A., 2004. *Listening as
a way of life: an introduction to
why and how we listen to young
children.* London: National
Children's Bureau.
CLARK, A., 2003. The Mosaic
approach and research with
children. *In:* V. LEWIS, M.
KELLET, C. ROBINSON, S.
FRASER and S. DING, (eds.)
*The Reality of Research with
Children and Young People.*
London: Sage.

mind more than its obvious materiality. What might also be considered
includes ritual, arrangements of bodies in space and choreography in
classroom practise – that is, lines, arms movements, eye movements, lining
up, pairs and groupings.

Eight children, each with cameras and map making equipment, worked
with members of the research cluster for one morning.

*'The age group we worked with was ideal. We also had a good range of
different children to work with. I was particularly impressed with the way
that the child with hearing problems (profoundly deaf) was able to take
a full part as a researcher with the aid of his hearing equipment and his
special friend.'*[4]

The opening discussion with the eight children set the tone. We talked
about research and we talked about the 17 researchers, adults and children
who together would explore the classroom and school during the morning.
We adopted a method employed by cluster member, Alison Clark, using
child-guided tours of meaningful spaces for them in classroom, school and
grounds.[5] Once again, attention was drawn to the children as experts of
and in their school environment. Not drawing attention to the differences
between child and adult seems to be important. But drawing attention
to the difference in scale and size seemed useful especially so that they
understood that they as children did indeed have a different 'view'.

 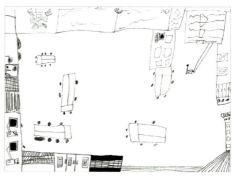

Figures 4 and 5,
left and right

Figure 4, Coat pegs, Norwich school, child's image. October, 2005
Figure 5, Drawing by boy showing detail at the edges and the 'public space' of desks and
chairs at the centre of the room. Norwich, October 2005

[6] BURKE, C. & GROSVENOR,
I., 2003. *The School I'd Like.
Children and Young People's
Reflections on an Education
for the 21st Century.* London:
Routledge Falmer.

[7] JT Bignold Notes

In the images that were produced by the children through the documentation of what is visual in the classroom, notice was taken of fine details. The tiny patterns on the table tops, the colours, the texture and patterns on the bricks and on the ceilings were brought into focus. Visual representations of identity and personal space were offered as these appeared to be significant in the material arrangements of classroom and school. In one classroom there did not seem to be a personal identifiable space beyond a chair and desk and a (ill-designed and malfunctioning) drawer. A conversation with one child about a coat hook was a powerful reminder of how material objects are infused with the memory of persons and events (the child showed us and photographed the coat hook that her older brother had once used!)

The mapping activity was revealing of perspectives, priorities and starting points. One child, when mapping his classroom space started with the sink at the edge of the classroom and carefully drew the spider in the sink while telling a detailed tale about the spider. Is this a suggestion that living things in the classroom are important for children reflecting many similar examples of this same message in the 'School I'd Like' archive.[6] Our own observations mirrored this perspective:

'The chairs and tables really dominate the classroom space. This means the edges of the classrooms become important; everything interesting happens around the perimeter. These edges are very rich, with display, interesting objects, storage cupboards, sinks, windows and so on. The middle part seems boring. The tables get in the way a lot of the time too, especially when the teaching method changes. The class I was in switched a lot from working as a whole class to small groups and individuals with a teacher/teaching assistant. The table and chair arrangement does not really support any of these activities well.'[7]

Our own visual record of the school building included the school wall – red bricks carved into over generations of children – leaving their mark – leaving their name in the brick – leaving their identity and the trace of themselves behind. The same wall corner was rounded, as if sandpapered smooth and was no longer sharp and right angled, curved and dented at just the same height as a child's shoulder. We were later told by a child that this could be explained by the fact that it was the route to the dinner hall.

In discussion, the children seemed uncritical, even unaware of the space. It is accepted as it is. There were only a few negative comments – noone liked the green toilets. Green does not seem to be a popular colour – one boy thought it was a very bad choice for the new carpet in his classroom. He would have preferred blue. The children were consulted about the colour but their views did not prevail. Interestingly green is used a lot in the school – the outside paintwork is green and inside there is pale green gloss used below dado level. There is a lot of yellow too. (Yellow looks like green if it is not directly lit.)

Reflections on the visual tour of the school included this from one of the research cluster members:

'I was struck by the discrepancy in size between adults and children. In some ways the building seemed to underline this rather than diminish it. It is an adult scale building – the doors and windows are big, with ironmongery mounted at adult rather than child height, so that children can't open the windows themselves. The window sills are mostly too high to give a view out when you are sitting down'.[8]

The view of the child is not usually taken into account in the design of spaces for children, either generally or specifically. Yet the children in their visual and spoken record revealed the importance of wall displays, coat hooks, secret gardens and what mattered most to them, which a designer would not normally find out about by other methods. In effect, in a very short time, it was possible to glean a series of spatial maps from the information given by the children, a reading of territories often invisible to adults and unintended by architects. We discovered that it is possible to 'read' the school in a series of applied layers that reflect spatial ownership so that, for example, the children's wall displays and personal territories are the result, to some extent, of their choice and intervention. The classroom as a whole reflects the teacher's choices in layout, perhaps even wall and carpet colours. A further layer concerns the question of who has which classroom in the school and who decides. Although it may not be possible for the architect to incorporate the child's layer specifically in the design, they can at least envisage how that contribution might be incorporated when it arrives.

The building we researched with the children is a compilation of layers in time, identifiable one by one going back to the Victorian original. As often in such cases later layers have obstructed the virtues of earlier parts, for example the daylight-driven Victorian rooms being destroyed by lowered ceilings and blacked-out or dark-glass windows, or the accidental creation

[9] BLUNDELL-JONES, P., 2005.
Notes. 15th October 2005.

[10] Ibid

of a main entrance which does not adequately declare itself as such. But the old school in its evolved and mixed-up form has two advantages: the first is that the fabric is embedded with memories and past encounters, an accumulation of gestures which has provided continuity between generations as opposed to a tabula rasa rebuild which would express only current styles, construction techniques and educational priorities. The second is the sheer untidy complexity of the whole, which allows for all kinds of interpretation and prompts various deliberate or accidental redevelopments, as a cumulative tradition in which each generation makes its mark in turn. A new building is by contrast likely to be simple, monothematic, unambiguous and almost devoid of memory.[9]

With schools like this the temptation is to declare the fabric inadequate and to destroy and rebuild, with a tendency to move fast, implementing a standardised solution which staff and pupils have to adapt themselves to, suddenly changing their ways of doing things but also losing the accumulated memory of the institution as defined in built form. If it is to be done well, there should be time for consultation, exploration, participation, both to produce an environment suited to pragmatic needs, and to get the users in tune with the idea of their new environment so that they feel empowered rather than oppressed. But if instead the old school is remade and maybe added to, it would be possible to preserve recent memories and to rediscover earlier ones: for example to restore the best parts of the Victorian buildings and their daylighting provision. Such a project could be a wonderful subject for historical research by staff and pupils into what the school had been like at various periods, and the conversion/extension could be done a wing at a time with detailed participation, allowing continuity. The complexity would be preserved, the pragmatic efficiency greatly increased, and the memories carried by the building would be selectively re-edited. 'We rebuild our school' is an educational vehicle full of enticing possibilities, and if parents become involved so much the better, especially in schools such as this one which has served two or thee generations of local families.[10]

Insights into the View of the Child

The early years theorist, Carlina Rinaldi suggests that we question, 'What is a school, who is the child?' and has said, 'These are not definitions you can find but ones you can build together.' Central to our discussions over the year has been the question not only how do children see school and bring to school a visual lexicon drawn from the landscapes in which they live but also, how do these ideas fit alongside community and professional answers to the same questions?

There is an honourable history of educationalists and architects
collaborating in the redesign of school buildings to realise advances in
pedagogy through the material and visual environment. The cluster
became more aware of this history as we progressed and the importance
of underpinning our projections of the future with a sound understanding
of the past. The exchanges during the year embedded the commitment to
participatory research with children and young people and enabled the
exploration and illumination of cross-disciplinary perspectives.
The significance of the visual culture of school is poorly understood and
children are certainly well placed to advise.

Can we design schools today that are inviting and stimulating places to
inhabit so that children are eager to enter and not wish to leave? The
cluster has explored how the view of the child and child-like perspectives
have been applied in the past by architects together with educators and
how these are consistent with what children and young people say their
need are today. We have argued that it is not enough to involve children
in partnership in the design process. This will always be tokenistic and
will fail if we do not also recognise that schools are places that continue
to be shaped and reshaped over time through habitation. Children and
young people can be engaged in that process if supported by those whose
thinking is 'spacious'. What unites the cluster is a belief in the value of
listening to children's ideas, views and experiences and how this can make
adults think differently. What we have learned is that in future projects
we must work to involve children as active participants where we can.
We must engage in action research projects that bring about change not
just comment on it. We need to act educationally whatever backgrounds
we bring with us to the study.

Orienting the Future: Design Strategies for Non-Place

Prof. Richard Coyne and Dr James Stewart (The University of Edinburgh)

[1] AUGÉ, M., 1995. Non-places: Introduction to an Anthropology of Supermodernity. London: Verso.

[2] KOOLHAAS, R., 2004. Junkspace. In: R. KOOLHAAS, Content, Köln, Taschen: AMO and OMA, 2004, pp. 162-171.

[3] MERRIMAN, P., 2004. Driving places: Marc Augé, Non-places, and the geographies of England's M1 motorway. Theory, Culture, and Society, (21) 4-5, 1 pp. 45-167.

[4] LEVIN, T. Y., FROHNE, U. and WEIBEL, P., (eds.), 2002. CTRL [SPACE]: Rhetorics of Surveillance from Bentham to Big Brother. Cambridge, MA: MIT Press.

[5] GIDDENS, A., 1999. Runaway World: How Globalisation is Shaping Our Lives. London: Profile Books.

[6] MEYROWITZ, J., 1985. No Sense of Place: The Impact of Electronic Media on Social Behavior. New York: Oxford University Press.

[7] WILLIAMS, R. and EDGE, D., 1996. The Social Shaping of Technology. In: W. H. DUTTON, (ed.), Information and Communication Technologies. Oxford: Oxford University Press, pp. 53-67.

In the concrete reality of today's world, places and spaces, places and non-places intertwine and tangle together. The possibility of non-place is never absent from any place.[1]

Overview

Our project brought together researchers from diverse disciplines to examine how designers create and ameliorate the effects of non-places, and to set in train a network of personnel and activities to research non-place themes. Non-places are the everyday spaces of late-capitalist cities: airports, malls, supermarkets, motorways, hotels, banks, call-centres, uncertain bureaucratic spaces, and so-called 'junk spaces'.[2] Orientation in non-places is guided and controlled by diverse forms of information that generate dense, overlapping way-finding and navigation conventions and technologies. We organised several workshops in non-places, and on non-place themes: a retail warehouse, an airport, and a bureaucratic site. We brought cross-disciplinary insights to bear in the formulation of a series of specific design research themes pertaining to social processes, technologies, organisational systems and architectures. We also produced articles, contributed to a major exhibition and started a network from which further research collaborations are being drawn.

The project began from a strong theoretical conceptualisation of non-place, supported by the writing of the anthropologist Marc Augé.[1, 3] As we anticipated, the theme of non-place was an appropriate stimulus for the cluster in its attention to contemporary design issues. Potential participants required reference to only a few examples to spark awareness of non-places. Across the spectrum of users, occupants, employees, managers, designers and academic theorists, we encountered both enthusiasm and criticism over the changes in contemporary environments

[8] TURNER, P. and DAVENPORT, E., 2005. *Spatiality, Spaces and Technology.* Dordrecht: Kluwer.

[9] POSTER, M., 2005. Digitally Local: Communications Technologies and Space. *In* K. NYÍRI, (ed.), *A Sense of Place: The Global and the Local in Mobile Communication.* Vienna: Passagen Verlag, pp. 31-41.

[10] WILLIAMS, R., STEWART, J. and SLACK, R., 2005. *Social Learning in Technological Innovation: Experimenting with Information and Communication Technologies.* Cheltenham: Edward Elgar.

[11] COYNE, R. and PARKER, M., 2005. Sounding Off: The Place of Voice in Ubiquitous Digital Media. *In: Proceedings of Seeing, Understanding, Learning in the Mobile Age, Budapest, 28-30 April 2005,* pp. 129-134.

[12] SHERRY, J. F. Jr., 1987. Cereal Monogamy: Brand Loyalty as Secular Ritual in Consumer Culture. *In: 17th Annual Conference of the Association for Consumer Research, Toronto, October 1986.*

[13] RELPH, E. C., 1976. *Place and Placelessness.* London: Pion.

[14] CAIRNS, S., 2003. *Drifting: Architecture and Migrancy.* London: Routledge.

[15] MEYROWITZ, J., 2005. The Rise of Glocality: New Sense of Place And Identity in the Global Village. *In* K. NYÍRI, (ed.) *A Sense of Place: The Global and the Local in Mobile Communication.* Vienna: Passagen Verlag, pp. 21-30.

[16] NYÍRI, K., (ed.), 2005. *A Sense of Place: The Global and the Local in Mobile Communication.* Vienna: Passagen Verlag.

ushered in by communications media, new security and surveillance protocols,[4] globalised consumption,[5] artefacts of the massification of travel and the bureaucratisation of citizenship.

Each discipline involved in the cluster brought insights and approaches to bear on the non-place problematic. The sociology of technology drew attention to the interrelation between social and technological systems of consumption, transportation and office work.[6,7] Information science encouraged thought about the unwieldy burden of communications and management systems for which non-places appear as symptoms.[8] Communications systems engineering introduced inventories of emerging systems, devices and components that affect how we interact with and use space, and identified technologies still looking for applications.[9,10] Architecture emphasised how aspects of gathering, communicating and working that were once accomplished by the configuration of floors, walls and furniture are now determined by supplementation from electronic systems and devices.[11] Graphic design brought awareness of signage, space, orientation and brandscape.[12] Human geography emphasised the complex relation between the local and the global.[13, 14, 15, 16] Marketing highlighted branding and 'flagship' retail[17] as non-place problematics, and cultural theory elaborated on the semiotics of place and the iconosphere.[18] Each cluster participant completed the project with an enhanced ability to research and communicate on the themes of place, non-place and design.

We held three main events and two supplementary events to advance the aims of the Designing for the 21st Century Initiative, that is, to foster the formation of a new diverse community with a common reference framework of theoretical concepts, cultures and languages pertaining to non-place; to stimulate new ways of design thinking about place; and to develop self-reflective, socially aware, and economically enterprising design research. The events were animated by engagement with specific sites commonly designated as non-places: a retail warehouse, an airport and a bureaucratic site. The conduct of the workshops evolved in concert with the stimulating activity-based Design21 workshops organised by Tom Inns and Vicky Hale.

Workshop 1: Consumer Non-Place

This workshop involved 'occupying' the demonstration area of the B&Q retail warehouse at New Craighall on the outskirts of Edinburgh by arrangement with the management [Figures 1 and 2]. We extended an invitation to potential participants, who were instructed by email and our website to document, map or 'itinerise' their journey to the store. Some of

[17] KOZINETS, R. V., SHERRY, J. F. Jr., DEBERRY-SPENCE, D., DUHACHEK, A., NUTTAVUTHSIT, K. and STORM, D., 2002. Themed flagship brand stores in the new millennium: theory, practice, prospects. *Journal of Retailing*, (78) 1, pp. 17-29.

[18] CHMIELEWSKA, E., 2005. Logos or the resonance of branding: A close reading of the iconosphere of Warsaw. *Space and Culture*, (8) 4, pp. 349-380.

these documents (wayfinding audits) were posted on the cluster website in advance of the workshop event. The day was structured around a series of activities involving photographic inventories, tours by the management, an account of how management design the store's information space, filling shopping trolleys with illustrative consumer items, interviews and reportage. Insights ranged across considerations of the implications of imminent RfiD tagging and stock control, signage, gendering, wayfinding, the deployment of local knowledge, personalised advice, the immediate urban context, the importance of shopping as an everyday leisure activity and the ways that B&Q managers work at making the environment culturally accessible. The event constituted an effective exercise in defamiliarisation, and seeded the growing repository of narrative assets and lore of the cluster.

Figures 1 and 2,
left and right

Figure 1, Workshop at B&Q
Figure 2, B&Q shopping aisle

Workshop 2: Transportation Non-Place

This took place in a staff training room beneath the main concourse of Stansted airport [Figures 3 to 7]. As if scripted, the flight from Edinburgh transporting the main organisers was delayed. So the day began with a non-place rendezvous among strangers and improvised introductions. Cluster participant Ann Light reports, 'We introduce ourselves – several people with an interest in motorway services, a few architecture academics, a couple of computer scientists, a sprinkling of artists – and leave quickly to explore more colourful parts. Small groups form and ours decides to follow trolleys around, establishing their routes through the airport to connect with new Arrivals or Departures traffic. Then we shadow a group of German marathon runners on their way out of the airport. . . we decide to navigate our way back at this level to our

Figures 3 to 7
left to right, top to bottom

Figure 3, Stanstead airport terminal building
Figure 4, Stanstead airport terminal building, interior
Figure 5, Stanstead airport terminal building, escape stair
Figure 6, Stanstead airport terminal building, arrivals door
Figure 7, Stanstead airport terminal building, public area

[19] LIGHT, A., 2005. Designing a workshop: A journey from design to use. Usabilitynews. Available at: http://www. usabilitynews.com/news/ article2396.asp.

[20] EDWARDS, B.,1998. *The Modern Terminal: New Approaches to Airport Architecture*. London: Routledge.

[21] BACK, L., FARRELL, B. and VANDERMAAS, E., 2005. *A Humane Service for Global Citizens: South London Citizens Enquiry into Service Provision by the Immigration and Nationality Directorate at Lunar House*. London: South London Citizens.

conference room. Would we meet trouble by stepping out of the paths meant for the public? No, but another group, following shortly behind us, is stopped by the police, reprimanded and made to fill out forms. . . This was the start of the second theme of the day: control and resistance.'[19] Other activities included an official tour, an extended passage through security checks, and discussion on themes of signage, shopping, surface, security and uses of airports by local communities. The workshop built on our lexicon of comparisons with other non-place encounters, including the more utilitarian environment and soft security of B&Q.

Workshop 3: Design and Non-Place

This was a consolidation event to advance the design issues raised by the airport visit. It included discussions led by Brian Edwards, who has written on airports,[20] Peter Adey (Aberystwyth) on the affordances of airports, Mike Rawlinson on the Bristol Legible City Project, Mark Perry (Brunel) on mobile working, Matthew Chalmers (Glasgow) on integrating infospace and physical space, and Alan Dix (Lancaster) on insider/ outsider orientation of place and signage and systolic flows.

Bureaucratic Non-Place Round Table Event

This involved a meeting of core cluster members with representatives of the South London Citizens Group (SLCG), including Les Back of Goldsmiths College UL, in Croydon, on Thursday 25th November 2005. The round table dealt with bureaucratic non-places, specifically those encountered by migrants, refugees and asylum seekers. SLCG recently conducted a Citizen's led Enquiry into the service and facilities at Lunar House.[21] The round table event explored the potential of design to contribute to the way such spaces operate and are experienced by clients who feel disoriented and alienated [Figures 8 and 9].

Workshop 4: Back-Door Design, Examining Commercial, Transportation and Public Service Hubs as Non-Place Exemplars

This summative workshop was held at the University of Edinburgh and provided further comparison and discussion on the themes of:

• Bureaucratic non-place. How stakeholders negotiate overstretched, regulatory bureaucractic systems.
• Design. The processes by which non-places are created and dismantled, designed and undone.

- Legibility. How the built fabric and information technologies interact to encourage or inhibit urban legibility, wayfinding and orientation.
- Identity. How selves and groups are configured and reconfigured in and through non-places.

Discussions were led by core team members and: Lorenzo Imbesi on remote control parasiting bodies and panoptic spaces, Peter Merriman on a critique of Marc Auge's theory of non-places, Peter Anderson (Interfield Design) on typography and the city, Frank Duffy (DEGW) on the future office, Yvonne Rogers on user-centred client interaction, Peter Excell on wireless technologies and signage and Pieter Boeder on urban screens.

Figures 8 and 9
left and right

Lunar House, Croydon. Images by Ray Lucas

Research Themes

In the course of our investigation we identified a series of themes for further research.

Appropriating non-place

Non-places seem to resist collective action. Bodies are individuated and rendered docile to the exigencies of the system, which is driven by technology and commerce. Commercial imperatives are often antithetical to personal freedoms. Our observations in non-place settings confirm that people are adept at creating a sense of place or being at home, even in alien environments. Are non-places resistant to a sense of place, culturally

[22] CLARK, A., 1997. *Being There: Putting Brain, Body and World Together Again.* Cambridge, MA: MIT Press.

[23] COYNE, R., 2006. Thinking through virtual reality: place, non-place, and situated cognition. *Techné*, 10 (3), Spring 2007, pp. 26-38.

rich in any case, or blank canvases? How do people make themselves at home, and what technologies do they deploy? How do people adapt non-places in the event of breakdown, for example, strike action by staff at an airport, disaster or excessive delays?

Non-place and cognition

Theories of the 'scaffolded mind,' suggest that thought and mind extend into the environment.[22,23] If places promote thoughtful action then what of non-places? Workshop activities were conducted in non-places. Apart from the inconvenience, did these strange settings abet or hinder the collective thought processes of the research cluster?

How does non-place function as a site of and for disruption? The use of artefacts in non-space entails a number of differences in the material ensemble by which work gets done. A particular device may have to carry a burden different to its design intention (for example, the phone compensates for the lack of a desktop), the ambient audience is different (strangers rather than colleagues), the presentation of self is altered (display and status assertion rather than self-effacing). So what kinds of work are attempted or achieved? How does the balance of transience and persistence work in these places? Can cognitive dissonance be creative?

Non-place, action and agency

Non-places are commonly considered the result of conspicuous design agency: masterplanning, control, regulation and a network of professionals. But they are also products of variable and uncertain agency: the designers of architectures and systems, and the designers of the myriad components that make up the environment, often with competing objectives. But who are the designers in non-places? What are the roles of users, tourists, itinerants, and the forces of socio-technological systems, bureaucracies, institutions and media?

How are the personae (or different actor actions) negotiated by individual actors at different times? How does a non-place function for the holiday-maker as opposed to the worker, consumer, client or patient? How does health care feature as non-place in the event of emergency, outpatient or long-term care?

Designing legible cities: text, context and orientation

Buildings and signs are codependent in the contemporary city. The materiality of the city (its architecture, pavements, buildings, streets and aisles) interacts with its informational systems (its street signs, maps, mobile information technologies, advertising and timetables) to establish the parameters for everyday life. At times, informational systems assist urban life, offering guidelines for movement, directions for action, instructions for use and the means of wayfinding. How effectively we use places, such as airports and supermarkets can depend on these informational overlays. The concept of non-place invites designers and researchers to think creatively about what is a 'legible city' in the contemporary context, and how built fabric and information technologies, old and new, combine in the design of a flexible and accommodating urbanism.

Signage and control

Non-places are reputedly dominated by textual signs. Signage is increasingly dynamic, and potentially can be targeted to specific users. What is the non-place sign in the emerging context of dynamic displays, user interaction, and mobile telephony? What is the relationship between text, image and voice in non-place design?

What is the role of mobile/personalised data systems for navigating non-places? Can these be designed to differentiate between naive and expert users? How does the differential availability of mobile information services influence our experience of non-places? What is it like to receive different navigational or instructive information than your neighbour using the same public space? What is the effect of the attrition of shared public-space iconic hardware, such as telephone boxes, postboxes and street signs? What will be their substitutes, and what are the emerging infrastructural place-markers?

The design of intimate artefacts

How do various kinds of design (architecture, digital and wireless technologies, dependable and ubiquitous computing, graphics, performance and visual art) enhance our everyday experiences of non-places? The aim is to devise new technologies and imagine new social conventions for more individually responsive and inclusive devices for orientation and wayfinding.

Branded meeting places

Some retailers and service providers create branded buildings, stores and places to give physical presence to their virtual businesses. Convention centres and other multi-purpose spaces are available for brand imprinting and rebranding. Increasingly, brand attributes are delivered to consumers through mobile devices, dynamic displays and other technologies. Branding clearly has a key role in marketing and retail. Office environments are also branded, and to move out of the office is to exchange one system of branding for another, or a single brand to a variegated brandscape. We can extend the concept of the brand to spaces where people gather to interact. Why do business people, clients, customers and service providers sometimes prefer to meet outside the office, shop or service centre to discuss, exchange ideas and transact business? It is not just convenience that draws us to certain places, but places lure us with meanings, and, increasingly, the layers of meaning in a place are indicated by branding.[24] Brands are icons, images and symbols that invoke a mood, ambience and a sense of loyalty to a product, service or place. Consumers identify with brands and sometimes let the brand do the work of colouring the meaning and authority of the activities that take place. Research on the theme of non-place and branding would focus on: the changing nature of commercial and business contexts, particularly with increased uses of networked communications in which many resources and transactions are accessed online; the changing nature of the office and other work environments, in which places are selected and used on the basis of their suitability as settings, particularly meetings, much as a stage set supports a performance; the increasing use of portable and mobile digital devices to supplement the operations of these environments, and make them more suitable for work processes and business transactions; commercial opportunities in targeted marketing to mobile phone users, so-called ambient intelligence through digital devices, personal signage systems, viral marketing and the increasing expansion of 'brandscapes.'

[24] LAEGRAN, A. S. and STEWART, J., 2003. Nerdy, trendy or healthy? Configuring the internet café. *New Media and Society*, (5) 3, pp. 357-377.

Voice and non-place

Auge's concepts of non-place focus on signage. We are told what to do and where to go, and, more characteristically, what we may not do. Non-places are structured less with walls, floors, windows and the paraphernalia of architectural organisation than with textual signs. Written or printed text belong arguably to the visual sense, but what of hearing? From the agora to the football stadium, spaces have evolved to take account of the characteristics of the human voice. Now the voice is mediated, modified and extended through digital and mobile networks,

[25] COYNE, R., 2005. Inflecting space. *Avatar: Dislocazioni tra Antrapologia e Comunicazione*, December 2005 (6), pp. 34-39.

[26] BULL, M., 2000. *Sounding Out the City: Personal Stereos and the Management of Everyday Life*. Oxford: Berg.

[27] BULL, M., 2005. The Intimate Sounds of Urban Experience: An Auditory Epistemology of Everyday Mobility. In: K. NYÍRI, (ed.) *A Sense of Place: The Global and the Local in Mobile Communication*. Vienna: Passagen Verlag, pp. 169-178.

[28] GRAF, R., 2005. Traces, Places and Self-evidence: Aspects of 'Space' on Cellular Phones. In: K. NYÍRI, (ed.) *Proceedings of Seeing, Understanding, Learning in the Mobile Age*, Budapest, 28-30ᵗʰ April 2005, pp. 97-102

[29] ZIZEK, S., 2002. Big brother, or, the triumph of the gaze over the eye. In: T. Y. LEVIN, U. FROHNE and P. WEIBEL, (eds.) *CTRL [SPACE]: Rhetorics of Surveillance from Bentham to Big Brother*. Cambridge, MA: MIT Press, pp. 224-227.

[30] HYDE, L., 1998. *Trickster Makes This World: Mischief, Myth and Art*. New York: North Point Press.

[31] COYNE, R., 2005. *Cornucopia Limited: Design and Dissent on the Internet*. Cambridge, MA: MIT Press.

[32] GEBBIE, G.C., JEBENS, S. E. and MURA, A., 1999. 'Not proven' as a juridical fact in Scotland, Norway and Italy. *European Journal of Crime, Criminal Law and Criminal Justice*, (7) 3, pp. 262-276.

[33] COYNE, R., 2006. Space without ground. In: M., BAIN, (ed.) *Architecture in Scotland*. Glasgow: The Lighthouse Trust, pp. 94-99.

as well as through the technologies of mass communications.[11,25] What are the subtle correlations now between spatial configuration and the voice modulated through public address systems, audio signage, mobile phones[26,27,28] and other paraphernalia of non-place?

Conclusion: A Litany of Trespass

According to Augé, the weight of signage in non-places is designed as if to accuse us: don't park here, have your passport ready, this is a quiet zone. Non-places are those over which the charge of trespass and violation hangs heavy through visible and invisible reproach and censure. We are in non-places under sufferance, and avoid any charge simply by dint of a legal technicality. We are in non-places on someone else's terms, and ready to be evicted.[29] Such spaces put us, the users, researchers and the critics, in the dock. We bear the burden of having to uphold our innocence. Whereas breaking into the off-licence or someone's home leads to incontrovertible guilt, in non-places we are never even sure we are trespassing. Non-place occupies the vexed threshold between innocence and guilt. The threshold is already the space of the trickster function, a site of duplicity and double-dealing.[30,31] At best we are neither entirely innocent nor guilty by virtue of the spaces we occupy, but the charge against us is 'not proven,' that is, has 'insufficient grounds.'[32,33]

'Not proven' has long been an option in Scots law unavailable in the rest of the United Kingdom. In Scotland a judge may pronounce you innocent of the charge, but if the evidence is insufficient for the charge to stick may resort to the third category of 'not proven'. Though the effect may be the same as innocence, technically the case can be reopened by other means. The condition of not proven is also known in France, where it is designated non-lieu, the literal translation of which is 'non-place.' Marc Augé's theories of place and non-place[1] derive in part from this coincidence of terms. Non-place has emerged as an obvious category to account for environments that are unhomely, alienating or blighted. But non-places are not places drained of meaning. Neither are they just the left over, overtly commercial, or systematic places of instrumental interaction and bureaucratic processes. Non-places are spaces in which it is only too easy to fall into a condition of trespass, as evident from the following catalogue of inhibitions and misplaced actions in the course of the cluster activities: arousing suspicion by perambulating and photographing the perimeter of a B&Q superstore in order to build a narrative about non-place and waste; guilt at leaving behind a shopping trolley filled with items which no one intended to purchase; wondering whether it is OK to have a picnic in the store's garden centre; being 2

[34] FREUD, S., 2003. *The Psychopathology of Everyday Life*. New York: Penguin Books.

[35] GARFINKEL, H., 1964. Studies of the routine grounds of everyday activities. *Social Problems*, (11) 3, pp. 225-250.

hours late for a non-place workshop on airports due to flight delays; being escorted from an airport car park by security personnel while seeking out plane spotters for interview; being interrogated by security for rattling a door labelled 'security'; having to speak by telephone to someone in an adjacent room, and under CCTV surveillance, to gain access to our meeting space; undergoing thorough search and security checks to pass from land to airside at an airport for fear that one of us might be a journalist concealing a weapon to publicise flaws in airport security; inhibited from accessing the Immigration and Nationality Directorate at Lunar House due to recent adverse press publicity surrounding Britain's dealing with asylum seekers.

These events seem to confirm the observation of many, from Freud[34] to Garfinkel,[35] that ordinary life is grounded on a sea of anxiety that surfaces with a breach of custom. Reiterating Augé, 'the possibility of non-place is never absent from any place'[1] [Figures 10 and 11]. Non-places become conspicuous as such when we use them for functions outside their narrowly defined operations. On the other hand, any space can reveal itself as non-place under the right conditions of transgression. Something similar applies to research. Research as transgression can be similarly invasive and revealing, especially a research that is based on action, and tuned to the challenges of the 21st century.

Figures 10 and 11
left and right

Edinburgh as Non-Place, G8 Summit, Summer of 2005

In resistance to the strictures of non-place, the cluster identified strategies for making public spaces more accessible, flexible, exciting, safe and inclusive (as exemplified in the Bristol Legible Cities Initiative). We explored how collective action can subvert the lines of hierarchical control often implicit in non-places, and identified the need to open non-place functioning to the creative agency of large numbers of users.

We saw how non-place actors can extemporise around non-place scripts through positive, creative action. The cluster also revealed the possibility of fruitful exchanges between disciplines able to contribute towards designing more legible and convivial spaces for the 21st century.

Acknowledgements

This work is supported by the Arts and Humanities Research Council and the Engineering and Physical Sciences Research Council (Designing for the 21st Century Initiative). We are very grateful to the other members of the core research team (and other participants) who have given generously of their time and ideas. This chapter draws on their insights in ways that go beyond what can readily be reflected by citation: Stephen Cairns, Elizabeth Davenport, Jane Jacobs, Ray Lucas, Dermott McMeel, Susan Turner, Robin Williams and Jennifer Willies.

Additional Reading

COYNE, R. and PARKER, M., 2006. *Voices Out of Place: Voice, Non-Place and Ubiquitous Digital Communications. Mobile Understanding: The Epistemology of Ubiquitous Communication.* Vienna: Passagen Verlag., pp. 171-182.

Screens and the Social Landscape: Digital Design, Representation, Communication and Interaction

Dr Carey Jewitt[1], Prof. Teal Triggs[2], and Prof. Gunther Kress[1],
([1]University of London and [2]University of the Arts, London)

Overview

'Screens' have played an important part in shaping the visual landscape of the 21st century. From the small flexible hand-held screen to the workplace computer and domestic television screens to the large-scale LED displays at Piccadilly Circus and Times Square, screens are fully integrated into our everyday experience.

The main aim of the research cluster was to enable a common language and process of collaboration to be established and communicated between the distinct disciplines represented within the cluster. That is, to move beyond building 'superficial' bridges which 'translate' between the 'languages' of culture of, for example, artists and computer scientists. In doing so we wanted to understand and identify the different principles and practices that underpin design as it is socially located and practiced, and to work towards a collaborative and multidisciplinary approach. In addition, the cluster sought to establish a shared set of communication and design principles focusing on the screen and related digital spaces with a particular focus on the urban environment, museums and galleries. Three main themes were used to focus our discussion:

- Social/Cultural History of the Screen.
- Screen as a Site of Display: Image, Work and Movement.
- Screen as Mediator of Interaction.

The cluster provided a space for us to think and explore ideas based on our varied experiences and discipline knowledge.

Rational and Previous Research

The research cluster understood screen as a designed interface (for example, television set, computers, information signage) with a central place in representation and communication of the social landscape, and the cultural and technological imagination, as well as having economic significance in the digital era of the 21ˢᵗ century. Traditional notions and functions of the screen are continuously shifting; a shift made all the more dramatic by the development of mobile and ubiquitous technologies. We explored the 'screen' and related information technologies and asked what its implications might be for how people communicate and interact in public spaces as well as in their display and function in the urban environment. This was achieved by bringing together professionals and academics working in the broad disciplines of design, computer science, digital technology, linguistics, sociology and cultural studies. 'Screen' was the common reference point.

Through in-depth workshops and public lectures we explored the different ways in which a range of disciplines understand and use the screen to communicate and engage visually either in the generation of their own messages or those of their 'clients'.

The concept of 'screen' resonates in important ways across disciplines in the changing communicational and representational landscape of the 21ˢᵗ century. It has implications for the practices of artists and designers working with screens, computer scientists and engineers, and more broadly the shaping of forms of knowledge, popular culture and technology-mediated interaction. This was explored through the changing notions of 'screen' in its broadest sense, including mobile and widely used technologies that are to a large extent transforming 'traditional' notions and functions of the screen. Through our multi-disciplinarity we were able to explore the many different roles of 'screen': in mediating activity and shared understanding in the work place; in public spaces as a site of engagement; as a site of communication such as information display; and the screen's resulting forms of representation as understood from a variety of perspectives relevant to design for the 21ˢᵗ century. These included human-centred systems design, socio-cognitive engineering, interaction studies, semiotics of design, multimodal communication theory, graphic design and typography, product design, design history and popular culture, fine art practices, technology used in everyday life and augmented technologies.

[1] LEVINSON, P., 2001. *Digital McLuhan*. London: Routledge.

[2] MANOVICH, L., 2002. *The Language of New Media*. Cambridge, MA: MIT Press.

[3] SCHWESIG, C., POUPYREV, I. C. and MORI, E., 2004. Gummi: a bendable computer. *CHI* 6(1): pp. 263-70.

Five key points (discussed below) emerged throughout the cluster circulating and weaving in and out of the presentations and discussions in different ways.

Changing Concepts of Screen provided a means for tracking the social history of technology. We asked what the screen is likely to become in the 21st century at the same time as exploring its current status and its previous history. We explored the interconnectedness of the 'old' and the 'new' and how they slip and slide over one another to produce change. The changing concept of the screen located in social/cultural histories offered us one way of exploring the forms of continuity and change that inform technology, screen and design.[1,2] This was the starting point for Charlie Gere's contribution titled 'Genealogy of the Computer Screen' in which he proposed that the modern computer screen is derived more from the radar screen than, as might be expected, the television screen, and that this has important ramifications for how the computer has developed and been understood; ramifications that are being obscured by the current drive towards the 'convergence' of television and computing.

Screen as a Site and Site as Screen enabled us to look at new screens that shrink and flex to fit in our pockets,[3] we examined how architects and artists transform public space into enormous screens in ways that impact on art, information display and popular culture. The screen as 'a site of public discourse' was also examined. We explored the points of intersection (and tension) between the small screen of the mobile phone and the transformation of buildings into large urban architectural screens. These intersections were particularly interesting in how they transform the private intimacy of the small screens kept in people's pockets into the larger-than-life displays of the public screens. The screen as a site of display was a feature of Kevin Walker's presentation on the place and function of screens in museums. Our conversations also led to examples of tools designed by and for artists and designers. This was an area that we have explored further in a special issue of the journal *Visual Communication* on 'screens'. A paper by the award-winning team of Casey Reas and Ben Fry, for example, reveals the significance of their tool 'Processing' (a Java-based Open Source programming environment and language) for artists and designers who want to 'find their way into a sort of more professional mode of programming'. Such tools, which allows artists to 'make their own tools', demonstrate that what goes on 'behind' the screen is equally as important as what is displayed on it.

⁴ TURKLE, S., 1997. *Life on the Screen: Identity in the Age of the Internet*. New York: Simon & Schuster.

⁵ BOLTER, D. J. and GRUSIN, R., 2000. *Remediation: Understanding New Media,* Cambridge, MA: MIT Press.

The 'Visibility' of Screen became increasingly key to our discussions. As screens change from stable, fixed, two-dimensional material objects to a range of more fluid, mobile, three-dimensional objects designed to inhabit the social world in ways that we barely notice. We discussed the implications of the visibility of screen (for example, wearable screens for mediating information-rich environments) on information display and interaction.

The 'designing out' of the screen is a feature of the i-shuffle that demands a change in use, a repositioning of the lack of choice of tune as an act of freedom; a randomness that frees the user from the demands of choice. Part of the visibility of screen also relates to how it features in our talk. Gunther Kress explored the everydayness of screen as a metaphor in his presentation 'Reflections of a Linguist'.

The 'screen' has become so pervasive in the landscape that it is no longer viewed as a physical, three-dimensional object. Instead, we concluded that we are now engaging with the visual landscape as a new augmented environment. This was taken up and elaborated in a paper by cluster members Ben Hooker, Niall Sweeney and Teal Triggs who explored the relation of the visual landscape and the digital screen much like Seurat had observed it – in dots, tones, resolutions and layers.

Screen as a Mediator of Human Interaction provided a focus on the relationship between people and technology and its uses in a range of settings, the cluster explored the implications for the design, development and deployment of screen technologies for identities[4] and for shared engagement and social experience. We asked the question of how identities are produced and mapped onto the physical landscape. Manovich[2] discusses how the general dynamic between spatial form and information functions differently in the computer culture of today in terms of 'augmented space' – a term he uses to refer to, 'the physical space overlaid with dynamically changing information', in which 'this information is likely to be in multimedia form and it is often localised for each user.' His focus is on the experience of the human subject in augmented space. These ideas provided a useful springboard for the research cluster.

The multimodal communicational landscape of the screen as a site of display allowed exploration of how do people use communicative modes – image, speech, music and movement and media to communicate and how does what is displayed on screen 'remediate' information?[5] This move in representation and communication was seen as a key aspect of learning

[6] JEWITT, C., 2006. *Technology, Literacy and Learning: A Multimodal Approach*. London: Routledge.

in a digital era.[6] These ideas were explored drawing on examples from art and museum studies. This aspect of our discussions was elaborated on in *Visual Communication* exploring the recent LED screen installation completed for the Nobel Field, Oslo's Nobel Peace Centre: a collaboration between the architects Adjaye/Associates and Small Design Firm and Timon Botez, which aimed to create responsive visual and aural spaces within a museum context where the screen at the same time became both 'content and artefact'.

Aims and Objectives

The main aim of the research cluster was to enable a common language and process of collaboration to be established between the key disciplines involved in the design, mediation, and creative interpretation of the screen. More specifically the key objectives of the research cluster were:

- to identify the forms and processes of communication and practices of different disciplines by examining the ways in which screen features in their work;
- to deliver a programme of innovative activities across a wide range of people working in screen and design;
- to develop working methods of collaboration at all stages of the screen-design process and product utilisation which will be disseminated and encourage interaction through the World Wide Web;
- to explore the changing concept of screen and its implications across the disciplines and the social landscape more broadly;
- to establish a framework of ideas relevant to the specific instance of screen and spaces of display (for example, museums and galleries);
- to engage in continuous dissemination of findings and key themes through a website and public events.

Activities and Outcomes

The research cluster was centred around four interrelated elements each of which helped to achieve our objectives. Each of these is described in some detail overleaf.

Workshops

A series of three 2-day workshops were held to facilitate the development
of effective working methodologies of collaboration across the
communication and practices, languages and cultures of the different
disciplines represented in the cluster. These focused on the three themes of
the project:

• The Social/Cultural History of Screen;
• Screen as a Site of Display: Image, Work and Movement;
• Screen as Mediator of Interaction.

The workshops involved group feedback and collaborative analysis of key
themes and action planning, development and agenda building towards an
understanding of the implications of design and screen in the 21ˢᵗ century,
a framework of research ideas on screen in museums and galleries, and
further collaboration and dissemination.

The events were video recorded and analysed to encapsulate the process
and key themes of collaborative design and edited and streamed on to
the cluster website. This supported the delivery and discussion of the
programme. Overall the workshops were especially effective in identifying
forms and processes of communication across disciplines and developing
ways of working. The use of objects and images as points for discussion,
and methods for discussing worked well, helping us to notice, investigate
and overcome crucial assumptions that talking can unwittingly keep
implicit and gloss over.

The workshops included a series of interactive presentations by the
participants and invited guests. These included presentations by leading
academics on topics such as: Screen and designing interaction; The social
and cultural history of the screen; Desktop evolution; Public authoring
systems (Urban tapestry); A lexicon of screen; Screens, painting and
digital art; Screens and display in museums and galleries; and Designing
the disappearing screen. Each of these presentations sparked off debate
and discussion that further extended our view of screens and ways of
talking with one another.

The sessions involving 'the analysis of objects' were an especially effective
aspect of the workshops. Small interdisciplinary teams (industry-based
designer, cultural historian, sociologist, psychologist, semiotician, and
a computer scientist) engaged in exploratory discussion of conceptions
of screen and 'analysis of objects' (for example, mobile phones, flexi-

screens, 3-D screens, wearable computers, and so on.) to address key questions and implications related to each focus point, for instance the increasing 'invisibility' of screens. This focus on objects provided us with a physical point of collaboration and thinking and helped us to establish a framework of ideas relevant to screens in the urban environment across our different interests and experiences.

'The building of a visual landscape' enabled us to engage with the screen as it features in the urban environment as opposed to 'extracting' the screen as an object from its place in the everyday. We structured this process into three stages: taking images, collaborative viewing and identifying emergent themes.

Working in small interdisciplinary teams with digital cameras we went out on to the streets of London to capture images of the screen in all its variety as it appears and functions in the city. These images were uploaded on to a computer and displayed on a large screen for collaborative viewing. Each small team displayed the images they had taken, described, explained, justified and defended their choice of images to the other participants. Through this process we built a collective visual catalogue of 'screen'.

A set of analytical concepts/categories and themes emerged through the collaborative critic and discussion of the images. These included: protection, surveillance, sectioning space, connecting space, hiding, revealing, layering, sorting, filtering, regulating, screening, remediating and information for action.

The images were edited and analysed thematically to identify patterns and connections and produce a visual landscape of the screen [Figures 1 to 4].

This process enabled us to examine how screens (and people's interaction with them) function in context. This visual focus introduced some features/dimensions of screen into the discussions more sharply. These were then designed to produce a visual landscape of the screen to visually reflect, contrast, and open up this as a visual space for further thinking about screen.

Figures 1 to 4,
left to right, top to bottom

These images are examples from one of the interdisciplinary workshops where cluster
members were asked to document in teams, what screen might mean in the urban
landscape. This collection of visual data formed the basis for group discussions around
what types of themes and analytical concepts/categories might be revealed through this
process including, as shown above: Filtering, Protection, Mediating and Sectioning.

Public lectures

Workshops were followed by a public evening keynote lecture drawing
upon the expertise of interdisciplinary 'visionaries' working with a
focus on the screen. Researchers, academics, design professionals,
representatives from industry and students (from the field of art and
design, education and computing) attended the lectures. (A total of
450 people attended and the lectures were also streamed on the project
website.)

Clive Dilnot (Parsons School of Design, New York, USA) focused on the
idea of 'Interaction Interface: Configuration, Negotiation'. He asked to
what extent does the artificial offer us the opportunity of a new way of
being human and to what extent does that opportunity devolve around
the possibility of reconceiving representation? He considered the extent to
which the artificial as we receive it today is undermining and transforming
the modern understanding of representational certainty. He argued it is

possible to see within some of the elements that press most closely against traditional notions of representation – interaction, interface, configuration – the outlines of a different model of representation, one that is not beholden to the strictures of the modern and which offers a different sense of how the technological may be thought and experienced.

The need to envisage and imagine futures we might want to inhabit was the focus of the second lecture, 'Bespoke Futures: Media Design and the Vision Deficit', given by Peter Lunenfeld (Institute for Technology and Aesthetics, Pasadena, USA). Drawing on examples from art, design and architecture he talked of the potential for 'creative misuse of scenario planning' as a means to guide media designers towards crafting visualisations, often interactive, immersive and augmented, which can inspire their realisation.

The assumption that the computer screen should be transparent: a window on to a world of information provided the focus for the third lecture, given by Jay David Bolter (New Media Center, Georgia Institute of Technology, USA). He argued that contemporary digital art offers an important alternative to the aesthetic and epistemological principle of transparency: the reflective interface. This introduced a productive tension across the workshop between these two ways of looking and knowing that characterises digital technology for our culture today.

Project website

An interactive website was designed (by cluster member Sweeney). The intent was to disseminate the findings of the workshops but also to provide a 'useable' document of the cluster's events and discussions. This would be key to future work in the area and provide a base for analysis. The activities of the cluster were video recorded and have been streamed on the website. The photographic evidence of one fieldwork 'task' is also presented as a series of visual screen categories.

Publications

 JEWITT, C. and TRIGGS, T., 2006. Screens and the social landscape. *Visual Communication* 5(2), pp. 131-140.

Key ideas from the cluster were expanded through the editing of a special issue of *Visual Communication* 5(2) on 'Screen and the social landscape'.[7] This provided an opportunity to build on and extend the cluster networks with an emphasis on international perspectives. This work will be developed further in the form of an edited collection (in preparation, 2007, Sage).

Teaching

The research cluster discussions moved beyond the workshop events and lectures and through our own teaching back into the college classroom. We were able to adopt some of the principles into our teaching such as the process of focusing on 'screen' as specific object/concept for analysis in order to facilitate an understanding of the multidisciplinary perspectives of the cluster membership. Triggs, for example, took such an approach as a tutor on the Postgraduate Diploma, Design for Visual Communication whose student's varied professional backgrounds and first degrees including sciences, architecture, fine art and design, presents an interesting challenge in the teaching of graphic design research methods. Discussions were also prompted about the screen-driven environment of the design classroom/ studio and the impact on student's learning. This has led Triggs to undertake further research in this area.

Interdisciplinary Investigation: Challenges and Opportunities

Communication across the disciplines within the cluster was positive and dynamic. However, at times it was patterned and clustered around shared disciplines and uses of academic language. The starting points for participants to express their ideas often differed: the economic, or the physical/material object, or questions of learning and meaning making. Perhaps as a result initially participants with a background in engineering and computer science found language that enabled them to exchange ideas relatively easily, and those from a semiotic background could do so with the cultural/social historians and so on, although this developed in many ways to cross over our disciplinary boundaries.

Early on we had noticed that the presence (or representation) of physical designed objects in the 'object analysis' sessions in the previous workshops provided a 'common node' for talking across disciplines, interests and experiences in a way that positively exploited our differences. The exploratory character of such conversation also served to open up the ways in which we talked.

Reflecting on this 'patterning' and the ways in which talk seemed to be most productive we decided to focus on object analysis and the building of a 'visual landscape' of the screen together as a process that would disrupt some of our usual ways of talking and give way to a visual way of thinking about screen and design. We focused more explicitly on the language and terminology of the screen. This enabled us to bring together different interests and build a more holistic way of looking at the concept of screen.

Historical analysis of the screen proved to be a particularly rich focus for exploring the different perspectives that participants brought to the analysis and understanding of screen. In particular the different explanations for why things were as they are – the 'evolution' of design – given by the participants enabled us to really understand our starting points and experiences of design: from the economic explanations, to the connections between old and new, to the ideas of design realising lifestyle and identities. An example of this is offered by our object analysis of MP3 players. This focused on the ways in which screen is designed 'in' and designed 'out' on different companies models, and the comparison of the i-pod (with screen) and the i-shuffle (screenless).

Insights and Reflections

The research cluster enabled academics and design practitioners to come together in common discussion in ways that they had not done before.

The results of the cluster activities prompted a broadening of the participants' conceptions of the screen. It furthered our understanding of what is meant by 'screen' and how language whether visual or verbal may be used to facilitate an understanding of a concept(s). It also further emphasised how our use and reception of screens is impacted on by context and mode; the links between design principles and practices; an understanding of multimodality; and language and collaborative working methods. In this way it established new ways of negotiation and facilitation taking into account interdisciplinary group dynamics. This was particularly useful for design practitioners who often lead interdisciplinary teams. This confirmed the value of interdisciplinary research as part of a design process that encourages 'lateral thinking' – specifically in solving complex design problems.

Ideas for Further Study

The research cluster generated a number of ideas for further study. In general our interest was to move this forward in the application of our findings to focused case studies which address the role of screens in the changing social landscape – specifically within the areas of information environments and educational practices.

The opportunity exists to examine further the iterative processes that occur between people and screens as 'objects' and their operational and social relationships to the built-environment. Questions which may be addressed include: what practice of confirmation, augmenting, annotation and reflection do screen designs enable? What are the possibilities for identity performance and production of community afforded by interaction with screen-based technologies? What scales and spaces of social interaction and connection does the design or screen produce and how does this mediate interaction? And, in what ways might the use of screens as an integrated element for information environments be more effective?

Research that continues to explore what communication tools and design methods might be developed that will assist designers and co-participants in their ability to anticipate factors such as 'accelerated time' and 'rapid change' in planning for the future is also suggested by the cluster. The focus on screen could usefully be expanded to explore the notions of community, communication, information and interaction via the concepts of territory, memory and common spaces moving towards the development of tools that respond to co-participation and change.

There continues to be a need to develop new ways of design thinking and design methods that are interdisciplinary and forward-looking in order to meet the demands of the 21st century for design.

Additional Reading

HEATH, C. and LUFF, P., 2000. *Technology in Action*. Cambridge University Press.

JACOBSON, R., (ed.), 1999. *Information Design*. Cambridge, MA: MIT Press.

KRESS, G. and VAN LEEUWEN, T., 2001. *Multimodal Discourse*. Arnold McMillan.

LUNENFELD, P., 2000. *The Digital Dialectic: New Essays on New Media*. Cambridge, MA: MIT press.

Technology and Social Action

Dr Steve Walker and Dr Andy Dearden, (Leeds Metropolitan University and Sheffield Hallam University)

Introduction

[1] BUTTON, G. & HARPER, R. H. R., 1993. Taking the Organisation into Account. *In*: G. BUTTON, (ed.) *Technology in Working Order: Studies of Work, Interaction and Technology*. London: Routledge.

[2] ORLIKOWSKI, W., YATES, J., OKAMURA, K. & FUJIMOTO, M., 1995. Shaping Electronic Communication: The Metastructuring of Technology in the Context of Use. *Organization Science*, 6(4), pp. 423-444.

[3] KYNG, M. & MATTIESSEN, L., 1997. Computers and Design in Context. Cambridge, MA: MIT Press.

[4] BROWN, J. S. & DUGUID, P., 2000. *The Social Life of Information*. Harvard: Harvard Business School Press.

[5] KLING, R., 2000. Learning about information technology and social change: the contribution of social informatics. *The Information Society*, 18(3), pp. 245-264.

The 'Technology and Social Action' (T&SA) project explored issues in the design and use of digital technologies and information systems in what we have termed 'social action' settings: settings where the purpose of using technology is oriented towards social change and social justice in one sense or another. This is in rather stark contrast to the business and consumer emphasis in most research into digital technology design and use. Since, as has been well established, the ways in which technologies are designed, implemented and used are intimately related to context[1,2,3,4,5] we might reasonably expect the characteristics which distinguish social action to be reflected in the design and use of the technology. There has been relatively little sustained engagement in this area by specialists from design-related disciplines such as human computer interaction (HCI), information systems (IS) and learning technology. Central to our work, then, has been the need to consider how as researchers, designers and practitioners we can contribute to more effective application of digital technology for social action purposes and/or in social action settings.

The remainder of this chapter is structured as follows: firstly, we provide an overview of the origins of the project in our earlier work on informatics in civil society, before giving a brief account of the activities of the cluster. We conclude with a discussion of the insights generated by these activities.

Overview

[6] DEARDEN, A. & WALKER, S., 2003. Designing for Civil Society. *In:* P. GRAY, H. JOHNSON and E. O'NEILL, (eds.) *Proceedings of HCI Vol II, Bath, 12-18th September 2003.* Bristol: Research Press International, pp. 157-158.

[7] WALKER, S. & DEARDEN, A., 2005. Design for Civil Society. *Interacting with Computers,* 17(1), pp. 1-8.

[8] CASTELLS, M., 1997. *The Power of Identity - The Information Age. Economy, Society and Culture Vol 2.* Oxford: Blackwell.

[9] HALL-JONES, P., 2006. *The rise and rise of NGOs* [online]. Public Services International. Available at: http://www.world-psi.org/.

[10] CASTELLS, M., 2000. *The Internet Galaxy: Reflections on the Internet, Business, and Society.* Oxford: Oxford University Press.

The T&SA project emerged from earlier work which sought to answer a question formulated variously as 'can there be a social movement informatics?'[6] or 'can there be a civil society informatics?'[7] In this work we suggested three conditions that would need to be satisfied in order to conclude that what we are now describing as 'technology and social action' would constitute a viable area of study:

- Is the area of social action use of digital technology sufficiently significant?
- Is the design and use of Information and Communication Technologies (ICT) in the context of social action sufficiently distinct from personal, governmental, commercial fields or other field of inquiry to warrant particular study?
- Is the field sufficiently coherent, in the sense that lessons learned from studies of one group or organisation might be applicable to other groups or organisations?

Briefly, we concluded that we could answer the first two of these questions positively. Digital technology use by individuals and groups engaged in social action is significant in two broad ways. Firstly, social action groups have become significant agents in shaping the world around us.[8] Even when measured in purely economic terms, one element of civil society – non governmental organisations (NGOs) – may be worth as much as a trillion dollars annually and employ 19 million paid workers (not counting the even larger number of unpaid volunteers).[9] Secondly, is that the contemporary significance of social action groups is at least partly associated with the use that they make use of ICT in general and the Internet in particular.[10]

Social action has a number of distinctive characteristics which we suggest will influence technology use. Among these are: heavy reliance on the work of volunteers; strong values of justice and inclusiveness; frequently rather restricted access to resources; a strong commitment to work with groups who themselves have relatively limited access to technology; and in many cases an involvement in some form of, more or less pronounced, social conflict. This is not an exclusive list, nor is it necessary that a particular case exhibits all of these characteristics. It is, though, likely that some of these characteristics will be present in most examples of technology use in social action settings. Examples of technology uses which reflect some of these characteristics are as

[11] MORRIS, D., 2004. Globalization and media democracy: the case of Indymedia. *In*: D. SCHULER & P. DAY, (eds.) *Shaping The Network Society: The New Role Of Civil Society In Cyberspace*. Cambridge, MA: MIT Press, pp. 325-352.

[12] BLYTHE, M. & MONK, A., 2005. Net neighbours: adapting HCI methods to cross the digital divide. *Interacting with Computers*, 17(1) pp. 35-56.

[13] DEARDEN, A., WALKER, S. & WATTS, L., 2005. Choosing Friends Carefully: Allies for CriticalComputing. *In*: O. W. BERTELSEN, N. O. BOUVIN, P. G. KROGH & M. KYNG, (eds.) *Proceedings of the 4th Decennial Conference on Critical Computing: Between Sense and Sensibility, Aarhus, 20-24th August 2005*. New York: ACM Press, pp. 133-136.

diverse as the 'smartmobs' that were prominent in protests at the World Trade Organisation meeting in Seattle in 1999, the Indymedia network which subsequently emerged as an independent online news network of the 'global justice' movement,[11] and the use of 'micro-volunteering' in enabling access to online shopping for elderly people.[12]

The answer to our third question, concerned with the extent of commonality in technology concerns between, say, international environmental NGOs, local community organisations and trade unions has remained open. The nature of an answer will of necessity be highly pragmatic. In order for what we have come to refer to as 'technology and social action' to represent a viable sub-discipline of design and technology requires in practice that enough designers and researchers recognise a benefit (primarily to their own practice) in sharing tools, methods and practices with others. One way of reading the following account of our experiences in the T&SA cluster is as a refinement of our understanding of the specific characteristics of technology design and use in social action settings that has allowed us more clearly to see the contours of the commonalities of concerns across these diverse organisational settings.

The T&SA project has also represented a further shift in our thinking, away from the structural contexts of social movements or civil society, to a more practice-centred approach. We are thus concerned less with whether the agents of social justice and social change can be characterised as belonging to civil society, distinct from state or market (and discussions of the often blurred boundaries between them). We are increasingly concerned with the practices of individuals and groups to encourage social justice and social change informed by values of emancipation and solidarity, while recognising that these terms are also highly contested in specific contexts. Here we have started to explore the relationship between our own work and developments in critical information systems and critical computing.[13]

Activities

The main activities of the cluster were a series of workshops bringing together practitioners and researchers in open-ended discussion and design activities aimed at uncovering concerns, priorities and understandings with the hope of developing common ground for research discussions. Initially we planned to hold three 2 day workshops throughout the year. As the project developed, this plan was modified so that eventually five distinct events were supported.

- An initial 2 day workshop was held in Leeds in March 2005. This brought together the network for the first time and used card-sorting and clustering activities to identify and select a small number of key themes that were recognised by participants as significant for technology and social action.
- A second workshop was held in Sheffield in June 2005. The participants in this workshop took the specific issues raised in round 1 and developed responses to those issues.
- A third 'feedback' workshop was held in November at the British Computer Society headquarters in London, where findings from the cluster activities were reported to a wider audience, and cross-cutting themes were explored.

As well as these three large workshops, the cluster arranged two other meetings to follow up on specific areas of work. The first was a 1 day workshop exploring issues of evaluation and organisational learning in Technology and Social Action. This was held in Loughborough in September 2005. The second was a meeting in Amsterdam with a number of European partners interested in Free/Libre Open-Source Software (FLOSS) in social action. This workshop explored the dynamics of 'commons-based peer production' (a generalisation of the FLOSS concept that takes into account all forms of cultural output). Participants from this meeting have been exploring opportunities for European funding of further research.

The workshop activities exposed two important issues for further research and design in this area. The first was a general ethical concern about the relationship between researchers and practitioners. Research involves both benefits and costs for all participants. Sometimes the benefits of research are long-term and ill-defined, rather than readily identifiable and immediate. For practitioners engaged in social action, the time and energy spent engaging with researchers may detract from their primary activities and goals and so represent a substantial 'opportunity cost'. Within the cluster this translated into difficulties for some practitioners in contributing the time and energy to cluster management that we had initially hoped. It was important to find ways for practitioners to engage in the process at many different levels – graduating from occasional contributions to an email list, linking to a wiki, through to active participation in planning, preparing and delivering workshops. It is also important to ensure that the design of activities considered both long-term and short-term payback for practitioners.

[14] Technology & Social Action. Available at: www.technologyandsocialaction.org

[15] esocialaction@email-lists.org

Secondly, many practitioners found the very open brainstorming and clustering exercises in the first workshops, where the cluster organisers were explicitly seeking to avoid imposing one particular perspective on the issues being discussed, were very unfamiliar and uncomfortable. On reflection, we consider that this discomfort was probably unavoidable given the goals of the workshop, but if we were to repeat such an exercise, we could plan some mitigating strategies.

In addition to the face-to-face workshops, the cluster used a number of online methods. The cluster organised an online 'delphi' consultation in which a selected group of experienced practitioners have engaged in discussion rounds identifying and exploring priorities for practice and for research. Two rounds of this consultation were completed and analysed within the year. A third round is currently being undertaken to clarify some outstanding uncertainties. The cluster established a wiki[14] and an email list.[15] Both of these remain active following the end of the project. The wiki is being used as a collaborative working area to share ideas and report findings. It includes links to a tool 'wikindx' in which we are developing a shared bibliography for Technology and Social Action. The mailing list is used for coordinating activities and distributing information about relevant developments elsewhere and continues to attract subscribers. Overall, this mix of activities appears to give scope to the graduated degrees of involvement that we sought. We aim to take these ideas forwards and consider the general factors in future projects.

Insights

Through the experience of the cluster, we have been able to generate a number of significant insights, which we discuss below in some detail.

A sociotechnical view

Perhaps the most significant, overarching, insight is that in using technology to effect social change, design must be understood as a profoundly sociotechnical process. Here, design is concerned as much with exploring the social and organisational arrangements of a technology-related intervention as with envisioning the technology itself. Conversely, activities related to designing must be understood as situated within the flow of other activities in the social and organisational context. While such observations have been repeatedly made in mainstream research into ICT and information systems design, in social action settings it frequently appears the norm for practitioners also to conceive of their work in sociotechnical terms.

[16] RITTEL, H. & WEBBER, M., 1973. Dilemmas in a General Theory of Planning. *Policy Sciences*, 4, pp. 155-169.

[17] CREANOR, L. & WALKER, S., 2005. *Trade Union Use of ICT in Learning.* London: TUC.

[18] LIGHT, A., 2005. *A World Usability Day Diary* [online]. Usability News. Available at: http://www.usabilitynews.com/news/article2790.asp

[19] Community Broadband Network. Available at: www.broadband-uk.coop.

The particular awareness of social aspects of technology use is likely to be linked to wider social concerns. However, the very nature of technology use in social action settings may also make the social dimensions of design and use rather more obvious. In social action contexts, applications are rarely either large-scale 'classical' information systems or highly commodified products. Rather, technology design and use become blurred as forms of bricolage and improvisation which bring together diverse materials and people in flexible arrangements to get things done. This further suggests that more open-ended design approaches and methods are required which can take account of the complex and dynamic interrelationships between people, organisations (both formal and informal) and technologies. Clearly, these design settings present many 'wicked' problems[16] which involve multiple stakeholders and have no single 'best' solution. Most of our subsequent observations are elaborations of, or supporting evidence for, our primarily sociotechnical perspective on design in social action settings.

Novel roles

Such a strongly sociotechnical view of design draws attention to the social and organisational arrangements in which technologies are designed and used. In particular, the significance of what became known within the cluster as 'novel' or 'emergent' roles[17] became evident. These terms refer to people who play new roles in orchestrating arrangements of people, practices and technologies, often resulting in (or from) innovative social or organisational forms. In some cases these practices may become institutionalised with organisations or communities of practice as identifiable roles. Particularly significant here are those people who are central in conceiving and designing new practices and forms, becoming 'architects of new sociotechnical relations'.[18] Within the cluster we heard of a number of examples, including 'network animateurs' in transnational trade union networks, who sought to facilitate new ways of distributed working in what had previously been rather bureaucratic settings. In doing so, they deploy a combination of technical, organisational, social and political skills. We heard from social entrepreneurs bringing together 'hard' technology networking skills, business methods and community development perspectives to set up wireless broadband networks for use by local communities.[19] We heard from people bringing together technology skills and approaches to community advocacy to develop technology-rich methods for the effective communication of concerns and grievances in urban communities. We hypothesise that these people, or in some cases roles, demonstrate varying combinations of facility with technology, creative design and use, domain expertise and social facilitation skills

[20] The Fiankoma Project. Available at: http://www.fiankoma.org/content.asp?page=home.

[21] Planning for Real® is a registered trademark of the Neighbourhoods Initiatives Foundation, www.nif.co.uk.

[22] TS3 Citizen Engagement for Safer and Stronger Communities. Available at: http://neukol.org.uk/sites/TS3/

[23] DEARDEN, A., LAUENER, A., SLACK, F., ROAST, C. & CASSIDY, S. 2006. Make it so! Jean-Luc Picard, Bart Simpson and the Design of e-Public Services. In: Proceedings of PDC 2006, Trento, Italy, 1st - 5th August 2006.

to achieve social action ends. Here, particularly, distinctions between the technology designer and the technology user become very blurred. Similarly, the notion of designer as 'auteur' breaks down as design outcomes emerge through complex, situated and collaborative dynamics between the individual and the collective.

Narrative

There was particular interest in the potential for narrative both in enhancing effective social action and in improving design practices. In enhancing social action there was a common finding that the ability to present personal and shared group narrative through new media can strengthen the voices of people who are often otherwise marginalised. Local politicians have reported how effective such narratives can be for communicating people's aspirations and values, in contrast to more traditional bureaucratic reports. Examples of using digital photography and video to compile such narratives came from run down estates in various UK cities, but also from rural Ghana.[20] In Middlesborough, the approach has been combined with the 'Planning for Real®'[21] technique to locate personal narratives within maps of a particular deprived area.[22] In accounts of narrative in the design process, we heard reports of the work of Blythe and Monk[12] and Dearden et al,[23] in successfully using Blythe's technique of 'Pastiche Scenarios' which employ fictional characters as the basis of interaction stories. Here, a concrete approach, using narrative methods to engage people from socially excluded groups in the design of complex technology for their own benefits, draws on shared knowledge of more complex and 'real' characters.

These narrative techniques are examples of how participation in design can be facilitated in practice. In social action settings, participation is widely seen as a good in itself, rather than simply as an instrumental means to improve the acceptability of design. This commitment to participation is a consequence of values of empowerment and emancipation inherent in social change and provides a link to work in the critical computing and critical information systems fields. Realising this commitment to participation raises practical issues, however. In many social action settings it is frequently easier to advocate participation than to achieve it in a meaningful way. This might be due, for example, to the lack of time and resources available to key stakeholders, lack of relevant skills or to geographic distribution. It has become clear during our work that technology designers might fruitfully learn from participation approaches used in community development. A further line of enquiry here was identified by participants raising issues of values in design practice more explicitly. In particular, gendered and culturally-specific assumptions about technology design and use may simply be replicated through participative design approaches without methods explicitly for identifying and reflecting upon them. Similar issues arise in discussions of evaluation (see below).

Free/Libre Open-Source Software

Exploiting Free/Libre Open-Source Software (FLOSS) has emerged as an important topic for several reasons. Pragmatically, it potentially offers low-cost options for obtaining software (though issues of total cost of ownership are not yet well understood). At a more political level, many social action technologists are attracted to the social arrangements of open source production, relying on contributions to a shared commons, and to its critique of conventional capitalist production and of the protection of one particular selection of the 'rights' that could be associated with intellectual 'property'. As one workshop participant put it, emphasising the collective nature of the FLOSS effort, 'FLOSS is a process not a product.'

The way that FLOSS plays out in practice varies significantly between different contexts. For example, we heard how campaigning groups in poorer countries might be tempted to use pirated software to cut costs, but may find that powerful actors could then use the legal system to silence their campaign efforts. Using FLOSS offers a form of security from such attacks. In the favellas of South America, we heard how FLOSS allows people with little money using repaired, recovered or recycled computers to access a fully featured operating system that is consistent and compatible with both old and new technologies. FLOSS also means that the barriers to entry to making a business in software development are more concerned with technical rather than financial capacity. Whilst these situations offer limited choice over whether or not to adopt FLOSS solutions, the situation in the rich industrialised countries is different. Many social action organisations benefit from preferential pricing deals from proprietary software providers. These discounts must be considered when evaluating total cost of ownership. Participants were also concerned that many social action organisations in the UK did not feel confident to make their first step into the FLOSS world, and were uncertain of where to get impartial advice. Recent moves funded by the UK government's ChangeUp initiative, and involving participants from the T&SA project have sought to provide support for FLOSS users in the voluntary sector, and will provide valuable practical lessons. One lesson already emerging is the need, when selecting FLOSS, to understand the network of actors supporting a chosen product and to determine whether both the product and the community have a sustainable basis for ongoing support.

More broadly, FLOSS organisation may also offer a useful model for the design and production of a wide range of other shareable, information intensive products such as graphics, video, sound archives or collective histories. Within the cluster we refer to this area of work as 'commons-based peer production'. Understanding the social arrangements that surround such production and design, and the extent to which practices originating in software development are replicable or adaptable in other areas represent important areas for future design research.

Evaluation and learning

A sociotechnical perspective on design immediately highlights its open-endedness and indeterminacy. Evaluation and organisational learning become pivotal within design. There are three reasons for this: firstly, evaluation is an integral part of the design process, providing a 'feedback' loop in these open-ended and complex situations. The outcomes of design interventions cannot be reliably foreseen when there are multiple possibilities for interaction. Formative evaluation provides a mechanism for 'in-flight' adjustments to sociotechnological interventions. Secondly, evaluations provide an opportunity to learn from others' experiences. Rigourous evaluation can be particularly significant in validating relationships between context, mechanism and outcomes, and in guarding against some of the more over-optimistic claims for the potential of technology made by some 'evangelists'. Thirdly, evaluation also has a role to play in helping decision making about the application of scarce resources. Design efforts here are ultimately driven by a search for value in terms of individual and collective capacity to deliver effective social action. This raises further research questions, such as how to treat the complex range of human values that drive social action which cannot readily be reduced to a single monetary measure. One way that we are taking this agenda forwards is by editing a special issue of the open-access journal *Human Technology*[24] on the subject of 'Quality, Values & Choice'.

[24] Human Technology Journal. Available online at: www.humantechnology.jyu.fi/

Other Issues

25 CUNLIFFE, D. & ROBERTS-YOUNG, D., 2005. Online design for bilingual civil society: a Welsh perspective. *Interacting With Computers*, 17(1), pp. 85-104.

26 WALKER, S. & CREANOR, L., 2005. Crossing complex boundaries: Transnational online education in european trade unions. *Journal of Computer Assisted Learning*, 21, pp. 343-354.

As well as the broad areas discussed above, a number of specific technology design problems were identified as prominent in, although not unique to, social action settings. Some of these, such as accessibility in design, are relatively well understood and practitioners here can draw on the growing bodies of knowledge already available. Other areas are perhaps of greater significance in particular contexts of social action, as for example with the development of bilingual websites in the context of defending minority languages.[25] Social action is frequently concerned with global, or at least transnational issues, bringing to the fore wider issues of multilingual and cross-cultural design.[26] An area of particular importance is the relationship between online and offline organisation, which emerged as an important, and again, 'wicked', design problem.

Within the cluster there was (initially surprisingly, for us at least) little practitioner concern with technologies qua technologies. There was very little explicit interest in evaluating and exploiting the implications of emergent technologies such as ubiquitous computing or the semantic web. The reasons for this are unclear but might reflect a lack of awareness of current developments; a more pragmatic focus on exploiting technologies which are already 'out there'; or perhaps indicate that attention remains focused on the social potential of existing technologies. Few participants expressed a primary need for specific hardware or software innovation. Even where this was expressed, as in the development of 'mesh' wireless community broadband networks it was part of a wider programme of establishing social enterprises. Development of social software (for example, shared bookmarks, wikis, blogs) appears primarily to be concerned with the integration and customisation of current applications in novel (social and technological) ways rather than the development of new applications *ab initio*. This finding, and the recognition of the central design questions as inherently sociotechnical, meant that our original intention of creating innovative conceptual designs for new devices or systems was not regarded as important within this community.

Concluding Remarks

The T&SA cluster has explored a new area for design research. Our findings raise a number of key parts of an ongoing research agenda. Notable amongst these are:

- Understanding the activities and roles of the 'architects of new socio-technical relations', how research and education might support their development, identifying practical resources to support their work, and investigating how their innovation initiatives propagate through the wider socio-technical networks of social action.
- Understanding the relations of 'designers' and 'users' in the complex webs of activity that emerge when technology related innovations are instigated in social action contexts.
- Developing new frameworks for evaluation and organisational learning in relation to technology interventions, with particular attention to the emancipatory human values that motivate social action and the exchange of knowledge between organisations.
- Exploring the potential of commons-based peer production (both in FLOSS software and in non-software products) as models for collective development and learning in social action.
- Developing effective methods to support participatory design in widely distributed organisations where key stakeholders have limited time.

The cluster has established a research agenda which is now informing new research interventions. This research agenda also provides a partial answer to, and elaboration of, the third question we set ourselves earlier: we can now claim to identify at least some areas where there is sufficient common concern among practitioners and researchers to provide a provisional basis for a 'social action informatics'.

Much, however, remains to be done.

Win-Win-Win-Win: Synergy Tools for Metadesigners
Prof. John Wood, (Goldsmiths, University of London)

From 'Design' to 'Metadesign'

[1] GIACCARDI, E., 2005. Metadesign as an emergent design culture. *Leonardo*, 38(4), pp. 342-349.

[2] GIACCARDI, E., 2005. Metadesign as an emergent design culture. *Leonardo*, 38(4).

[3] MATURANA, H. R., 1997. *Metadesign* [online]. Available at: http://www.inteco.cl/ articulos/006/texto_ing.htm.

[4] FULLER, R. B. & APPLEWHITE, E. J., 1975. *Synergetics: Explorations in the Geometry of Thinking*. New York: Macmillan Publishing Company, Inc.

Our initial context for the 'Design Synergy in the 21ˢᵗ Century' cluster project was the belief that 'Eco-design', and 'Design for Sustainability' have so far failed. We wondered, therefore, whether some form of 'metadesign' practice might become the basis for a more effective alternative. Our preliminary conclusion is that 'metadesign' is a consensual, systemic and holistic mode of design practice that replaces 'design as planning' with 'design as a seeding process'.[1] In this sense, 'metadesign' behaves as a 'systems integrator'.[2] Philosophically, it would function as a living system that actively 'languages' its own ethical identity.[3] We envisage that it would be managed using teams that include all the relevant, design-related practices. In wondering how to evaluate the effectiveness of such a complex system we asked whether it could be assessed by using 'synergy' as a performance indicator. Society would certainly benefit from new levels of synergy that might emerge from within, between and across many social, political, ideological, economic and biological boundaries. Here, Buckminster Fuller's grand vision of a 'synergy of synergies'[4] was helpful. I would define it as a totally comprehensive equilibrium that emerges from manifold diversities and mutual adaptabilities. In order to evolve a suitable understanding of 'metadesign' itself, we built our group out of individuals representing 14 different disciplines. We also consulted with Dr Lisa Giaccardi of Boulder University.

Can 'Metadesign' Save the World?

[5] GORNICK, N., 2006. Convergence: new management imperatives and their effect on design activity. *Design Management Review*, 17(2).

[6] SCHUMACHER, E. F., 1973. *Small is Beautiful: A Study of Economics as if People Mattered*. London: Abacus Penguin Books.

[7] WACKERNAGEL, M. and REES, W. E., 1996. *Our Ecological Footprint: Reducing Human Impact on the Earth*. Philadelphia: New Society Publishers.

Importantly, the implied focal point in our study was the future role of the designer. We believe that designers can, and should, play a greater role in transforming society. Recently, the way designers think has become increasingly interesting to scholars, business managers and other professionals. This is because it is often seen to be more radical, creative and holistic than the way that specialist bureaucrats, lawyers or managers tend to think. One of our team, Prof. Naomi Gornick has been charting the convergence between design thinking and management thinking.[5] Another of our experts from design research, Prof. Martin Woolley, showed how synergies already exist within good practice, but that we need to develop better methodologies to enhance them. This suggests that, even though, as designers, we have the potential to work at a higher level of organisation, we are not yet trained to do so. One reason for this is that our education system still insists on creating specialists. Profs. Naomi Gornick and Karen Blincoe explored the implications of metadesign for design education and corporate practice, concluding that there would be significant advantages in locating it right at the centre of the curriculum. This has enormous implications. What if metadesign teams were to run governments, farms and banks? This is a highly ambitious, entrepreneurial and, perhaps, even subversive idea. Nevertheless, it is worthy of consideration. Whilst we would not want to erode existing traditions of professional practice, society needs to change very rapidly if we are to avoid the impending environmental calamity that is looming.

The Failure of Eco-Design

Few environmentally aware designers find a way to follow their conscience whilst thriving economically at the professional level. Most see little option but to apply their skills in support of market forces. Unfortunately, these forces are manipulated to proliferate more and more products within a rapidly expanding market. Unwittingly, designers have therefore helped to create a society driven by over-consumption and waste. Since the 1950s we have tried to create a 'sustainable' world by 'reforming the environment,'[4] reducing the scale of enterprise,[6] or creating biodegradable, longer lasting products. However, although we now understand far more about the damage we are doing to the eco-system[7] this knowledge has failed to wean us away from specialist design practices, and to establish a common environmental discourse across the industry. Perhaps the most promising work in the 'design for sustainability' movement has already been edging towards metadesign by advocating a more enterprising,

[8] MURRAY, R., 2002. *Zero Waste.* Greenpeace Environmental Trust.

[9] MCDONOUGH, W. & BRAUNGART, M., 2002. *Cradle to Cradle: Remaking the Way We Make Things.* Emmaus, PA: Rodale Books.

[10] HAWKEN, P., LOVINS, A. B. & LOVINS, L. H., 1999. *Natural Capitalism.* Earthscan.

[11] ROMER, P. M., 1987. Growth based on increasing returns due to specialization. *American Economic Review,* 77(2), pp. 56-62.

adaptive, 'zero-waste' society.[8] In this system, production would operate as a 'cradle-to-cradle' system,[9] that offers more and more opportunities for sustainable enterprise.[10] Despite the heroic efforts by the pioneers of 'eco-design', 'design for sustainability' and so on, global carbon emissions continue to rise, and bio-diversity levels are falling at an alarming rate. This is because neither 'eco-design', nor 'design for sustainability' have been powerful enough to tame an economic system designed for limitless growth. This is why 'metadesign' is needed.

Future Research Issues

However, where 'metadesign' is potentially vast in scale, the range of our project was limited by its brevity and modest scale. We could not, for example, address paramount issues such as food production and transport policy. Today, more than half the world's population live in cities. Although poor urban communities spend an average of 30 per cent more on food than their rural counterparts, they consume fewer calories. This is not just because of low incomes and high fuel prices. In many of these areas between 10 and 30 per cent of food produce is lost or spoiled on long journeys and because of poor infrastructure. Without a 'metadesign' vision, our energy-dependent systems of intensive farming and long-distance transportation will begin to fail us. We need a new discourse that is able to explain how things work in a more holistic and relational way. This, in turn, would be needed in order to promote a more consensual, decentralised system of governance. Whatever system of metadesign we adopt will therefore need to make individuals more creatively responsible and ecologically attuned. But, even if we could find one, how would we evaluate the efficacy of such a complex and interdependent system? One way to do this, we concluded, would be to look for processes that fulfil the 'law of increasing returns',[11] and to measure their synergy levels as well as we can.

The Economic Dimension

One of our researchers is the 'eco-economist', Richard Douthwaite, who helped us to articulate a possible role for economics as a fundamental aspect of metadesign. Over the past 30 years, the rate of economic growth and the rate of discovery of oil reserves have followed almost identical upward curves. This has facilitated a waste-based society that has camouflaged its lack of synergy by doing everything at an accelerating pace. However, despite the optimism of some oil executives, this trend will falter, perhaps in the next few years. When this happens, the 'endless growth' model will lose all credibility, and we may then feel inclined to

[12] DOUTHWAITE, R., 2006. Economic Synergy. *Journal of Landscape and Urban Planning, Landscape Ecology, Planning and Design* (at press).

[13] Peabody Trust. Available at: http://www.peabody.org.uk/pages/GetPage.aspx?id=179.

envision how we really want to live. My view is that we will then see the rise of 'super-creative banking' systems, by which resources will be valued and orchestrated using ingenious new processes of sharing and exchange. In his nine preliminary recommendations, Richard showed how scarce resources could be rationed fairly, partly by encouraging local initiatives on a truly sustainable basis. This is something that an unregulated world economy is ill equipped to do. We would redesign the way that money is put into circulation, and we would cease to use debt as a way to maintain productivity. Richard suggested that governments, rather than banks, might sponsor two types of currency, one for savings, one for trade. By prudently spending the exchange currency into circulation and taxing it back again, governments would be able to move us slowly toward zero inflation. Eventually, we would establish a genuine world currency (rather like what used to be called 'paper gold', or 'SDRs'). This would be distributed on the basis of population numbers and global sustainability, rather than on economic power. It would be issued into circulation on a scale that would allow the reserve currencies to be returned to their countries of origin to clear international debt.[12]

The Architectural Dimension

In seeking to explore a wide range of practical and theoretical issues, we made a brief case study of 'BedZed', a pioneering and acclaimed 'zero-carbon' housing project in the South East of England. This project was created by one of our researchers (the eco-architect, Bill Dunster). We discovered that Bill had already considered incorporating an economic dimension by considering a local currency system within early plans for his BedZed housing scheme.[13] His practical experience proved useful for our research, especially at the economic, entrepreneurial level. For example, Bill had found it important to demonstrate the financial and political viability of environmental improvement schemes. For example, by 'leaving the rich to be rich', whilst 'rewarding the poor', we might transform otherwise damaged environments into fertile and pleasant areas. This highly pragmatic aspect of metadesign emphasises its dynamic and creative nature. Bill advocated a mixture of building solutions, in order to achieve a rich mixture of styles and possibilities. Some entrepreneurs might want to build more, in return for using more carbon reducing technologies. This welcoming of difference and heterogeneity seemed to be an important feature of what we understand as 'metadesign'. For one thing, it is realistic. Where some people wish to devise conspicuous and innovative ways of 'eco-living', others might live in unremarkable houses, quietly transforming them into zero carbon zones.

Working with Super-Complex Systems

Some of Bill Dunster's work entailed managing the efficiencies of energy conservation and generation. This aspect of his work dovetailed with the findings of two other of our researchers, a building scientist and a practising architect. Prof. Philip Jones, a buildings scientist, uses laboratory methods to improve the conservation and management of energy in very large buildings around the world. His work is closely integrated with the designs of architects and planners, to ensure that synergies at one level can be maintained by synergies at another. A disadvantage of discrete, specialist design practice is that it offers incomplete solutions. Hence, the advantages of living in a low-energy house would easily be cancelled out by driving long distances to work, even in a 'low energy' car. Jan-Marc Petroschka, our expert in social housing, is also an innovator in the design of live-work dwellings in London. Under his guidance we discussed the feasibility of 'scaling-up' the suburban BedZed agenda to become a fully interdependent urban 'living style'. This is because greater economies of scale can be achieved within cities. Some of Jan-Marc's ideas on space-saving 'live-work' architecture are shown in his critically acclaimed housing project (Astra House, MacDonald Egan & Partners), recently completed in the Deptford area of London. Whilst neither the BedZed, nor Astra House projects have required significant technical innovation we were interested to know why pioneering initiatives like these often take a great deal of time to gain acceptance, or even to inspire imitations. We developed several mapping methods that facilitate close inquiry into such a question. In one example [Figure 1], the early difficulties in gaining acceptance for a novel scheme can be grasped by monitoring the actions of four 'players' and the six relations that co-sustain them.

Whilst useful, this is an inadequate way to represent the vast number of tiny, but significant factors that are, to a significant extent, reciprocally self-creating. In short, it may not contain enough information to be effective. Complexity must therefore be apprehended as a whole entity. In this case, for example, BedZed needed to gain the support of a cluster of interested parties, each of whom may have a different 'vested interest'. The support of a given individual is usually, also, influenced by the perceived views and likely actions of others within the cluster. Figure 2 shows all of the above eight players (the dots on the diagram) linked together (by lines) in a minimum set of 28 links. If we are to represent all of the possible relations within the system, it would be wise to explore each link in turn, using a positively creative, opportunistic and open-minded

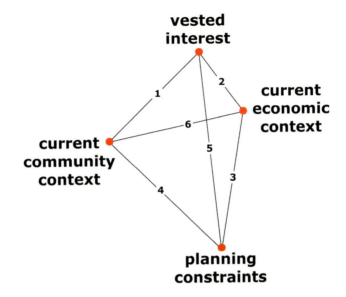

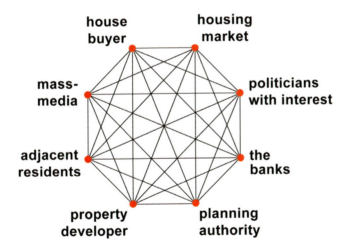

Figures 1 and 2,
top and bottom

Figure 1, Simplified (four-fold) model of the challenges in housing innovation
Figure 2, The 28 possible relationships in an eight player system

approach. This may mean that the 28 links can also be represented as 56 relational viewpoints. By using this map opportunistically and creatively it is possible to design points of critical intervention, and to devise new solutions to this kind of complex problem. We believe that this mapping system can enable complex 'vicious circles' to become transformable into more 'virtuous circles'. As such, it is a useful tool for metadesigners.

The relational mapping method we used in Figure 2 was inspired by some original research by another of our researchers, (Dr Vadim Kvitash). Vadim holds many patents on a comprehensive system for evaluating something that is akin to the 'equilibrium', or 'balance' of whole systems within a medical context. His system of 'Relonics'[14] offers a powerful, systemic language of complex, interdependent relations. In one application he finds a use for the otherwise discarded data taken from laboratory analysis of the blood samples. Arguably, in orthodox medicine, if the experts only look for 'abnormal' levels of particular chemicals associated with a given illness most of this data is ignored. In Vadim's system, we are also interested in the total set of relations between each individual factor, and each other factor. As the number of factors increases the resulting number of relations rises exponentially. This means that when we use a reduced set of isolated indicators to make a judgement, we are overlooking some of the information. Mathematically, the number of factors in a given set determines, with 100 per cent accuracy, the finite number of relations implied. At this level of logic, we can therefore know exactly how many relations are possible. How we interpret them is another matter, but Dr. Kvitash can forecast, with 95 per cent accuracy, whether a patient will live or die within 3 years of a heart operation. Where more discrete, analytical methods tend to look for single, identifiable parameters, his system plots relations against a non-statistically derived set of self-balancing norms (he calls 'relons'). We have evaluated his system using urban planning situations, rather than medical data, concluding that it is likely to be just as useful.

[14] KVITASH, V., 2004. *Balascopy System and Method with Improved Sensitivity.* United States Patent Application 6,768,948.

Dealing with Intangibles in a Complex System

In our project we also addressed the issue of complexity by considering the emergent nature of real urban spaces, and its potential for facilitating creative evolution and change. Where Vadim's work sought a high level of predictability, other researchers (Prof. Milan Jaros, a theoretical physicist, and Hannah Jones, an artist and design theorist) both explored the more volatile and marginal features of our spatio-temporal environment. Each, in their different ways, acknowledged the need for a new, non-Kantian, non-Cartesian understanding of space and time. Milan, for example, explored the way that individual self-identity is, to an important extent, enabled by the 'spatio-temporal instabilities, or warps' between the virtual and the material worlds. In other words, the citizen finds or 'creates' herself at the boundaries between what he calls, 'an assemblage of the self, place and interactions (narratives) binding them dynamically together.' Although the responsible designer cannot dare to 'design' in any deterministic or predictive sense, at this level, metadesign teams might nevertheless be wise to reflect upon the complex socio-political insights that Prof. Jaros's work has generated. If we were to ignore this level of understanding we may find that we may impair our ability to facilitate and/or to cultivate a creatively adaptive society.

Future Research Issues

Hannah Jones looks at the potential for sustainable urban planning by seeing the spaces between buildings as possible sites of unintended potential. By describing these unconsidered zones as 'awkward spaces', she acknowledges the inescapable ambivalence between that which is planned and that which inevitably follows as a by-product of the logic of form and flow. At a time when the public rhetoric of 'iconic buildings' is used to totalise an ethic of grace and power, Hannah prefers to celebrate the maladroit, the uncanny, the chaotic and the dissipative. In working to establish a comprehensive language of urban incompleteness, she opens up unforeseen possibilities for the metadesigner. One of the aims of her project is the prospect of transforming 'vicious circles' into 'virtuous circles' [Figure 3].

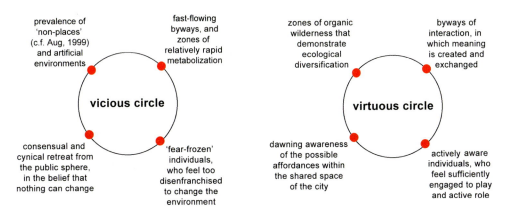

Figure 3, Transforming a 'vicious circle' into a 'virtuous circle'

Going Beyond Symbiosis

In seeking to integrate the best aspects of all of these belief systems, the idea of a 'win-win' situation is useful because it is so familiar. A 'win-win' situation is usually conceived of as two players in a symbiotic relationship. However, a metadesign team might multiply this idea by seeking to 'seed' new environments in which there are many more 'winners' than 'losers'. Although the language of 'winning' and 'losing' has some dubious implications, in the short term it is useful. Implicitly, Adam Smith's original idea that self-interest yields shared benefits for all[15] is very appealing because it makes a 'win-win' (that is, at least doubly attractive) offer. Unfortunately, evolved into a contagious ethic of consumption in which individual self-gratification is rewarded because we believe it will energise the economy, and, ultimately, reward everyone. By contrast, the logic of 'sustainability' appears to offer a 'lose-win' scenario in which citizens must curb their desires in deference to future generations of consumers. Here, we may be attracted to an eco-mimetic model in which, say, when several tasks are undertaken in parallel there is a possibility that one may help the other without disadvantaging itself. It is customary to identify individual gains and losses as 'categories of advantage' as follows:

[15] SMITH, A., 1993. *The Wealth of Nations*. Indianapolis: Hackett Publishing Company.

1) **Mutually damaging**
(— / —)
(Disadvantaging each another in pursuing exclusive advantage)

2) **Parasitic**
(— / +)
(High dependency on the fitness of one, rather than on both partners)

3) **Symbiotic**
(+ / +)
(Mutually supportive collaboration)

4) **Super-symbiotic**
>(+ / +)
(Symbiosis that also enhances context, or that acts 'for' additional beneficiaries who share the same eco-system yet may be unknown or beyond comprehension)

Unfortunately, faced with this kind of choice, humans frequently disregard the negative consequences of their immediate actions by seeing them as a choice between a single, strong, immediate, personal gain, versus a small (that is, when shared collectively), unspecific, long-term loss.[16]

[16] HARDIN, G., 1977. The Tragedy of the Commons. In: G. HARDIN and J. BADEN, (eds.) *Managing the Commons*. San Francisco: W. H. Freeman and Co.

The idea of two individuals who share a mutually beneficial relationship is familiar [Figure 4], but what happens when we bring in additional players to introduce new synergies into an existing symbiotic relationship? Here, we face the problem of how to manage increasingly complex systems. Nevertheless, it can be shown that the possible advantage increases significantly, even for a relatively small increase in the number of symbiotic players.

Figure 4, The 'win-win' scenario mapped as a single relationship

Let us take four players, rather than two, and represent them a tetrahedron [Figure 5]. Buckminster Fuller noted the unique properties of the tetrahedron in 1975. They are implicit in Euler' Law (1752), which states that the number of vertices plus the number of faces in any polygon will always equal the number of edges plus two (that is, V + F = E + 2). This '2' is what Fuller called the 'constant relative abundance'. However, because this surplus becomes increasingly trivial as complexity increases, we may note an auspicious balance between the tetrahedron's simplicity (that is, mnemonic convenience) compared with its relational richness (that is, in its high ratio of edges to vertices). Thus, there are six times more peer relationships (that is, edges) between four players (that is, faces, or nodes) than there are between two players [Figure 5]. Hence, by merely doubling the number of 'players' from two to four, we achieve a six-fold increase in the number of mutual relations that can be utilised. In short, the tetrahedron is special because it combines a graspable, non-hierarchical topology that offers possible symbiotic advantage to each of the four players. This can be presented to untrained users as a 'win-win-win-win' situation.

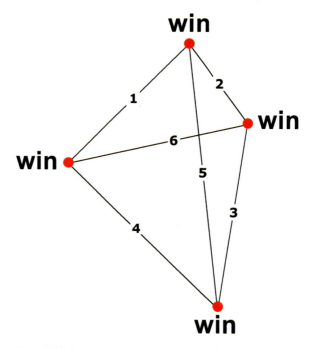

Figure 5, The 'win-win-win-win' scenario mapped as six paired relations

Mapping Synergy

Although the concept of 'synergy' appears to be well understood in management, and elsewhere, its definition is surprisingly vague. This is partly because synergy itself is elusive and changeable. Indeed, all of the definitions we found were too generic to be useful. In seeking measurable outcomes, we therefore defined four fundamental 'orders' of synergy that would help us to map, and to manage the complexity of a practical system. This scheme regards Peter Corning's[17] observation that some bioeconomic synergies include 'information-sharing' capabilities. I adopted this as our 'second order' synergy, the added 'data-storing synergy' (first order), 'knowledge-sharing synergy' (third order) and 'knowledge-sharing synergy' (fourth order). This tool makes it possible to 'metadesign' for complex conditions by mapping them as manageable task domains that can subsequently by reintegrated within the whole.

[17] CORNING, P., 1983. *The Synergism Hypothesis*. London: McGraw-Hill. Available at: http://www.complexsystems.org/publications/pdf/synselforg.pdf.

Figure 6 shows a crude mapping of our four Orders of Synergy. It reflects four levels of complexity intended to encompass and 'synergise' a wide range of other synergies. Where, for example, the 'data-sharing' level might include, say, smart metallurgical synergies, the 'information-sharing' level might facilitate sophisticated energy management systems. Where the 'knowledge sharing' level might be used to guide the cultivation of shared social benefits, the 'wisdom-sharing' level would probably include highly ephemeral and emergent phenomena, perhaps at the eudemonic, or spiritual level.

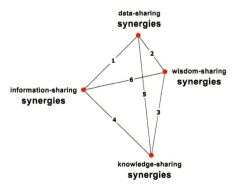

Figure 6, Using our four Orders of Synergy to map a 'Synergy-of-Synergies'

In seeking to ensure excellent communication at many cognitive levels we preceded some of our meetings with a dance workshop run by a choreographer. These proved to be extremely effective in reminding ourselves of the embodied nature of thinking, also in facilitating a rapid rapport between each, and every other researcher. Much of our theory behind our mission was underpinned by the multifaceted research of another of our research team, Dr Otto van Nieuwenhuijze. Van Nieuwenhuijze's work includes some of the topological insights that informed communication issues, including co-authorship.[18] Some of the methods or tools we used emerged partly as a response to difficulties of interpersonal relations that, for a short time, threatened our momentum when conducting practical workshops. Here, we used a corresponding, but different mapping system. Assigning each researcher to one of four levels reduced unhelpful conflict, thereby enabling them to play an optimum role. We created four levels of collaboration, each represented by a 'group' for holding the identity of one of the four roles.

[18] NIEUWENHUIJZE, O. & WOOD, J., 2006. Synergy and sympoiesis in the writing of joint papers; anticipation with/in imagination. *International Journal of Computing Anticipatory Systems*, 10(August), pp. 87-102.

Complexity	Role/Group	Approach/Mode of Inquiry
HIGHER ⇑	NEW KNOWING	intuitive/spontaneous/anticipatory
	ENVISIONING	imaginative/critical/self-reflexive/tactical
⇓	LANGUAGING	discursive/interpretive/adaptive/facilitating
LOWER	PUSHING/DOING	hands-on/decisive/resourceful/managerial

Figure 7, The four groups and their roles

Where the 'New Knowing' group acted as a kind of unconscious mind for the whole team, the 'Languaging' group was able to create new meanings that would promote better communication. Where the 'Pushing and Doing' group focused on the delivery of specified outcomes, the 'Visioning' group's role was to anticipate possibilities, and to present options.

We developed this idea into a practical management tool that mooted co-creative roles for synergy management [Figure 8], developed for 16 individuals on four tables [Figure 9].

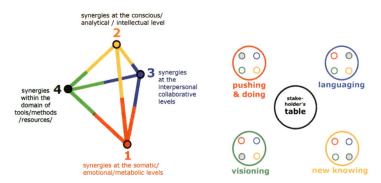

Figures 8 and 9,
left and right

Figure 8, The Four Collaborative Roles
Figure 9, Layout of tables for the workshop

At each table there was one permanent member of the group. The other three were each assigned the task of liaising with another table. This ensured that the maximum number of interdependent conversations could take place with the minimum of confusion or conflict. On March 21ˢᵗ 2006 we gave the system a final test in the presence of a stakeholder, Andrew Carmichael, of the Creative Lewisham Agency. The workshop was extremely successful. During the 5 hour workshop we used the above tool to deliver several innovative solutions to Andrew's practical problem.

Acknowledgements

We are grateful to Prof. Tom Inns and Vicky Hale for managing the Design for the 21st Century Initiative, and to the EPSRC and AHRC for their support. Warm thanks are extended to Ann Schlachter and Hannah Jones, for organising the research events with an extraordinarily positive spirit. We are also indebted to our researchers:

Prof. Karen Blincoe, Andrew Carmichael, Dr Caroline Davey, Richard Douthwaite, Bill Dunster, Prof. Naomi Gornick, Hannah Jones, Prof. Phil Jones, Prof. Milan Jaros, Dr Vadim I. Kvitash, Dr Otto van Nieuwenhuijze, Jan-Marc Petroshka, Prof. Martin Woolley.

We are grateful to our expert visitors and supporters who made a significant contribution. These include: Jonny Bradley, Jonathan Chapman, Dr Ken Fairclough, Alistair Fuad-Luke, David Heldt, Will Jones, Duncan Kramer, Julia Lockheart, Anette Lundebye, Bim Malcolmson, Jae Mather, Denis O'Brien, Fabiane Perella, Dr Garth Rennie, Paul Taylor and Mathilda Tham.

Additional Reading

JAROS, M., 2006. Towards re-definition of space-ness in the post-mechanical age: methodological notes. *Journal of Landscape and Urban Planning, Landscape Ecology, Planning and Design*, (at press).

JONES, H., 2006. Sustainable future cities: how can re-evaluating the potential of awkward spaces in the city lead to a creative and sustainable urban design of london? *Journal of Landscape and Urban Planning, Landscape Ecology, Planning and Design*, at press.

JONES, P., 2006. Modelling the environment in cities. *Journal of Landscape and Urban Planning, Landscape Ecology, Planning and Design*, at press.

WOOD, J., 2004. The tetrahedron can encourage designers to formalise more responsible strategies. *Journal of Art, Design & Communication*, 3(3), pp.175-192.

WOOD, J., 2005. (How) Can Designers Learn to Enhance Synergy within Complex Systems?. *Presented at the DESIGNsystemEVOLUTION Conference, Bremen, March 2005.*

WOOD, J., 2006. Synergy city. *Journal of Landscape and Urban Planning, Landscape Ecology, Planning and Design*, at press.

Embracing Complexity in Design

Prof. Jeffrey Johnson[1], Katerina Alexiou[1,2], Dr Anne Creigh-Tyte[3], Dr Scott Chase[4], Prof. Alex Duffy[5], Dr Claudia Eckert[6], Damian Gascoigne[3], Prof. Bimal Kumar[7], Prof. Eve Mitleton-Kelly[8], Michael Petry[9], Dr Sheng Fen Qin[10], Prof. Alec Robertson[11], George Rzevski[1,10], Prof. Necdet Teymur[12], Avril Thompson[5], Prof. Robert Young[13], Mateo Willis[9], Theodore Zamenopoulos[1,2].
([1]The Open University, [2]University College London, [3]Kingston University, [4,5]Strathclyde University, [6]Cambridge University, [7]Glasgow Caledonian University, [8]London School of Economics, [9]Museum of Contemporary Art, [10]Brunel University, [11]De Montfort University, [12]University of Dundee, [13]Northumbria University)

Overview

In recent years there have been major advances in the science of complex systems that are clearly relevant for the theory and practice of design. It is now recognised that the objects of most domains are 'complex systems', including natural systems, social systems and artificial systems. The science of complex systems cuts across the particular domains, seeking principles and methods that can be applied to complex systems in general.

Science is increasingly concerned with what *could be*, as an extension of what *is*. For example, biology blurs the distinction between a dispassionate study of plants and animals, and the desire to apply the knowledge gained in medicine, industry, agriculture and ecosystem management. Increasingly science is motivated by the need to design and manage complex socio-technical systems whose behaviour depends on interactions between physical laws and human behaviour. Science is increasingly concerned with the artificial and the synthetic, and the science of complex systems is increasingly motivated by *design*.

Although, there is no universally accepted definition of what it means for a system to be complex, there are some widely accepted characteristics of complex systems. These include:

- some deterministic systems are inherently unpredictable over long periods of time:
  - chaotic systems are very sensitive to initial conditions;
  - path dependent systems depend on their particular history;
  - systems may have co-evolving subsystems, or co-evolve with their environment;
  - emergence: new order may emerge from existing system states;
  - systems may adapt to unpredictable changes in their environment.

- some systems are discrete and cannot be solely represented by numerical equations:
  - computationally irreducible systems cannot be modelled by solving equations;
  - system dynamics may be constrained by network connectivity and topology;
  - self-organisation: system behaviour can emerge from agent interactions;
  - multilevel dynamics: the behaviour of systems may depend on many discrete levels;
  - emergence: wholes can have properties not possessed by their parts.

In parallel to developments in complex systems science, there have been many advances in design research and design practice motivated by the recognition that complexity exists across every aspect of design. Research in this field has been initiated by different groups around the world: in the USA (Braha and Bar-Yam at NESCI, Suh at MIT), in Australia (Gero at Sydney University) as well as in Europe and UK (including members of our cluster). In these studies the relation between complexity and design has been interpreted in a variety of ways. Our project identified four ways in which complexity impacts on design:

- many designed products and systems are inherently complex, for example, aeroplanes, buildings, cities, microchips, information systems, manufacturers and organisations;
- designers need to understand the often complex dynamic processes and supply chains used to fabricate and manufacture products and systems: design, products and processes co-evolve;
- the social and economic context of design is complex, embracing market economics, legal regulation, social trends, mass culture, fashion and much more;

• the process of designing can involve complex social dynamics, with many people processing and exchanging complex heterogeneous information over complex human and communication networks, in the context of many changing constraints.

We call these more-or-less orthogonal axes the *four pillars of complexity and design*. Design projects involve them all, for example, designs may fail due to (i) the system not being adequately understood, (ii) failures in fabrication or manufacture, (iii) the environment not being favourable, or (iv) the design team failing to deliver. Most likely, projects fail for interactions between all four, reflecting the complexity that is the everyday challenge in design.

A better understanding of complexity and a better synergy between complexity and design will be essential for the design research and practice in the 21st century. Our main objective was to bring individuals and groups together to develop a research agenda in complexity and design. Although designers deal with complexity in their everyday practice, many are still unaware of the benefits of embracing complexity thinking, and incorporating complex systems methodologies and tools in design practice. Thus another objective of the cluster was to create a framework where advances in research on complexity and design can be communicated, and to investigate new ways of communicating our research findings through exhibitions and events.

Our method of research involved taking a multidisciplinary view across the design disciplines, investigating how the principles from complex systems science can be applied in particular design domains. We were able to do this because the cluster had experts in architecture and environment design, information systems design, engineering design, electronics design, knitwear design, systems design, organisational design, and art. During our meeting it was clear that, despite particular specialisms, the group shared a common 'design culture', being familiar with the same issues and literature. This made communication very effective and allowed us to focus on the issue of complexity as it relates to design.

Activities of the Cluster

In general, there were three kinds of activities organised, corresponding to different objectives: *Tutorials and Seminars* where the aim was to learn from each other and establish a common communication language; *Workshops and Conferences* in order to communicate and share research findings with the wider design and complexity communities, provide a forum for multidisciplinary exchange at a national and international level and initiate original publications; and *Exhibitions* in order to extend collaboration with design practitioners and artists, and to experiment with different ways to disseminate to researchers and practitioners.

Sheng Feng Qin at Brunel University organised our first *International Conference* on *Embracing Complexity in Collaborative Design and Solutions*. Some of the themes explored in papers included: complexity in design, communication and tools for supporting design decision making in distributed design, holistic design, complex networks between design teams, users and markets. Papers presented at the conference were published in a book of proceedings while selected papers were published in a special issue in *Co-Design*.

Another international workshop, entitled 'Design Out of Complexity', was organised by Katerina Alexiou, Theodore Zamenopoulos and Elena Besussi from UCL, as part of CUPUM, an international conference on Computers in Urban Planning and Urban Management, held in London. The aim of the workshop was to explore the hypothesis that design is a natural capacity that is derived by the complexity and organisation of large social or socio-technical systems such as cities or human-computer networks, where the focus is not on an individual designer but on the system as a whole. Another important issue discussed was the nature and role of design in the face of complexity. Two journal special issues with papers from this workshop are in preparation, one in *Futures* and the other in *Environment and Planning B: Planning and Design*.

Finally, we also organised an 'International Workshop' as part of the 'European Conference of Complex Systems' in Paris. The objective of this workshop was different to the previous ones as the focus was to communicate with the complexity science community and collect together state-of-the-art research exploring the connections between complexity and design. From this conference we produced proceedings published by the Open University.

Apart from these larger conference-type workshops, we also organised smaller scale workshops more focused on exploring directions of research in a particular subject area.

Another kind of activity was organising exhibitions with the aim to collaborate with artists and explore the relation between complexity and art.

[1] ECiD. Available at: www.complexityanddesign.net

[2] TEYMUR, N., 2002. *Re: Architecture – Themes and Variations*. London: ?uestion Press.

[3] KAUFFMAN, S., 1993. *The Origins of Order: Self-Organisation and Selection in Evolution*. USA: Oxford University Press.

[4] KAUFFMAN, S., 1995. *At Home in the Universe*. USA: Oxford University Press.

[5] KAUFFMAN, S., 2000. *Investigations*. USA: Oxford University Press.

[6] HOLLAND, J., 1995. *Hidden Order: How Adaptation Builds Complexity*. Addison Wesley.

[7] HOLLAND, J., 1998. *Emergence: From Chaos to Order*. Addison Wesley.

[8] WALDROP, M. M., 1992. *Complexity: The Emerging Science at the Edge of Order and Chaos*. Penguin.

[9] GELL-MANN, M., 1994. *The Quark and the Jaguar: Adventures in the Simple and the Complex*. WH Freeman.

[10] ALLEN, P. M., 1997. *Cities & Regions As Self-Organising Systems : Model of Complexity. Environmental Problems & Social Dynamics Series, Vol 1*. Gordon & Breach Science Publications.

[11] GOODWIN, B., 1995. *How the Leopard Changed Its Spots*. Phoenix.

[12] WEBSTER, G. and GOODWIN, B., 1996. *Form and Transformation: Generative and Relational Principles in Biology*. Cambridge University Press.

[13] AXELROD, R., 1990. *The Evolution of Cooperation*. Penguin Books.

This began by participating in a workshop on 'Art, Complexity and Technology' held in Torino.

Eve Mitleton-Kelly organised another workshop in London under the title 'Art, Complexity and Design'. It focussed on issues of representation and interpretation and their role in science and art. The discussion was motivated by the exhibited works of the artists Mateo Willis, Michael Petry and Gail Troth. It also included video recordings of presentations at the Torino meeting by John Fraser and Luc Steels.

The 'Complex Embrace' exhibition at the Picker Gallery at Kingston University investigated communicating concepts in complex systems science through art, in this case a series of animations by the artists Damian Gascoigne projected onto three large vertically aligned screens. This exhibition was well received as an artistic event and the indications are that art can be used as a means of communicating scientific ideas.

Our 'Grande Finale' held at the Royal College of Art in December 2005, 'More is More' was a 2 day celebration of the project with members of the cluster, the design research community and practicing designers. Organised and designed by Alec Robertson, based on his interests in 4D design and issues of design research dissemination, the event provided a forum that enabled cluster members to reflect upon the ideas emerging from their activities, and to begin a discussion with design researchers and professionals. Held within an environment more intimate than the usual conference, workshop or exhibition, the event encouraged artistic, designerly and scientific minds to communicate and understand each other.

Materials from all these events can be found on the cluster website.[1]

Insights

'DESIGN' – Complex Definitions

In his paper *'DESIGN' – Complex Definitions* presented at the Paris workshop, Necdet Teymur showed how the word 'design' is used in many disciplines, with the word denoting an activity, a noun, a mode of graphical representation and many other things too. He comments that, 'If architecture were any simpler, we wouldn't be able to understand it any better.'[2] This divergent approach to embracing complexity in design is shown in Figure 1, which illustrates the many ways one can interpret the word 'design' in the context of complexity.

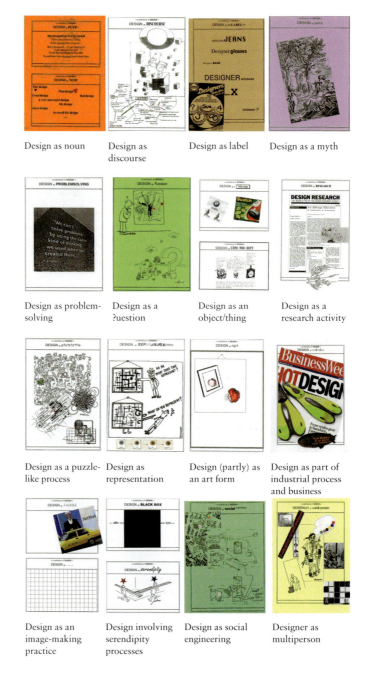

Design as noun

Design as discourse

Design as label

Design as a myth

Design as problem-solving

Design as a ?uestion

Design as an object/thing

Design as a research activity

Design as a puzzle-like process

Design as representation

Design (partly) as an art form

Design as part of industrial process and business

Design as an image-making practice

Design involving serendipity processes

Design as social engineering

Designer as multiperson

Figure 1, 'DESIGN' – complex definitions, (from Teymur, 2005)

Dialogue on complexity and design

[14] AXELROD, R., 1997. *The Complexity of Co-operation: Agent-Based Models of Competition and Collaboration.* Princeton University Press.

[15] AXELROD, R. & COHEN, M. D., 2000. *Harnessing Complexity: Organisational Implications of a Scientific Frontier.* Free Press.

[16] CASTI, J., 1997. *Would-be Worlds.* Wiley.

[17] BONABEAU, E., DORIGO, M. & THERAULAZ, G., 1999. *Swarm Intelligence.* Oxford University Press.

[18] EPSTEIN, J. M. & AXTEL, R., 1996. *Growing Artificial Societies: Social Science from the Bottom Up.* Brookings Institution Press.

[19] FERBER, J., 1999. *Multi-Agent Systems: An Introduction to Distributed Artificial Intelligence.* Addison Wesley.

[20] PRIGOGINE, I. & STENGERS, I., 1985. *Order Out of Chaos.* Flamingo.

[21] NICOLIS, G. and PRIGOGINE, I., 1989. *Exploring Complexity.* WH Freeman.

[22] PRIGOGINE, I., 1990. Time and the Problem of the Two Cultures. *First International Dialogue on the Transition to Global Society,* Landegg Academy, 3-9th September 1990.

[23] NICOLIS, G., 1994. Physics of Far-from-equilibrium Systems and Self-organisation. *In:* P. DAVIES, (ed.) *The New Physics.* Cambridge University Press.

[24] VARELA, F. and MATURANA, H., 1992. *The Tree of Knowledge.* Shambhala.

[25] LUHMAN, N., 1990. *Essays on Self Reference.* New York: Columbia University Press.

Our first tutorial seminar meeting was organised by Eve Mitleton-Kelly from LSE. The purpose of the meeting was twofold: as tutorial on fundamental principles of complex systems for those less familiar with the science of complexity, and to establish a common language between cluster members. A particular aim was to explore how concepts such as emergence, self-organisation or co-evolution can be seen in design research and practice. The tutorial began with a useful review of recent research in complex systems science. Although there is no single unified Theory of Complexity, there are several theories arising from natural sciences studies of complex systems, such as biology, chemistry, computer simulation, evolution, mathematics and physics. This includes the work undertaken over the past four decades by scientists associated with the Santa Fe Institute (SFI) in New Mexico, USA, and particularly that of Stuart Kauffman,[3,4,5] John Holland,[6,7] Chris Langton[8] and Murray Gell-Mann[9] on Complex Adaptive Systems (CAS), as well as the work of scientists based in Europe such as Peter Allen[10] and Brian Goodwin;[11,12] Axelrod on cooperation;[13,14,15] Casti,[16] Bonabeau et al,[17] Epstein & Axtel[18] and Ferber[19] on 'modelling and computer simulation;' work by Ilya Prigogine,[20,21,22] Isabelle Stengers,[20] Gregoire Nicolis[21,23] on 'dissipative structures;' work by Humberto Maturana, Francisco Varela[24] and Niklaus Luhman[25] on autopoiesis;[26] as well as the work on chaos theory[27] and that on economics and increasing returns by Brian Arthur.[28,29,30]

The tutorial introduced the 'Ten principles of complexity' for Complex Evolving Systems (CES).[31] Such systems are characterised by the 'creation of new order.' Non-CES systems (like machines with multiple interrelated parts) do not have this capacity and are therefore not 'complex' within the meaning of the term – but 'complicated'. These ten generic principles of CES have been tested for appropriateness and relevance to human systems in collaborative research projects with business partners since 1997. The left of Figure 2 summarises five main areas of research on (a) CAS at the Santa Fe Institute (centre for CAS research in the USA) and Europe; (b) dissipative structures by Ilya Prigogine and his co-authors; (c) autopoiesis based on the work of Maturana in biology and its application to social systems by Luhman; (d) chaos theory; and (e) increasing returns and path dependence by Brian Arthur and other economists.[32,33] The right of Figure 2 shows the ten generic principles of complexity. Since the ten principles incorporate more than the work on CAS, Mitleton-Kelly uses the term CES.[10]

[26] MINGERS, J., 1995. *Self-Producing Systems: Implications and Applications of Autopoiesis.* New York: Plenum Press.

[27] GLEICK, J., 1987. *Chaos: Making a New Science.* Cardinal, McDonald & Co.

[28] ARTHUR, B. W., 1990. Positive feedbacks in the economy. *Scientific American,* 262 (February), pp. 92-99.

[29] ARTHUR, B. W., 1995. *Increasing Returns and Path Dependence in the Economy.* Michigan.

[30] ARTHUR, B. W., 2002. Is the information revolution over? If history is a guide, it is not. *Business 2.0* (March). Available at: http://demo.ebusiness.uoc.gr/content/downloads/

[31] MITLETON-KELLY, E., 2003. Ten Principles of Complexity & Enabling Infrastructures. *In:* E. MITLETON-KELLY, (ed.) *Complex Systems & Evolutionary Perspectives of Organisations: The Application of Complexity Theory to Organisations.* Elsevier.

[32] HODGSON, G. M., 1993. *Economics and Evolution: Bringing Life Back Into Economics.* Polity Press.

[33] HODGSON, G. M., 2001. Is Social Evolution Lamarckian or Darwinian? *In:* J. LAURENT and NIGHTINGALE, (eds.) *Darwinism and Evolutionary Economics.* Cheltenham: Edward Elgar, pp. 87-118.

[34] MAGUIRE, S. & MCKELVEY, B., (eds.), 1999. Special Issue on Complexity and management: Where are we? *Emergence,* 1(2).

[35] LANE, D. A. & MAXFIELD, R., 1997. Foresight, Complexity and Strategy. *In:* B. W. ARTHUR, S. DURLAUF & D. A. LANE, (eds.) *The Economy As an Evolving Complex System II: Proceedings, Santa Fe, September 1997.* Reading, MA: Addison-Wesley.

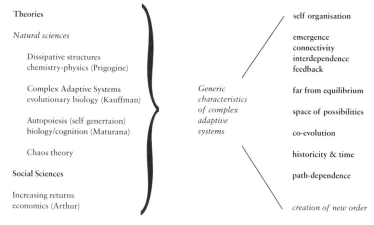

Figure 2, Mitleton-Kelly's five areas of research and ten Principles of Complexity

By comparison with the natural sciences there was relatively little work on developing a theory of complex social systems despite the influx of books on complexity and its application to management in the past decade (an extensive review of such publications is given by Maguire & McKelvey[34]). The notable exceptions are the work of Luhman on autopoiesis, Arthur in economics and the work on strategy by Lane & Maxfield,[35] Parker & Stacey[36] and Stacey.[37,38,39,40] A theory in this context is interpreted as an 'explanatory framework that helps us understand the behaviour of a complex social (human) system'. Such theories may provide a different way of thinking about organisations, and could change strategic thinking and our approach to the creation (design) of new organisational forms – that is, the structure, culture and technology infrastructure of an organisation.

Multilevel systems in design

Our second tutorial-seminar, given by Jeff Johnson, addressed the issue of multilevel systems. It aimed to introduce concepts and tools for the modelling and understanding of networks and hierarchies in artificial and natural systems. The premise of this tutorial was that design problems (including design teams, design products and also the very process of design) are structured into different levels of abstraction with complex interconnections. The tutorial introduced new mathematical structures for multi-level representation of design problems.

[36] PARKER, D. & STACEY, R. D., 1994. *Chaos, Management and Economics: the Implications of Non-Linear Thinking.* Hobart Paper 125, Institute of Economic Affairs.

[37] STACEY, R. D., 1995. The science of complexity: an alternative perspective for strategic change processes. *Strategic Management Journal,* 16(6), pp. 477-495.

[38] STACEY, R. D., 1996. *Complexity and Creativity in Organisations.* Berrett-Koehler.

[39] STACEY, R. D., 2000. *Complexity & Management.* Routledge.

[40] STACEY, R. D., 2001. *Complex Responsive Processes in Organisations.* Routledge.

One of the major outstanding problems in the science of complex systems is to find a way of representing the dynamics of multilevel systems. It is easy to point to parts of systems as lying at difference levels, for example, atoms, molecules, crystals in chemistry; cells, organs, organisms in biology; individuals, households, communities in social science; buildings, neighbourhoods and cities in regional science. Despite this there is no well established theory in any domain that adequately addresses the interactions between the micro-, meso- and macro-levels, and certainly no adequate theory of how the dynamics interact between levels.

The approach begins with the observation that the design process ends with a blueprint for putting together the 'right' parts in the 'right' way to achieve desirable emergence. Fabrication then involves bringing together the set of parts and *assembling* them to form a whole.

For example, artefacts like cars have a multilevel part-whole structure. Components like carburettors themselves are assembled from sub-components, and assembled into intermediate components such as the power unit. Often the assembly relations are expressed in pictorial form such as exploded diagrams, such as that in Figure 3. These diagrams show the *set of parts*, and how *they should be assembled*.

Whereas constructing systems involves the bottom-up assembly of parts, designing systems also involves top-down processes. The design in Figure 3 is fully instantiated, with all the parts explicitly shown, and the way they should be assembled explicitly shown. Generally it is not possible to

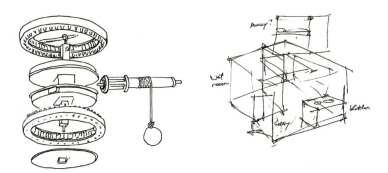

Figures 3 and 4,
left and right

Figure 3, A sketch showing Leonardo's method of showing sets of parts and assembly relations
Figure 4, A sketch as an uninstantiated way of representing intermediate parts and wholes

go from a statement of requirements to the final design, and usually the design process involves a co-evolution between requirements, specification and candidate design solutions until one candidate is declared *the* preferred solution.

[41] JOHNSON, J. H., 2005, Complexity science in collaborative design. *CoDesign*, 1(4), pp. 223- 242.

Johnson[41] presents a theory of design in which designers begin with an ill-specified notion of 'the system' at a highest level of aggregation, and knowledge of available parts and assembly processes at low and intermediate levels of aggregation. Large parts of the design are *uninstantiated*, meaning that they are hazy constructs expressed in words, or a few marks on paper. For example, in the sketch of a small apartment in Figure 4 the designer has written the word 'kitchen' to represent an ambiguous function related to an ambiguous space.

Designers necessarily reason about the objects and systems they are creating using very loose language. It is not possible to start with every part of the design fully instantiated, and large parts of the design are represented by a few sketched lines, a few uttered generalities or a sweep of the arm. Designers make hypotheses that uninstantiated parts will fit together in certain ways and have certain emergent properties, even though nothing is determined in detail.

Building a vocabulary of *intermediate words* to represent and reason about parts and their interactions is essential in the design process. The top-down approach creates and deals with abstractions, to be instantiated at lower levels, until the whole design is grounded in real things and fully instantiated as a blueprint.

In this context, designers of new systems are the first scientists to accumulate knowledge about them, and the methods of design may offer a lot to the science of complex systems.

Embracing complexity in engineering design

The cluster members from the Engineering Design Centre of Cambridge University provided some very concrete examples of how complexity impacts on design.

Designing a really complex engineering product, such as a helicopter or a jet engine, is an exercise in taming complexity. Millions of person-hours are required to design thousands of parts fulfilling a number of often conflicting constraints and requirements to a tight deadline and with a tight budget. The goal of the research in the Cambridge EDC is to

[42] EARL, C. F., ECKERT, C.
M. & CLARKSON, P. J., 2005.
Predictability of Change in
Engineering: a Complexity
View. In: 17th Design Theory
and Methodology Conference
Proceedings of the 2005 ASME
Design Engineering Technical
Conferences & Computers and
Information in Engineering
Conference, Long Beach, 24-28th
September 2005. American
Society of Mechanical Engineers.

[43] ECKERT, C. M., KELLER, R.,
EARL, C. F. & CLARKSON,
P. J., 2006. Supporting change
processes in design: complexity,
prediction and reliability.
Reliability Engineering & Safety
Systems, 91(12), pp. 1521-1534.

[44] WYNN, D., ECKERT, C.
M. & CLARKSON, P. J.,
2006. Applied Signposting:
a Modeling Framework to
Support Design Process
Improvement. In: Proceedings
of ASME 2006, International
Design Engineering Technical
Conferences and Computers
and Information in Engineering
Conference, Chicago, 5-10th
November 2006. American
Society of Mechanical Engineers.

support designers and design managers in their endeavour to design better products faster. An important aspect of this is to help them to understand and visualise the processes that they will need to employ and predict likely problems and bottlenecks. This requires a suitable degree of abstraction. Neither product models with tens of thousand of components nor process models with tens of thousands of individual task entries are suitable to product-designers and managers with the required overview.

The Cambridge group aims to find a medium level of abstraction to model design processes to support design process planning and risk assessment as well as give designers an opportunity to scrutinise and thus improve their processes; and products to help designers to assess the impact of changes to particular components or subsystems on the rest of the system. Both require connectivity models, linking parts of products and process to each other.

This immediately raises some of the fundamental questions of complexity research:

• finding suitable descriptions for hierarchical, almost decomposable systems;
• understanding the potential effects of very detailed changes on the behaviour of the overall system;
• predicting the behaviour of a complex and highly connected system.

The research in the Cambridge EDC has led to the development of two tool kits, which are both currently deployed in industry:

• the CPM (change prediction method) tool,[42,43] which models product connectivity in a dependency matrix, capturing both the type of the link and the likelihood and impact of the change from one component to another. This allows the designer to calculate the risk of change propagation and to display a product as a highly connected network [Figure 5].
• the P3 signposting tool,[44] which enables designers to model processes through hierarchical building blocks and simulate the behaviour of processes to generate risk assessment and find potential process plans in the form of Gantt charts with provide possible sequences of tasks.

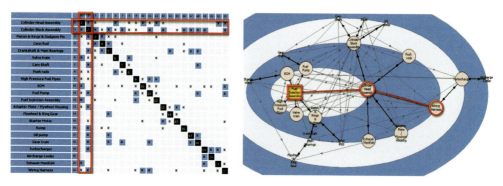

Figures 5a and b,
left and right

Figure 5a, The Change Prediction Method Tools, a dependency matrix
Figure 5b, The Change Prediction Method Tools, a highly connected product network

Complex is beautiful

At an early cluster meeting, George Rzevski shocked everyone by
arguing that design needs to embrace more complexity – contrary to the
conventional wisdom that good design involves reducing complexity – less
parts, less interactions, fewer complications and fewer failures.

To explain his ideas, Rzevski gave a tutorial 'Complex is Beautiful'
arguing that designing adaptive artefacts is important since the
environment in which they operate may become ever more complex and
unpredictable. Thus there is a need to equip artefacts with the necessary
complexity to be able to self-organise and adapt. Every system has a
minimum degree of complexity and variety, and simplifying beyond this
creates a different system.

Rzevski presented some principles and methodological decisions for
designing complexity into artefacts. His approach involves the design
of *multi-agent systems*, where each agent is autonomous and interacts
with others in its 'neighbourhood'. He gave the example of his company,
Magenta Technology, developing a family of multi-agent schedulers for
10 per cent of the world's oil tankers. 'Ocean fleet scheduling involves
planning multi-billion dollar cargoes, where the cost of even the smallest
mistake is very high. A single ocean vessel journey may cost half a million
dollars and bring to the operating company a return of two million
dollars, or more.'[45] Due to weather, political and economic volatility,
such tankers operate in conditions of great uncertainty that make it

[45] RZEVSKI, G., HIMOFF,
J. and SKOBELEV, P., 2006.
*MAGENTA Technology: A
family of multi-agent schedulers.*
Workshop on Software Agents
in Information Systems
and Industrial Applications
(SAISIA). February 2006.
Fraunhofer IITB.

necessary to continually replan their schedules. The inherent complexity of such systems pre-empts conventional methods of analysis. In contrast the agent-based approach allows the many parts of the system to be represented by autonomous agents, each with their own 'local' rules for interactions with other agents, and the behaviour of each agent *emerges* from these interactions.

It is not helpful to simplify such systems by using small numbers of agents. On the contrary, all agents that affect the system must be included. Although increasing the number of agents may make the system more complex, the multi-agent approach can cope with this and be used to design high added-value system. Thus, Rzevski concludes, 'complex is beautiful'.

Embracing complexity in collaborative design and solutions

Sheng Feng Qin writes, 'Collaborative design is a process to result in physical artefacts such as cars, rockets, washing machines and chairs, as well as information artefacts such as software, organisations, business processes, services and plans and schedules. The design is performed by many participants (representing individuals, teams or even entire organisations) with different tools, knowledge, languages, methodologies and processes working on different elements of the design. All participants interact with others independently. How do we measure the complexity in collaborative design?'

His answer to this question involves the development of a network model supporting information flows. First he identifies *system complexity* relating to describing the microstates of the system (for example, numbers of designers, budgets, previous experience, number of layers in decision making, available design tools); *algorithmic complexity* relating technical issues in modelling, computation and communication; *behaviour complexity* as the number of actions in response to the environment; *decision making complexity* which depends on the number of decisions to be made to complete tasks and the amount of information needed to support decision making; and *negotiation complexity* as the amount of negotiations having to be made with collaborators. These factors give complexity measures on the nodes of the network, which can be used to give an overall system complexity which depends on the network connections at any time.

Design out of complexity

Katerina Alexiou and Theodore Zamenopoulos consider design as a
fundamental issue in complexity research. Their particular aim is to
understand and formalise design as a characteristic capacity of complex
systems due to their distributed nature. In the CUPUM workshop they set
up a 'game' in order to introduce their view and discuss its implications.
The venue had been left without a particular arrangement (layout of
chairs) apart from a projection screen which was placed at one end of
the long side of the rectangular room. The chairs were assembled at
the perimeter. The participants were asked to take a chair and place it
wherever they wanted to. Very quickly a horseshoe configuration of chairs
emerged.

This configuration emerged with no central controller or top-down
designer. Each participant acted as an individual agent spontaneously or
according to their individual goals, memories and expectations. For an
external observer, the system constitutes a typical instance of a complex
adaptive system. However, two further observations about the task can be
made:

First, the chair-placing process led to the construction and social
recognition of a functional artefact – a design object. The resulting
configuration had a clear effect: it reduced the complexity of
the environment and, importantly, it was then used to structure
communication between the participants. The constructed configuration
had an (intended) function.

Second, this capacity to construct and recognise a design artefact was by
and large distributed; the configuration was a collective realisation and
to a great extent independent of the design abilities of the individuals
involved. This can lead us to assume that design can be considered as a
capacity derived by the organisation (and complexity) of the system.

These observations are relevant to cities, design teams, political systems,
organisations, ant colonies and social systems in general (human or
animal). A lot of the subsequent discussions at the workshop touched
in many ways on this central theme and the spawning questions around
function, intentionality, social construction, the role of individual action,
or intervention, as well as the role of observation and meaning-giving.

[46] ZAMENOPOULOS, T. and ALEXIOU, K., 2003. Computer-aided Creativity and Learning in Distributed Cooperative Human-machine Networks. *In:* M-L. CHIU, J-Y. TSOU, T. KVAN, M. MOROZUMI and T. JENG, (eds.) *Digital Design: Research and Practice, Proceedings of the 10th International Conference on CAAD Futures 2003, Tianan.* Dordrecht: Kluwer Academic Publishers, pp. 191-201.

[47] ZAMENOPOULOS, T. and ALEXIOU, K., 2004. Design and Anticipation: Towards an Organisational View of Design Systems. CASA Working Paper 76, University College London, Centre for Advanced Spatial Analysis. Available at: http://www.casa.ucl.ac.uk/working_papers/paper72.pdf.

[48] ZAMENOPOULOS, T. and ALEXIOU, K., 2005. The Problem of Design in Complexity Research. *In:* P. BOURGINE, P. KEPES and F. SCHOENAUER, (eds.) *ECCS'05 Conference Proceedings, Paris, 14-18th November 2005.* European Complex Systems Society, pp. 137-138.

[49] DUFFY, A. H. B., DUFFY, S. M. and ANDREASEN, M. M., 1995. Using Design Complexities in Validating the Design Coordination Framework. *In: Proc. Joint Final Conference of ESPRIT Working Groups CIMMOD and CIMDEV: CIM at Work Conference, Kaatsheuvel, 30th August 1995,* pp. 16-20.

[50] CHASE, S. and MURTY, P., 1999. Evaluating CAD complexity. *Int J. of Design Computing,* 2. Available at: http://wwwfaculty.arch.usyd.edu.au/kcdc/ijdc/vol02/dcnet/chaseFrameset.htm

Katerina and Theodore's research, focusing exactly on such questions, follows two parallel routes: experimentation with computational simulations, and mathematical modelling. In the first case, the particular problem of coordination in distributed design settings in studied.[46] In the second, the formal language of category theory is used to model design problems.[47,48]

Complexity and complexity measures in design management

Avril Thomson from the University of Strathclyde organised a workshop on problems related to the management and measurement of complexity in design. The Scottish sub-cluster includes three areas: complexity within design projects, complexity within design teams and design complexity within a Computer Aided Design environment. For them, complexity often implies many parts, many relationships between those parts, with the parts producing combined effects that are not easily predicted and which may be novel.

The group's framework for measuring the complexity of design projects is based on a library of project activities, subtask selection modules, information measuring modules, and information processing modules (consisting of a library of justifying factors) and a complexity index generator based on entropy concepts. Duffy *et al,*[49] suggest the map shown in Figure 6 as the factors and issues of design complexity. The main features are: the artefact being designed, the design activity itself, the actors involved, the decision-making process, the considerations impinging on the design, and the knowledge and sources used and generated. 'Focusing on Computer Aided Design, complexity can be defined in terms of Design Complexity (the appearance of the object to be measured) and CAD Complexity (the actual CAD embodiment of the design, as CAD data, CAD structure and Application Software). It is suggested that being able to identify CAD complexity at the beginning of a project can: aid CAD organisation at the planning stage; give deeper understanding of the CAD model organisation; match project complexity to knowledge and skill levels more accurately; and control modulation of complexity during the course of a project.'[50]

Many approaches to measuring complexity have been suggested in the literature. They include measuring the number of symbols necessary to represent a system, counting the number of parts, counting the number of interactions, and so on. Defining complexity measures relevant to design is seen to be an important research direction for design management.

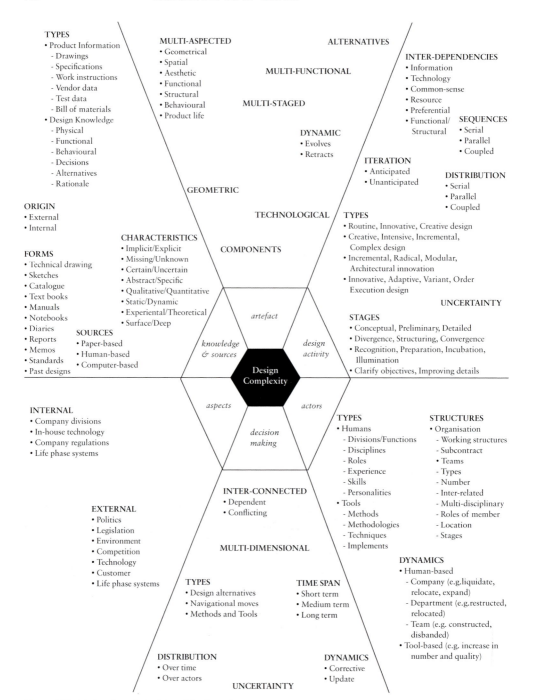

TYPES
• Product Information
  - Drawings
  - Specifications
  - Work instructions
  - Vendor data
  - Test data
  - Bill of materials
• Design Knowledge
  - Physical
  - Functional
  - Behavioural
  - Decisions
  - Alternatives
  - Rationale

MULTI-ASPECTED
• Geometrical
• Spatial
• Aesthetic
• Functional
• Structural
• Behavioural
• Product life

ALTERNATIVES

MULTI-FUNCTIONAL

MULTI-STAGED

DYNAMIC
• Evolves
• Retracts

INTER-DEPENDENCIES
• Information
• Technology
• Common-sense
• Resource
• Preferential
• Functional/
  Structural

SEQUENCES
• Serial
• Parallel
• Coupled

ITERATION
• Anticipated
• Unanticipated

DISTRIBUTION
• Serial
• Parallel
• Coupled

GEOMETRIC

ORIGIN
• External
• Internal

TECHNOLOGICAL

TYPES
• Routine, Innovative, Creative design
• Creative, Intensive, Incremental,
  Complex design
• Incremental, Radical, Modular,
  Architectural innovation
• Innovative, Adaptive, Variant, Order
  Execution design

CHARACTERISTICS
• Implicit/Explicit
• Missing/Unknown
• Certain/Uncertain
• Abstract/Specific
• Qualitative/Quantitative
• Static/Dynamic
• Experiental/Theoretical
• Surface/Deep

COMPONENTS

FORMS
• Technical drawing
• Sketches
• Catalogue
• Text books
• Manuals
• Notebooks
• Diaries
• Reports
• Memos
• Standards
• Past designs

SOURCES
• Paper-based
• Human-based
• Computer-based

UNCERTAINTY

STAGES
• Conceptual, Preliminary, Detailed
• Divergence, Structuring, Convergence
• Recognition, Preparation, Incubation,
  Illumination
• Clarify objectives, Improving details

artefact

knowledge
& sources

design
activity

Design
Complexity

aspects

actors

INTERNAL
• Company divisions
• In-house technology
• Company regulations
• Life phase systems

decision
making

TYPES
• Humans
  - Divisions/Functions
  - Disciplines
  - Roles
  - Experience
  - Skills
  - Personalities
• Tools
  - Methods
  - Methodologies
  - Techniques
  - Implements

STRUCTURES
• Organisation
  - Working structures
  - Subcontract
  - Teams
  - Types
  - Number
  - Inter-related
  - Multi-disciplinary
  - Roles of member
  - Location
  - Stages

INTER-CONNECTED
• Dependent
• Conflicting

EXTERNAL
• Politics
• Legislation
• Environment
• Competition
• Technology
• Customer
• Life phase systems

MULTI-DIMENSIONAL

DYNAMICS
• Human-based
  - Company (e.g.liquidate,
    relocate, expand)
  - Department (e.g.restructed,
    relocated)
  - Team (e.g. constructed,
    disbanded)
• Tool-based (e.g. increase in
  number and quality)

TYPES
• Design alternatives
• Navigational moves
• Methods and Tools

TIME SPAN
• Short term
• Medium term
• Long term

DISTRIBUTION
• Over time
• Over actors

DYNAMICS
• Corrective
• Update

UNCERTAINTY

Figure 6, The Design Complexity Map of Duffy et al.

Art and complexity

Our cluster had a number of sessions discussing complexity and art. We participated in the meeting 'Art, Complexity and Technology' at Villa Gualino, Torino, Italy, in May 2005, in which Michael Petry used the participants to create his self-organising *Superstring* installation [Figure 7], and in a session on Art and Complexity organised by the artist Mateo Willis at the 2005 Liverpool conference on 'Complexity, Science and Society'.

Art can be complex in many ways, as illustrated by Willis' picture shown in Figure 8. In this case the complexity is related to the physics of the way the material interact, as induced and guided by the artist. A number of scientists have analysed works of art, effectively mapping the artwork into symbolic systems such as distributions of numbers. One such example is the work of Richard Taylor[51] who determines fractal indices of paintings, and who has been involved in analysing and authenticating pictures attributed to Jackson Pollock.

[51] TAYLOR, R., MICOLICH, A. P. and JONAS, D., 1999. Fractal analysis of Pollock's drip paintings. *Nature*, 399(3 June).

A question asked by some in the cluster was whether art can contribute anything to the science of complex systems? Can art tells us things that we don't already know? Of course it can: for many years artists have experimented in what today is cognitive science. Our perception and cognitive systems have some remarkable properties exposed by artists, long before scientists appropriated the knowledge they generated. And this process continues to this day, with many art installations and exhibitions giving the viewer new insights into the way they perceive and reconstruct their environment. Thus some members of the cluster believe that art may give us new scientific insights into complex systems.

Figures 7 and 8,
left and right

Figure 7, Michael Petry's The space between Superstring installation II (Calabria)
Figure 8, Oil-on-water image by Mateo Willis

One example of this is Mitleton-Kelly's use of an artist when collecting information on organisations, alongside more usual instruments. After listening to what people say, and by looking at an organisation, the artist produces pictures which express what he has seen and heard. These may give information on the organisation not captured in other ways, but more importantly they encourage people to say things they might not say otherwise. Thus in this case art can be used an as instrument to elicit information about social systems.

In the cluster we performed an experiment to investigate the relationship between complexity and art, resulting in Damian Gascoigne's 'Complex Embrace' exhibition at the Stanley Picker Gallery in Kingston, London. The exhibition resulted from many discussions between the artists, Anne Creigh-Tyte and Jeff Johnson, and addressed the question whether one can communicate concepts from complex systems science through art. Two themes running through the installation are emergence and non-repeating dynamics. Figure 9(a) shows a sequence of drawings, which Gascoigne produced one after another. This contrasted to his usual practice, as an animator, of drawing objects on top of others, frame by frame. In this way he felt new kinds of graphic objects emerged that could change the way he worked.

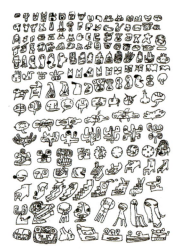 

Figures 9a & b,
left and right

The video installation Complex Embrace by Damian Gascoigne The Stanley Picker Gallery, Kingston, Dec 2005

Figure 9a, Temporal development of objects
Figure 9b, Photograph of the video installation

The installation itself had video projectors trained on three screens. Initially the sequence of images is synchronised, but due to variations in the mechanisms replaying the images they drift out of sync. This raises the question whether the sequence of images ever repeats, or is this an example of a chaos? The conclusion from this exhibition, which was well received as an artistic event, is that that art can be used as a means of exploring and communicating scientific ideas.

Conclusion

The activities of the cluster reinforced the original premise that complexity is pertinent to design products and processes as well as the environment and context of the design activity. However, the meetings also helped cultivate a sense of community and motivated members to continue working on the advancement of a 'complexity in design' research agenda.

A lot of new ideas and interesting research questions also emerged from these meetings. Complexity can offer tools, methodologies and theories for analysing, representing and modelling design processes and products, supporting and augmenting design communications and interactions, as well as supporting innovation and creativity. Also, there is scope for establishing a greater synergy between art, design and science and to investigate new directions for collaborative working. Art and design can offer new insights to the understanding, modelling and managing of complex socio-technical systems (such as organisations, human-computer networks or cities), and make major contributions to the emerging science of complex systems.

Additional Reading

ALEXIOU, K. and ZAMENOPOULOS, T., 2002. Artificial Design and Planning Support: Interactive Plan Generation and Coordination in Distributed Decision-Making. *In*: H. TIMMERMANS & B. DE VRIES, (eds.) *Design and Decision Support Systems in Urban Planning, Proceedings of the 6th International Conference on Design and Decision Support Mechanisms, Eindhoven, 7-10th July 2002.* Ellecom, pp. 1-11.

ASHBY, W. R., 1956. *Self-regulation and Requisite Variety in Systems Thinking.* Penguin.

BRAHA, D. and BAR-YAM, Y., 2004. Topology of large-scale engineering problem-solving networks. *Phys. Rev. E.*, 69, 016113-1-7.

CLARSON, J. & ECKERT, C., 2005. *Design Process Improvement: A Review of Current Practice*. London: Springer Verlag.

GERO, J. S. and KAZAKOV, V., 2004. On measuring the visual complexity of 3D objects. *Journal of Design Sciences and Technology*, 12(1), pp. 35-44.

KLEIN, M., SAYAMA, H., FARATIN, P. and BAR-YAM, Y., 2002. A complex systems perspective on computer-supported collaborative design technology. *Communications of the ACM*, 45(11), pp. 27-31.

LEWIN, R., 1993. *Complexity: Life at the Edge of Chaos*. London: J M Dent Ltd.

MITLETON-KELLY, E., 2000. Complexity: Partial Support for BPR? *In:* P. HENDERSON, (ed.) *Systems Engineering for Business Process Change*. Springer-Verlag.

MITLETON-KELLY, E. & PAPAEFTHIMIOU, M-C., 2000. Co-evolution and an Enabling Infrastructure: A Solution To Legacy? *In:* P. HENDERSON, (ed.) *Systems Engineering for Business Process Change*. Springer-Verlag.

MITLETON-KELLY, E. & PAPAEFTHIMIOU, M-C., 2001. Co-evolution of Diverse Elements Interacting Within a Social Ecosystem. *In:* P. HENDERSON, (ed.) *Systems Engineering for Business Process Change*. Springer-Verlag.

MAIMON, O. and BRAHA, D., 1996. On the complexity of the design synthesis problem. *IEEE Trans. on Systems, Man and Cybernetics*, 26, pp. 142-151.

SUH. N. P., 1999. A theory of complexity, periodicity and the design axioms. *Research in Engineering Design*, 11, pp. 116-131.

Journal special issues, conference proceedings and DVDs published by the cluster

QIN, S. F. & JOHNSON, J., (eds.), 2005. Editorial: Special Issue on exploring complexity in collaborative design and solutions. *International Journal of CoDesign*, 1(4), pp. 219-221.

ALEXIOU, A., JOHNSON, J. & ZAMENOPOULOS, T., (eds.), 2007. *Environment and Planning B: Planning and Design*. Special Issue on Complexity and Design, at press 2006/2007.

ALEXIOU, K. and ZAMENOPOULOS, T., at press. Design as a social process: a complex systems perspective. *Futures*, Special Issue on Design out of Complexity.

QIN, S., JOHNSON, J. and ARIYATUM, B., (eds.) *Proceedings of the International Workshop on Exploring Complexity in Collaborative Design*.

ALEXIOU, K., BESUSSI, E. and ZAMENOPOULOS, T., 2005. *Proceedings of CUPUM-ECiD Joint Workshop on Design out of Complexity, 2nd July 2005, UCL.*

JOHNSON, J., ZAMENOPOULOS, T. and ALEXIOU, K., 2005. *Proceedings of the European Conference on Complex Systems Satellite Workshop on Embracing Complexity in Design, ECCS'05, Paris, 17th November 2005.* ISBN: 978-0-74921-545-3.

JOHNSON, J., ZAMENOPOULOS, T. and ALEXIOU, K., 2006. *Proceedings of the European Complex on Complex Systems Satellite Workshop on Embracing Complexity in Art and Design, ECCS'06, September 2006.* The Open University.

ROBERTSON, A., (ed.), 2005. More is More: Video Proceedings of the *Embracing Complexity in Design Grande Finale*, Royal College of Art, 16-17th Dec 2005 [DVD]. Available from: *Department of Design and Innovation*, The Open University, MK7 6AA.

Emergent Objects: Design and Performance Research Cluster
Alice Bayliss and Joslin McKinney, (University of Leeds)

Overview

[1] LOVE, T., 2002. Constructing a coherent body of theory about designing and designs: some philosophical issues. *Design Studies*, 23, pp. 345-361.

[2] BUCHANAN, R. & MARGOLIN, V., 1995. *Discovering Design: Explorations in Design Studies.* London and Chicago: University of Chicago Press.

The 'Emergent Objects Design and Performance' research cluster provides a platform for the inter-disciplinary exploration of the relationship between design and performance. In the first phase of operation it brought together researchers and practitioners from the fields of robotics, performance, new media, digital arts and urban regeneration to investigate the role that performance knowledge could play in relation to understanding contemporary design, the practice of designing and its outcomes.

The proposal for the cluster identified that although various disciplines within the spectrum of design (from art to engineering) have developed knowledge and theories within their areas, there is a perceived need for a more overarching concept of designing that is cross-disciplinary.[1,2] Terence Love, for example, calls for the creation of a unified body of knowledge and theory to inform developments in research, teaching and practice (both the practice of design and the consumption of design). He examines how design has drawn from other disciplines (the natural, physical and environmental sciences, ergonomics, management and aesthetics, for example) in the search for core design knowledge. He does not explicitly consider performance in relation to this but he is clearly concerned that any unified theory of design be able to address more affective aspects; feelings, experiences, and that which might be considered to be beyond conventional analysis, such as intuition.

Richard Buchanan too, argues for an over-arching concept of design 'as a humanistic enterprise.'[2] His particular suggestion models design on rhetoric:

3 MULLER, M. J., 2002. Participatory Design: The Third Space. *In*: J.A. JACKO and A. SEARS, eds. *HCI, The Human-computer Interaction Handbook: Fundamentals, Evolving Technologies and Emerging Applications.* Mahwah, NJ: Lawrence Erlbaum Associates, Inc., pp. 1051-1068.

4 IACUCCI, G., IACCUCI, C. & KUUTTI, K., 2002. Imagining and Experiencing in Design, the Role of Performances. *In*: O. BERTELSEN, S. BROEDKER and K. KUUTTI, (eds.) *Proceedings of the Second Nordic Conference on Human-computer Interaction, Aarhus, 19-23rd October 2002.* New York: ACM Press, pp. 167-176.

5 CARLSON, M., 2004. *Performance: A Critical Introduction.* 2nd ed. London and New York: Routledge.

6 MCAULEY, G., 2000. *Space in Performance: Making Meaning in the Theatre.* Ann Arbor: University of Michigan Press.

'Design is an art of thought directed to practical action through the persuasiveness of objects and, therefore, design involves the vivid expression of competing ideas about social life.'[2]

We proposed that performance knowledge and practice might provide a lens through which design, especially where it is seen to be an agent of cultural expression and discourse, might be viewed. Furthermore, focusing on instances where performance and design understanding overlap might provide new thinking and techniques to enhance interdisciplinary design processes.

Standard performance devices (such as role-play, games or scenarios) have long been employed directly and indirectly by design researchers, primarily as a means of accessing and understanding human factors within the design process, particularly in participatory design[3] and in the design of interactive systems.[4] Whilst endorsing the value of such techniques, the Emergent Objects cluster aims to mobilise a deeper understanding of the value of performance knowledge as a means of enhancing design practice and thinking about design.

The discipline of Performance Studies concerns itself with the irreducibly 'performed' aspects of human interaction. As Marvin Carlson puts it, performance is:

'. . . a specific event. . . presented by performers and attended by audiences both of whom regard the experience as made up of material to be interpreted, to be reflected upon, to be engaged in – emotionally, mentally, and perhaps even physically. This particular sense of occasion and focus as well as the overarching social envelope combine with the physicality of theatrical performance to make it one of the most powerful and efficacious procedures that human society has developed for the endlessly fascinating process of cultural and personal self-reflection and experimentation.'[5]

Crucial to the performance event is the relationship between performer and spectator and the way physical places of performance become spaces of interaction. Stage space may be 'rendered meaningful by the presence of the performers',[6] but the simultaneous presence of the audience means they are active agents in the creative process. The experience of performance is primarily a spatial one and the essential condition of performance is the 'phenomenological experience of being there, of the space in relation to oneself, of one's self *in* the place. . .'[6]

⁷ SHEPHERD, S. and WALLIS, M., 2004. *Drama/Theatre/Performance*. London and New York: Routledge.

⁸ ROBERTSON, A. and WOUDHUYSEN, J., 2000. 4D Design: Applied Performance in The Experience Economy. *Liminality and Performance Conference, Brunel University, 27-30 April 2000*. Available at: http://people.brunel.ac.uk/bst/documents/alecrobertson.doc

⁹ Practice as Reearch in Performance. Available at: www.bris.ac.uk/parip/

¹⁰ POPAT, S. and PALMER, S., 2005. Creating common ground: dialogues between performance and digital technologies. *International Journal of Performance Arts and Digital Media* 1(1), pp. 47-65.

Performance is both an inclusive term covering genres such as music, dance, theatre and performance art, and 'a paradigm for the investigation of culture at large'.⁷ Other disciplines have deployed models of performance to investigate how societies and individuals interact and express themselves. Performance understanding thus offers a perspective on design and its operation. In particular, key concepts of performance such as embodiment, empathy and expression allow us to explore design as an agent of interaction and experience, as suggested by Robertson and Woudhuysen.⁸

Like design, performance is an emergent and hence dynamic and pliable interdisciplinary field. It has developed out of dialogue with a wide range of disciplines, crossing the arts and humanities as well as the social, medical and physical sciences. It is also characterised by active links between the academy and the creative industries, independent artist-practitioners, theorists and social agencies. Like design, performance has been actively engaged in exploring research methods which serve both the academy and industry. Performance is newly being applied as a practice-based research domain. The AHRC-funded 'Practice as Research in Performance' project⁹ has been a focus for performance academics and practitioners to share and examine methods of research aimed at constructing experience through embodied cognition and disseminating insights through the practice itself. Practice-based methods in performance tend to adopt iterative patterns of development where research can progress within parameters which allow for the creative context. Research questions established at the outset are typically open and it is through practice that research aims are refined and developed¹⁰ and further practice is pursued. Each phase of work involves mediating between tacit

Figures 1 and 2,
left to right

Dancer working with 'Zephyrus' in an embodiment workshop (Performance Robotics Research Group)

11 SCHÖN, D. A., 1983. *The Reflective Practitioner: How Professionals Think in Action.* New York: Basic Books, Inc.

12 TRIMINGHAM, M., 2002. A methodology for practice as research. *Studies in Theatre and Performance*, 22(1), pp. 54-60.

knowledge, reflection-in-action[11] and *post hoc* objective understanding. Successive cycles of work result in better articulated research questions and deeper research insights in what has been described as a 'hermeneutic spiral'.[12]

With iteration as a guiding principle, members of the cluster brought with them knowledge from research projects which had been established previously but which were seen to exemplify important principles for how notions of performance might help design. For example, The Performance Robotics Research Group, a joint initiative between the University of Leeds, an academic partner now at Nottingham University and the Shadow Robot Company, aims to establish a common language between robotics engineers/technologists and performers with a view to designing socially and aesthetically acceptable robots. A series of participatory workshops between robot designers and engineers and performance specialists in dance, puppetry and performance theory were set up to explore how knowledge could be exchanged between disciplines to mutual benefit. In one, a dancer/choreographer engaged in an embodiment exercise, where she aimed to gain a feel for the essence of a prototype air-muscle controlled robot, Zephyrus, and to translate that experience into her own body. She took on the movement qualities and restrictions of the robot and experimented with its considerable physical limitations. Over a series of encounters with the robot, her movement became richer and more complex and it became apparent that her growing familiarity with its restrictions (and its possibilities) was leading her to develop movements that were currently beyond Zephyrus, but which could potentially be realised through changes in the robot's design. Using sketches and notes the robot's designers translated the dancer's movements into ideas for the development of the design. The robot engineers eventually set the dancer the challenge of investigating how Zephyrus might manage to stand and, using a combination of her embodied understanding of the robot and her knowledge as a dancer/choreographer, she improvised using the robot's insistent rhythmic hisses and clicks (from the air-muscle technology) to finally achieve a standing position.[10]

This and other examples of research at the interface between performance and design provided a starting point for identifying principles and practices of performance that would benefit design practice and design thinking.

Accordingly, key aims for the first phase of the cluster's work were:

- to hold seminar and practice-based workshops during the life of the cluster to provide an opportunity for synthesis and reflection with the objective of identifying the current state of knowledge, the identification of gaps in that knowledge and the identification of research and practice opportunities in this field;
- to establish an online database for the collection and dissemination of case studies, data and intelligence on the value of performance knowledge to design;
- to develop a strategy for research and practice beyond the life of the research cluster.

Activities

Emergent Objects: Design and Performance research cluster symposium

At the first event in Hinckley, 21ˢᵗ and 22ⁿᵈ April 2005, cluster participants witnessed each others' research through a series of workshops and performance activities. Ideas on and examples of working practices, collaboration, theoretical frameworks and common key terms were exchanged in order to begin mapping the basis for researching the design/performance relationship. This first event used performance as the predominant mode of interdisciplinary communication and exchange.

A Grand Tour of Hinckley's Cultural Future introduced participants to key places in Hinckley's cultural regeneration plan. Using cameras, audio recorders and GPS systems, we chose a place, moment or object and recorded it or left a 'blue plaque' to remember it. This activity, led by the Strategic Arts Manager and Masterplan Coordinator for the Hinckley and Bosworth Borough Council, invited performative interaction with Hinckley as a means to engage with design possibilities within the context of urban development and community involvement and ownership. A subsequent round table discussion on urban regeneration examined how performance techniques are being used to develop meaningful engagement between planners, architects and the community. This discussion drew on experiences in Hinckley and Bosworth and Newham Sixth Form College's partnerships with professional arts organisations in community based and regeneration focused projects. Notions of responsivity and shared ownership were seen to be an important part of the way performative figurings and interventions could help develop the notion of design as enablement, facilitating creative engagement across the network of various stakeholders.

The Projecting Performance project (a collaboration between University of Leeds and KMA Ltd) enables computer operators to perform alongside dancers through the medium of projected digital sprites. At the symposium, a workshop allowed cluster members to experience how controlling the sprite via a graphic tablet and pen could either respond to or lead the performance of a live dancer so that the technical operator becomes as much of a performer as the dancer herself.

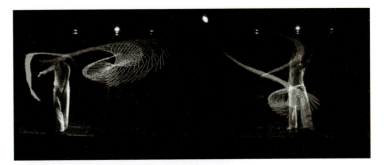

Figures 3 and 4,
top and bottom

Projecting Performance Workshop exploring the interaction of a performer and computer generated sprites (Dr Sita Popat and Scott Palmer, University of Leeds and KMA Ltd, York)

Following this, a further workshop drawing on research into the way design for theatrical performance (settings, costumes, objects and lighting) communicates to an audience, asked participants to record their response to the experience of watching and performing the digital sprites. Through image-making they were able to access and begin to articulate their response to the colour, form, material and movement of the sprite and the dancer. Performance events and designed objects were seen to operate spatially, visually and experientially.

Other sessions focused on the way technology can be playfully and performatively appropriated in art and in gaming. Stuart Nolan (University of Huddersfield) demonstrated how stage magic can be a productive guiding principle in the design of video games and gave an insight into a magician's understanding of various techniques such as manipulating a narrative, focusing and diverting audience attention and (apparently) transforming matter. The notion of play was seen to be a key characteristic of the relationship between performance and design, not only in game design but in much of the other work in which cluster members were engaged.

As a finale, a team of practitioner-researchers from the Central School of Speech and Drama devised a performance based on sound and images collected from the workshops. The aim was to use performance as a means of reflecting on what seemed to be emerging. Using the vocabulary of contemporary performance (juxtaposition, repetition and collage) they devised a piece which highlighted some of the interests and concerns expressed by the cluster. The nature of the human/technology interface was the central theme, but this performance also raised questions about communication, translation and documentation which were then extended through a post-performance discussion. In particular, this contribution provoked questions about the dissemination of research in this area and the extent to which performance provides an effective means of presenting new knowledge.

At this event and at subsequent meetings, the cluster began the process of trying to identify key terms and practices in order to build a shared language that might bridge the disciplines and facilitate further work. This then led to the development of a glossary for the website and the second workshop.

Design-perform-provoke

The 'design-perform-provoke' seminar, hosted by the Digital Research Unit at the Media Centre, Huddersfield on 14ᵗʰ October 2005, invited key practitioners in the fields of performance and design to present on and debate three concepts seen to be of mutual interest to design and performance: play, space and translation-communication.

Play

[13] HUIZINGA, J., 1955. *Homo Ludens*. Boston: Beacon Press.

[14] TURNER, V., 1982. *From Ritual to Theatre: The Human Seriousness Of Play*. New York: Performing Arts Journal Publications.

[15] SUTTON-SMITH, B., 1997. *The Ambiguity of Play*. Cambridge, MA: Harvard University Press.

[16] CSIKZENTMIHALYI, M., 1975. *Beyond Boredom and Anxiety: The Experience of Play in Work and Games*. San Francisco: Jossey-Bass.

[17] BAYLISS, A. J., SHERIDAN, G. and VILLAR, N., 2005. New shapes on the dance floor: influencing ambient sound and vision with computationally augmented poi. *International Journal of Performance Art and Digital Media*, 1(1), pp. 67-82.

One of the cluster's points of convergence is that play sets the foundation for fruitful relationships between design and performance. The world has now entered decisively the 'ludic turn' envisaged by 20th century play theorists such as Johan Huizinga,[13] Victor Turner[14] and Brian Sutton-Smith.[15] We live in an increasingly ludic society where understandings of play, its place within culture and the values we attach to it are becoming ever more significant, not only in the leisure industry and within the creative field but also in the work place and in everyday interactions between groups and individuals.

The amphibolous nature of play and the inherent dualities and ambiguities it presents makes it resistant to any complete and satisfactory definition and remains one of its enduring qualities. In any attempt to pin it down, it is often described in terms of what it is not, rather than what it is (that is, not serious, not work, not productive). As Simon Shepherd and Mick Wallis point out, as a cultural formation playing has had 'a pejorative status' in the Western tradition, being dismissed as regressive, against reason, childish and wasteful.[7] However, psycho-sociological frames have more recently repositioned play as a force for change where participants can imagine alternatives, create possibilities and experience the loss of self through 'a flow state' where the activity has no extrinsic reward beyond its own existence.[16] Play is, in itself, a 'reframing activity', a state of mind which allows us to access the intuitive and to envisage the (im)possible. As such, play permeates performance and design practice at all stages – conceptualisation, development and realisation all depend on what Sutton-Smith calls 'the potentiality of adaptive variability' offered by this affective state of mind.[14]

Many of the projects brought to the cluster have play as a guiding principle in terms of their designed process and performed outcome. Work such as the iPoi Project (a collaboration between University of Leeds and Lancaster University) have developed analytical models for evaluating playful behaviour within what has been termed the 'playful arena' of club culture.[17] In this context the club is seen as a playing space hedged off from the world of the everyday and imbued with certain characteristics such as risk, unpredictability, fluidity and malleability that make it a fruitful, lived context for research in this area.

Figure 5,
Club performance and poi:
exploring creative collaboration
using hi-tech computing in a
playful environment, (Alice
Bayliss, University of Leeds
and Jennifer G. Sheridan,
Lancaster University)

[18] VAN VEEN, T. C., 2002.
It's Not A Rave, Officer, It's
Performance Art: Art as Defense
from the Law and as Offense
to Society in the Break-In Era
of Rave Culture. Conference
Manuscript, University of
Alberta, 31ˢᵗ October 2002.

[19] BACHELARD, G., 1994. *The
Poetics of Space.* Boston: Beacon
Press.

[20] MCKINNEY, J., 2005.
Projection and transaction:
the spatial operation of
scenography. *Performance
Research,* 10(4), pp. 128-137.

How play infuses working methods and the quality of designed and
performed objects, is a central feature of the cluster's inquiry and, as such,
attempts to investigate the paradox of intentionality when using play in a
'telic' rather than an 'auto-telic' manner. How designers and performance
practitioners position themselves in relation to the rhetorics of play
suggested by Sutton-Smith and how play might afford us
'psychotopological cracks'[18] within which to create new work are
questions that will be carried forward.

Space

Processes of both performance and design draw on our knowledge of and
articulation through space. 'Bodystorming' techniques in design have a
parallel in improvisation and devising processes in performance. Mock-
ups and stand-ins provide means of modelling and investigating the way
objects perform in space.

However, designed objects and performance events are, crucially,
mediated through space in such a way that space becomes a medium of
expression and understanding. At the interface of user/object or audience/
performance, our embodied understanding of space is mobilised. Our
memories and imaginations, as Gaston Bachelard[19] describes, augment real
spaces and we experience the designed world at a phenomenological level.

The research performance 'Homesick' (presented at University of Leeds,
2005) is an example of a designed performance environment which aimed
to implicate and involve the imaginations of its audience. Using sound,
light, objects and performers the work investigated the way audiences
responded to and augmented scenographic constructions. Through
drawings, audience members recorded and projected their experiences
of the sensory and the metaphoric impact of the designed space.[20]

Figures 6 and 7, Research performance exploring the notion of 'scenographic exchange' (Joslin McKinney, University of Leeds)

[21] PUGLISI, L. P., 1999. *Hyper Architecture: Spaces in the Electronic Age*. Basel, Boston and Berlin: Birkhäuser.

[22] LEFEBVRE, H., 1991. *The Production of Space*. Malden, Oxford and Carlton: Blackwell.

[23] DELEUZE, G., 1993. *The Fold: Leibniz and the Baroque*. Minneapolis: University of Minnesota Press.

Considering architecture, Luigi Prestinenza Puglisi has called on the notion of projection as a means of exploring and arriving at new ideas. Techniques in art (such as those employed by Marcel Duchamp) use the presentation of objects in space to both articulate the nature of the thing itself and to explore how they can go beyond their obvious and immediate use opening up new meanings and possibilities.[21]

Meanwhile, Henri Lefebvre's account of space asserts that it can be both an actual location, a means of seeing oneself in a particular position and in relation to others and at the same time, a space of mediation, where one seeks to apprehend something else beyond the plane surface, beyond each opaque form.[22] In this way, space is a means of experiencing, articulating and understanding.

Translations/communication

Basic to the work of the cluster is the translation of performance knowledge into terms understandable to people working in design and vice versa. This knowledge exchange, situated at the heart of the creative design process and actively explored, for example, by the Shadow Robot Company, was coined translation/communication.

The rubric of translation/communication also addresses the role of performance in improving access for public and other client constituencies to creative design processes and their being enfolded into the design process as a whole. One of the several models and figures relating to translation/communication was Gilles Deleuze's concept of the 'objectile'. Deleuze[23] distinguishes between object as event and the objectile as occupying an in-between state in the dissolved nothingness of space and time. The performance of embodied knowledge informs this liminality. What happens, for instance, when a community and urban designers share the notion of a building as objectile?

Puglisi's notion of projection again figures in this context, as design content is translated from one system of notation, representation or embodiment to another. The lens of performativity can help in understanding both the nature of specific projections and the re-articulation of the design content.

Finally, performance theorists and practitioners have joined architects and others since the mid-90s in reappropriating Heidegger's specification of *technè* as a mode of revealing.[24] Here, craft, art and the understanding of materials, formal principles, purpose and context are addressed at a phenomenal rather than perspectival level. We asked how might thinking of the performance/design dialogue in terms of *technè* help us in designing for the 21st century?

[24] HEIDEGGER, M., 1977. *Questions Concerning Technology and Other Essays.* New York: Harper and Row.

The performativity of metaplay in emergent technology design

The Emergent Objects cluster's third meeting 'The Performativity of Metaplay in Emergent Technology Design' was held on the 9th and 10th February, 2006 at the University of Huddersfield. This event continued the metalevel mapping process using play as a means of identifying methodological intersections and overlaps in the varying fields of performance, game design, interaction design and digital media. Presentations focused on notions of gaming culture, the role of the digital space as performative context, hapticity in digital software design and place-making through interactive performance using GPS.

The cluster's concern with playfulness as a central tenet was further developed by Stuart Nolan. He proposed that play is used to describe both the working styles of designers and the quality of designed objects themselves. Designers now actively seek to be playful and employ approaches to design practice that attempt to foster playfulness. However, the literatures of play research firmly define play as intrinsically auto-telic. As such it cannot be intentionally harnessed for the production of value artefacts which clearly raises issues for researchers and industry alike. By looking at areas of metacognition, creativity, intuition, organisational play and identity construction we can ask whether these activities are actually forms of metaplay and can then begin to consider the role of performativity in them.

The following questions formed the basis of the final summary and discussion;

- What designed/ performed and/or emotional objects are emerging in your practice?
- How is play contributing to this process?

Common ideas such as the importance of play in the creative design process and the interrelationship of play, intuition and ambiguity began to concretise as the event drew to a close. The following were identified as contexts likely to support cooperative research projects as the cluster began to look to the future and Phase 2 research projects: open-source software, product design, software, visual performance, unfinished objects, hyperphysical instruments, robotics, participatory design and the evaluation of creative work.

Emergent Objects website

[25] Emergent Objects. Available at: www.emergentobjects.co.uk

Running alongside the workshops, the Emergent Objects website[25] exists to facilitate communication between existing cluster members, provide information and invite external users to engage with the cluster's work. It is an information hub on performance and design which contains details of cluster projects and activities, a message-board, external links and a bibliography and glossary.

The website has helped draw in potential new partners and has provided, through the glossary, a focus for examining how key terms and concepts are being used in the various design/performance projects that members represent and in moving towards a shared understanding of the theoretical territory which most usefully supports the cluster.

A broad range of practice-based knowledge and practice as research is represented in the cluster and knowledge exchange through practice has taken place between engineers and artists, the academy and the commercial sector. The work of the cluster so far has been enhanced by our attempts to maintain a hands-on approach to exploring and disseminating new knowledge whilst simultaneously pursuing a metalevel discussion which allows local knowledge to be considered in a broader context.

Insights

Interdisciplinary collaboration through performance

²⁶ RUST, C., 2004. Design enquiry: tacit knowledge and invention in science. *Design Issues,* 20(4), pp. 76-85.

²⁷ WALLIS, M., 2005. Thinking through technè. *Performance Research,* 10(4), pp. 1-8.

What is clear from the first phase of the Emergent Objects project is that performance processes can facilitate a high level of interdisciplinary communication and collaboration in a design context. Key to this facilitation is the mobilisation of tacit knowledge. Chris Rust has argued that in interdisciplinary research teams, designers can be the means by which this mobilisation occurs. Providing images and artefacts can create an environment where tacit knowledge can be accessed and imaginations set to work so that 'the gap between our existing situation and the new world we wish to inhabit' can potentially be bridged.²⁶ In the Emergent Objects examples, the tacit dimension, particularly through kinaesthetic perception and embodied understanding, has been significant. The Performance Robotics Research Group workshop demonstrates that in a design context leaps of the imagination can be facilitated by the translation from one mode to another, in this case the translation of the movement of a prototype robot into the language of movement and choreography. The translation is also a projection or an articulation in space; a representation of the thing itself but also a new perspective and a proposal of how things might be in the future.

The notion of translation/communication can be considered, in a very practical sense, as a central aspect of the role of designers, but it also opens up the consideration of using interdisciplinary translation to consider the role of design at a more philosophical level. Drawing on Heidegger's notion of *technè*, Mick Wallis has argued that the theatrical apparatus can be considered a 'collective subject' which offers a collaborative platform for the embodied understanding of the human-crafted environment.²⁷ In the context of Emergent Objects, this points to a metalevel articulation of performance and design which informs and is in turn informed by concrete examples of the performance/design interface.

Emergent, responsive objects

The particular focus of Emergent Objects case studies has been the way interdisciplinary exchange and collaboration allows fluidity and responsiveness in uncertain design contexts.

As notions of design are shifting from a linear product/user-oriented perspective towards a more open-ended and participatory practice, the concept of emergence has an affinity with approaches that acknowledge the complex and shifting context of design practice. Design thinking and performance knowledge intersect particularly where we consider the potential for an expressive and affective interaction between the designed object and the human subject. From this perspective, the designed object is seen as the Deleuzian 'objectile', where the temporal modulation of the object implies the beginning of a continuous variation of matter and a continuous development of form: the object becomes an event, always in the process of emerging and becoming.

Over-inflated claims for the 'interactive' nature of products have been countered recently by redefinitions of the possible and desirable relationships between users and designed artefacts or systems. Thus, Susan Kozel[28] calls for 'responsive' interactions between system and participant. Applying performance thinking to design processes would seem to allow a moving beyond transparent interfaces and into the realm of invisibility through direct kinaesthetic engagement and playful, embodied experiences. The possibility here would be to avoid submission to technology, whether through fetish or by disconnection, in order to design responsive systems which can support creative, participatory engagement between designed objects and their users and also between designers and users. The spatial, phenomenological experience of design (in particular in theatre design or scenography) suggests an intersection of imaginations between the designer and the 'consumer' such that the experience can be configured as an exchange rather than a transmission.[20] Applying this idea of exchange to other participatory and open-ended contexts of design prompts questions about the extent to which users can be participants and co-creators. Performance knowledge could help us design interfaces that are fluid, malleable and emerging, to promote human engagement with technological objects as an expressive, communicative and creative act.

An iterative methodology

Practice-based methodologies which are increasingly being used in research into performance practice can also be usefully applied to the design process. The practice-based projects which formed the basis of enquiry for phase 1 of Emergent Objects were investigated in the cluster using practice as a vehicle. The principle of being there together and experiencing through the initial practical workshops was an important means of knowledge exchange. This embodied knowledge was then brought into dialogue with the developing theoretical framework and further workshops were then developed in the light of this.

[28] KOZEL, S., 2005. Revealing practices: Heidegger's techne interpreted through performance in responsive systems. *Performance Research*, 10(4), pp. 33-44.

This model of iteration between the local projects and a metalevel discourse was felt to be a productive and dynamic means of investigating the performance/design interface.

The Next Phase

For the next phase of the Emergent Objects project, the core team has identified three sub-projects which address notions of emergence and interface in separate but interpenetrative ways. These projects constitute a braid of knowledge development which is iterated and articulated via a metalevel engagement with overarching questions of design. At the local level the sub-projects will deliver specific knowledge in the areas of robotics, product design and human-computer interaction (HCI). The metalevel activity will enable the mapping and articulation of concepts, methods and language from performance useful to design practice. The synaptic web formed by the sub-projects and the metalevel framework will explore models of interdisciplinary collaborative practice where performance knowledge is used to benefit design; investigate notions of emergence and interface; and interrogate the role of design and designers, role of user or participant, embodiment and tacit understanding.

Principal objectives will be to:

- influence design thinking and practice through exploration and articulation of the emergent and performative nature of the interface between technological object and human and;
- investigate how performance knowledge can help us to understand and facilitate emergence in the context of design processes and how performance practice and theory facilitate interdisciplinary communication, knowledge exchange and collaboration in a design context.

In particular, it will be important to establish how engaging with embodied experience and kinaesthetic understanding can inform the design of invisible interfaces between humans and technological objects, leading to interfaces which are fluid, malleable and emerging and offering expressive and creative engagement between the user and the designed object or system.

Additional Reading

POPAT, S., RAMSAY, G., TRIMINGHAM, M. and WALLIS, M., 2004. Robotics and Performance: A Phenomenological Dialogue. *In*: *Proceedings of Pixelraiders 2 Conference, Sheffield, 6-8th April 2004* [CD-ROM].

Designing Physical Artefacts from Computational Simulations and Building Computational Simulations of Physical Systems
Prof. Mark d'Inverno and Prof. Jane Prophet, (Goldsmiths College, University of London)

Introduction and Overview

Designing in the 21st century often necessitates high-level knowledge or use of computational systems. These are increasingly being used to model and simulate the world in which we live both in physical and social terms. In contemporary art and design practice these computational systems are frequently embedded in products that have a physical presence in the real world. However, even though design is increasingly dominated by computation, it is not clear that the relationship between these previously disparate disciplines is fully understood or exploited.

In this project, therefore, the cluster members were interested in exploring the following questions:

- How do we as users of computational devices perceive and relate to computational systems in the physical world?
- What does it mean to simulate the real world in a computational environment?
- How can computational simulations and visualisations be exploited in the design of physical artefacts?
- How can the emergent properties of distributed systems be harnessed in design? (In very simple terms a system can be thought emergent if its behaviour is surprisingly complicated or sophisticated in some way.)
- How can designers, academics and users best explore and subsequently evaluate new modes of design thinking arising from the work of inter-disciplinary teams from art, design and science?
- What models can be used to enable interdisciplinary teams to work together more productively?

The cluster was specifically interested in two types of computational systems known as Cellular Automata Systems (CAS) and Multi-Agent Systems (MAS) and how they could be used in design. CAS systems typically consists of a fixed grid of cells, where each cell has a state (for example a number between one and five) and rules for working out what the 'next' state should be, based both on its own current state and the state of other neighbouring cells. On every tick of a clock the state of each cell is updated according to these rules. Visualisations of the state of a cell usually assign a colour to each of the individual states. As this system evolves patterns or shapes emerge at the system level. In a multi-agent system, the individual processing units can move within a space, and do not have fixed grid locations. However, how an agent behaves is determined by its internal state and local environment. The cluster was interested in how both these related but distinct approaches could be used in modelling natural systems and in generative design. One example, seen in Figure 1, is of an existing mathematical model of how stem cells might behave.[1] Here a grid can be black (space), white (stem cell) or red (blood cell).

[1] AGUR, Z., DANIEL, Y. and GINOSAR, Y., 2002. The universal properties of stem cells as pinpointed by a simple discrete model. *Jour. Math. Biol.*, 44(1), pp. 79-86.

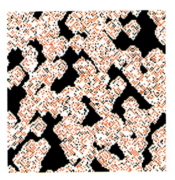

Figure 1, A Visualisation of a Cellular Automata Model of Stem Cell Organisation. Courtesy of Mark d'Inverno and Rob Saunders

The beauty of cellular automata lies in their relative simplicity for novices and the general public to use in order to understand the concepts involved. The rules in the figure above are very simple yet the overall behaviour is extremely sophisticated. It would be fascinating to a wide range of observers to be able to see and/or hear how sets of simple rules can generate non-intuitive system outcomes. In the future a whole variety of visual and audio artefacts could be designed that harness this concept of emergence.

CAS models can be implemented in many guises. The most obvious is on a 2D screen as seen in Figure 1. However, CAS can also be created as 3D lattices (maybe employing LED studded surfaces). The work undertaken by the research cluster was focused on using these principals to produce artefacts that comprise a place (or installation) where virtual and real worlds meet and interact, similar in spirit to Jon McCormack's *Eden*,[2] these would take advantage of sensor information fusion, emerging behaviour, miniaturisation, portability and rudimentary massively parallel actuating capabilities.

[2] MCCORMACK, J., 2001. Eden: An Evolutionary Sonic Ecosystem. *In*: J. KELEMEN & P. SOSÍK, (eds.) *Advances in Artificial Life, 6ᵗʰ European Conference ECAL 2001, Prague, 10-14ᵗʰ September.* Springer, pp. 133-142.

Activities

The main aim of the cluster project was to form a new research community focused on simulation and digital art and design. The disciplines, originally represented by the co-investigators were multi-agent systems (Mark d'Inverno), art and design (Jane Prophet), robotics (Chris Melhuish) and cellular automata (Andy Adamatzky).

Our activities included creating a website and a newslist, forming a new community and holding an introductory symposium (a collective series of ten design challenges proposed by members). Then through a 2 day workshop, and a series of design meetings with cluster members and a professional design house, the design and engineering of a prototype for an art work which exploits multi-agent simulation. Finally we created a glossary to help artists and scientists work together, and finally the launch of this prototype and a review meeting to determine what would be done next.

Through the activities of the cluster a team of experts from a range of different disciplines, who had not worked together before, came together in order to design and specify a series of artefacts based around the use of computational simulation.

Through the initial meetings of the cluster the idea of *design challenges* emerged. Issues under investigation by individuals or teams, which related to the cluster's themes, were posted to the web and considered by a multi-disciplinary team during a 2 day workshop. The following challenges, where theory and practice are strongly connected, were proposed and posted to our website well in advance of the workshop:

- *Net Work*, An artwork of light emitting buoys, Jane Prophet.
- The Visualisation and Simulation of Stem Cells, Mark d'Inverno.
- The Aesthetics of Cellular Automata, Adamatzky.

- Designing Real Time Reactive Environments, Jon McCormack.
- Embodiment of a Live Music Algorithm, Tim Blackwell.
- Evolving a Robot That Can Draw, Paul Brown.
- Visualising Hierarchies of Complex Systems, Neil Theise.
- Interaction with Virtual Musical Agents, Fredrik Olofsson.
- Growing Architecture, Sana Murrani.
- Creating a Meaningful 'Virtual' Experience of Microfossils Foraminifera, Catherine Watling.

Most of these challenges centred on the distinction between the physical and computational world. Through discussion it was decided that design challenge one should be pursued through the cluster. In this, Jane Prophet proposed to build a prototype for an artwork entitled *Net Work*. The proposed artwork consists of a grid of around 2500 autonomous, computational, light-emitting buoys, sensitive to their environment and the activity of other neighbouring buoys. Jane Prophet's rendering of a smaller 8 by 8 grid, as seen at different times in the day, is shown in Figure 2.

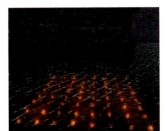 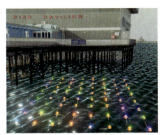 

Figure 2, Jane Prophet's Net Work, Daylight and Dusk Courtesy Jane Prophet

The specific algorithms driving *Net Work* were developed through investigations by members of the cluster to understand and simulate the collective behaviour of stem cells in the adult human body. Mark d'Inverno and Rob Saunders designed visualisations of these simulations of stem cell behaviour [Figure 3]. Of note here is that the simulation and visualisation is a MAS one as opposed to the CAS model shown earlier. Through engagement in this activity it became evident just how important the design of a visualisation might be for biology. Indeed it may be that visualisations of computational systems of stem cells will end up being the 'Trojan Horse' for scientists engaged in conceptual modelling. This is especially true for those biologists whose culture is to work full-time in wet lab (experimental) conditions, and who may not have had an opportunity to consider more of a 'system view'.

Figure 3, A visualisation of Stem Cells in the Adult Human Body, based on
an agent-based extension the Roeder/Loeffler Model of Self-Organisation.[4]
Courtesy of Mark d'Inverno and Rob Saunders

Some Insights

[3] SUSMAN, G. I., 1983. *Action Research: A Sociotechnical Systems Perspective*. G. MORGAN, (ed.) London: Sage Publications, pp. 95-113.

[4] ROEDER, I. and LOEFFLER, M., 2002. A novel dynamic model of hematopoietic stem cell organization based on the concept of within-tissue plasticity. *Exp. Hematol.*, 30, pp. 853-61.

[5] PROPHET, J. and D'INVERNO, M., 2006. Transdisciplinary Research in CELL. *In:* P. FISHWICK, (ed.) *Aesthetic Computing*. Cambridge, MA: MIT Press.

Throughout this project there was discussion about how to develop a
hybrid methodology using existing methods from both the arts and
sciences that includes process-based research methods, where goals are
not specifically predetermined.[3] Specifically, how are interdisciplinary
teams built so that they are sustainable? How can we as individuals learn
to develop empathy for each other's disciplines and culture? How can we
move towards a common language and a common understanding and a
common conceptual framework? How can we ever get to the point where
there is a shared understanding of disparate theoretical concepts, cultures,
methods and languages?

As the cluster activities progressed they grew momentum and became
self-sustaining, as people developed a clear sense of ownership. Whilst the
cluster was successful it could very well not have been. We clearly need
to build models and methods for engaging in successful interdisciplinary
research in general.[5] Our experience suggests that effort is needed to set up
certain initial conditions and then provide the right growth environment
for an emergent collaborative process to take place.

The authors experience in another current project called CELL,[5] was
of researchers and artists collectively converging on an agreed subject;
then engaging, collectively and individually, in sustained enquiry (using
methods suitable to each researchers' discipline); and lastly diverging

to produce a range of outputs such as academic publications, products, patents, simulations, artworks and so on. Central to this notion of the importance of divergence is that the collaborative research produces at least one output that can stand up to peer review in each of the disciplines involved in the collaboration.

One of the successes of the cluster from our perspective was how members gave their time freely in order to produce designs at both the computational and physical levels. For example, Figures 4a, 4b and 5 are snapshots of some of the to drive the physical prototype by Jon Bird. First we started with an 8 by 8 grid to ensure how an intermediate version of *Net Work* could operate and then this was reduced to a 3 by 3 version for the layout of the *Net Work* prototype that was launched at Wapping Station.

In order to realise the practical ideas generated by the cluster it was necessary to hire an experienced technician, Paul Hammond. One of his first contributions was to build the basic rig to support the light-emitting buoys and to immediately post photographs to the cluster's newslist shown in Figure 6.

Our belief is that, 'collaborative, interdisciplinary research challenges existing modes of thinking and radical new ideas and products can freely emerge.' In our project our investigation was centred on the development of a series of self-powering artefacts that run without the need for any direct human intervention. These artefacts will function continuously and autonomously, responding to the physical environment, which includes human users 'participating' with the system. The prototype for *Net Work*, which had these characteristics, was launched towards the end of the cluster project at Wapping power station as shown in Figure 7.

Even though there was some notion of the issues we (as co-investigators) wanted to explore in the cluster, we had no strict plans or schedules that told us how we should go about our activity. Despite setting up a newsgroup and website, and putting out various calls to join our community, the traffic on the website was initially very low. However, we did organise several meetings of a very heterogeneous set of people (artists, designers, computer scientists and engineers) and decided that in order to explore the issues it would be best to actually build a physical artefact that had computational and generative elements. We believe the theory practice divide worked well and focused activity and debate.

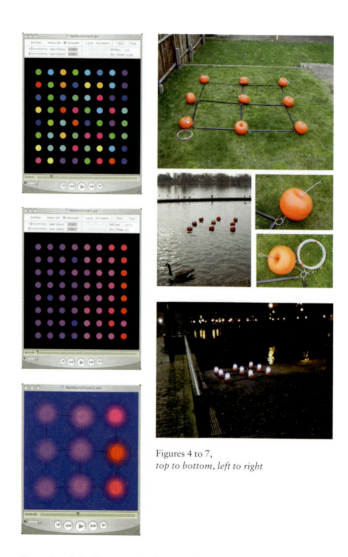

Figures 4 to 7,
top to bottom, left to right

Figure 4a and 4b, Computer Simulations and Visualisation of an 8 by 8 Version of Net Work based on Homeostasis. Courtesy of John Bird.
Figure 5, Visualisation of the 3 by 3 Simulation. Courtesy of Jon Bird.
Figure 6, First construction of the Network Buoys. Photos courtesy of Paul Hammond. Layout by Jane Prophet
Figure 7, The Final Physical Artefact: A 3 by 3 prototype of *Net Work*. Photo courtesy of Trevor Graham

At the end of the workshop where the ten design challenges were presented, a vote was taken to make a prototype of *Net Work*, Jane Prophet's proposed interactive installation. Because members of our group felt a sense of ownership, not only of the goal to collectively build a physical artefact, but also of the design process, the traffic on the newsgroup increased significantly. Many members of the cluster gave their time freely to argue and consider the best way to build the *Net Work* prototype. The joint sense of ownership of its process was the key ingredient in establishing and maintaining the momentum of the cluster's activities.

Whilst there may be effort to build models of successful interdisciplinarity, there is no doubt that it all hinges on the people that are involved. Of course one can always aim to set up the right initial conditions and environment, but it is including those people that are empathetic, enjoy learning from others, who are happy to have their ideas challenged and enjoy sharing their knowledge with others from different backgrounds, that brings success. Moreover, they need to be patient as results can often seem a long way off.

In another strand of the cluster themes outlined in the first section, insights were also gained into how computational simulation relates to the physical world in the form of visualisations of biological systems, these need to be sufficiently close to a biologists view of the world, but not so much that they are 'photorealistic'. This level of simulation allows the 'liveness' of a system to be investigated. This is often not possible in the wet-lab, as experiments are typically with dead tissue. Moreover, it is not possible to observe the interaction of stem cells within the adult human and so simulation provides scientists with a useful tool. Moreover, as computational agents are programmed at a 'behavioural' level, this is often intuitive to biologists and this allows negotiation to take place between modelers, visualisation designers and biologists and can, in itself, aid interdisciplinarity.

One of the other insights gained from this work is how humble it is necessary to be when simulating the real world. This is especially true in biology where many of the mechanisms that allow for sophisticated and robust self-organisation are simply not understood at all. Whilst it is clear that the simple models that are run on a computer will give us an understanding of (say) basic cell-cell interactions, it is not the case that there is any claim to any 'reality'. Computational models are incredibly simple in comparison to the reality of the biology, but nevertheless, there are reasons – both for scientific understanding and for producing new ideas in design – why they are worth exploring.

The advantage of having a large number of collaborators, with a broad range of artistic, computing and engineering skills was evidenced by the large number of potential solutions offered to software and engineering problems, the subsequent high-level debate, and the speed at which the research cluster solved many of the challenges associated with building *Net Work*. The distributed collaboration prompted the lead artist Jane Prophet to further develop and clarify her core idea and the project evolved as collaborators introduced and argued for new elements. Having built a prototype, there are still several outstanding technical challenges to be solved and the design will evolve further through collaboration.

Setting up the website was time consuming, but a necessary signpost and a useful focus for both national and international researchers, especially given the visual nature of many of the themes. More recently it became key in presenting material relevant to the design challenges posted by the individual members. The newslist was useful to communicate details of events and challenges though our expectation of a high level of use was not met initially. It was only once members felt a stronger sense of ownership and community that volume was significant. The co-investigators spent a lot of time 'priming' the list and the website, especially for our events which all proved very successful. Transcription necessitated good quality recording of the day requiring additional organisation but this was worthwhile. For the chosen design challenge, a prototype has been designed and is now being produced. Working with a design company to design and engineer the chosen design has proved difficult and time consuming at first. However, this has now become more efficient and effective through learning each others working practices.

There is now a lasting community though and the website will be up to date. We have put in further grants to continue this work and there is now a continuing collaboration between academic and the professional design house involving the use of multi-agent systems in design. Our cluster has bought academics and professional designers, from a range of different areas of expertise, into contact to form important new communities for future sustained collaboration.

Acknowledgements

We especially want to thank our co-investigators Andy Adamatzky and
Chris Melhuish. We would like to thank all members of the IRC that
were involved in the development of the *Net Work* Prototype especially
Michael Bacon, Adrian Bowyer, Trevor Graham, Paul Hammond, Jon
McCormack, Luke Nicholson, Fredrik Olofsson, Ben Pirt, Rob Saunders,
Neil Theise and all members of the interdisciplinary research cluster. We
would also like to thank the EPSRC and AHRC, the Design House More
Associates, along with Tom Inns (who provided some very useful feedback
for this chapter) and Vicky Hale.

Additional Reading

D'INVERNO, M., THEISE, N. D.and PROPHET, J., 2006. Mathematical
modelling of stem cells: a complexity primer for the stem cell biologist. *In*:
C. POTTEN, J. WATSON, R. CLARKE and A. RENEHAN, (eds.) *Tissue
Stem Cells: Biology and Applications*. Marcel Dekker.

D'INVERNO, M. and PROPHET, J., 2006. Biology, Computer Science
and Bioinformatics: Multidisciplinary Models, Metaphors and Tools.
In: E. MERELLI, P. GONZALES and A. OMICINI, (eds.) *LNCS
Transactions on Computational System Biology*. Springer, Chapter 1.

D'INVERNO, M. and PROPHET, J., 2004. Creative conflict in
interdisciplinary collaboration: interpretation, scale and emergence. *In*:
E. EDMONDS and R. GIBSON, (eds.) *Interaction: Systems, Theory and
Practice*. ACM Press, pp. 251 - 270.

D'INVERNO, M. and LUCK, M., 2004. *Understanding Agent Systems*.
2nd edition. Springer.

D'INVERNO, M. and SAUNDERS, R., 2005. Agent-based modelling of
stem cell organisation. *In*: S. A. BRUECKNER ET AL., (eds.) *Engineering
Self-Organising Systems: Methodologies and Applications*. Springer.

PROPHET, J., 2004. Re-addressing practice based research: funding and recognition. *Digital Creativity*, 15(1).

PROPHET, J., 2002. Performativity, Repetition and Acting Out. In: S. KIVLAND, (ed.) *Transmission: Speaking and Listening*. Sheffield Hallam University and Site Gallery.

PROPHET, J., 2001. TechnoSphere: 'real' time 'artificial' life. *Leonardo: The Journal of the International Society for The Arts, Sciences and Technology*, 34(4).

Understanding and Supporting Group Creativity Within Design

Dr Hilary Johnson, Prof. Peter Johnson, and Tim Coughlan,
(University of Bath)

Introduction

[1] 2005. *International Journal of Human Computer Studies*, 63 (4-5), pp. 363-536.

[2] SHNEIDERMAN, B. et al., 2006. Creativity support tools: report from a U.S. National science foundation sponsored workshop. *International Journal of Human Computer Studies*, 20(2), pp. 61-77.

[3] STERNBERG, R. J., LUBART, T., KAYFMAN, J. C. & PRETZ, J. E., 2005. Creativity. In: K. J. HOLYOAK & R. G. MORRISON, (eds.) *Cambridge Handbook of Thinking and Reasoning*. Cambridge University Press, pp. 351-369.

[4] CSIKSZENTIMIHALYI, M., 1996. *Creativity: Flow and the Psychology of Discovery and Invention*. New York: Harper Collins.

[5] BODEN, M. A., 1990. *The Creative Mind: Myths and Mechanisms*. London: Weidenfeld and Nicolson.

[6] WALLAS, G., 1926. *The Art of Thought*. New York: Harcourt Brace.

What do we mean by creativity in design? What distinguishes a creative design process or artefact from one that is not? How can we develop theories, methods and tools that support creativity? These fundamental questions need addressing through research into design creativity. However, this is a significant challenge for individual disciplines, or single industries. Only by adopting multidisciplinary and interdisciplinary perspectives can we rise to this challenge.

The development of a multidisciplinary research cluster to investigate creativity in design is necessary and timely given the complex issues, and growing awareness of the importance of creativity in our daily lives. Governments and industries are conscious of the need for creativity and innovation in design. A corresponding academic interest exists, evidenced by the Creativity and Cognition Conferences, special issues of journals on Creativity[1] and a US Government sponsored workshop on Creativity Support Tools.[2]

This chapter describes the issues generated by members of a multidisciplinary 'Creativity in Design', research cluster. Section 2 describes previous creativity research in Human Computer Interaction (HCI). Reviewing this work previously for an HCI journal paper was a motivating factor in initiating the cluster proposal. Section 3 outlines the cluster motivations, aims and objectives. Section 4 describes the activities undertaken to achieve the aims and objectives. Finally, section 5 reports the findings and insights of the cluster activities undertaken within the 1 year time frame.

Previous Creativity Research

[7] NUNAMAKER, J., APPLEGATE, L. and KONSYNKI, B., 1987. Facilitating group creativity: experience with a group decision support system. *J. Management Information System*, 3, 4.

[8] CANDY, L. and EDMONDS, E., 1997. Supporting the creative user: a criteria-based approach to interaction design. *Design Studies*, 18, pp. 185-194.

[9] JOHNSON, S., 1997. *Interface Culture: How New Technology Transforms the Way we Create and Communicate*. New York: Harper Collins.

[10] EDMONDS, E., 2000. Artists augmented by agents. In: H. LIEBERMAN, (ed.) *International Conference on Intelligent User Interfaces*. ACM Press.

[11] GREENE, S. L., 2002. Characteristics of applications that support creativity. *Communications of the ACM*, 45(10), pp. 100-104.

[12] PEPPERELL, R., 2002. Computer Aided Creativity: Practical Experience and Theoretical Concerns. In: *Proceedings of the 4th Conference on Creativity & Cognition, Loughborough*. New York: ACM Press, pp. 50-56.

[13] JOHNSON, H. & CARRUTHERS, L., 2006. Supporting creative and reflective processes. *International Journal of Human Computer Studies*, 64(10), pp. 998-1030.

[14] LUBART, T., 2005. How can computers be partners in the creative process: Classification and commentary on the special issue. *International Journal of Human Computer Studies*, 63, pp. 365-369.

[15] ELAM, J. and MEAD, M., 1990. Can software influence creativity? *Inf. Syst. Res*, 1(March), pp. 1-22.

Documenting previous research into a topic as pervasive and ubiquitous as creativity in design is not easy since 'creativity' is not 'owned' by a single academic discipline. Psychologists study human behaviour in creating problem solutions, artists consider the 'practice' and 'craft skills' involved in creating works of art, and researchers in HCI consider technologically supporting creative processes. Consequently, our review focuses principally on our backgrounds in HCI. The review underpins the need to establish a multidisciplinary Creativity in Design cluster, and the motivation to understand issues involved in defining and supporting creativity.

There are commonalities and differences in how creativity is characterised within diverse disciplines. Within psychology, there have been many approaches to understanding creativity and creative design processes. An excellent review is provided by Sternberg et al,[3] who distinguish between mystical, pragmatic, psychodynamic, psychometric, cognitive, social-personality and social-cognitive, evolutionary and confluence approaches.

One widely referenced psychological approach providing inspiration for HCI (c.f. Shneiderman[2]) is that of Csikszentmihalyi.[4] Other work widely acknowledged (for example, Boden[5]) describes creativity as involving exploration and transformation of conceptual spaces. In 1926, Wallas[6] described four creative stages: preparation, incubation, insight and verification, which are still widely cited today. More recently, Csikszentmihalyi[4] outlined five stages which overlap and recur – preparation, incubation, insight, evaluation and elaboration.

How creative design processes are described is important within HCI since the overriding goal is to support users in designing creative artefacts *with ease, enjoyment and engagement*. Consequently, several researchers have considered the role(s) computers could play in creative design.[1,2,7,8,9,10,11,12] Johnson and Carruthers[13] review the work of Lubart[14] who outlined four roles computers could adopt – nanny, pen-pal, coach and colleague.

A number of researchers have proposed principles, guidelines and/or requirements for designing support tools for creativity.[11,15,16,17] Similarly, Shneiderman et al[2] report the outcomes of a workshop on Creativity Support tools which developed 12 principles for designing creativity support tools.

[16] ERICKSON, T. D., 1990. Interface and the Evolution of Pidgins: Creative Design for the Analytically Inclined. *In:* B. LAUREL, (ed.) *The Art of Human-Computer Interface Design.* New York: Addison-Wesley.

[17] BONNARDEL, N., 1999. Creativity in Design Activities: The Role of Analogies in a Constrained Cognitive Environment. *In: Proceedings of the 3rd Creativity and Cognition Conference, Loughborough, 11-13th October 1999.* New York: ACM Press, pp. 158-165.

[18] SHIPMAN III, F. M. & MCCALL, M., 1994. Supporting Knowledge-base Evolution with Incremental Formalisation. *In:* B. ADELSON, S.T. DUMAIS, J. S. OLSEN, (eds.) *Conference on Human Factors in Computing Systems, CHI 1994, Boston, 24-28th April 1999.* ACM Press, pp. 285-291.

[19] SHIPMAN III, F. M., MARSHALL, C. C. & MORAN, T. P., 1995. Finding and Using Implicit Structure in Human-organised Spatial Layouts of Information. *In: Proceedings of the Conference on Human Factors in Computing Systems, CHI 95, Denver, 7-11th May 1995.* ACM Press, pp. 1-14.

[20] LIN, J., NEWMAN, N. W., HONG, J. I. & LANDAY, J. A., 2000. DENIM: Finding a tighter fit between tools and practice for web site design. *CHI Letters,* 2(1), pp. 510-517.

[21] VAN DE KANT, M., WILSON, S., BEKKER, M., JOHNSON, H. & JOHNSON, P., 1998. Patchwork: A Software Tool for Early Design. *In: Extended Abstracts of the Conference on Human Factors in Computing Systems, CHI 98, Denver, 18-23rd April 1998.* AMC Press, pp. 174-5.

Finally, within HCI, there are general-purpose applications that could facilitate creativity, and also creativity support tools. Shipman and McCall[18] developed an application to formalise informal information expressed by users. This may facilitate creativity by enabling and supporting idea refinement, and the formalisation of informal ideas. Another tool[19] facilitates users in noticing and expressing regular information structures such that new associations are perceived, leading to inspiration and innovative combinations of elements.

The problem of the creator's need for imprecision, and the computer's need for precision led to the development of DENIM,[20] which allows designers to defer making premature decisions about precision. DENIM has an emphasis on free-form sketching. (See also 'Patchwork' reported in van de Kant et al[21] and the sketching tool developed by Sedivy and Johnson.[22,23]) The electronic cocktail napkin,[24,25,26] also supports free hand drawing, and early creative activities such as 'tinkering' and 'doodling' can be undertaken. The tool also provides intelligent design critiquing, simulation and information retrieval.

Another tool, Designer's Outpost[27] combines the 'affordance' of paper and large physical workspaces with the advantages of electronic media. The tool manipulates and organises information, and supports brain storming at different refinement levels.

Nakakoji et al.[28] claim to have developed a tool allowing users to find the 'right' balance between creativity and usefulness. eMMa (Environment for MultiMedia Authoring), is a knowledge-based computational system that volunteers information relevant to current design situations, thereby potentially augmenting the user's creativity. Low-level suggestions aid users in becoming aware of new features for their design tasks, leading to innovative artefacts. The system criticises a user's partial designs for improvement and the knowledge-base is shared and evolved by a community of users. Other tools support the creative processes of hypothesis-testing. Terry et al.'s[29] Parallel Paths facilitates the generating, manipulating and comparing of alternative solutions inherent in evaluative or verification creative stages. An earlier tool, Sideviews,[30] supports near-term experimentation and evaluation by displaying previews of future states or the results of 'experiments'.

Most tools function to support individual users, however, Fischer et al.[31] have developed tools for social creativity. Additionally, Coughlan and Johnson[32] developed the 'Sonic-sketch-pad', to allow musicians working individually or in groups to capture composition ideas [Figure 1].

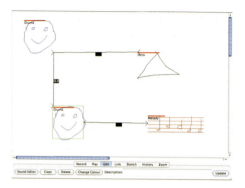

Figure 1, Sonic-sketch-pad, developed by cluster member and investigator

[22] SEDIVY, J. and JOHNSON, H., 1999. Supporting Creative Work Tasks: The Potential of Multimodal Tools to Support Sketching. *In: Proceedings of the 3rd Creativity and Cognition Conference, Loughborough, 11-13th October 1999.* New York: ACM Press, pp. 42-49.

[23] SEDIVY, J. and JOHNSON, H., 2000. Multimodal tool support for creative tasks in the visual arts. *Knowledge Based Systems on Creativity and Cognition,* 13(7-8), pp. 441-451.

[24] GROSS, M. D. & YI-LUEN DO, E., 1996. Ambiguous Intentions: A Paper-like Interface for Creative Design. *In: Proceedings of the 9th Annualk Symposium for User Interface Software and Technology, UIST 96, Seattle, 6-8th November 1996.* ACM Press, pp. 183-192.

[25] GROSS, M. D. & YI-LUEN DO, E., 1996. Demonstrating the Electronic Cocktail Napkin; a Paper-like Interface for Early Design. *In: Conference on Human Factors in Computing Systems, CHI Demonstrations, Vancouver, April 13-18th, 1996.* ACM Press, pp. 5-6.

[26] GROSS, M. D., 1992. Graphical Constraints in CoDraw. *In: Proceedings of the IEEE Workshop on Visual Languages, Seattle, 15-18th September 1992.* IEEE Computer Society, pp. 81-87.

The development of technological support for enhancing individual and group creativity requires a substantial investment from researchers and developers. Supporting users necessitates understanding creative processes across disciplines such that the designed support can be principled and well informed.

Cluster Motivation, Aims and Objectives

Motivation

The motivation underpinning the establishment of the cluster is that creativity is a research area lacking in cross-fertilisation of knowledge, methods and tools but ripe for interdisciplinary exploitation and exchange of ideas. Moreover, there is an increase in dispersed group working to exploit devolved skill sets, and yet generally available tool support is poor, hindering rather than enhancing creativity. Consequently there is a need for new, usable tools to aid creative design – an activity that sells products and services, at which the UK, whilst it cannot compete on labour costs, can compete and excel. The cluster aimed to address this acknowledged problem of lack of knowledge and cross-fertilisation.

The rationale for the cluster activities relates to identifying the fundamental research questions, priorities and agendas raised by the cluster participants in considering how to address the need for a better understanding of creativity and creative practices in design, across disciplines. Currently, there is too little cross-disciplinary fertilisation of design ideas and understanding. Developing a leading and competitive edge to design means dynamic, evolving and timely use of new and current design practices being applied to new design problems. New ways of envisioning design problems and increasing computational power and storage capacity mean that computing technology can be the enabling vehicle for developing creative design solutions. Given the extent of

[27] KLEMMER, S. R.,
NEWMAN, M. W., FARRELL,
R., BILEZIKJIAN, L. &
LANDAY, J. M., 2001. The
Designers' Outpost: A Tangible
Interface for Collaborative Web
Site Design. *In: Proceedings
of the 14th Annual ACM
Symposium on User Interface
Software and Technology,
Orlando, 11-14th November
2001.* ACM Press, pp. 1-10.

[28] NAKAKOJI, K., SUZUKI, K.,
OHKURA, N. and AOKI, A.,
1997. A Framework to Support
Creativity in Multimedia
Information Design. *In:* S.
HOWARD, J. HAMMOND
and G. LIINDEGAARD,
(eds.) *Proceedings of the 6th
IFIP Conference on Human
Computer Interaction,
INTERACT '97, Sydney, 14-18th
July 1997.* Laxenburg, Australia:
IFIP, pp. 212-219.

[29] TERRY, M., MYNATT, E. D.,
NAKAKOJI, K. YAMAMOTO,
Y., 2004. Variation in Element
and Action: Supporting
Simultaneous Development
of Alternative Solutions. *In:
Proceedings of the Conference
for Human-Computer
Interaction, CHI 2004, Vienna,
24-29th April 2004.* ACM Press,
pp. 711-718.

[30] TERRY, M. & MYNATT, E.
D., 2002. Recognising Creative
Needs in User Interface Design.
In: E. A. EDMONDS, L.
CANDY, T. KAVANAGH and T.
T. HEWITT, (eds.) *Proceedings
of the Creativity and Cognition
Conference, Loughborough,
13-16th October 2002.* ACM
Press, pp. 38-44.

[31] FISCHER, G., GIACCARDI,
E., EDEN, H., SUGIMOTO,
M. & YE, Y., 2005. Beyond
binary choices: integrating
individual and social creativity.
*International Journal of Human
Computer Studies,* 63,
pp. 482-512.

localised and dispersed group working, developing technologies which enhance, enable and create new potential for group creativity is crucial to the success of future design projects. Therefore, it is important that a principled and informed approach is taken to the design of interactive software to support creative design. Good user interaction design is the result of a participatory process by which users, clients and designers all play a role in the developmental process. Computer use in design for the 21st century will act as the lynchpin for the majority of creative design activities. The design of the technology must save user (physical and cognitive) effort and also create new ways of working and envisioning, allow greater dissemination of information and designed artefacts, and enable increased social inclusion of stakeholders.

Aims and objectives

The cluster was established with three broad aims. First, to establish a multidisciplinary cluster community with the goal of identifying contributions to theoretical, methodological and applied problems in creative design and subsequently cross-fertilising these contributions.

Secondly, to identify and prioritise research issues to be addressed in existing and emerging challenges of understanding and supporting group creativity in design in the 21st century.

Finally, to stimulate new interdisciplinary research to generate a better understanding of group creativity and understand how group creative design processes could be supported by 21st century computing technology.

Developing improved technological support for innovative and creative design by teams of designers is a formidable goal. To achieve these aims there were two related sets of objectives, to establish the cluster community and to outline the research objectives the community would address.

The objectives to establish the community were:

- to bring together researchers from different disciplines to identify contributions to theoretical, methodological and applied problems in creative design;
- to establish new research collaborations to address the current and emerging challenges of understanding and supporting group creativity;
- to provide a research and information exchange for research in creative design.

[32] COUGHLAN, T. &
JOHNSON, P., 2006. Ideation
in Creative Tasks: Ideation,
Representation and Evaluation
in Composition. *In: Proceedings
of the Conference on Human
Factors in Computing Systems,
CHI2006, Montreal, April
22-27th 2006*. ACM Press.

The research objectives for this community were:

- to consider the nature of group creativity and identify how the represented design disciplines could contribute to a fuller understanding of creativity;
- to establish principles, models, methods and tools used within the different contributing disciplines to support teams engaged in innovative and creative design, and identify opportunities and challenges;
- to identify how the different disciplines understand, teach, model and assess creative design and the resulting solutions;
- to address the research problems of assessing current technological support for group creativity in design, and developing future design-support tools;
- to formulate a prioritised agenda of research issues on group creativity in design supported by 21st century technology.

A series of activities were undertaken to achieve these aims and objectives.

Cluster Members and Activities

The backgrounds and disciplines of cluster members who took part in the activities included: cognitive science, computer science, philosophy, mechanical engineering, mathematical sciences, industrial design and manufacture, psychology, statistics, electrical engineering, industrial sociology, ergonomics, architecture, change management; film makers, performance and installation artists, fashion designers, textile designer/researcher in digital printing techniques, sculptors, digital artists/painters, actors, dancers, arts facilitator, directors of galleries, arts tutors and glass makers.

Activities

In order to satisfy the cluster objectives, four themed workshops were held throughout the year. The workshops consisted of presentations from international experts; invitees from learned societies; presentations from members of the creativity cluster, and other clusters; two artists' forums; a poster session; extensive discussions; and also individual and group activities related to each workshop. The different themes of each workshop, the workshop objectives and activities undertaken are outlined below.

Workshop 1: Understanding creativity and creative processes in design

The objectives of the first workshop were to develop, i) a better understanding of creativity in design research issues within the different disciplines, ii) an awareness and reflection of disciplinary, interdisciplinary and participant perspectives, and iii) a mechanism for exploitation and/or cross-fertilisation of ideas.

To achieve these objectives, there were presentations from attendees, a poster session, group activities, report back and discussion sessions.

Figures 2 and 3,
left and right

Figure 2, 'Draig', a digitally printed silk artwork produced and discussed during the artists' forum by cluster member Cathy Treadaway, exhibited in 'Digital Perceptions', Kansas City USA and Collins Gallery, Glasgow

Figure 3, 'Yu', a digitally printed silk artwork produced and discussed during workshop 3 by cluster member Cathy Treadaway, exhibited in 'Digital Perceptions', Kansas City USA and Collins Gallery, Glasgow

Workshop 2: Studying creativity across disciplines

The objectives of the second workshop were to i) establish the approaches and tools used within different disciplines to support people engaged in innovative and creative design, ii) identify how the different disciplines teach and assess creative design solutions, and iii) generate a list of emerging research themes.

To achieve these objectives, there were presentations from an industrial design engineer, an architect and a fashion designer to investigate how diverse disciplines approach and generate creative design solutions. Additional activities included individual and group activities related to best practices representative of the different disciplines, identification of possible impacts and benefits to society of creativity research, and matrix activities. The matrix activities provided a platform for effective discussion of the following dimensions of creativity across disciplines:

- methods and tools used to support creativity;
- teaching creativity;
- assessing creativity.

Three different matrices were presented to the attendees. The attendees used coloured marker pens to indicate important topics for their discipline. They were also asked to prioritise the items. The matrices were then used to discuss the commonalities, differences and priorities across disciplines.

Workshop 3: Technological support for creativity

The objectives of the third workshop were to i) educate the cluster about the different creativity support tools available, ii) outline the role of the computer, from an HCI perspective, in supporting creative design iii) educate the cluster about how artists from different disciplines create works of art and, iv) begin development of research collaborations and proposals [Figures 2 and 3].

To achieve these objectives, a presentation of HCI research in creativity was given. This was followed by an artist's forum and a group activity where the research issues identified as important in the previous workshops were discussed, with the aim of producing research proposals.

Workshop 4: Prioritisation and development of research issues and collaborations

The objectives of the fourth workshop were to i) appreciate an international perspective on creativity research and practice, ii) understand the role of the computer in artists' practice [Figure 4], and, iii) generate research plans providing effective responses to funding opportunities for researching creativity in design supported by 21st century technology.

Figure 4, Broadway Set Print, an example of work from Ernest Edmonds, who gave the keynote talk at workshop 4

The objectives were achieved through a number of activities which included invited talks from international speakers, and a representative of the Bath Rennie Mackintosh Society, an artists' forum which addressed the theme of the role computers currently play in artistic practice, and group activities which included development of research proposals. The workshop provided the basis for ongoing collaboration beyond the life of the funded cluster [Figure 5].

Enquiry methods adopted

There were different goals for each workshop thus necessitating the use of a variety of enquiry methods. The work of the cluster meant that members had to be educated about the underlying philosophy, knowledge, and practices of different disciplines from academic, practitioner and industrialist perspectives. Additionally, a range of activities allowing discussion about important topics in the diverse areas was needed along with recognition of commonalities and differences. It was also important to build a community of people from different disciplines and perspectives working together on common themes over a period of time. Developing a shared dialogue that could provide the foundation for new and future collaborations was of paramount importance. Finally, frameworks had to be provided to focus, but not stifle, 'creative' conversations and discussions. Often conflict and breakdowns in communication are the inspiration for creative empowerment.

Image 5, The 'cluster-in-action', cluster members make notes during Ernest Edmonds keynote address

Some enquiry methods proved more successful than others, but the success or failure of the activities resulted from more than the methods adopted. Presentations from people from diverse backgrounds, from a user group, and presented within a short time frame were successful. Other successful activities included the artists' forums where practitioners described their computer usage, good and bad points of technology, and the role computers played in their work. Individual work activities where cluster members in isolation answered questions about their respective disciplines thus providing the basis for later debate, were not enjoyed regardless of the fact that the later discussions were stimulating.

Success of the enquiry methods can be measured in different ways. Some activities produced significant and important outputs but were enjoyed less – the matrix and wheel activities fell into this category. Discussions continuing long after the close of workshops were clearly enjoyable but with less 'tangible' outputs, those being greater understanding and relationship building. This indicates a balance of activities is needed, and achieving this balance might be the work of a cluster activity – a metaactivity.

Enquiry method success depends on cluster membership – involving industrialists, academics from different disciplines and also a user-practitioner population is important, along with forging relationships under time pressure.

Conducting interdisciplinary research is complex. The greatest barrier initially is lack of knowledge and understanding. Another barrier relates to finding a language to educate and be educated in, and finally in developing a common debating language. Whilst debate is stimulating, it raises not only awareness but polite conflict which needs resolution and also a means to overcome disciplinary 'defensiveness'. Moreover, the 'interdisciplinary' insights have to be more than insights from individual perspectives, or the summing of insights from different individual perspectives – it means working together towards a common goal.

Insights Gained from the Cluster Activities

In this section we review new insights gained and research questions generated, as a result of the workshop activities. One output from an early session regarded 'What is creativity?' It was agreed that diversity in how people from different backgrounds understood 'creativity', was a strength of a multidisciplinary cluster, and forcing consensus was not to be attempted. The aim was not that we do not define 'creativity' at all but rather that we educate cluster members about how the term might be used in the different disciplines and from different perspectives, and not compromise by rigidly applying a universal, consensual definition.

Another output from a group and report-back activity investigated the likely impact of research into improving tool support for group creativity in design. The following impact features were outlined by cluster members: improved quality of life, richer understanding, personal development, better products, encouragement of exploration, more adventure, increase UK's position for leading design, improved quality and quantity of creative designs. A further series of outputs from group activities were concerned with identifying commonalities and differences in the group members' understanding of creativity and creative processes. The following is a snapshot of one group's contribution to the report-back and discussion session.

- Creativity is for . . .
  - Survival.
  - Personal identity forging.
- Creativity may be inspired but cannot be taught. It is a trait-based notion.
  - Everybody has a potential for creativity.
  - The relevant tools can be provided, but creativity cannot be taught. The role of the tools is to allow expression, inspire rather than teach creativity.

- Many of the designs with 'Designer of the Year' awards neither solved anything nor fix anything, but are still creative.
- Without 'problem solving', how do we decide what is creative and what isn't? But there can be situations where there is no problem to solve.
- If function is not the point of creativity, why did someone create something? Is putting our personal stamp, or to become known, a reason?
- In art being 'good' or 'bad' does not matter. If function is important 'good'/'bad' design matters. The difference is that for art aesthetics is enough, but for design and user interface design, aesthetic and function are needed.
- What is the relationship between 'Group Creativity' and 'Group Identity'?
- What would be a metric for measuring creativity?
- Who decides that an idea is good and bad?
- The most creative people have 'loosely associative' thinking. They create new ideas using existing ones, but connecting them differently.
- The implication of process constrains creativity.

From the group discussions, commonalities were found to exist across disciplines in how creativity is understood. The main differences exist in the approaches and methods used to generate creative solutions in design, and cluster members were given information from different perspectives concerning methods about which they were previously unaware. There were also found to be common high-level design activities undertaken, but frequently given different terms or labels.

Outputs from another workshop activity included a set of emerging research questions, to be addressed by future creativity research. The emerging research questions which were extensively discussed at the workshops, include:

- How do we support the development of a creative culture?
- How do we encourage cross-fertilisation of qualitative and quantitative creativity approaches? And how do we apply them?
- How do we support/encourage collaboration in creativity?
- What fuels the creative leap?
- What is the bridge between environment and methods/tools used?
- How can we provide a risk-enabling environment to support exploration and experimentation of creative design?

- What is the transition between individual and group creativity?
- What elements are needed to create an environment that leads to creativity?
- How do you teach managers the skills?
- What can be learnt from case studies?

A further series of outputs came from the artists' forums. The forums consisted of 12 artists giving short presentations. Particular features of these presentations relate to fun, laughter, entertainment, pleasure and optimism.

Commonalities existed across artists in trying out ideas on different versions, hypothesis testing, and in how everyday life (actions, pictures, stories/themes and photographs) led to inspiration. Computer usage was varied. Computers held different and multiple roles in each artist's creative process. Using the computer in a particular role meant that it should involve either making something entirely new possible or make an existing task easier.

Support for non-linear working methods in the interface is key to allowing artists to continue the creative processes that they expect to follow. Creativity involves exploratory behaviour to identify what is possible with the tool, what can be expressed, and how. Environments must be complex yet their workings transparent, combined with this they must offer quick results to provide a satisfactory learning process.

Making use of computers requires accurate input and feedback, and this is not always available in the desired form, for example, the lack of tactile feedback available, thus hampering idea evaluation. A lack of physicality emerged as a major reason why many of the artists did not make more use of the computer as a medium. On the other hand, the computer can offer an approximation of the medium without the associated constraints, and can take existing work as inspiration providing unexpected new perspectives. The twin requirements of tools to aid exploration appear to be lower exploration costs, but enhanced exploration in new directions.

Several artists felt that usable tools to organise large collections of multimedia material in a meaningful way were required, particularly, when work is temporal or temporary (for example, a dance performance or installation).

Collaboration between artists required communicative ability in the work medium or through an acceptable representation. Additionally, many artists need to build relationships with their audience, and technology can provide new mechanisms to enable this.

The final set of workshop outputs related to initial development of research proposals to address high priority research questions. The following research problems, aims and objectives of proposals were generated:

- How to overcome communication breakdowns in collaborative creative design processes.
- To investigate the practices that allow creative process to function.
- How do we demonstrate the value of creativity to society?
- The edgy environment – define the characteristics of appropriate methods for exposing and reflecting on artists' ongoing work.

These research issues could each have an important impact on group creativity in design in the 21ˢᵗ century. Taking the first research issue as an example, better support for communication, and facilitating breakthroughs from breakdowns, should lead to a more streamlined design process and more creative products. For this to happen, interdisciplinary research must be conducted into the nature of breakdowns and breakthroughs. This research will provide the basis for developing technologies by which conflict resolution and breakdown and breakthrough management strategies, are supported.

Whilst we might like to think each of artistic, academic and engineering 'creativities' as truly unique, the work of the cluster has shown that many aspects of creativity in design in these communities are shared.

Acknowledgements

We are grateful to the members of the 'Creativity in Design' cluster for participating in the cluster activities. We thank AHRC and EPSRC for funding this research.

Additional Reading

CANDY, L. and EDMONDS, E., 1999. Introducing Creativity to Cognition. *In: Proceedings of the ACM Conference on Creativity and Cognition '99, Loughborough.* ACM Press, pp. 3-6.

SHNEIDERMAN, B., 2000. Creating creativity: User interfaces for supporting innovation. *ACM Trans. on Computer-Human Interaction,* 7(1), pp. 114-138.

Nature Inspired Creative Design – Bringing Together Ideas from Nature, Computer Science, Engineering, Art and Design

Thorsten Schnier, Russell Beale, Xin Yao, Bob Hendley and Will Byrne, (University of Birmingham)

Overview

The 'Nature Inspired Creative Design' cluster brought together people from three main areas: Nature and Biology, Art and Design, and Science and Computing. It aimed to establish a forum for cross-fertilisation between disciplines, within the overall topic of adopting nature inspired approaches to creative design. Its members explored a wide range of subjects, including evolution, growth and development, emergence and self-organisation, robustness, natural structures, and human design behaviour and performance.[1]

[1] This is an extended version of a paper originally published in: *Proceedings of the 7ᵗʰ Conference on Adaptive Computing in Design and Manufacture, ACDM 2006, Bristol, 25-27ᵗʰ April 2006.*

This chapter presents the background and ideas of the cluster, predominantly from a computational viewpoint. It also presents some of the result of the initial 1-year funded phase of activity.

Nature Inspired Creative Design

Nature is the ultimate designer. Every species, every individual, can be seen as the result of an implicit design process. At the same time, the results of this design process perform extremely well, in whatever measure of performance one might want to use. Often this includes aesthetical measures – there are many extremely beautiful species on earth.

The main goal of the network was to explore what can be learned from Nature for human design and engineering activities. However, this is not a one-way process. The nature of the funding put an emphasis on applications to design, and this chapter will maintain this emphasis. However, there is potential for transfer of ideas between all the groups who participated in the cluster [Figure 1].

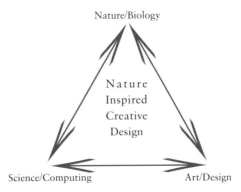

Figure 1, Nature Inspired Creative Design cluster

Promises of nature inspired design

The design process is becoming increasingly complex and demanding, and will continue to do so into the future. Individual designs are composed of more and more parts; designs are subject to more and more requirements and constraints; at the same time the rapid technical innovations and shorter lifespans increase the demand for new designs. By adopting nature inspired methods, we hope to solve some of these problems. Nature inspired methods have a number of potential contributions, as described in the following sections.

Produce better designs

Comparing natural and artificial designs, it is clear that natural designs often have a number of advantages. For example, natural designs are usually:

- Resource efficient: through continuous adaptation, natural designs have become parsimonious in their use of resources.
- Resilient to faults: artificial designs often fail when individual components break. Natural designs, on the other hand, usually show graceful degradation: a small injury is usually not fatal to an animal, and the death of a number of individuals will not seriously endanger a colony of insects.
- Adaptable: natural designs are usually able to adapt to the environment; sometimes this happens as part of the development process from genetic code to individual, sometimes this happens during the lifetime as physical change, or as behavioural change.
- Extremely varied: natural design processes have produced individuals

that span a massive range of scales, complexities, shapes and forms. They can be found in a vast range of environments. Nature inspired processes can help designers to create very novel designs.

Create better design processes

By taking inspiration from nature's methods, we will be able to find processes that are:

- More scalable: nature has developed systems that show a very high complexity: human nervous systems, colonies of insects, large eco-systems are all examples. Very often, these systems are composed of a large number of elements with complex interactions. Designing artificial systems of similar complexity is usually a very difficult process.
- Better parallelizable: in natural evolution, there is no top-down design process – every species evolves on its own, and individual parts of a design (for example, the beak of a Darwin Finch) can often be optimised fairly much independently of other parts.
- More reliable: a very simple system consisting of 10 components interacting in 10 different ways has the state space of 10,000,000,000 possible states. A designer using conventional tools simply does not have the time to search the entire state space. Natural systems have developed various emergent methods for searching the state space of the system.
- More efficient: natural design processes are unsupervised processes – no conscious designer is involved. Instead, processes of evolution, emergence, self-organisation and interaction with the environment determine the outcome. Together with the increasing availability of fast computer clusters, nature inspired approaches have the potential to provide efficient alternatives to labour-intensive manual design processes.

Create better design tools

Nature inspired design tools have the potential to:

- Allow the user to search a larger design space: designers are often limited to a small subset of the total design space, for a variety of reasons: lack of knowledge, lack of time and lack of design methods. Nature inspired methods may be able to help produce designs in a larger search space, and help in evaluating these solutions.
- Provide better support: systems that know about the design process, and learn the user's preferences, will be able to provide better support to the designer. Nature inspired techniques can provide both languages to describe designs, as well as the learning algorithms.

Provide knowledge about human design activities

[3] EIBEN, A. & SMITH, J. E., 2003. *Introduction to Evolutionary Computing*. Berlin: Springer Verlag.

[4] BENTLEY, P., 1999. *Evolutionary Design by Computers*. Morgan Kaufmann Publishers.

[5] SCHNIER, T. and GERO, J. S., 1998. From Frank Lloyd Wright to Mondrian: Transforming evolving representation. *In*: I. C. PARMEE, (ed.) *Adaptive Computing in Design and Manufacture*. Springer-Verlag, pp. 207-219.

- Humans are a part of nature. They are also a result of an evolutionary process – our artistic perception, and our creative abilities, are formed by this process. By studying aspects of human design activities, we can learn more about human and animal creative processes. Human creativity is a multi-faceted process, and attempts at creating creative computer programs can benefit from emulating one or more of these attributes. Human creativity is also of course a result of human evolution.
- Capture design knowledge. Human designers have developed a large pool of knowledge about design, both explicit and implicit. This knowledge can be applied in other disciplines, for example in data visualisation.
- Gain insights into ethical aspects of design. Natural life has survived many drastic changes, in terms of climate changes, natural disasters and or rapid evolutionary changes. Studying natural design dynamics may give us some ideas about possible interactions between the natural and human designed worlds.

Areas of Interest

With about 40 members with a variety of backgrounds actively participating in the cluster, a wide variety of subjects were discussed. The following sections attempt to categorise and summarise these subjects.

Evolution

The process of evolution has inspired a whole ecosystem of algorithms, generally referred to as Evolutionary Computation (EC)[3] or Evolutionary Algorithms (EA). There is also an extensive body of work for EC in the art and design area. Most of this work is in the area of design optimisation. While there may be many technical challenges for any particular application, it is very straightforward to map the EC paradigm to design optimisation problems.

Creative design and art using EA (evolutionary art) [Figure 2], has also been explored.[4] The difficult issue here is generally finding a suitable fitness function; most often this is solved by 'human in the loop' approaches.

Representation of the problem is also not straightforward, as any particular representation used will define a fixed design space. In some cases, representations can be learned from examples.[5]

Evolution is probably the most prominent natural design process. As an unsupervised design process, with very successful results, it is an attractive proposition. However, it is important not to forget that evolution has had more than 800 million years to develop. Natural evolution is also extremely parallel: every individual in existence is essentially one fitness evaluation.

Representation and fitness, the two crucial parts of any EA, also featured in the work of the cluster. The subject of suitable 'natural' fitness functions, particularly automated evaluation according to aesthetical criteria, was one of the cluster topics. Another topic of interest to the group was more natural representations for design. Co-evolution of different species can also provide a possible model of co-evolution between design and user preferences, and possibly be used to model user trends.

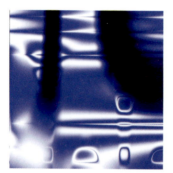 

Figures 2 and 3,
left and right

Figure 2, Evolutionary Art: image created using user preference as fitness (Thorsten Schnier and Kennon Ballou)
Figure 3, 'Feedback' (Gail Troth, detail): scales and wave boundaries use self-organisation properties of paints of different viscosity

Self-organisation and emergence

Emergence is generally the result of the interaction of a large number of individual entities. Both emergent behaviours (for example, sorting behaviours of ants) and emergent structures (for example, patterns on sea shells[6]) are possible. Emergent phenomena are generally very robust, for example sorting ants will still be able to sort if half of them are killed, or if obstacles are placed in their way. They also mainly rely on local, one-to-one communication, and are therefore also very scalable.

[6] MEINHARDT, H., 1995.
The Algorithmic Beauty of Sea Shells. Berlin: Springer-Verlag.

[7] KAUFFMAN, S. A., 1993. *The Origins of Order: Self-Organisation and Selection in Evolution.* Oxford: Oxford University Press.

[8] BENTLEY, P., 2003. *On Growth, Form and Computers.* Academic Press.

[9] MILLER, J. F., 2004. Evolving a Self-Repairing, Self-Regulating, French Flag Organism. *In*: DEB et al, (eds.) *Proceedings of the Conference on Genetic and Evolutionary Computation, GECCO 2004, Part I, Lecture Notes in Computer Science 3102, Seattle, 26-30th June 2004.* Springer Verlag, pp. 129-139.

[10] PRUSINKIEWICZ, P. and LINDENMAYER, A., 1990. *The Algorithmic Beauty of Plants.* Springer Verlag.

Because of the often non-linear interactions, it is often very difficult to predict and engineer emergent behaviours and structures. Evolution (and EC) may be one of the best mechanisms available. Systems displaying emergent behaviours can often be simulated on computers. This includes models of human behaviours, for example evacuation of crowds from buildings.

Self-organisation is a related phenomenon, in which higher-level order arises from the interaction of lower-level parts.[7] Self-organisation and emergence may also suggest methods of teamwork in humans. Finally, self-organisation can also be used in art, as explored by one cluster member [Figure 3].

Development and growth

Development is the process that transforms a set of genetic information (genotype) into an individual (phenotype). Biological development, especially of higher-order individuals, is a highly complex process, involving non-linear interactions of a large number of parts. It can be an extremely robust process – for example faults in the process (any kind of small birth defects) can still lead to viable individuals. Environment plays a strong role – the process can be robust to some environmental changes, but other environmental factors may be highly critical (for example, egg temperature). It can also take advantage of and adapt to the environment; for example bone growth depends on the loads on the bone.

There is interest from the biological side in the dynamics and robustness of the process. But there is also a very strong interest from the computing community.[8] For example, conventional evolutionary computation uses very direct genotype-phenotype transformations. EC researchers are very interested in representations that involve a development process, and result in robust processes, which can be influenced by the environment for example, French-flag work by Miller.[9] One development model, based on plant growth, is so-called L-systems.[10] An interesting question is also how indirect, growth and development based representations change the evolutionary dynamics – do they make it easier or harder to evolve complex genotypes?

Robustness

11 ATHERTON, M. and
BATES, R., 2005. Robustness
and Complexity. *In*: M. W.
COLLINS, M. A. ATHERTON
and J. A. BRYANT, (eds.) *Design
and Nature*. Southhampton:
WIT Press.

12 VINCENT, J. F. V., 2002.
Stealing ideas from nature. *In*: S.
PELLEGRINO, (ed.) *Deployable
Structures*. Vienna: Springer,
pp. 51-58.

13 TRACTINSKY, N., KATZ,
A. and IKAR, D., 2000. What is
beautiful is usable. *Interacting
with Computers*, 13,
pp. 127-145.

Robustness is a design quality that is abundant in natural design, but often very difficult to achieve with conventional design processes.[11] Robustness issues have already been explored in the previous two sections. However, there are other mechanisms nature uses to achieve robustness. One mechanism explored by the network is the combination of compliant (flexible) structures with active control.

Existing structures in nature

The previous sections all discussed *processes* in nature that are interesting from the design point of view. Another source of inspiration for art and design are the *structures* employed by nature. The growing field of biomimetics is concerned with identifying particular design solutions in nature, and converting them into usable artefacts – essentially 'stealing' design ideas from nature.[12] For example, the egg-laying organ of the wood wasp can inspire new drill designs, and the surface structure of lotus leaves can be 'copied' to create new, liquid-shedding surfaces.

Humans and design

We can learn a lot about design by looking at 'natural' human design processes.

One example is our sense of aesthetics. In order to create an artificial aesthetics measure, we need to understand the nature of the human sense of aesthetics. Individual development and experience plays a role, but some of it is innate. One of the research projects coming out of the cluster is interested in the evolutionary origins of aesthetics. Understanding this will not only increase our understanding of humans, but may also provide important hints in how to design artificial selection methods for aesthetics. Interestingly, work on interactive systems has demonstrated a link between aesthetics and usability.[13]

Another interesting aspect is the difference in human reaction to natural and artificial objects, what features make an object appear natural, and how this can influence the design process.

In ambient art, artistic methods are used to present elements of information from the environment to the user. Recent research aims to explore the role of ambient art as both a new approach to artistic

[14] SKOG, T., LJUNGBLAD, S. and HOLMQUIST, L., 2003. Between Aesthetics and Utility: Designing Ambient Information Visualisations. Presented at the *9th IEEE Symposium on Information Visualisation, InfoVis 2003, Seattle, 19-21st October 2003.*

[15] BEALE, R., 2005. Ambient Art: Information Without Attention. Presented at the *11th International Conference on Human-Computer Interaction, HCI 2005, Las Vegas, 22-27 July 2005.*

expression, and in understanding the process of creating it which allows us to transfer knowledge from the artistic domain into more technical and scientific domains.[14,15]

The cluster was also interested in the influence of human design on nature, including a number of ethical questions: how will human and natural designs interact? How far can we go in manipulating natural design?

The Network

The initial AHRC/EPSRC funded cluster period was from 1st April 2005 to 31st March 2006. Throughout this time, we have had very positive reactions to the interests and goals of the cluster, both from members and from the public, through the website and public presentations. There appears to be a large community of people interested in the broad subject, from all disciplines represented in the cluster. The growing mailing list membership, and the success of the workshops, also attest to this. The cluster will continue to be run for the foreseeable future, based on the website and mailing list, with one to two meetings per year.

Cluster membership

During the 1-year funded period of the cluster, it grew from an initial membership of 20 to 40 active members. The mailing list continues to grow, and at the time of writing contains more than 90 members. The cluster membership comprised artists, designers, design scientists, biologists, engineers and computer scientists. Active members came from all over the UK; some of the mailing list members are in other countries.

Cluster meetings

The cluster organised three successful meetings, each one generating a lot of lively discussion, debate and new ideas. Meetings included presentations from members as well as demonstrations of work, ideas and experiments, and we also had some nature-inspired art on display. At all three meetings we had a good cross-section of attendees representing diverse disciplines and viewpoints. This cross-fertilisation of ideas is at the heart of our aims and activities, and will drive the research proposals and future initiatives coming out of the cluster.

¹⁶ Nature Insprired Creative
Design. Available at:
www.nature-inspired.org.

Cluster website

The cluster has its own website.[16] This website has been used to distribute
information about cluster events, collect resources and advertise the
network. It is set up as a collaborative resource using wiki technology,
which allows all registered members to add material.

Cluster links

The cluster benefited from strong links with a number of organisations.
Three of the four Co-Investigators are part of Cercia, a Centre of Excellence
that specialises in applications of natural computation. Cercia is part of the
School of Computer Science, University of Birmingham, which offered the
first Natural Computation MSc, including the (at the time of writing) only
Computer Science course in nature inspired design. Cercia sponsorship will
allow the cluster to continue after the end of the funding period.

In addition to links to all the organisations represented by the
members, the cluster has particularly strong links to other regional arts
organisations, especially the Birmingham Institute of Art and Design
(BIAD), the Jewellery Industry Innovation Centre and DesignGap.

Outcomes

Proposals

The cluster produced three significant concepts that were developed into
research proposals. These were:

- creative mass customisation;
- morphogenic design;
- ambient art: information without attention.

Nature inspired approaches to creative mass customisation

New manufacturing technologies have the potential to revolutionise the
manufacturing industry. Digitally controlled manufacturing processes,
such as rapid prototyping (RP) machines and modular assembly, allow
manufacturing models where each item produced is customised for
an individual user, without introducing significant additional costs.
The Internet provides a widely available interface, and a number of
manufacturers have recently started offering mass customised products,
including such high profile companies as Nike, Lego and Dell. Currently
the customisation available to the customer before the product leaves
the factory is very limited and often superficial. In one common model

in the clothing industry, the user has no real design influence at all – the customisation concerns the sizing, and the system automatically adapts the shapes of the items (clothes, shoes). The user has slightly more influence in systems where they can chose between a number of predefined options (for example, parts of different colour) in a modularised manufacturing process. At best, the user can upload images that are then printed on to the object.

The manufacturing technologies to take customisation further and integrate it with the design and manufacturing process itself are now available, and there is a considerable market opportunity. What is missing is a suitable design process, which can allow the user to creatively modify a design but ensure the result still incorporates the functionality and design characteristics of the professional designer's original. This project will develop a novel, computer supported design process which combines designer and user input into a final artefact; developing new manufacturing models where the customer can be involved together with the designer in a creative design process.

Evolutionary design processes with user selection are limited in the outputs they can produce. The inclusion of a bio-inspired development process removes this limitation: while the evolution always operates on the same, simple set of data (or genes) the development process can transform this data into highly complex forms. Most importantly, style and other properties of the resulting design are determined or at least strongly influenced by the particular transformation used. With an appropriate transformation, we can ensure that all designs the system produces conform to a style developed by the designer; while functionality, manufacturing and other constraints are also enforced. Style and external constraints can additionally form part of the selection process: the evolutionary system can produce far more potential designs, while only those that the system determines to conform to the constraints are presented to the user.

Morphogenic design

Design is driven, not just by function, but also by the manufacturing processes that are available. Nature uses very different construction methods from those used for man-made objects, and that is why it is generally very easy to distinguish between natural and man-made items. Natural morphogenesis is a highly complex, nonlinear process. There are a number of different mathematical and computational models that attempt to model aspects of morphogenesis at different levels of abstraction – for example Cellular Automata, Reaction-Diffusion (R/D) systems, and Lindenmayer systems. We propose a novel design approach based on natural designs, where the designs are defined in terms of particular reaction-diffusion equations, and artificial evolution is used to derive these equations. R/D systems are very powerful models, which have been successfully used to model two and three dimensional formation of form and patterns. In two dimensions, they have been used to model the generation of stripes and other patterns on animal coats, and the formation of fingerprint patterns. In three dimensions, R/D based models have been successfully used to show patterns of limb formation equivalent to those in chickens. As a result of the non-linearities involved, it is generally very difficult or impossible to 'reverse-engineer' a particular R/D system from the desired or observed output. The system we suggest uses artificial evolution to construct R/D type systems with particular user-defined properties. The output of these R/D systems can be interpreted in a physical form, and one or more user-defined performance values generated. These values in turn serve as 'fitness' to guide the artificial evolution. The artificial evolution will work on two levels, co-evolving the equations and the parameters of those equations. The final designs can currently be implemented using modern 3D manufacturing, and computer-controlled machining. A longer-term aim is to use the design process to design for new manufacturing processes based on real processes that can be described as R/D systems.

If we can use some of the principles of natural morphogenic processes to drive our design process then we have a route to developing naturalistic designs that are significantly different from conventional ones, both in terms of appearance and performance. We can also use the same design processes to construct models of natural structures from a limited amount of data.

Ambient art

We are becoming increasingly exposed to more and more digital information streams, and need effective ways to monitor these without being overwhelmed and distracted from our real-world experiences and primary goals. This is particularly relevant for long-term interactions with almost invisible technologies, which are part of the 2020 future, which will tell us for example where our children are, how our investments are doing, what the state of the power plant is, and so on.

We cannot spend all our time looking at this, but need to know when things are OK, and when they are not. If this information is to be permanently displayed in our periphery, it has to be aesthetically pleasing – we have to want to have it around, and to enjoy interacting with it. Nature provides the inspiration for the design approach we will follow: it offers many forms that are aesthetically pleasing to us, and has processes such as evolution that produce pleasing, effective solutions. The project proposes to investigate how to provide aesthetic informative representations via three strands:

- natural representations (for example, images from nature, which appeal to us somehow);
- nature-inspired representations (for example, evolutionary art pictures) which develop according to nature-inspired rules;
- human-created art, inspired by natural scenes or processes.

Each will be used to represent complex, large-scale information without presenting all the details. The project will then evaluate these approaches, looking at both their aesthetic qualities, the increased awareness of the information presented engendered in the observer, the degree of attention required by the observer (that is, do they have to actively concentrate on the images, or can they simply absorb the information without any conscious attention?) The project also uses the opportunity to investigate the psychological mechanisms of non-attentive displays through its experimental process. This work is the first detailed attempt to understand the mechanisms behind the effective use of non-attentive information displays from both an artistic and a cognitive perspective.

Cluster dynamics

The cluster showed an interesting split in the commitment and contributions. On one side, the cluster meetings succeeded extremely well in engaging members. On the other hand, it was very difficult to get contributions from cluster members between the meetings. The collaborative potential of the website was never used, and only a small number of members contributed to meeting preparations and mailing list discussions. One reason for this was the density of events in the 'Designing for the 21st Century' Initiative, with 21 clusters holding meetings, and a large overlap in cluster membership.

Summary

There is a large potential for nature inspired ideas in a range of design activities. This cluster has been very successful in bringing together a group of interested professionals from diverse fields. While it has generated many ideas, it has yet only scratched the surface of the possibilities. It remains for future cluster activities and research partnerships to explore these ideas further.

Acknowledgements

The authors wish to thank the AHRC and EPSRC for funding the cluster, and all the cluster members for their contribution to the success of the network.

Additional Reading

SCHNIER, T. et al., 2006. Nature Inspired Creative Design. Available at: http://www.nature-inspired.org

Spatial Imagination in Design
Dr Jane Rendell and Dr Peg Rawes, (Bartlett School of Architecture, UCL)

Overview: Situating Spatial Imagination in Design

[1] The 'frivolous' imagination associated with buildings by architects such as Ron Herron, Imagination Building, (London, 1989) or Alsop Architects, Peckham Library (London, 1999), and Ontario College of Art and Design (Toronto, 2004).

[2] Aldo van Eyck, children's playgrounds in Amsterdam (1947-1978), or Mark Dudek's Kindergarten Architecture: Space for the Imagination (Spon Press, 1995) in which children's games represent 'unconscious' design activities that inspire professional, modern architectural design of playgrounds and schools.

[3] Frank Lloyd Wright, An Autobiography [1932] (Horizon Press, 1987), refers to his childhood fondness for Fröbel's blocks, suggesting an early aptitude for imaginative spatial design awareness.

This cluster developed out of a conversation between Peg Rawes and Jane Rendell which highlighted our theoretical, historical and practice-led interest in the role of the imagination in spatial design practices. Through our conversation we identified how the imagination is frequently misunderstood and/or overlooked in both professional and academic discussions in the spatial and architectural design disciplines that prioritise determined or predicted relations between the designer, users and products. From this perspective the built product is seen to demonstrate (or prove) the intellectual and 'reasoned' control of the design process by the designer, the responses of the user, and the economic, intellectual or professional success of the product. The imagination features here as a neglected constituent of the cultural, social and historical value of architectural and built environments, and in many cases the spatial imagination is considered in what we would call negative terms, for example: as indicative of uncritical, populist or frivolous modern architectural design;[1] as a sign of amateur or immature design processes – those that relate to either the untrained or unprofessionalised production of design, or to the responses of an 'immature' reason, for example, play or a child's engagement with spatial design and environments;[2] as evidence of 'irrational' intuition – despite the positive 'all-in-one-grasping' which an intuitive understanding of spatial design might designate, the imagination is more frequently allied to knowledge which is 'unruly' or 'unreasonable', and is therefore positioned in opposition to the production of design through deterministic, rational and reasoned thought;[3] as gender-specific – linked to 'feminine' or therefore 'inadequate' concepts

[4] Christine Battersby, Gender and Genius: Towards a Feminist Aesthetics (Pluto Press, 1989) provides a critique of the masculine and feminine forms of imagination which excluded 18th women from having access to 'reason'.

[5] An examination of Leibniz's 'fictional' geometry in: RAWES, P., 2007. Plenums: Rethinking Matter, Geometry and Subjectivity. In: K. LLOYD-THOMAS, (ed.) Material Matters: Architecture and Material Practice. Routledge.

[6] DAVENPORT, G., 1997. The Geography of the Imagination: Forty Essays. David R. Godine Publishers.

[7] The philosophical writings of Walter Benjamin, including, One Way Street (Verso, 1992), explore how temporal narratives are produced by the individual in the modern 20th city.

[8] RAWES, P., 2007. Reflective subjects in Kant and architecture. Journal of Aesthetic Education, 41(1), pp. 74-89.

[9] PEREC, G., 1997. Species of Spaces and Other Pieces Penguin. Where Perec suggests how mathematical procedures are also creative qualities in the spatial design of the built environment and literary texts.

or codes of behaviour, for example values inherited from 18th century European understandings of 'genius';[4] as disembodied and fantastical – in opposition to the empirical, material manufacture of design, and thereby relegated to general rather than specific designs of an idea, space or artefact.

In response to these common cultural, social and historical perceptions which continue to inform understandings of design (even in the 21st century), we set out to develop the project in order to address each of these negative associations. In particular, we propose the following counter-arguments through which to reconstitute the spatial imagination in design as an active and critical research environment, enabling the imagination to be understood as a positive and productive constituent in the design process.

First, that the spatial imagination needs to be uncovered from within, or introduced into, the professional and academic design context. Here we suggest that prioritising the imperative of reductive scientific or axiomatic design procedures to produce 'clear truths' or 'complete' objects conceals the *actual* indeterminacy of these complex cultural processes.[5] Second, that the spatial imagination is politically and culturally specific.[6] Here we propose that understanding specific cultural and political imaginations as belonging to the individual designer and user, enables the imagination to positively inform understandings of the design process, and as a result, such understandings of the imagination may therefore inform and reflect the specific cultural, historical and political diversity and value of the architectural and built environment to the design community and beyond. Third, that the spatial imagination may be a temporal form of design. Here we argue for the production of a narrative that enables understandings of spatial processes in relation to temporal conditions, for example, the relationship between an individual's lived experiences and memory in relation to the spatial organisation of the modern city.[7] Fourth, that the spatial imagination contributes to the designer's and user's embodied experiences and understandings of the urban and built environment. Here we demonstrate that an individual's sensory and perceptual engagement with an environment or space is, in part, constructed by their powers of imagination.[8] Finally, we critique the spatial imagination as a design agent which augments scientific understandings of design that are generated by deterministic design procedures, and offer instead self-reflective modes of practice-led knowledge to academia, the design professions and the public at large.[9]

Activities

Processes of Spatial Imagination in Design

Our cluster was composed of 15 members, drawn from architecture, exhibition, product and interactive design; fine and public art; psychotherapy, history, economics and philosophy; structural engineering and construction management, with project partners Kate Trant of CABE (Commission for Architecture and the Built Environment) and Greg Cowan of the RIBA (Royal Institute of British Architecture). Through a series of three workshops, each one devised and led by cluster members, and held at 3 monthly intervals throughout 2005, we explored the spatial imagination as a mode of perception and tool of production in the experience and design of space, through particular design processes of: 'modelling', 'writing' and 'drawing'.

Starting with visits to two very different exhibition collections, the modelling workshop focused on 'immersion' and allowed us to investigate how various qualities of the spatial imagination – critical, intuitive, perceptual, temporal – produced a range of relationships to objects and places. The cluster was divided into two groups. One visited the Museum of Childhood, the other the Hornimann Museum plus the Dulwich Picture Gallery designed by Sir John Soane. Subsequent experiments – responses to our 'immersion' in the museum environments – drew on a range of images and materials to produce new objects that provided the opportunity for conversations concerning chance, wandering and performance in the design process to emerge.

The writing workshop took further our nascent interests in how imagined space exists simultaneously and dialectically with real space. Such concerns were encouraged to unfold during our walk through London led by environmental artists Platform, following the colonial expansion of the East India Company. At certain sites, imaginative projections – geographical and historical – were superimposed onto, and at the same time triggered by, our understandings of 'real' or material space. An accompanying writing workshop utilised principles of juxtaposition to create writing modes where objective and subjective experiences were combined. Artist Brigid McLeer asked participants on the walk to collect found words, from signs, packaging and other graphic sites, and to write more experiential accounts at certain moments through the day. These two collections of words – those 'found' in the city and those written by the authors – were then put together as a collection of material for all to draw on to combine in various configurations during the following day's workshop.

The drawing workshop took the form of a group 'crit' where each cluster member presented their work in progress for the forthcoming exhibition. The intention was to present the research in such a way that it exposed the soft underbelly of the design process – in opposition to the usual form of the design 'crit' where in anticipation of a difficult critique, the presenter adopts a defensive position, negating the possibility for any 'real' development or discussion of the issues raised through the work we produced a situation conducive for the emergence of critically-engaged dialogues. Each workshop participant presented concepts for their projects in the form of questions to the audience, inviting their colleagues to participate in the creative process by making suggestions for the completion of the work.

Products of Spatial Imagination in Design

Over the year, the development and design of the website by Stuart Munro played an important role in communicating our ongoing activities to an internal and an external audience through two routes, one which 'explains' the cluster's research processes to the user, and another which allows the user to 'discover' places in which to get lost, drawing strongly on more intuitive and less determined states such as curiosity and uncertainty.[10]

[10] Spatial Imagination in Design. Available at: http://www. spatialimagination.org.uk/ .spatiaimagination.org.uk

From the outset it was the group's intention to develop our understandings of the spatial imagination through the production of artefacts. The site chosen for the exhibition of these works, the Domo Baal Gallery, housed in an 18ᵗʰ century house in Clerkenwell, London, provided an important context for the development of the research – this was a location that provoked our spatial imagination, both through the architectural features of the original design, but also through patterns of historical and contemporary occupation.

The building was designed between 1730 and 1750. The textured edge and central rose of the white ceiling in the main first floor room of the gallery were the most evocative manifestations of the delicacy of spatial imagination in the rococo, an architectural style connected with this historical period. The initial occupation of the building as a family home and a solicitor's office had left traces, hinting at the complex negotiations between domestic and institutional space which continue in the building today, where the everyday life of a family coincide closely with the ongoing activities of an art gallery.

This place provided an opportunity for each cluster member to make a new work drawing on understandings gained from previous conversations, visits and walks, yet informed by each individual's own particular interest in the spatial imagination in design. The final works took the form of proposals and exhibits – including sound pieces, texts, drawings and models – that operated across the disciplines of art, design and architecture communicating the spatial imagination through a configuration of material designs [Figure 1].

The three workshops provided places where participants could exchange ideas for the development of their final artefacts. The curatorial process also allowed the crossovers between individual projects to be exploited. Participants were invited to suggest ideal locations for their projects in the gallery and Penelope Haralambidou presented her early plan for the distribution of objects in the gallery to the group for debate in the final workshop. But it was really on site, in the gallery, surrounded by the finished items, and a changing group of participants, that final decisions were made concerning the articulation of the relationships – visual, audio, tactile and conceptual – between works – involving a consideration of the framed yet changing views presented of the spatial imagination on

Figures 1 and 2,
left and right

Figure 1, View of Exhibition showing the work of Peg Rawes to the left, Katja Grillner to the right, and Rory Hamilton in the distance, Spatial Imagination, (London: The Domo Baal Gallery, 2006). Photograph: David Cross of Cornford & Cross

Figure 2, Faye Carey, 'Cum Nimis Absurdum: Perverse Imagination/Endless Solution', Spatial Imagination, (London: The Domo Baal Gallery, 2006). Photograph: David Cross of Cornford & Cross

a journey through the building. The editorial of the catalogue, written before the design of the exhibition, anticipated and suggested a number of connections evident in the interests and art and design processes adopted by participants. However, it was in the aftermath of the exhibition that unexpected yet common understandings of the spatial imagination emerged. These came to the fore in the form of responses by cluster members to comments made by external critics, as well as through the dialogues with our partner organisations and an invited audience drawn from various different academic disciplines and the architectural profession which took place at the final symposium. As editors we attempt to describe below how, out of the production and dissemination of these art and design works, three key thematics emerged.

First, a number of projects looked at the use of the imagination in the operation of political power – both as a tool of oppression and of resistance. For example Faye Carey's work, taking the form of a textile printed with symbols used to identify Jews, examined how the imagination has been used as a 'perverse' legal power by societies to divide, conceal and repress Jewish communities into 'ghettos', raising questions about the responsibility of the spatial imagination in architectural construction [Figure 2]. The walking-works of collaborative environmental and interdisciplinary artists' group Platform, presented as an audio piece in the gallery, invited the participant to imagine the production, management and labour embedded in the built environment

Figures 3 and 4,
left and right

Figure 3, Brigid McLeer, 'A Jealousy', Spatial Imagination, (London: The Domo Baal Gallery, 2006). Photograph: David Cross of Cornford & Cross

Figure 4, Penelope Haralambidou, '3 John Street, 1:50', Spatial Imagination, (London: The Domo Baal Gallery, 2006). Photograph: David Cross of Cornford & Cross

and in so doing to animate the imagination as critical tool. For Katja
Grillner, critical theorist Walter Benjamin's notion of 'distraction'
suggested the power of the peripheral imagination to rethink architectural
and landscape criticism from a political perspective, shifting the critic's
gaze and attention to what is out of, rather than in, focus.

Second, a number of works combined the traditional design processes of
drawing, writing and modelling. For example, Brigid McLeer's 'writing-
as-drawing', located in a gap between two doors, in rewriting Alain
Robbe-Grillet's novel La Jalousie (1957), explored how the emotion of
jealousy heightens the perception of space between individuals [Figure 3].
In various works the architectural drawing was reconfigured. While Peg
Rawes retrieved the technical geometric imagination through the aesthetic
experiences of drawing while thinking, in Christine Hawley's architectural
drawings the imagination provided a principle of transposition, which
connected the different notational modes of presentation with the
material and physical properties of the architectural process and form.
In what she calls a 'drawing-as-model' Penelope Haralambidou's work
demonstrated the extent to which the imagination produces multiple
space-times. In placing the architectural model she produced as a design
tool for curating the exhibition in the corner of the gallery, she made a
mis-en-abyme or a space within a space [Figure 4].

Third, an understanding of imagination as a space of ambiguity between
designer and user could be seen in a number of works. For Jonathan Hill,
drawings operated as 'ambiguous objects' indicating the power of the
18th century imagination to connect the individual with architecture and
the landscaped garden, while Metaphor's miniature models of landscape
furniture existed in the contemporary moment but also led the viewer
back into the imaginative re-enactment of an 18th century pastoral
landscape [Figure 5]. In Rory Hamilton's work the imagination animated
space in moving silhouettes, which oscillated between legible and illegible
images, while in the drawing instruments that Nat Chard produced, the
imagination negotiated an indeterminate relation with architectural space
[Figure 6]. In repeatedly writing the word 'purdah' (a word which refers
to a screen or architectural element as well as a veil or item of clothing)
Jane Rendell transformed the window – an architectural site of visual
connection – into a screen – one of separation. Where the definition of
purdah in certain versions of the Koran, demands covering as a response
to female embellishment, 'An Embellishment: Purdah', suggested that
artifice structures rather than decorates divisions in the gendering of
space [Figure 7].

Figures 5 to 7,
left to right, top to bottom

Figure 5, Metaphor, 'Hardwick Park: Paradise Restored', Spatial Imagination, (London: The Domo Baal Gallery, 2006). Photograph: David Cross of Cornford & Cross

Figure 6, View of Exhibition showing, from the left, the work of Penelope Haralambidou, Jonathan Hill, Nat Chard and Yeoryia Manolopoulou, Spatial Imagination, (London: The Domo Baal Gallery, 2006). Photograph: David Cross of Cornford & Cross

Figure 7, Jane Rendell, 'An Embellishment: Purdah', Spatial Imagination, (London: The Domo Baal Gallery, 2006). Photograph: David Cross of Cornford & Cross

[11] RAWES, P. and RENDELL, J., (eds.), 2005. *Spatial Imagination*. The Bartlett School of Architecture, UCL.

[12] BUCHENAU, M. and SURI, J. F., 2000. Experience Prototyping. In: *Proceedings of the Conference on Designing Interactive Systems, DIS '00, New York, 17-19th August 2000*. ACM Press. Available at: http://www.ideo.com/media/info.asp?x=6

And finally, all the works converged in their desire to critique conventions of architectural design practice through productive methods. The exhibits were physical statements but ones that did not seek to be understood as demonstrations or applications of pre-existing theoretical ideas. Rather these were provisional works, which registered the importance of discovery in the process of production. Each piece was an example of the materialisation of the spatial imagination in action.

An accompanying catalogue played a key role in providing a more focused and complementary view of each of the 15 contributors' works in progress. In the editorial we offered a framework for thinking about the ways in which the cluster's research interests ran through the different practices, methods and works in the exhibition. And through image and text, each cluster member contributed their own perspective on the various ways in which the spatial imagination is both a tool for investigation and proposition in the design of objects and spaces.[11] In a symposium, 'Spaces of Exchange', held at CABE, with speakers from the cluster, partners Kate Trant and Greg Cowan, and Nathalie Weadick from The Architecture Foundation, Daisy Froud from 'Agents of Change' and developer Lee Mallett, we discussed in more detail the role of the imagination in both academic and professional design research.

Reflections

Spatial Imagination in Design as a prototype

Spatial Imagination in Design has enabled us to generate a new understanding of the 'prototype' in contrast to its meaning in engineering-based design processes. Taking place in the second workshop of the project, Rawes, together with the artist Hamilton and engineer Jon Rogers, introduced ways in which 'immersive' understandings of spatial design related to the imagination. Hamilton and Rogers introduced the group to the notion of 'prototyping', a discussion which the design consultancy IDEO has transformed out of the rigid rules of testing in laboratory experimentation into testing design products in the everyday world.[12] Taking pictures of the everyday with throw-away cameras, the group developed a series of spatial narratives in response to three museum collections which showed how prototyping is a design activity that is not just demarcated by scientific or technical procedures of iteration. Instead, this workshop revealed how spatial imagination is embedded throughout the design process.

The role of the prototype is evident on a number of different levels; for example, the prototype is a kind of aesthetic structure for the production of the design drawing, text or model. Rogers' exhibit in the exhibition was a plinth that contained a digital animation of a foggy walk in Scotland and showed how an Ordnance Survey map operates as a disfunctional prototype of the actual geographical location when it is used to navigate a walk in inclement weather [Figure 8]. Alternatively, Yeoryia Manolopoulou's model of shutters for a house in Greece operates as both a 1:1 model in itself, but also as prototype for the actual construction of this structure in the building [Figure 9].

Figures 8 and 9,
left and right

Figure 8, Jon Rogers, 'Unmarked Path', Spatial Imagination, (London: The Domo Baal Gallery, 2006).
Photograph: David Cross of Cornford & Cross

Figure 9, Yeoryia Manolopoulou, 'Shutters, House F', Spatial Imagination, (London: The Domo Baal Gallery, 2006). Photograph: David Cross of Cornford & Cross

Moreover, the project showed that prototyping also constructs relationships between the activities of the designer and user. First, the designer's intentions provide an initial prototype. Second, multiple variations of the prototype are generated by the user's own interaction with the building, space or environment. Third, each contributor's exhibit represents a distinct, original prototype of spatial imagination during the project, one that also endures beyond the boundaries of the 1-year project in the development of an individual's spatial design practice or theory. Fourth, the project showed that the exhibition is an additional, sometimes

[13] ARTS AND HUMANITIES
RESEARCH COUNCIL, 2003.
*The RAE and Research in the
Creative & Performing Arts*
[online]. Available at: http://
www.ahrb.ac.uk/about/policy/
response/the_rae_research_in_
the_creative_performing_arts.
asp

[14] For an extended discussion
of points one and two see for
example: RENDELL, J., 2004.
*Architectural Research and
Disciplinarity*. ARQ, 8(4),
pp. 141-7.

[15] SCHÖN, D., 1987. *Educating
the Reflective Practitioner*
[online]. Available at: http://
educ.queensu.ca/~ar/schon87.
htm

difficult, prototype of the design process. As a result, the cluster generated multiple ideas, artefacts, tests or prototypes through its activities, further underscoring the material diversity of the imagination in spatial design and the world at large.

Spatial Imagination in Design as research

The year of research activities comprising Spatial Imagination in Design serve to embed the following observations concerning interdisciplinary and practice-led research.

First, the value of practice-led research is its role in questioning and redefining modes of research traditionally developed in the sciences and humanities. In 1993, The Royal College of Art, London, published Christopher Frayling's paper 'Research in Art and Design', where Frayling put forward a tri-partite model of 'in', 'through', 'for', in order to clarify the complex set of relationships between design and research. In the last decade, research 'for' and 'into' design has developed non-problematically, partly because such work can easily be positioned within existing disciplinary modes in science and the humanities. Research 'through' design has produced more debate and is currently being further developed in discussions around the relation between theory and practice. In 1999 the AHRB put forward a set of criteria for assessing the extent to which practice-led funding proposals could qualify as research. This required that a proposal be defined according to four elements – questions, methods, contexts and modes of dissemination. This has been widely adopted across the research community as a 'definition' of practice-led research.[13] However, it has become increasingly clear, and the creative processes adopted by the practitioners in Spatial Imagination in Design clearly indicate, that practice-led work differs from more traditional 'academic' text-based research in its sequencing of the four elements of research processes.[14] For example, in much practice-led research, the process operates through generative or propositional modes, producing works that may then be reflected upon, along the lines of Donald Schön's 'Reflection in action'.[15]

Second, research 'through' architectural design operates between the architectural profession and its educational and academic counterpart – the university. This is a site of intersection that often operates according to differing value systems, and so it is vitally important that we examine carefully the expectations and methodologies of design research in these different contexts and for these divergent user groups. For example, while 'critique of concepts' might count for an academic audience as the

¹⁶ KRISTEVA, J., 1998.
Institutional interdisciplinarity
in theory and practice: an
interview. In: A. COLES and A.
DEFERT, (eds.) *The Anxiety of
Interdisciplinarity, De-, Dis-,
Ex-*, vol. 2. Black Dog
Publishing, pp. 3-21 & pp. 5-6.

¹⁷ For an extended discussion
of points three and four see for
example: RENDELL, J., 2006.
*Art and Architecture: A Place
Between*. IB Tauris.

most original form of new knowledge to be gained in design research, the 'application of concepts' might be considered more viable to a client based in industry. The precise mechanisms, therefore, for exchanging knowledge between different parties in the production of new research understandings cannot be underestimated.

Third, research aims and methodologies vary across different forms of practice-led research, namely art, design and architecture, as well as those of theoreticians who view writing and criticism as a form of practice-led research. For example, as became apparent in the development of works for the Spatial Imagination exhibition, artists and designers are frequently interested in gaining different kinds of knowledge and do so through diverging forms of acquisition and dissemination. If traditionally, design has tended to define its methodology in response to a brief, where the creative outcome is the solution to a posed problem, as a growing number of artists adopt design-like working methods, producing objects that 'look like' designed artefacts, the distinctions between art, design and architecture are becoming more complicated. At the same time, designers are taking on the basic tenets of conceptual art, which we might define as a critique of the terms of engagement of the brief, and so moving towards modes of practice traditionally associated with fine art, and so further increasing the complexity of interdisciplinary practices.

Fourth, it is important that we define carefully what the terms interdisciplinarity and multidisciplinarity mean in the current research context. In both academic and arts-based contexts, the term interdisciplinarity is increasingly used interchangeably with multidisciplinarity, yet historically the terms have been used to refer to quite different modes of research: multidisciplinarity to a mode of research where a number of disciplines are present but that each maintains its own distinct identity and methods; interdisciplinarity to a mode of research where individuals move between and across disciplines and in so doing question the basic tenets of their own disciplinary procedures, including legitimate objects of study, contexts, terminologies and methodologies. Given the complex terrain of interdisciplinary practice noted above in point three, it is vital that the critical context for interdisciplinarity as defined in 1998 by Julia Kristeva is maintained.¹⁶ Interdisciplinary work is not simply procedural but demanding emotionally and politically, as well as intellectually, because this way of working requires researchers and practitioners to be open to transformation and change.¹⁷

Additional Reading

ABBOTT, E., 1983. *A Flatland: a Romance of Many Dimensions [1884]*. HarperCollins.

ARAGON, L., 1994. *Paris Peasant [1926]*. Exact Change.

BAL, M., 2001. *Louise Bourgeois' Spider: the Architecture of Art-Writing*. University of Chicago Press.

BARTHES, R., 2000. *Camera Lucida: Reflections on Photography*. Vintage.

BENJAMIN, W., 1992. *One Way Street*. Verso.

BLOOMER, J., 1993. *Architecture and the Text: the (S)crypts of Joyce and Piranesi*. Yale University Press.

BRETON, A., 1987. *Mad Love*. University of Nebraska Press.

BURGIN, V., 2004. *The Remembered Film*. Reaktion Books.

BURKE, E., 1970. *A Philosophical Enquiry into the Origin of Our Ideas of the Sublime and the Beautiful [1757]*. Scholar Press.

BYATT, A. S., 2001. *'Old Tales, New Forms', On Histories and Stories*. Vintage.

CALVINO, I., 1997. *'Cybernetics and Ghosts', The Literature Machine*. Vintage.

CARDIFF, J., 1999. *The Missing Voice*. Artangel.

FEHN, S., 1962. *Pavilion of the Nordic Nations*. Venice Biennale.

BURNS GAMARD, E., 2000. *Kurt Schwitters' Merzbau: the Cathedral of Erotic Misery*. Princeton Architectural Press.

HANKINS, T. L. and SILVERMAN, R. J., 1995. *Instruments and the Imagination*. Princeton University Press.

KANT, I., 1974. *Anthropology from a Pragmatic Point of View*. Masrtin Nijhoff.

IGLESIAS, C., 1999. *Tilted Hanging Ceiling* [exhibition]. Whitechapel Art Gallery. See BLAZWICK, I., (ed.), 2003. *Cristina Iglesias*. London: Whitechapel Art Gallery.

PILE, S., 1999. *The Body and the City*. Routledge.

PROUST, M., 1941. *Remembrance of Things Past*. Chatto and Windus.

SUH, D-H., 1999. Seoul Home [exhibition]. Serpentine Gallery. See, for example, CORRIN, L. G. and M. KWON, (eds.), 2002. Do-Ho Suh. London: Serpentine Gallery.

Spatiality in Design

Dr John Stell, Prof. Lynne Cameron and Prof. Kenneth G Hay,
(University of Leeds)

The Landscape of Spatiality

Spatiality permeates the whole field of design and, if we accept the view
of Johnson-Laird,[1] all thinking, 'The evidence indeed suggests that human
reasoners use functionally spatial models to think about space, but they
also appear to use such models in order to think in general.' Rather than
attempt to encompass all the aspects of the topic, the 'Spatiality in Design'
cluster drew its initial motivation from the observation that there are
new and developing investigations of spatiality outside design that have
considerable potential for use within it. This potential is not only for the
specific contributions that these developments can make, but also for their
role within the use of spatiality as an organising principle for design
research as a whole. The cluster activities were organised to explore these
and other new developments in spatiality in the context of design, and
also to generate interactions among participants which would allow ideas
for new research directions to emerge.

In this first section of this chapter we give an overview of three specific
aspects of spatiality which provided the cluster's starting point. These
come from computer science and mathematics, from linguistics, and
from fine art, and are explored in the three subsections below. In the two
subsequent sections, we summarise the activities promoted by the cluster
and conclude with an area for research suggested by one activity.

Qualitative space

The computer is a valuable tool for many design processes – it operates
in general by manipulating virtual objects. That is, objects are given
numerical descriptions and by working with these, the designer is given
the illusion of working with objects themselves. The kinds of space

[1] JOHNSON-LAIRD, P. N.,
1996. Space to Think. In: P.
BLOOM, M.A. PETERSON, L.
NADEL, & M.F. GARRETT,
(eds.) *Language and Space*.
Cambridge, MA: MIT. Press,
pp. 437-462.

² SPUYBROEK, L., 2004. NOX: *Machining Architecture*. London: Thames and Hudson.

³ BOOTHBY, W. M., 1986. *An Introduction to Differentiable Manifolds and Reimannian Geometry*, 2ⁿᵈ (ed.) San Diego: Academic Press, pp. 4.

⁴ EVANS, R., 1995. *The Projective Cast. Architecture and Its Three Geometries*. Cambridge, MA: MIT Press, pp. 352.

⁵ NOWAK, G., 1996. The Concepts of Space and Continuum in Poincaré's Analysis Situs. In: J-L GREFFE, G. HEINZMANN & K. LORENZ, (eds.) *Henri Poincaré: Science et philosophie. Congrès International, Nancy, 1994*. Berlin: Akademie Verlag, pp. 365-387.

thus manipulated are, however, quite restricted. The simplest case is the two- or three-dimensional grid in which points are specified by numerical coordinates. Within this framework, elaborate curves and surfaces as well as lines and planes are sets of points which can be readily represented and manipulated. In computer graphics and in computer-assisted design this approach to space has been remarkably effective, and the computer harnessed to the numerical representation of space has enabled new shapes to be used in design. As Spuybroek[2] writes of one architectural project, 'In the past this kind of curvature would have been inconceivable in architecture. . . the mathematical information of the complex geometry can be passed directly from the computer to the CNC machine.'

The space captured by the grid-like numerical coordinate model is generally called 'Euclidean space' although, as Boothby[3] reminds us, 'Euclid and the geometers before the seventeenth century did not think of the Euclidean plane or three-dimensional space. . . as pairs or triples of real numbers.' Lines and planes were originally entities in their own right, rather than sets of coordinate points. Whichever approach is taken, however, there have long been objections to the idea that Euclidean space is a good model of the space we experience. These objections are not just of interest to philosophers, but are of practical relevance to designers creating physical objects and environments. Euclidean space is a metric space, once a unit of measurement is agreed there is a good notion of distance between any two points. But, in many everyday spatial situations, for example moving about in a room or drinking a cup of coffee, these exact distances play no role; they are artefacts of the way the world is represented, not intrinsic features. Mach, quoted in Evans,[4] held that, 'Haptic space, or the space of touch, has as little in common with the metric space as the space of vision. Like the latter, it also is anisotropic and non-homogeneous.' The discrepancy between experienced space and the classical mathematical formalisation of space also concerned Poincaré, quoted in Nowak,[5] 'Space when considered independently of our measuring instruments, has therefore neither metric nor projective properties.'

Representations of space within the computer require some form of mathematical formalisation. Such formalisations of new kinds of space are relevant to design in that they permit computer implementations which can then be used by designers. One specific example is qualitative space. This does not deal with points or distances, instead it uses relationships between regions which model common linguistic descriptions: that one object is next to another, that something encloses something else, that one region is separated from another and so on. The idea of space based on

[6] STELL, J. G., 2000. Boolean connection algebras; a new approach to the region-connection calculus. *Artificial Intelligence*, 122, pp. 111-136.

[7] LEFSCHETZ, S., 1949. *Introduction to Topology.* Princeton: Princeton University Press, pp. 3.

[8] POSTON, T., 1971. *Fuzzy Geometry.* PhD thesis, University of Warwick.

[9] BURKE, K., 1945. *A Grammar of Motives.* New York: Prentice Hall.

[10] CAMERON, L., 1999. Operationalising metaphor for applied linguistic research. In: L. CAMERON & G. LOW, (eds.) *Researching and Applying Metaphor.* Cambridge: Cambridge University Press, pp. 3-28.

[11] LAKOFF, G., 1993. The Contemporary Theory of Metaphor. *In:* A. ORTONY, (ed.) *Metaphor and Thought,* 2nd ed. New York: Cambridge University Press, pp. 202-251.

regions in this way has a long history, outlined by Stell,[6] and is now often referred to as mereotopology. This name indicates that the relation of parthood (studied in mereology) plays a fundamental role. There are now a number of formalisations of aspects of mereotopology, and studies of how to implement reasoning with spatial relations, but there seems to have been little awareness from fields such as design and architecture of the work in this area and its potential applications.

Mereotopology is quite different from topology which provides a mathematical notion of space which is also less detailed or less rigid than Euclidean space, but which, in the case of 'general topology', is based fundamentally on points. Lefschetz[7] notes, 'Topology begins where sets are implemented with some cohesive properties enabling one to define continuity.' The cohesion may be achieved in various ways and consists of additional structure which can be thought of rather like glue sticking the points together. Mereotopology proposes an alternative, one justification for which is that in our experience of space points play no role.

Another example of a space motivated to some extent by considerations of human experience is Poston's notion of 'fuzzy geometry' or 'tolerance space'.[8] This deals with the issue that at a certain level of detail we may be unable to distinguish things and builds a theory of space on a relation of indistinguishability. This and other novel mathematical formulations of space reflect spatial properties of the world that designers have to address more fully than some of the more well-known accounts and one of the aims of the cluster was to raise awareness among design researchers of work in this area.

Metaphor and spatiality in discourse

The second of the cluster's motivations came from metaphor. Metaphor is a core and basic human process and ability in which one thing is seen in terms of another.[9] Metaphor involves language, thought and emotions as it requires us to find similarities across difference.[10]

Metaphor then is a human resource that appears indispensable in discourse around abstract ideas, such as space and spatiality. It a key tool employed in talk and text as people express their ideas and as they negotiate understandings with others. Some would go further and suggest that our understandings are sometimes metaphorically structured and cannot exist or develop without metaphor.[11] Metaphors become conventionalised as ways of talking about whole domains, so that, for example, success is characterised in terms of movement upwards through

¹² GIBBS, R. W., 1994. *The Poetics of Mind: Figurative Thought, Language and Understanding*. Cambridge: Cambridge University Press.

¹³ EVANS, V., 2004. *The Structure of Time: Language, Meaning and Temporal Cognition*. Amsterdam: John Benjamins.

¹⁴ CAMERON, L., 2007. Patterns of metaphor use in reconciliation talk. *Discourse & Society*, 18(2), pp. 197-222.

¹⁵ CBABALLERO, M. d. R. R., 2003. Metaphor and genre: The presence and role of metaphor in the building review. *Applied Linguistics*, 24(2), pp. 154-167.

¹⁶ CAMERON, L. & STELMA, J., 2004. Metaphor clusters in discourse. *Journal of Applied Linguistics*, 1(2), pp. 7-36.

space, as in expressions such as 'climbing the career ladder', 'moving on up', 'reaching the dizzy heights of fame'. Here, space is used as a source domain for metaphors, and theories of metaphor that emphasise the embodied nature of cognition would predict that our physical experiences of moving through space, of orientation in space, of occupying space and of our material being serve as the basis for metaphorical description of less concrete experiences and ideas.¹² We speak of time in terms of space, when we say that 'the future lies in front of/ahead', when we 'put a bad experience behind us'.¹³ We speak of 'breathing space', 'emotional space', 'mental spaces' and 'safe spaces', this latter meaning trust between former enemies in a post-conflict context.¹⁴ Our physical experience of space will be reflected in our use of spatial metaphors.

Space and spatiality are abstract concepts and so are themselves talked of metaphorically. Caballero¹⁵ has studied metaphor use in building reviews produced by architects, and found design processes described in terms of 'making music or textiles'.

The architect's interpretation of the spirit of the place is restrained and lyrical, and the delicacy with which he has stitched the new to the old recalls Foster's work at the Royal Academy.

Strong image metaphors were frequently used in descriptions of buildings.

Fixed glass skylights span each of the side arches; beneath those, a bonelike cage of steel ribs, controlled by pneumatic struts, can open and close like an eyelid, revealing the sunken, tile-encrusted orb of the IMAX to the outdoors.

We would also expect to find metaphors used in negotiations between design professionals and lay people, for example, designers and clients or users of space, or between design and other professionals. Critical points in talk are often signalled by clusters of metaphors as people attempt to resolve misunderstandings or explain complexities.¹⁶ Metaphor analysis offers a tool for investigating discourse and a window on concepts and understandings.

Artistic potentials of post-industrial space

The involvement of artists in urban space was the origin of the cluster's third area of motivation. In a recent study of urban space and representation, Maria Balshaw and Liam Kennedy observe that:

[17] BALSHAW, M. & KENNEDY, L., 2000. *Urban Space and Representation*. London: Pluto.

[18] FOUCAULT, M., 1980. *Power/ Knowledge: Selected Interviews and Other Writings 1972-1977*. New York: Pantheon.

[19] LEFEBVRE, H., 1991. *The Production of Space*. Oxford: Blackwell.

[20] SOJA, E., 1989. *Postmodern Geographies: The Reassertion of Space in Critical Social Theory*. London: Verso.

'. . .the city, as a universal object or category of analysis, has been demythologised and positioned as a site of spatial formations produced across diverse discursive regimes and everyday practices.'[17]

Where previously, the city had been studied in terms of social history, demographics and architectural history, space, and in the context of this paper, urban space has become increasingly reconfigured as a metaphor for investigations resultant from the convergence of the humanities and social sciences, in the wake of the post-structuralist analyses of Michel Foucault, Giles Deleuze and Felix Guattari, Homi Bhabha, Fredric Jameson and others. The new interdisciplinarity, itself reflected in the academic exchange within this cluster, spans mathematics and physics, linguistics and art practices, computer science and architecture. New generations of vocabularies are reframing questions of identity, positionality, diaspora, interstitiality, and these convergences have not (yet) resulted in a unitary method, lexicon or focus. Perhaps this is as it should be. In the ongoing process of (inter)disciplinary repositioning, urbanism too has embraced the freedom of malleability.

Where space, in the common understanding of pragmatic everyday life, is simply 'just there', as a neutral and ill-defined arena for our physical being, for Foucault and others, it is to be seen as anything but transparent or natural. Rather, it is the site where social power and knowledge are literally constructed and continually reconstructed.[18] Henri Lefebvre and Edward Soja make this aspect more explicit, describing how space becomes 'filled with politics and ideology' which both ascribe and conceal the contradictions of global capitalism.[19,20]

For Lefebvre, the material practices of social life (which are, in turn, 'spatial practices') actually 'construct' spatiality such that the traditional dualities of physical space and mental space are superceded in the very production of social space. What is useful in the current context in Lefebvre's conception, is the prioritisation of the visible and legible in spatial interpretations, 'Reading follows production in all cases except those in which space is produced especially in order to be read.'[19] Urbanism is primarily an experience (lived and social), which only later gives rise to its interpretation. Both Soja and Lefebvre are concerned that the social reality of urbanism is eclipsed by the 'will to power' of theory. In such instances, 'Social space folds into mental space, into diaphanous concepts of spatiality which all too often take us away from materialised social realities.'[17,20]

Aims and objectives for the cluster

As we have seen, mathematicians and computer scientists, linguists and artists are exploring aspects of spatiality which have resonances with the uses of spatiality in design. Our perception that these explorations were not widely known in the design world led us to propose a cluster with the following objectives:

- Promote novel interactions and partnerships among design researchers, and enable existing research questions to be seen from new viewpoints through the use of spatial concepts as an organising principle for design research.
- Introduce new spatial ideas into design (from areas including artificial intelligence, applied linguistics and fine art), and to develop a cross-disciplinary community of designers and experts in aspects of spatiality from other disciplines.
- Map out the topography of spatiality in design: drawing in people and groups related to spatiality research and proposing new research challenges for design in the 21st century.

Our aim was to achieve these objectives through a series of meetings and other means of communication, supported by the development of electronic resources. In the next section we describe some of the cluster's activities, and focus on two areas which were not originally planned as part of our activity, but which emerged as important during the period of cluster operation.

Activities

Meetings

The principal activity of the cluster was the organisation of meetings bringing together interested parties. There were six of these events and they were designed to inform the participants of areas of research and also to stimulate interaction through a mixture of informal discussions and more organised working groups. We held four, half-day, meetings in February, May, October and December and two longer 2-day events: a workshop in April and our Spatiality Marketplace in July.

The April workshop

The April workshop was held at the Round Foundry media centre in Leeds. We do not have space here to summarise all the various parts of the programme, so we, rather unfairly, single out two topics. One of these was

[21] LABAN, R., 1966. *Choreutics*, 2nd ed. London: MacDonald and Evans Ltd.

[22] HERNANDEZ, D., 1994. Qualitative representation of spatial knowledge. *Lecture Notes in Artificial Intelligence*, vol. 804. Berlin: Springer Verlag.

space in choreography. Jim Schofield from Bedford Interactive exhibited a large-scale model of a polyhedron which he explained overcame some of the difficulties with the icosahedron used by Laban[21] to describe a dancer's movements. He can be seen holding a much smaller model in Figure 1. It was noted in the discussions that using polyhedra in this way was similar to the use of qualitative directions in geographical information,[22] and that there was potential here for interaction between the choreographers and the community examining qualitative spatial reasoning in Artificial Intelligence. The other topic to note here was the recording of motion in three-dimensional space. Two demonstrations provided hands-on experience for cluster members: *3D drawing* (Ben Hammett) and *3D gesture for performing arts* (Kia Ng). This was the first occasion that most of the participants had seen the three-dimensional drawing system which become a particular focus for later activities and is described in more detail below.

Figure 1, Jim Schofield at our April workshop

The Spatiality marketplace

Our main meeting was a 2-day event held at the Yorkshire Sculpture Park. The name 'marketplace' signalled that participants would bring their own expertise and problems in spatiality. We hoped that they would leave having learnt new ways to address their problems while having imparted their own spatial expertise in exchange. To facilitate this interchange, we allocated more time to group activities than in our other events while still providing a stimulating range of presentations. A list of the presentations gives a good indication of the wide range of topics that were covered. The speakers were: Prof. Mike Worboys (Maine) 'Spatio-temporal information representation for a pervasive computational world'; Prof. Kushi Katsuhiko (Kyoto) 'The need to explore across borders: finding the lost piece of the design process'; Claude Heath (London) 'Drawing in three dimensions'; Prof. Tom McLeish (Leeds) 'High dimensional spatiality and design in molecular biology'; Daniel Banaczek (Krakow) 'Embodied space in the physical environment'.

Topics

As a result of the cluster meetings, two specific topics emerged as important and were developed by cluster participants outside the meetings. One of these, the convergence of high dimensional thinking with interior design, was exactly the kind of unexpected interaction that we hoped the cluster would generate; the other was drawing in three-dimensional space. This exploration of drawing had been initiated before the cluster, but it was only through the cluster activities that new people were involved and the analysis of the way the artists used spatial metaphor when talking about their three-dimensional drawings was articulated.

Interior design

One of the cluster's aims was to bring together designers and others working with space to generate new interactions that would result in the transfer of novel ways of thinking about space from one discipline to another. This was most notably achieved in the interaction we enabled between Prof. Tom McLeish, from the School of Physics and Astronomy at Leeds University, and students of Interior Design at Leeds College of Art and Design. This arose from the participation of Tom McLeish and Eleni Tracada, from Leeds College of Art and Design, at our Spatiality Marketplace. In October 2005, as part of a module for the Year 3 interior design students, Tom McLeish gave a presentation on complexity in design, drawing on his own experience of spatial thinking in research. This contributed to a module designed to facilitate and reinforce students reading and understanding of buildings and spaces. Working in teams, the students were required to explore, through visual, historical and theoretical research, two selected interiors, one monumental and one small-scale. Feedback from the students showed that they valued the input from Tom McLeish, and Eleni Tracada has written about the experience.[23] The students' work on this module formed part of the College's contribution to GIDE – the Group for International Design Education – an international consortium of higher education design schools, which work together in order to enrich the experience of students in the areas of

[23] TRACADA, E., 2006. Reading buildings and translating places: 'a place to. . . '. In: J. G. STELL, L. CAMERON and K. HAY, (eds.) *Explorations in Spatiality*. Leeds: Spatiality in Design, Chapter 3.

[24] HAMMETT, B. J., 2005. *Drawing in 3D Space.* Final Year Undergraduate Project Report, School of Computing, University of Leeds.

[25] PATRIZIO, A., 2003. Perspicuous by Their Absence: the Drawings of Claude Heath. *In*: A. KINGSTON, (ed.) *What is Drawing.* London: Black Dog Publishing Ltd., pp. 32–57.

3D, architectural and interior design. Besides the Leeds College of Art and Design, the group consists of four other main partner colleges in Belgium, Italy, the Netherlands and Germany. Selected work from the module was exhibited in February 2006 in Breda, the Netherlands.

Three-dimensional drawing

Drawing typically marks a flat, two-dimensional, surface and these marks can represent spaces of three and higher dimensions. This use of one kind of space to communicate features of another is an important aspect of spatiality. A similar situation can be seen in the use of spatial metaphor, where the experience of the space used metaphorically affords the conveying of ideas from another domain. The cluster explored both these topics through the involvement of artists in a system for three-dimensional drawing, and a subsequent analysis of how they used spatial metaphor in talking about their experiences. We used a system built in the School of Computing at the University of Leeds by Ben Hammett.[24] During the cluster's year, two artists spent several days making drawings: Claude Heath, who is known internationally for his work in novel approaches to drawing,[25] and Patricia Cain a PhD student from Glasgow School of Art. At the end of the year, for our final meeting in December, Lynne Cameron conducted interviews with the artists which were later transcribed and their use of spatial metaphor analysed. The results of this process have been described in more detail below.

The drawing system is shown in Figure 2. The artist works within a volume, roughly a 2m cube, containing the low table shown in the figure. A drawing instrument, which can be seen on this table, is linked by a cable to a magnetic tracking system. The box shown suspended from the ceiling in the figure creates a magnetic field, and the drawing instrument is able to detect its position within this field and the trajectories of the drawing instrument held in the artist's hand are represented in a virtual space on the computer. These trajectories are displayed in a visual representation of the virtual space on a monitor, the large screen in the illustration, which is capable of creating a three-dimensional illusion when the appropriate stereo glasses are used. The lines in virtual space are represented in an internal format in the system, but this can be exported to produce a VRML file. These VRML versions do not fully preserve the appearance of the drawings, but using a VRML viewer, the images can be manipulated in three-dimensions in a web browser.

Figures 2 and 3,
left and right

Figure 2, System for 3D drawing, School of Computing, University of Leeds
Figure 3, 'Ben Nevis' 3D drawing, Claude Heath 2005

26 CAMERON, L., HEATH, C. & CAIN, P., 2006. The Practice of Drawing in Three Dimensions. *In:* J. G. STELL, L. CAMERON and K. HAY, (eds.) *Explorations in Spatiality.* Leeds: Spatiality in Design, Chapter 2.

27 Tacitus Research Project. Available at: www.eca.ac.uk/ tacitus. *Hands On: Concept Innovation.* Available at: www.eca.ac.uk/hands_on

Some of the drawings made by Claude Heath are illustrated in Figures 3, 4, and 5. Of course, in two-dimensional images we can only show one view of the three-dimensional drawing. Figure 3 shows a drawing made from a stereo-pair of photographs of Ben Nevis. Some of the series of Ben Nevis drawings were included in Heath's exhibition 'In Aere Aedificare, Built in the Air' at the Galerie für Zeichnung, Berlin, 2005. The image in Figure 4 was transcribed from an astronomical atlas of the Universe which was itself printed to be viewed with red and green glasses to give the illusion of three dimensionality. The final image of the three was also constructed by a transcription process, this time from a musical score. In this case the three planes visible in the drawing were drawn in the same physical location, but the virtual space supporting the drawing was rotated in between drawing each one. Further illustrations of drawings made with the system can be seen in Cameron.[26]

There have been a number of other systems for drawing in three-dimensions. One is the 'Hands On' (originally known as Tacitus) project at Edinburgh.[27] This differs from the system we used in providing haptic feedback, and consequently requiring the artist to draw on a smaller physical scale. Our system did allow drawing with whole-body movements, and produced marks that were relatively crude. This attribute of the marks did not seem to be a disadvantage, and the artists found that it was very straightforward to begin making marks in a direct way.

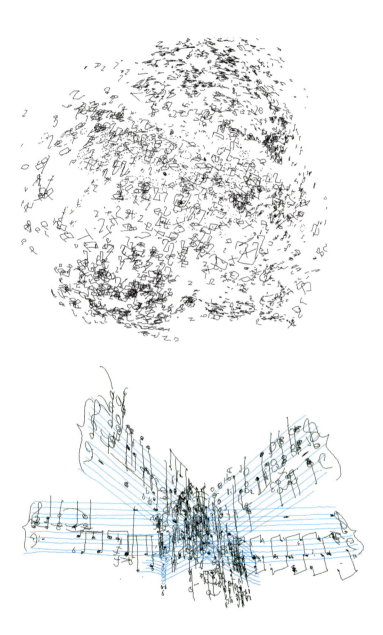

Figures 4 and 5,
top and bottom

Figure 4, 'Universe' 3D drawing, Claude Heath, 2005
Figure 5, 'Quest (1935)' 3D drawing, Claude Heath, 2005

Conclusions and Further Work

To conclude we outline our vision for the way forward in just one topic. Design depends on effective communication among the various parties involved. New developments in technology have provided new ways to produce and to experience the visual, but such technological advances do not automatically produce advances in communication. The significance of our three-dimensional drawing for design is that drawing is a primary means of visual communication and one which is still of enormous importance, especially informal sketching and even doodling where ideas are fluid and evolving. The three-dimensional is often seen as delivering greater fidelity for representations, and much virtual reality work and computer modelling is also driven by a desire to construct representations which appear close to our perception of the real world. Our experience suggests that the opportunity of the three-dimensional is perhaps not in realism but as a support for new notations which can communicate effectively without necessarily being representational. One area for further exploration is thus the ways in which the ability to make three-dimensional marks provides a new means of exploring spatial concepts and communicating them. In the context of mapping as a process of collecting 'found marks' in space, one possibility is indicated by drawings as illustrated in Figure 6. These are constructed by the artist moving through space and the relationship of these to three-dimensional drawing is considered in.[28]

[28] Stell, J. G., 2006. Drawing in Three Dimensions. *In*: J. G. STELL, L. CAMERON and K. HAY, (eds.) *Explorations in Spatiality*. Leeds: Spatiality in Design, Chapter 1.

Overall the cluster provided an exciting year, but one of the greatest challenges was how to generate concrete proposals for work, and specific questions for research, from a topic as general as spatiality. Our events clearly succeeded in generating new and unexpected interactions and ideas for many of the participants, but to get beyond the excitement of new ideas to the formulation of concrete plans to work with the ideas was often difficult. The ideas that we did follow up proved sufficient to generate fruitful activities, so the fact that many apparently promising notions fell on stony ground has not been too much of a problem. In this

Figure 6, 'Bingley map: places 14 - 26' digital image, John Stell, 2006

[29] STELL, J. G., CAMERON, L. & HAY, K. G., (eds.), 2006. *Explorations in Spatiality*. Leeds: Spatiality in Design.

[30] Spatiality in Design, proposal for a SiD website. Available at: www.leeds.ac.uk/SiD.

chapter, we have only been able to outline a few of the cluster's activities. For more information, there is our book *Explorations in Spatiality*,[29] which contains essays expanding on the activities in three-dimensional drawing, interior design, and post-industrial space; there is also our website.[30]

Additional Reading

BANACZEK, D. & SZREBER, J., 2004. *Nowa Sztuka W Nowej Hucie* (New Art in Nowa Huta).

BLOOM, P., PETERSON, M. A., NADEL, L. & GARRETT, M. F., (eds.), 1996. *Language and Space*. Cambridge, MA: MIT Press.

BRUNO, G., 2002. *Atlas of Emotion. Journeys in Art, Architecture and Film*. New York: Verso.

CAMERON, L., 2003. *Metaphor in Educational Discourse*. Continuum.

DODGE, M. & KITCHIN, R., 2001. *Atlas of Cyberspace*. Addison-Wesley.

DODGE, M. & KITCHIN, R., 2001. *Mapping Cyberspace*. London: Routledge.

DOYLE, M. et al., (eds.), 2002. *Drawing on Space*. London: The Drawing Room.

EISENMAN, P., 1999. *Diagram Diaries*. London: Thames and Hudson.

GÄRDENFORS, P., 2000. *Conceptual Spaces: The Geometry of Thought*. Cambridge, MA: MIT Press.

PENZ, F., RADICK, G. & HOWELL, R., (eds.), 2004. *SPACE in Science, Art and Society*. Cambridge: Cambridge University Press.

WILLATS, J., 1997. *Art and Representation. New Principles in the Analysis of Pictures*. Princeton: Princeton University Press.

Discovery in Design: People-centred Computational Issues

Prof. Ian Parmee,[1] Prof. Lisa Hall,[2] Prof. John Miles,[3] Dr Jan Noyes,[4]
Christopher Simons[4] and Dr David Smith,[5] (University of the West of
England,[1] University of Cambridge,[2] University of Cardiff,[3] University of
Bristol,[4] University of Wales[5])

Overview

This chapter introduces the activities and associated output of the
'Discovery in Design: People-centred Computational Issues (DiD)' cluster
established in March 2005 under the UK EPSRC 'Designing for the 21ˢᵗ
Century' Initiative. Over a 12-month period this highly multidisciplinary
cluster has investigated the requirements for the development of generic
user-centric computational systems that support the early conceptual
stages of design. The DiD cluster objective has been to identify
primary research aspects concerning the development of people-centred
computational design environments that engender concept and knowledge
discovery across diverse disciplines and domains. Such systems would
represent a new generation of generic computational support for
conceptual design relating to many disciplines.

Introduction

Current computer-aided design and decision support tools support
the later, well-defined stages of design where a product or objective is
physical, tangible and comprehensible. More abstract concept formulation
and development is poorly supported, especially where uncertainty is an
inherent characteristic. Furthermore, computer-aided design tends to be
domain specific with little or no exploitation of cross-domain experience.
Research and development agendas to redress both these imbalances are
required.

[1] GOEL, A. K., 1997. Design, analogy and creativity. *Intelligent Systems and their Applications*, 12(3), pp. 62-70.

[2] SISK, G. M., MILES, J. C., MOORE, C. J., 2003. Designer-centred development of a GA-based DSS for conceptual design of buildings. *Journal of Computing in Civil Engineering*, 17(3), pp. 159-166.

[3] PARMEE, I. C., BONHAM, C. R., 2000. Towards the support of innovative conceptual design through interactive designer/evolutionary computing strategies. *Artificial Intelligence for Engineering Design, Analysis and Manufacturing*, 14, pp. 3-16.

[4] MILES, J. C., FOLEY, A. & MOORE, C. J., 2000. Metaphors and cost significance in a conceptual design decision support system. In: G. GUDNASON, (ed.) *Construction Information Technology*, IBRI Reykjavik, pp. 640-649.

[5] GERO, J. S., 1998. Conceptual designing as a sequence of situated acts. *In*: I. SMITH, (ed.) *Artificial Intelligence in Structural Engineering*. Berlin: Springer, pp. 165-177.

[6] MILES, J. C. & SCHLAICH, J., 2005. Conceptual design - how it can be improved. *Structural Engineering International*, 15(4), pp. 122-128.

[7] SU, N. P., 1990. *The Principles of Design*. New York: Oxford University Press.

The utility of established and emerging computational intelligence, enabling computational technologies and people-centred issues have been investigated across a diverse set of problem domains relating to widely differing disciplines to identify synergies and to separate and distill peculiarities. Collaborations across engineering, drug design, software engineering, biosensors and material design, graphical, media product and wearable technology design have provided a basis for study. Cluster membership has ensured specific expertise in each of these areas with some members active across several. Views and approaches from practitioners and researchers that are not normally considered in the same time-frame and context have thus been investigated.

There is a well-established history of conceptual design research within architecture and engineering literature.[1,2,3,4,5,6,7] Broad aspects of such research have been presented at the various workshops described in this chapter and have been taken into account to varying extents during discussion. Care has been taken, however, not to allow such discipline-specific research to dominate in order to avoid the dampening of new perspectives emerging from the multiple disciplines represented within the cluster.

The strength of the cluster has been in the collaboration of seemingly disparate cognitive disciplines that require a common core expertise to support decision-making processes. The result has been the initial identification of primary aspects of mutually symbiotic design environments that create new potential interfaces for capturing and enabling discovery and innovation.

Why 'People-Centred'?

During the early stages of design and decision making, people play a major role processing both qualitative and quantitative criteria in a manner that they may find difficult to articulate. In this activity, differing dependent problem spaces need to be concurrently considered that is, those relating to:

- underlying variables, constraints and objectives;
- higher, human-based knowledge and experience;
- the environment for which we are designing;
- the people affected by our designs/decisions.

[8] PARMEE, I. C., 2002.
Improving problem definition
through interactive evolutionary
computation. *Artificial
Intelligence for Engineering
Design, Analysis and
Manufacturing*, 16(3),
pp. 185-202.

[9] PARMEE, I. C. &
ABRAHAM, J. R., 2004.
Supporting implicit learning via
the visualisation of coga multi-
objective data. *IEEE Congress
on Evolutionary Computation*,
Portland, 20-23rd June 2004,
pp. 395-402.

In terms of the decision space defined by all possible solutions, aspects that contribute to overall complexity include:

- problem representation;
- number of variable parameters;
- non-linearity and discontinuity;
- high modality that is, many local optima;
- soft and hard constraints;
- multiple conflicting quantifiable objectives;
- qualitative criteria with no machine-based representation.

Inherent uncertainty and poor problem definition initially exacerbate the situation. Preliminary machine-based problem representations may comprise fuzzy concepts and sparse information. Further, representations change as information and knowledge accumulates from initial search and exploration and associated human assimilation. It is this complex, dynamic environment that engenders the discovery of new, sometimes seemingly unrelated information which can lead to innovative and creative solutions to problems.

Human experience plays a major role in terms of meaningful evaluation of data and the introduction of external information. People-centred systems are required that meld such knowledge with machine-based simulation, search and exploration, data processing and data visualisation. The decision maker should become immersed in the system playing a major role in an iterative process of data generation; evaluation and analysis; subsequent design space reformulation and further exploration of the redefined space. Such an interactive environment may lead to the capture of experiential and tacit knowledge within this iterative reformulation process.[8, 9]

Cluster Activities

The cluster's activities have concerned the identification of people-centred computational issues including:

- problem representation and simulation;
- problem space search and exploration;
- data mining and processing;
- computationally intelligent systems;
- machine-based enabling and bridging technologies;
- data visualisation and presentation.

[10] Discovery in Design. Available at: www.ip-cc.org.uk/did

[11] PARMEE, I. C., HALL, A. E., MILES, J. C., NOYES, J. & SIMONS, C., 2006. Discovery in Design: Developing a People-centred Computational Approach. *In: Proceedings of Design 2006 Conference, Dubrovnic*, pp. 595-602.

Complementary investigation of areas of human-computer interaction and cognitive issues have included:

- assimilation of information relating to multi-variate, multi-criteria and constraint relationships;
- knowledge extraction and knowledge capture;
- subjective solution evaluation;
- implicit learning and generation of tacit knowledge;
- supporting innovative and creative thinking.

Cluster workshops

Four, 2-day workshops were held during the 12-month operating life of the research cluster. These involved presentations from industry and academe with associated round-table discussion and sub-group working to address both global and specific issues. This has allowed complex characteristics of each design domain; their people-centred aspects and computational strategies to be identified. Typically, attendance at each workshop comprised delegates from civil and mechanical engineering, biotechnology and the pharmaceutical industry, software and communication engineering, computer science, fashion and media product design. The final cluster event was the evening launch of the Institute for People-centred Computation (IP-CC) and a subsequent round-table meeting on the following day to plan future activities and direction.

More detailed descriptions of the workshop activities can be found at the cluster website[10] and in reference.[11] Final reports from each workshop will be available at the IP-CC website in the near future. These reports have been developed from flip-chart material and the extensive notes of three 'scribes' whose specific task at each workshop was to capture as much information as possible. Brief descriptions of each workshop follow.

Workshop 1

The main objective of workshop 1 was to establish a common language and a mutual understanding of the diverse concepts relating to both discovery and people-centered computation. An initial overview of the cluster's objectives and planned activities was followed by short presentations. Interim discussion and debate highlighted problems with regard to differing terminologies and requirements across the cluster's diverse design processes. Much initial confusion diminished over the first day as a better understanding of each other's domains emerged. The final task of the day was for each delegate to identify primary issues relating to

[12] SIMONS, C. L., PARMEE, I. C. & COWARD, D., 2004. 35 years on: to what extent has software engineering design achieved its goals? IEE Proceedings. *Software*, 150(6), pp. 337-350.

[13] SHAW, D., MILES, J. C. & GRAY, W. A., 2004. Genetic programming within civil engineering. In: I. C. PARMEE, (ed.) *Adaptive Computing in Design and Manufacture* VI. London: Springer-Verlag, pp. 51-62.

[14] SHARMA, B., PARMEE, I. C., WHITTAKER, M. & SEDWELL, A., 2005. Drug Discovery: Exploring the Utility of Cluster Oriented Genetic Algorithms in Virtual Library Design. In: *Proceedings of the IEEE Congress on Evolutionary Computation, Edinburgh, 2-4ᵗʰ September 2005*.

[15] HALL, A. H., 1998. Biosensors. In: R. KELLNER et al, (eds.) *Analytical Chemistry*. Wiley-VCH.

[16] NOYES, J. M., 2001. *Designing for Humans*. Hove: Psychology Press

people-centred computation and design discovery that had arisen during the day. Analysis of these issues revealed a high degree of commonality indicating that the cluster was already grasping primary generic issues. Major aspects were identified and these provided topics for break-out groups on the second day.

Workshop 2

The intention of workshop 2 was to investigate the softer, human-centred aims of the cluster and more detailed descriptions of the problems facing engineering, product, software, drug and sensor designers. The workshop comprised presentations from external speakers and from cluster members followed by extended discussion.

Pat Jordan (Contemporary Trends Institute) focused on lifestyle trends and how they relate to technology and innovation where trends represent the spirit of the times in terms of behaviours, attitudes and lifestyles. Creativity was addressed by Ian Jones (Cardiff University) who suggested that to be creative we may have to work against our training as people may become increasingly creatively redundant as they become more specialised. Chris Simons (Bristol UWE) discussed the complexities of the software design process and the difficulties associated with working with abstract entities that are difficult to design and specify.[12] The weaknesses of early expert systems for civil engineering design were discussed by John Miles (Cardiff University) before he moved on to current applications of evolutionary computing.[13] Chris Jofeh (Ove Arup) addressed issues faced by designers in the industry where tools that collate and appropriately present information are a primary concern. Computational intelligence techniques for the pharmaceutical and biotechnology domains were discussed by Ian Parmee (Bristol UWE)[14] and Lisa Hall (Cambridge University). User interaction is essential to capture chemists' tacit knowledge. Examples of the integration of evolutionary computation with drug design and potential integration with sensor design were presented.[15] Jan Noyes (University of Bristol) concentrated on human factors. Over-automation and removing the human from the loop tends to result in failure, however automate too little and the benefits of a complex system will remain unutilised.[16]

Questions, resulting discussion and round-table sessions over the 2-day period generated much diverse information which was duly recorded by the workshop scribes. Each day ended with a summary of the primary items that had emerged during the day. The presentations in workshop 2 were particularly diverse and wide-ranging which resulted in a considerable number of primary items plus many comments and observations. All of these were noted and collated for further analysis during workshops 3 and 4.

Workshop 3

The intention was to identify:

- stages and/or aspects of the design process that have proved difficult to support computationally;
- gains and losses through attempting to formalise design via specific computational tools;
- our 'wish list' for future computer-aided design systems;
- what, with appropriate research agendas, would be possible in the short, medium and long term taking into consideration the outputs from workshops 1 and 2?

Tom Karen (former director, Ogle Design) an intuitive designer of several UK design icons including the Reliant Scimitar GTE, Bond Bug and the Raleigh Chopper always stores potentially useful information that is processed via his 'butterfly mind' that jumps from one observation to another always attempting to map observed good design onto other, less successful examples. David Smith (University of Wales, Newport) discussed issues elating to the design of human-centred information systems.[17] Designers should think in terms of human purpose rather than business. Simeon Barber (Open University Planetary and Space Sciences Research Institute) presented details of the Beagle 2 Mars Lander design process which involved an interdisciplinary science and engineering team. This presented significant problems relating to transfer of tacit knowledge. Paul Mortenson (Evotec) described objectives and processes relating to drug design. Manual design introduces bias based on user's past experience whereas automation limits design to implementation/strategic issues. Both limit opportunities for creative thinking.

During the round-table discussions that took place over the 2-day period it became apparent that the group's ideas, concepts and understanding were beginning to converge. It was very tempting at this point to disturb this consensus and deepen explorations. However, given the overall objectives of the cluster in terms of the Designing for the 21st Century Initiative (that is, to identify primary research issues for the initial call for funding) and the time left to realise these objectives it was decided to concentrate on what had been achieved.

[17] SMITH, D. J., 2002. Communicating Tacit Knowledge Across Cultures: A Multimedia Archive of The Bankura Dhokra Craft Industry of West Bengal as a Case of the Artificial. In: M. NEGROTTI, (ed.) *The Yearbook of the Artificial*. Bern: Peter Lang.

By the end of the workshop 3, five primary issues had been identified which required concurrent and significant research effort if a generic people-centred computational environment for conceptual design is to be achieved. The five issues are:

1. Knowledge Extraction/Knowledge Capture
2. Search and Exploration
3. Enabling Environment
4. Representation
5. Understanding humans

Workshop 4

The mass of information gathered during the previous three workshops required further collation, analysis and classification. Around 350 relevant comments, ideas and issues had been identified from the scribes' notes and flip charts and these had been classified into 29 groupings as shown in Table 1.

Workshop 4 was devoted to the analysis of this information in terms of the manner in which these groupings relate to the five identified key issues. Ten two-dimensional graphs comprising the constituent couplets of the five key issues were generated (for example, 1-2, 1-3, 1-4, 1-5, 2-3, 2-4, 2-5, 3-4, 3-5, 4-5). With increasing relevance represented on each axis.

These graphs were distributed around three delegate sub-groups (Blue, Green and Orange) who were asked to discuss and then place the numbered groups in the most appropriate positions on each chart. Examples of the completed charts from the differing groups are shown in Figures 1 to 4. These provide a visual aid (Figure 5) for subsequent discussions.

Over the course of the 2-day workshop we identified the main factors associated with each of the five key issues. Results from this preliminary analysis are shown in Table 2.

Figure 5, Display of the 2D representations of the Five Key Issues and 29 classes

1. Learning for example, support of implicit/subconscious learning; learning from nature; discovery and insight; multiple uses – teaching tool?

2. Form for example, Looking good, functioning well, easy to make; aesthetics; patterns – re-use versus blank canvas; perspective in software design.

3. Capturing/extractinge/obtaining knowledge for example, qualitative and tacit knowledge; user experience; formalising designer's internal model; mapping tacit knowledge; capturing disparate types of knowledge.

4. User Support for example, generating hypotheses – induction; pattern recognition – GOOGLE versus Amazon model; questioning element; focus/diversify in response to user action; software agency- based guides that contradict, prompt, confuse?

5. Visualisation and/or Senses Stimulation for example, graphics, visualisation, tactile; non-visual cues; haptic feedback – smells and sounds stimulate creativity?

6. Representation for example, system generated approaches; problem reformulation; evolution of objectives; informal expressions/definition – translation into design space; road-mapping to define problem space; representations at expert and customer level.

7. Evaluation for example, quantative versus qualitative judgement; give something to n experts get n differing answers.

8. End User Issues for example, customer's role in conceptual design (differing disciplines); get under skin of your customers; ethnographic commentator/ anthropological modeller; methods for explaining design to the end user.

9. Multi-users and/or Multi-user Interaction for example, scale and discipline; overall interactive system architecture $\rightarrow$ self adaptive to suit χ scenarios; types of info $\rightarrow$ interdisciplinary requirement/ format – communication between designer and machine; interactions between customers, designers and the system.

10. Re-use/deconstruction/ecology for example, design for consumption/ecology; Un-design environment – deconstruction; re-use and improve.

11. Cooperation and Collaboration for example, cross-field impact; synergy – crossdiscipline learning and re-use; language; transferring ideas; sharing design experiences; allow all stakeholders to interact; transparency across design teams; skill propagation within teams.

12. Interface for example, context dependent stakeholder interface; protocol – who is allowed to do what and when; satisfy access criteria; intuitive to users from disciplines; context provides levels of entry to the system; interface to allow definition of a model via code, numbers, rules, fuzzy logic and so on.

13. Creativity and Innovation for example, thinking nonsense breaks down historical/ cultural barriers; creativity by contradiction; machine-based questioning of user hypotheses/assumptions; modeless software – butterfly mind?; can you search the unknown?

14. History and Traceability for example, historical tracking of all activity, decisions, failures, interesting 'dead-ends'; rhizomic structure; identify areas which have, or have not been, searched.

15. User-centric Issues for example, exciting and engaging design systems; subjective, user-based and machine-based evaluation; multiple contexts/context switching – info that stimulates all senses; user in control but challenged by system; mind meld; 'hive mind'; emotional tagging; design psychology/cognitive aspects.

16. Drivers for example, design influences (demographics/environmental)'

17. Briefs for example, managing open briefs; brief extraction; breaking tight design brief.

18. Data Requirements for example, identify gaps in knowledge/limits of knowledge/ what we don't know/what's not there – intuition driven?; smart dust → real data – {pseudo/virtual} smart dust; knowledge market – ability for the designer to discover facts, ideas and so on. accommodation of differences; hierarchy of I/O GUI/code/ docs/pics – delivery of info at different levels depending on user; flexibility – Solution filters; data mining massive data sets.

19. Trends for example, don't base design on current views – extrapolate trends; influence trends to drive objectives; lifestyle versus work trends; trends may render sense into nonsense; global culture driving design/economics driving design rather than trends?; imagine a future – opposite of trends.

20. Validation and Risk for example, design feasibility (and cost) 'relevant' data output trust?; force us to question solutions; validate robustness of model; checks and balances; new design hard to accept; detect errors before they occur; ethical constraints/alerts.

21. Examples for example, observing examples of good and bad design – analysing differences; exemplars – case studies; irrelevance engine.

22. User Interaction for example, machine/software influences RH/LH side of brain; interactive process must stimulate both sides of the brain (equally?); computer given permission to think?

23. Usability for example, what it is to be human; consideration for human needs; non-tedious – system must not cause fatigue in the user; techno fear trend; flexibility in systems; functions must be in 'near' real-time; less frightening; accessibility; simple is best; transparency; quantifying human responses/sensations.

24. Emergence for example, dynamic real-time design – 'emergent'; consequences – understanding good/bad aspects of emergence? predict emergent properties; implied information ≡ generating the problem.

25. Protocol for example, 'design champion' does the system know who is initiating design? human-system divide – what and when.

26. Modelling for example, machine-based tool to assist people to describe their model; constant, cyclic modification of model; information transfer from abstract to definable; holistic versus modular; Intangible/tangible → transparent (how can the machine help us)?

27. Science/Engineering for example, hypothesis versus concept; science versus engineering; design versus research.

28. Search and Exploration for example, human versus machine-based – which and when or collaborative? exploration versus exploitation; stochastic/evolutionary processes; large scale vs small scale.

29. Technology for example, representation – powerful modules to provide visualisation and interactive exploration of the search space; gaming technologies; play 'what if?'; machine/agency based learning plus cognitive model; grid technology; changing machine's personality → 'dice man'.

Table 1, The 29 groupings with samples of their component ideas/comments

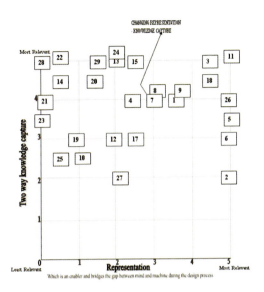

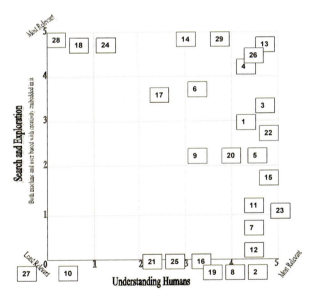

Figures 1 and 2,
top to bottom

Figure 1, Blue group: Two-way Knowledge Capture versus Representation
Figure 2, Green group; Search and Exploration versus Understanding Humans

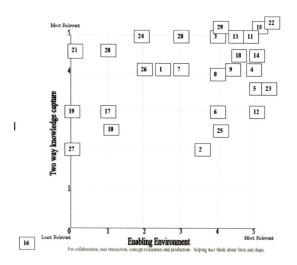

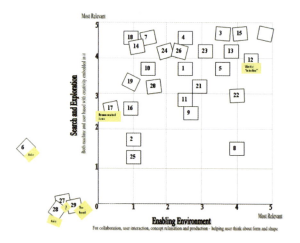

Figures 3 and 4,
top to bottom

Figure 3, Blue group; Two-way Knowledge Capture versus Enabling Environment
Figure 4, Orange group: Search and Exploration versus Enabling Environment

Knowledge Extraction and Capture	Search and Exploration	Enabling Environments	Representation	Understanding Humans
Cooperation and collaboration; capturing/ extracting knowledge; enabling computational technologies; emergence; history and traceability; modelling; data issues; creativity and innovation; user support; learning.	User support; creativity and innovation; modelling; emergence; history and traceability; capturing/ extracting knowledge; data Issues.	User-centric issues; cooperation and collaboration; useability; user interface; creativity and innovation; multi-users and multi-user interaction; capturing/ extracting knowledge; user support; user interaction.	Visualisation/ senses stimulation; form; modelling; capturing/ extracting knowledge; cooperation and collaboration.	Usability; visualisation/ senses stimulation; user interaction; validation and risk; multi-users and multi-user interaction; creativity and innovation; interface; user-centric issues; user support; end user issues; learning; form; cooperation and collaboration.

Table 2, Classification of key issues in terms of the five identified research areas

Continuation of Cluster Activities

The final activities of the cluster included the launch of the Institute for People-centred Computation in early March 2006. The Institute is a developing entity that will provide focus for a new highly multidisciplinary community of academic and industrial researchers/practitioners. The DiD cluster group is providing an initial core for this larger, growing community. The aim of the Institute is to support a significant expansion by moving the focus of the group from design processes to the early stages of decision-making processes in general. This expansion is being supported by a Network Grant from the EPSRC exploring 'People-centred Computational Environments for Design and Decisionmaking'.

The objectives of the Institute are to develop agendas for research and development that will result in user-centric computational environments that:

- support human/machine-based information discovery that will lead to innovative and creative solutions beyond those typically produced by decision makers alone or by decision makers supported by current computational systems;
- through human interaction reduce uncertainty and associated risk during the early stages of design and decision-making processes;
- capture experiential and tacit knowledge whilst supporting implicit learning and an improved understanding of complex problem relationships;
- develop collaborative multidisciplinary proposals for this research and development and subsequently implement programs that will ultimately deliver generic commercial systems;
- concurrently support workshops, seminars, special interest groups summer schools and training events. These will ensure a better under standing of the domain and the requirements, both human and machine-based, of the perceived people-centred computational environments whilst also disseminating new knowledge to those involved in their development and utilisation;
- develop a portal for UK industry to access interdisciplinary expertise in all aspects of people-centred computation;
- ensure that the UK develops and maintains a strong position in the area of human-centred computation for early design and decision-making processes.

The long term aim is to develop collaborative multidisciplinary proposals for research and development and subsequently implement programs that will ultimately deliver generic commercial systems. Further information can be found at www.ip-cc.org.uk.

Conclusions

One of the main outcomes of the cluster activities has been a very significant increase in awareness across the members and their particular disciplines of design issues relating to many differing forms and levels of complexity. It is generally agreed across the cluster that each discipline has come away with new knowledge that is of benefit to their research and/or current practice. The workshops have been extremely information rich. The data presented has provided excellent visual stimulation for workshop activities and has given a strong indication of the relevant issues.

A significant proportion of the generated knowledge is however tacit and will require more 'teasing-out' through further interactive sessions. The establishment of the Institute for People-centred Computation and the associated Network funding will support this activity and the further analysis of the cluster data which will also contribute significantly to initial Institute workshops.

Bringing together such a diverse set of disciplines with varied backgrounds over a 9-month period through workshops and other activities to discuss design, computational and people-centred relationships is probably unique. There is no doubt that, with hindsight, we would have organised our activities a little differently but the outcomes have been entirely satisfactory in terms of the objectives both of the cluster and the Designing for the 21st Century Initiative. The overall benefits in terms of a learning exercise and an opportunity to move closer to the establishment of people-centred conceptual design environments have been significant.

Acknowledgements

We wish to acknowledge and thank the AHRC and EPSRC for their support.

Design Imaging

Gordon M Mair and Kevin Miller, (University of Strathclyde)

Overview

Design is carried out as a preliminary action to the creation of: *artefacts* – such as products and architectural structures; *systems* – such as social and transport; and *processes* – such as chemical and business. The 'Design Imaging' project was formed with the intention of encouraging the use of the senses to inspire new perspectives in all areas of design and for all participants. The project aimed to develop a stimulating and exciting environment that would provoke a change in how the design process is implemented. It brought together people with diverse expertise from a variety of backgrounds, but all with a common focus on design and an interest in creating something new and better than the status quo.

Multimodal Imaging

In order for a designer to communicate their ideas to colleagues, customers and the public, images are often used to augment or replace text and the spoken word – these images are normally visual and monoscopic. It is, however, possible to generate stereoscopic, volumetric and immersive visual images. It is also possible to produce surround, environmental and binaural sound. Increasingly, sophisticated haptic (tactile and force) images can also be created as can solid physical representations through rapid prototyping. In the future, all of the sensory modalities may be utilised to produce mixed modality images that will afford an extremely stimulating and information rich environment. To this end, the notion of 'multimodal images' was proposed as a means of enhancing communication, cooperation and creativity in design.

Objectives

[1] MCCULLOUGH, M., 1998. *Abstracting Craft: The Practiced Digital Hand*. Cambridge, MA: MIT Press.

[2] SEVALDSON, B., 1999. Research on Digital Design Strategies. Presented at the *Useful and Critical Design Research Conference, University of Industrial Arts, Helsinki*.

[3] TERRY, M. and MYNATT, E. D., 2002. Recognizing Creative Needs in User Interface Design. In: *Creativity and Cognition: Proceedings of the Fourth Creativity and Cognition Conference, Loughborough, 2002*. New York: ACM Press, pp. 38-44.

[4] Transparent Telepresence Research Group. Available at: www.telepresence.strath.ac.uk

[5] Design Imaging. Available at: www.dmem.strath.ac.uk/designimaging/

[6] The Centre for Comminication and Information Technologies. Available at: http://www.paccit.gla.ac.uk/public/goals.php

Specifically, the cluster was established to develop the concept of 'multimodal images', in all of their forms, as a means of improving the design process through consideration of: a) how existing and emerging technologies can be utilised to improve the design function; b) the design process, to determine whether there are new ways, without regard to real or anticipated technological limitations, of communicating ideas and designs; c) the identification of appropriate research directions resulting from a) and b); and d) one or more possible projects that could lead to world-class research in the field of design imaging.

Cluster Membership

While technological developments present exciting opportunities and seductive solutions in some of the above areas, they are not always sympathetic to the nature of artistic and design practice.[1,2,3] As creative practice and the benefits of working with others of differing skills were particular concerns of the project, an effective investigation (and the development of sensitive solutions) necessitated exploitation of knowledge from many realms.

A multidisciplinary cluster was, therefore, assembled with members of the initial core cluster having backgrounds in design, computer graphics, virtual reality, visual and musical arts, communications, psychology and telepresence. Cluster membership grew as the project progressed and attracted the interest of researchers from other disciplines – demonstrating the potentially significant contribution of the Design Imaging concept. The following list constitutes the original core members plus the enthusiasts who joined after its inception:

The Principal Investigator, Gordon Mair is a Senior Lecturer in the Department of Design, Manufacture, and Engineering Management at the University of Strathclyde in Glasgow, he is also the founder and Director of the Transparent Telepresence Research Group,[4] a multidisciplinary research group interested in all aspects of multi-modal communication. Kevin Miller, a full time Research Assistant who created the cluster web pages and forum,[5] recorded and analysed all workshop meetings, carried out literature searches, and assisted with publication and dissemination. Prof. Anne Anderson is from the Department of Psychology at the University of Glasgow, where one of her roles is manager of the Multimedia Communications Group[6] that researches technologically

⁷ Jane Harris. Available at: www.
janeharris.org

⁸ Digital Design Studio.
Available at: http://www.gsa.
ac.uk/gsa.cfm?pid=12

⁹ rootoftwo. Available at: www.
rootoftwo.com/bios.htm

¹⁰ Advanced VR Research
Centre. Available at: http://avrrc.
lboro.ac.uk/

¹¹ Human Computer Interaction
Research Group, University of
Glasgow. Available at: http://
www.dcs.gla.ac.uk/research/
index.cfm?resgroup=HCI

mediated human communication. Dr Jane Harris is a Senior Research Fellow at Central Saint Martins College of Art and Design and visiting lecturer at Goldsmith's College, University of London,[7] her artistic research was very relevant to the project with one aspect related to the aesthetic fabrication of digital textiles. Mairghread McLundie of the Digital Design Studio, Glasgow School of Art[8] brought a broad range of artistic experience to the project. Dr Wolfgang Sonne is a Lecturer on the history and theory of architecture in the Department of Architecture and Building Science at the University of Strathclyde and his research focuses on 20ᵗʰ century urban design and how different factors influence the form of the city. John Marshall,[9] a sculptor and designer. Prof. Allan Bridges is from the Department of Architecture at Strathclyde University. Prof. Roy Kalawsky, Director of the Advanced Virtual Reality Research Centre at Loughborough University,[10] has published widely in the fields of virtual reality and virtual environments with a wide breadth of knowledge of multimodal systems. Dr Neil Houston is a Lecturer in Music in the Aesthetic Studies group of the Department of Curriculum Research and Development at the School of Education at the University of Edinburgh. Prof. Marc O Cavazza of the School of Computing, University of Teesside has particular interests in Intelligent Virtual Environments including psychology and the human computer interface. Prof. Stephen Brewster of the Human Computer Interaction Research Group[11] in the Department of Computing Science, University of Glasgow. He has a broad interest in multimodal interaction and has had a variety of past and present projects funded in this area. Finally Prof. Jian Zhang is Head of Research in the National Centre of Computer Animation at Bournemouth University where his research interests range from 3D computer graphics, physics based computer animation, to medical visualisation and simulation.

Background

We are multisensory creatures. For example we can form images in our mind based on music, and a pleasingly constructed pictorial image can portray a visual symphony. Our perception of the world, and our relationship to it is experienced and formed through a large number of senses, viz. our five Aristotelian senses of vision, audition, olfaction, taction and gestation, plus our kinaesthetic sense and others. In fact, we usually experience the world, and form our opinions of it, based on an integration of one or more of these senses. It is important, therefore, to consider senses of the participants in the design process and potential means of using them for the benefit of design.

There are many good examples of consideration for the senses in product design. Touch, for example, is of importance in the design of small, hand-held products such as mobile phones, MP3 players and cameras. Indeed, modern, digital cameras also take advantage of audition to improve interaction – an artificial shutter noise is included in some to make the user feel more confident that the photograph has been properly taken. The car is an example of a product that demands consideration of all the senses [Figure 1].

Visually, the shape and colour of the body, the internal displays and fascia and general appearance of the whole assembly will be important. *Aurally*, the sound of the exhaust and engine, road noise, sound insulation and door closing, and locking sounds, will all contribute to a sense of quality and performance. With respect to *taction*, attention is given to the texture of the upholstery and the surface of the steering wheel while, with respect to our *kinaesthetic* sense, the forces required to operate the power steering, gear change, foot controls and door handles are all relevant. The *vestibular* sense is considered through concern for the performance of the suspension system to ensure a comfortable, nausea free, experience. An extreme example that demonstrates the importance of the senses regarding *olfaction* is cited by Lindstrom[12] where, because modern materials, manufacturing methods, and safety regulations prevented the modern 'Silver Cloud' from smelling the same as the 1965 original, Rolls

[12] LINDSTROM, M., 2005. Sensing an Opportunity. *The Marketer*, February, 6-11th.

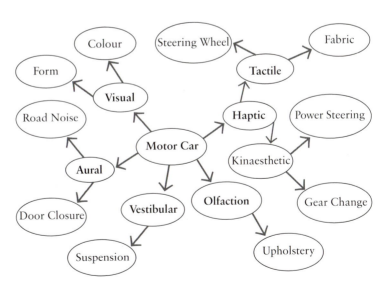

Figure 1, Multimodal automotive design

Royce spent hundreds of thousands of dollars on artificially recreating the smell of the original upholstery. While these are all good examples of design *for* the senses, we ask – what new insights could be gained if we were to introduce the senses into the design process and design *with* the senses?

Activities

The cluster operated throughout the year predominantly through scheduled workshops, email communication, presentations at dissemination events and publication of conference papers. A summary of these activities is given in chronological order below:

Workshops

At the first meeting of the cluster (held in February at the University of Strathclyde), the Principal Investigator provided the introductory presentation in which he outlined the aims of the project in relation to the context of the Designing for the 21ˢᵗ Century Initiative. Each of the core cluster members similarly gave short presentations of their own work and research interests and their relevance to the project. An open discussion ensued concerning what each member could contribute and the likely course of the work over the next year. In relation to multimodal imaging in design, some aspects considered were:

- the translation of tacit knowledge;
- removal of disciplinary boundaries;
- development of new tools;
- supporting creativity;
- aiding understanding of user needs;
- enhancing communication and presentation;
- the use of multimodality to promote inclusion in design and improve learning.

With the March workshop being hosted by the Glasgow School of Art's Digital Design Studio, the group considered different aspects of design tools: the translation of tacit knowledge was examined more closely and ways of supporting the development of tacit knowledge, as opposed to capturing it all, were considered. The possibility of designing new tools that did not simply emulate existing, manual processes was therefore explored. The group discussed the notion of multirepresentational tools and ways in which individuals could use these in order to develop their own approaches, techniques and methodologies. The question of whether existing design tools emulated and/or empathised with natural/intuitive non-technologically mediated ways of being creative was explored. Finally, the group considered whether we could use multimodal imaging to fully indicate implications of a design without the need for explicit detail – thus affording a range of representations in the same model.

Held in May at Loughborough University's Advanced Virtual Reality Research Centre and with only six attendees, this was the smallest of all meetings – yet it proved to be one of the most focused. The group had an in depth discussion on multimodality with respect to the arts and the sciences. Regard was given to who currently used multimodality, for example, visual and tacitle senses are important in fabric design, filmmakers are concerned with vision and sound, sculptors use vision and touch, art installations are often multimodal and advertising and marketing are increasingly exploiting all of the senses. Two specific ideas for further work emerged from this meeting that were informed by discussions from the previous workshops: 'multimodal metaphors' to improve the design process and the possibility of using multimodality to help individuals with sensory impairment to participate more in the design process and facilitate design education.

The July workshop (held at the University of Strathclyde) was intended to build on the work to date and the success of the smaller number at the previous meeting, the 12 attendees were therefore split into three groups. Following a plenary session, the members divided into the groups in the morning and early afternoon and the day was concluded with a plenary meeting in which the groups reported their conclusions. The first group addressed the question 'How can multimodal design improve design creativity?', the second 'How can multimodal imaging improve interdisciplinary communication in design?', and the third 'How can multimodal imaging improve HCI in design?'

The October workshop welcomed a number of new members that had joined as a result of presentations at earlier conferences. A considerable amount of time was spent in this workshop discussing the role of multimodal imaging in relation to design education for children and how technological mediation can influence their development. Questions of a shared language for communication and the potential for achieving a common conceptual framework between disciplines were also returned to.

¹³ MAIR, G., MILLER, K. and ANDERSON, A., 2005. Multimodal Design Imaging. In: P. ROGERS, L. BRODHURST and D. HEPBURN, (eds.) *Crossing Design Boundaries. Proceedings of the 3ʳᵈ Engineering and Product Design Education International Conference, Edinburgh, September 2005*. London: Francis & Taylor, pp. 27-32.

¹⁴ MAIR, G. and MILLER, K., 2005. Multimodal Metaphors for Design Engagability and Inclusion. In: J. KNIGHT and J. SHERIDAN, (eds.) *Proceedings of International Design Engagability Conference (IDEC), Part of HCI 2005, September 2005*. ISBN 1-904839-01-0.

¹⁵ MAIR, G., MILLER, K. and SONNE, W., 2005. The Evocation of the Unseen in Architecture Through Multimodal Imaging. In: J. HALE and B. STARKEY, (eds.) *Book of Abstracts: Models and Drawings: The Invisible Nature of Architecture, AHRA Conference at the University of Nottingham, November 2005*, pp. 96-97.

¹⁶ MILLER, K. and MAIR, G., 2006. Multimodality – A Stimulant to Design Creativity? *In: Proceedings of the 4ᵗʰ Engineering and Product Design Education Conference, Salzburg, 6-8ᵗʰ September 2006*.

¹⁷ SCAIFE, M., CURTIS, E. and HILL, C., 1994. Interdisciplinary collaboration: a case study of software development for fashion designers. *Interacting with Computers*, 6, pp. 395-410.

The final workshop (held in December) focused in more detail on the development of proposals for projects that would build on the research areas that had been discussed throughout the year. The group identified six topics that merited further research and some of these are outlined in the insights section below.

Dissemination

Throughout the year, the work of the cluster was also presented at conferences across disciplines. Presenting at different conferences proved to be a valuable activity that led to a greater appreciation of the problem, encouraged different perspectives and new insights. It introduced a wider audience to the research and, through the forming of new relationships, helped broaden our understanding of the topic and increased cluster membership. The papers tackled inclusivity and human factors in design, education and architecture.[13,14,15,16]

Insights

With such diverse membership, workshops were pivotal to the development of a shared understanding and cohesion within the cluster. While large workshops helped establish the general nature of the work and provided depth to the investigation (with boundaries being defined and promising directions being identified), small workshops afforded the opportunity to focus on specific aspects of these broader issues and gave the investigation depth. This dynamic between workshops ultimately led to a detailed conception of the problem area.

Interdisciplinarity

The problem of communication between disciplines, viz. the arts and the sciences, was particularly salient and so became the first area to which the concept of multimodality was applied. The issue was manifest through experience within the cluster itself and through anecdotes, related by cluster members, of previous collaborations. We found that because participants in the cluster came from such different backgrounds in the arts, humanities and sciences, they expressed themselves very differently and there was considerable opportunity for ambiguity and even misinterpretation between them.

In contrast to multidisciplinary approaches that simply bring together separate skills,[17] the interdisciplinarity the cluster aimed to achieve and support, demands the integration of different disciplinary perspectives.

[18] ROGERS, Y., SCAIFE, M. & RIZO, A., 2001. Isn't Multidisciplinarity Enough? In: S. DERRY, D. MORTON & A. GERNSBACHER, (eds.) *Problems and Promises of Interdisciplinarity: Perspectives from Cognitive Science*. Earlbaum Associates.

[19] HEY, J., 2004. *Metaphors We Design By*. Creativity Assessment Report. Berkeley: University of California.

[20] SCHON, D., 1983. *The Reflective Practitioner*. Cambridge, MA: MIT Press.

[21] COYNE, R. and SNODGRASS, A., 1995. Problem Setting within prevalent metaphors of design. *Design Issues*, 11(2), pp. 31-61.

[22] CASAKIN, H., 2004. Metaphors in the Design Studio: Implications for Education. In: P. LLOYD, N. ROOZENBURG, C. MCMAHON and E. BRODHURST, (eds.) *Proceedings of the 2nd International Engineering and Product Design Education Conference, EPDE04, Delft*.

[23] DAY, S., 1996. Synaesthesia and synaesthetic metaphors [online]. *Psyche*, 2(32). Available at: http://psyche.cs.monash.edu.au/v2/psyche-2-32-day.html [Accessed 27th June 2006].

[24] RAMACHANDRAN, V. and HUBBARD, E., 2001. Synaesthesia – a window into perception, thought and language. *Journal of Consciousness Studies*, 8, pp. 3-34.

[25] SHIMOJO, S. and SHAMS, L., 2001. Sensory modalities are not separate modalities: plasticity and interactions. *Current Opinion in Neurobiology*, 11, pp. 505-509.

[26] BRETONES, C., 2001. *Synaesthetic Metaphors in English*. Technical Report TR 01-008. Berkeley: International Computer Science Institute.

Such interdisciplinary enterprises entail the development of new theoretical and applied approaches that the traditional frameworks of separate disciplines do not permit.[18, 13]

Overcoming disciplinary barriers, then, was essential and a need for some form of *lingua franca* was proposed[13] – a means of talking about concepts that could be understood by all involved. The cluster initially conceived of this as a problem concerning language – specifically, the ineffable nature of tacit knowledge and how to articulate this to those unfamiliar with creative practice. The group envisaged a more engaging interaction, where participants play an active role, provoking reciprocal learning in interdisciplinary design teams. Investigation of metaphor proved to be a crucial approach to the problem of communication and of multimodality in design in general.

Multimodal metaphors

The study of metaphor was not only appropriate because of their role in making the unfamiliar familiar, but also because metaphors are considered as intrinsic to design, particularly divergent thinking during the 'conceptual phase'[19] – being referred to by Schon[20] as 'generative metaphors'. They are key to the structuring of problems and have even been regarded as constituting a 'cognitive strategy' in design.[21,22] Three applications of metaphor have been identified in design:[19]

- the switching of metaphors;
- the extension of existing metaphors; and
- the introduction of novel metaphors.

The concept of 'multimodal metaphor' was inspired by the linguistic phenomenon of 'synaesthetic metaphors' where experience in one sense is described in terms of another[23,24] and other, more sophisticated examples of sensory manipulation (such as the Geiger counter, which uses sound to communicate radiation levels).[14] Such phenomena implied complex sensory relationships – relationships which could, perhaps, be exploited to 'introduce a sensory logic at the semantic level',[25,26] thus affording articulation of multisensory creative practice.

[27] LAKOFF, G. and JOHNSON, M., 1980. *Metaphors We Live By*. Chicago and London: University of Chicago Press.

[28] FAUCONNEIR, G. and TURNER, M., 2002. *The Way We Think: Conceptual Blending and the Mind's Hidden Complexities*. New York: Basic Books.

[29] TORGNY, O., 1997. Metaphor: A Working Concept. In: *Proceedings of the 2ⁿᵈ European Academy of Design Conference, EAD97, Stockholm, 23-25ᵗʰ April 1997*. The Swedish Industrial Design Foundation.

[30] JOHNSON, M. and LAKOFF, G., 2002. Why cognitive linguistics requires embodied realism. *Cognitive Linguistics*, 13(3), pp. 245 – 263.

[31] LAKOFF, G. and JOHNSON, M., 1980. *Metaphors We Live By*. Chicago and London: University of Chicago Press.

Further investigation, indicated that metaphor was 'not just a matter of language, but of thought and reason'[27,28] – indeed, research suggested that it is increasingly regarded as fundamental to human cognition. Just as metaphor is driven by similarities and differences, so too, whenever we are confronted by a new experience, we try to understand it in terms of previous and similar experiences. [29,14]

Conflations are situations in which source and target domains are experienced simultaneously.[30] They develop a system of hundreds of basic conceptual metaphors that structure our thought. For example, verticality and quantity are both active when liquid is poured into a container or when objects are piled on top of one another[31] [Figure 2]. Such experiences are thought to determine the way in which we conceive of and communicate other experiences.

Visual metaphors can be particularly powerful. Two images are shown below from one of the author's work on telepresence. The first, [Figure 3] has the connotation of the human senses being projected elsewhere via technology through the integration of human and machine. The second, [Figure 4] conveys the fragile benefits of technology, the robotic arm is grasping an egg with the Chinese symbols for the English word 'crisis', these are comprised of elements which represent 'danger' and 'opportunity'.

Both [Figures 3 and 4] are particularly relevant to the Design Imaging project and perhaps to the Designing for the 21ˢᵗ Century endeavour in general. For example one interpretation of the arm and egg image is that today we have many opportunities to use technology in design but we must be careful not to stifle the creative process by its unsympathetic application.

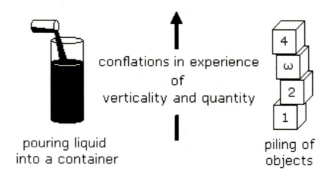

Figure 2, Development of basic conceptual system via conflations in experience.

Multimodal imaging

[32] GEDENRYD, H., 1998. *How Designers Work*. PhD Thesis. Cognitive Studies Department, Lund University, Sweden.

[33] SUWA, M., GERO, J. S. and PURCELL, T., 1999. Unexpected Discoveries and S-invention of Design Requirements: A key to creative designs. *In:* J. S. GERO and M. L. MAHER, (eds.) Computational Models of Creative Design IV. Sydney: Key Centre of Design Computing and Cognition, University of Sydney, pp. 297-320.

[34] EIMER, M., 2004. Multisensory integration: how visual experience shapes spatial perception. *Current Biology*, 14, pp. 115-117.

[35] SHILITO, A. M., PAVNTER, K., WALL, S. and WRIGHT, M., 2001. Tacitus project: identifying multisensory perceptions in creative 3D practice for the development of a haptic computing system for applied artists. *Digital Creativity Journal*, 12(5), pp. 195-203.

[36] CANDY, L. and ERNEST, E., (eds.), 2002. *Explorations in Art and Technology: Intersections and Correspondence*. London: Springer Verlag.

[37] EDMONDS, E. A., TURNER, G. and CANDY, L., 2004. Approaches to Interactive Art Systems. *In:* S. N. SPENCER, (ed.) Proceedings of the *Proceedings of the 2nd International Conference on Computer graphics and Interactive Techniques in Australasia and South East Asia, GRAPHITE 2004, Singapore.* ACM Press, pp. 113-117.

Design is inherently conceptual, but different modalities will be emphasised depending on the nature of the design activity.[13] Vision, through sketching, pervades engineering and architectural design,[32,33] but the arts and crafts are dominated by other senses. The sculptor's intuitive capacity for conceiving and understanding in three dimensions will, for example, have developed through the senses of touch and vision.[34,35] 'Multimodal Imaging' emerges from the intersection between such creative practice and technology – where artists and designers are eager to explore new technologies that could support their traditional practices and help invent new techniques that allow for the 'artistic satisfaction' experienced when working with materials[1,36,37,38]

For the sculptor, or any individual, to practice creatively, information must be acquired and skills must be practised for knowledge to become tacit and tool use transparent[39] – in the applied arts, this is referred to as 'intelligent making'.[35] Having developed the notion of metaphor and its role in human reasoning (cf. Multimodal Metaphors), the cluster came to consider creative practice as the acquiring of 'embodied knowledge.'[16] Concepts and images are not born separate to technological mediation, but are formed as artists physically work with tools in all guises [Figure 5] and materials, as they experiment with variation and continually reflect on strategies.[40,41]

Figure 3, The Telepresence Concept

Figure 4, Technology – Danger and Opportunity

[38] SENER, B., VERGEEST, J. and AKAR, E., 2002. The Future Expectations of CAD Users of New Generation Computer-Aided Design Tools: Two Related Research Projects Investigating the Future Expectations of Designers. In: Proceedings of the 7ᵗʰ International Design Conference- Design 2002, Dubrovnik. Volume 1, pp. 539-545.

[39] TREADAWAY, C., 2004. Digital Creativity: The impact of digital imaging technology on the creative practice of printed textile and surface pattern design. Journal of Textile and Apparel, Technology and Management [online], 4(1). Available at: http://www.tx.ncsu.edu/jtatm/volume4issue1/vo4_issue1_abstracts.htm [Accessed 27 June 2006].

[40] DI SCIPIO, A., 1998. Questions concerning music technology. Angelaki, 3(2), pp. 31-40.

[41] SCHON, D., 1983. The Reflective Practitioner. Cambridge, MA: MIT Press.

[42] ROBERTS, J., 2004. Visualization equivalence for multisensory perception. Computing in Science and Engineering, 6(3), pp. 61-65.

[43] GIBSON, J. J., 1979. The Ecological Approach to Visual Perception. Boston: Houghton Mifflin.

[44] RAMACHANDRAN, V. and HUBBARD, E., 2005. Hearing colours, tasting shapes. Scientific American Mind, 16(3), pp. 16-23.

[45] GARDNER, H., 1983. Frames of Mind: The Theory of Multiple Intelligences. New York: Basic Books.

A primary concern of the cluster, then, became the cognitive and communicative roles perceptual representations play in the design process, rather than the means of producing them. In this way, the necessary technology would be determined by the requirements identified as opposed to the requirements being constrained by technology. An increased appreciation for the careful design of perceptual representations holds many advantages:[42]

- information becomes more accessible to the sensory impaired;
- different modalities can be more effective for representing different data, for example, sound is best used to express time;[42]
- using multiple channels may prevent cognitive overload and improve interaction (consider affordances);[43]
- potential to communicate the ineffable;
- stimulation of different modalities could evoke novel concepts.

Regarding the stimulation of novel associations, note the similarity between this function and that of metaphor in design (cf. Multimodal Metaphors) – a similarity not unobserved, with studies indicating a higher incidence in synaesthesia and metaphor use in artists.[44] Also, consider the prospects for learning through the use of different forms of data representation.

In addition to Gardner's theory of multiple intelligences where learning styles have been defined in sensory terms,[45] it has recently been proposed that the use of multiple sensory channels can lead to more effective learning.[46,47]

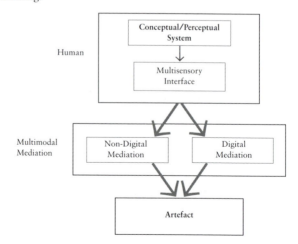

Figure 5, Sensory and modal route to design

Cluster questions

46 SANKEY, M., 2003. Visual and Multiple Representation in Learning: An Issue of Literacy. *In*: M. LAWRENCE, (ed.) *Create.ed 2003: Elearning for the Creative Industries*. Melbourne: RMIT University.

47 STOKES, S., 2002. Visual literacy in teaching and learning. *Electronic Journal for the Integration of Technology in Education* [online], 1(1). Available at: http://ejite.isu. edu/Volume1No1/Stokes.html [Accessed 27 June 2006].

48 LOFTIN, R. B., 2003. Multisensory perception: beyond the visual in visualization. *Computers in Science and Engineering*, 5(4), pp. 565-568.

49 KOFFKA, K., 1935. *Principles of Gestalt Psychology*. New York: Harcourt, Brace & Co.

50 CHANDRASEKARAN, B., 1999. Multimodal Perceptual Representations and Design Problem Solving. *In*: M. PETRE, H. C. SHARP and J. H. JOHNSON, (eds.) *Visual and Spatial Reasoning in Design*. Cambridge, MA: MIT Press. ISBN 1-86487-090-7.

Despite this potential, the complexity of sensory interdependencies, the ability of metaphor to restrict as well as broaden conceptual scope[21] and the absence of a viable theory of multisensory perception[48] make it difficult to prescribe a means of designing adequate perceptual representations.

The cluster's investigation, then, ultimately generated more questions, including: How can we effectively present information for different senses? Can we apply design principles from one modality, for example, Gestalt principles of vision,[49] to another? Are there different rules for reasoning in each modality?[50] Could better metaphors be used to aid conceptualisation in design? Can metaphors be used to develop more intuitive designs and design tools? What are the most effective metaphors to use in design and in what context? Can metaphors help to successfully transmit the embodied knowledge of artists and designers to others? How can we use the senses and metaphor to broaden the language of design, support communication and enhance creativity in interdisciplinary design environments?

Multimodal Design Imaging expects to contribute to this endeavour by answering these questions and continuing the work to explore the field and exploit the senses in design.

Future Plans

We intend to continue to broaden the spectrum of the disciplines involved to ensure that the arts and the physical, human and social sciences are all represented and make a significant contribution. As a means of achieving this, the cluster identified six possible research directions:

- Multimodal Metaphors
  An investigation into how metaphors that utilise all of the senses can be utilised to enhance design practice.
- Multimodal Representation of Space
  Can multimodality be used for the exploration and evocation of the unseen?
- Multimodal Design Literacy
  An investigation into the possibility of interpreting the quality of a design using multimodal criteria.

- Coherence in Design through Multimodal Imaging
  Can multimodal images be used to achieve 'coherence' – a goal of the
  creative processes in many disciplines?
- Enhancing Design Education through Multimodal Imaging
  An investigation of the sensory education of children as a means of
  encouraging their engagement and appreciation of the natural world.
- Design Inclusivity via Multimodal Imaging
  To be an investigation of how multimodal displays and controls can be
  used to engage the sensory impaired in the design process and design
  culture.

Two project proposals have been developed further and submitted for
AHRC and EPSRC review: 'Multimodal Representation of Urban Space'
and '*In-Mind* – Investigating Multimodal Metaphors for Interdisciplinary
Design'.

Multimodal representation of urbanspace

In 'Multimodal Representation of Urban Space' we plan to tackle the
long-standing problem of representing space that occurs not only in the
arts but in architecture, civil engineering and urban planning. In our
proposal we will investigate the suitability of multimodal imaging to
create a sense of space during the design process that will truly represent
the sense of space experienced in the final real world situation. The
part sensor fusion plays will be investigated by integrating visual, aural,
olfactory and tactile stimuli. We propose to do this without the use of
large scale expensive technological aids or installations but rather by
identifying low cost solutions that could easily be adopted by small
design, engineering or architectural companies.

Multimodal metaphors for interdisciplinary design

'In Mind' addresses an aspect of interdisciplinary working that became
apparent from our cluster activities – the need to understand each other's
'language'. An investigation into where, why, how and what multimodal
metaphors are currently used in the design process in the arts and sciences
has been proposed. The proposed project asks whether the use of these,
or new, metaphors can be transferred across the traditional boundaries
between the arts and sciences in order to improve understanding between
participants in the design process, encourage interdisciplinarity in an
integrated manner in design, and facilitate creativity.

Conclusion

The proposed work therefore hypothesizes that the identification and application of multimodalality and metaphors, capable of being used by both artists and scientists, through the integrative means of design practice, will support more effective interdisciplinary collaboration. Furthermore, the exploration of different multimodal images and metaphors will facilitate the inclusion of individuals and groups often excluded from the design process due to sensory impairment, but with valuable, indeed unique, contributions.

At a time when our experience is increasingly mediated by representations (consider CAD) it is appropriate to ask how we reintroduce a sensory understanding to design. Continuing the research and answering the questions generated has implications not just for novelty and creativity in design, but also for communication and learning. The use of multimodal images has great potential that could help us achieve effects, express intentions and conceptualise in new ways that develop the skills and knowledge base for the future of design in the 21st century.

Sensory Design and its Implications for Food Design and Presentation

Brent Richards, (University of the Arts)

Overview

We live in a world dictated by the eye, with a predominance of the visual over the other senses. We see, perceive and in turn visualise the world through a plethora of images, and whether these are represented through the still of photography, or the moving digital imagery of TV/laptop or mobile phone screen, they provide an edited version of our environment, that is largely abstracted and selected.

This is also true of much of our contemporary lifestyle, whether it is travel, architecture, fashion or food. It is first presented in an idealised format that is stylised, choreographed and landscaped in a particular fashion to appeal, seduce, and to reflect the latest cultural consensus.

However, this was not always so. Previously, our experiences of the world, and therefore our understanding of it, were more physically orientated, connected by interaction, transmitted through a tactile relationship and translated through touch; the modularity of our skin as an extension of our tactile senses. (As Gaston Bachelard says 'the polyphony of the senses'.)[1]

[1] BACHELARD, G., 1971. *The Poetics of Reverie*. Boston: Beacon Press, pp. 6.

Indeed, all the senses including vision are physical extensions of this tactile sense, (whether our tongue, nose, ears or eyes) and all our sensory experiences are modes of 'touching' or sensing, related to tactility and interpreting our habitat. Within this haptic realm of contact and engagement (reinforcement and response) lies our primary medium for communication. Touch integrates our experience with that of ourselves, our sense of reality and self. It is through the sense of self that we engage with our emotions, dreams, imagination, and with desires. Notably in the case of food, the ability to engage in this manner is vital, if we are to experience the act of dining, and to find emotional as well as physical reward from eating collectively. In the wider culinary world, it can be said that vision has usurped our intellectual cognition of the sensory realm. From the traditional dominance of French Haute Cuisine as a 'state of the art', to the rise of the visual art of Nouvelle Cuisine, to the mass adoption of the technology in process of Fast Foods, to the adoption of global culture within Fusion Foods; these approaches have become dominated by an articulation of the visual media over the other senses.

Our encounters and desires for food recipes and food product branding are now indoctrinated by the contemporary 'TV/Cook' culture, as well as the mass communication of associated media tie-ins, 'TV chefs' come raconteurs, as well as the ranges of cook books, and epicurean ready meals now available.

But like advanced computer imaging, which turns the process of design into a passive visual manipulation, the emphasis on visual representation has so separated out our real experience (and the opportunity of the other senses to encounter the taste/flavour/aroma/sound of the foods) with simulated representation, that it has led to a suppression of the natural stimuli that otherwise consume our emotional engagement with the food.

Consequently, we are transformed into mere salivating spectators, lacking the normal sensory stimulation, being left devoid of the haptic encounter with the ingredients, food process, which are enacted on the TV screen like a transitory mirage before us. As pure entertainment this is arguably justified, but as an erosion of our human empathy with our world, and as a doctrine of take-away food in a uniform pre-packed perfect format, this is having a devastating (and some would say immediate) effect on the lives of our children, the well being of future generations and our planet.

Our cluster project within 'Designing for the 21st Century' sought to consider a Futurescape© for food, remapping how we can better accommodate all our senses and to realise how we can benefit from articulating a more sensorial experience in food delivery. Our ambition is to transform ways of experiencing food through design and thereby promote changes in food attitudes, habits and practices.

Molecular Gastronomy

Part of this research considers the role of 'Molecular Gastronomy' – that is how science can better inform the art of food preparation, cooking and presentation, and in so doing re-engage with the senses and to review its implication on food design, presentation and food environments; in this case, primarily for incorporation into public restaurants. (Though it will have similar implications for schools, prisons, hospitals, the travel industry; as well as direct applications for the domestic environment.)

Areas of investigation included: food cognition, alchemy, and synthesis, as well as the possibilities for interdisciplinary discourse, and the potential for future innovation in food rituals, by exploiting the synergy between the senses and celebrating the art of deliciousness [Figure 1].

The Design Laboratory's previous experience in molecular gastronomy stemmed from commercial design work with Pierre Herme in Paris and the brand of Henri Charpentier/Cool Earth, with the launch of a new flagship store in Kobe, Japan in 2004. This led our investigations to the key practitioners of molecular gastronomy in France, Spain and the UK, and we became involved in research into the applicability and significance of sensory design for food/food presentation, food branding and packaging.

The Molecular Gastronomy revolution that has taken place over the past 15 years, was founded by Nicholas Kurti, a Hungarian physicist working in Oxford, UK in 1969, and popularised by his then scientific collaborator, Herve This (France) in his 1988 thesis.[2] Kurti introduced the importance of understanding the science of food preparation and the cooking process, which led to a new movement in thinking about the interdisciplinary nature of food, not only as the gastronomic (the relationship between culture/arts and food), but also in the application of scientific knowledge to food [Figure 2].

It was Kurti's term 'Molecular Gastronomy' that was to inspire a new generation of chefs, ranging from Pierre Gagnaire (France), Ferran Adria (Spain), Heston Blumenthal (UK) to Thomas Keller (USA). These chefs gradually challenged the high traditions of French Haute Cuisine, being more open to new forms of innovation, experimentation and with a quest for finding authenticity in food flavours, taste, aromas, combined with new textures and forms; perceiving food more as an 'alchemic art for

[2] Introduced by Nicholas Kurti (Physicist) and Herve This (Chemist): 'scientific exploration of culinary, and more generally, gastronomical transformations and phenomena.' KURTI, N., 1994. Physics and Chemistry in the Kitchen. Sci. Am, 270(4), pp. 44-50. *The First International Workshop on Molecular and Physical Gastronomy, Erice, 1992.* Later published as THIS, H., 1995. *La gastronomie moleculaire et physique.* PhD Thesis, University of Paris VI.

Figures 1 to 3,
left to right, top to bottom

Figure 1, Snail Butter – Image that accompanied Heston Blumenthal's Snail Porridge recipe

Figure 2, Table Landscape – The landscape of the table is a blank canvass where art, science and food, interface in a narrative of emotions. and memories.

Figure 3, Science of Cooking – Where the molecular and the physical meet. Science is one more tool in the search for excellence and the perfection of deliciousness

All by Cameron Watt ©Food Photographer

the senses', but supported by sound scientific principles. Notably, Ferran Adria at his El Bulli Restaurant in Roses, Catalonia, has led this revolution for some 10 years, closely followed and now shared by the English Chef Heston Blumenthal at his Fat Duck Restaurant in Bray, Berkshire [Figure 3].

These highly influential chefs represent a profound interest in continuous experimentation, combining texture, playing with memories, invoking the role of nostalgia and giving importance to experiencing food through flavour. Flavour involves all our senses and it comes about through a complex set of interactions caused by stimuli and sensations that take place when we eat – the eyes, mouth, nose, tongue and ears all contribute to the vital experiential connection made through the receptors to our brain .The brain then provides the cognitive understanding that permits us to interpret and emotionally respond to what we have tasted. Our reward is then measured in what we more commonly express as the 'deliciousness' of the food!

This Designing for the 21st Century cluster project has its foundations in an active creative and design collaboration (founded in summer 2004, through a meeting at the International Workshop on Molecular Gastronomy at the Ettore Majorana Center for Scientific Culture in Erice Sicily) between architect and designer, Brent Richards of The Design Laboratory at the Innovation Centre, Central Saint Martins College of Art and Design in London, (part of the University of the Arts, London) and the three starMichelin chef, Heston Blumenthal of the Fat Duck Restaurant, UK (and his own earlier collaborative work with the food scientist, Harold McGee.

Whilst this earlier collaborative work proved highly influential it lacked the opportunity to address the wider cultural context, and the chance to research more holistically into how these interdisciplines might develop in the future. With this in mind, from the outset the research cluster comprised a combination of disciplines, represented by cultural historians, an anthropologist, curators, psychologists, medical doctors, research scientists, architects, designers, artists and chefs.

Activities

The aim of the cluster was primarily to provide an interdisciplinary
platform for dialogue and exchange, exploring three basic research
territories:

- *Molecular Gastronomy*: To define sensory design in relation to
  molecular gastronomy and to consider its implications for food design
  in the new millennium.
- *The Senses*: To investigate the role of the senses in the appreciation,
  perception and understanding of food.
- *Sensory Design*: To consider what the interaction between food/sensory
  design and innovation might be and to evolve a contemporary taxonomy
  for sensory design.

We held five cluster workshops over a period of 9 months during 2005,
culminating in a Symposium on the subject of sensory design in December
2005. The cluster sessions were orchestrated and usually facilitated by
the team from the Design Laboratory, but members of the cluster were
elected to take turns in presenting the subtopics as the work progressed.
(In addition, 'guest visitors' were invited to certain sessions supplementing
this approach, they enlivened debate and ensured that workshops were
balanced and representative.) Given the breadth of topics, the sessions
followed a gradual process of iteration, building a focus and seeking
definitions and detail as time progressed.

The cluster workshops explored:

- Futurescaping
- Food Habits and Rituals
- Sensory Deprivation
- Smart Technologies and New Materials
- Nostalgia and Sensory Alchemy

All workshops were orchestrated according to a pre-agenda, they were
video recorded, and notes of the discussions were taken and distributed
to those attending. However, conversations were not minuted, rather
captured for reference purposes.

Members of the cluster:

- Brent Richards – Architect, designer and Founding Director of the Design Laboratory, University of the Arts London, Principal Investigator.
- Dr. Peter Barham – Reader in Physics, University of Bristol, Co-Investigator.
- Heston Blumenthal – 3 star Michelin chef of Fat Duck Restaurant, Bray, Berkshire.
- Prof. Farida Fortune – Professor of Medicine Queen Mary University London, Co-Investigator.
- Dr Hamish Park – Anthropologist and Photographer, Co-Investigator.
- Prof. Marina Wallace – Art historian and Director of Artakt, University of the Arts London, Co-Investigator.
- Dr Marianne Moore – Chemist and designer, Design Laboratory and Research Fellow University of the Arts London, Co-Investigator.
- Dr. Caterina Albano – Cultural Historian and Curator, Artakt University of the Arts London, Co-Investigator.

Invited guests:

Dr Charles Spence – Psychologist, Oxford University.
Ranjit Sondhi – Social Scientist, Board of National Gallery.
Chris Sanderson – Director of the Future Laboratory.
Dr Mark Miodownik – Lecturer in Engineering and NESTA Fellow for Materials Science, Kings College London.

Workshop 1 – Futurescaping© (April 2005)
Session facilitator: Brent Richards; Venue: Innovation Centre, Central Saint Martins

The first workshop was planned to be a provocative vision of the future of food, to set the scene and to act as a catalyst for subsequent discussions. For this purpose there was a guest participant: The trend mapping consultancy – Future Laboratory, London (which was not part of the formal cluster) were commissioned to undertake some initial in depth research on food nutrition, health consciousness, obesity, food technology and contemporary lifestyle and its relationship to food design, branding, and products. Following a formal presentation with images, a lively debate ensued and this created a rich context for the other workshops to follow.

Whilst this encouraged early interaction between the cluster members, the topic revealed the inhibitions of respective disciplines and produced both wide-ranging and tangential views. These relied heavily on respective discipline cultures in terms of nomenclature and perspective.

Workshop 2 – Food Rituals (May 2005)
Session facilitators: Prof. Marina Wallace and Dr Caterina Albano;
Venue: SOAS Brunei Gallery

The second workshop examined cross-cultural traditions, customs and the rituals of eating and dining across major European cultures through an examination of European art. It explored the relationship to new eating customs being introduced into the western tradition, such as 'raw food', fusion of cross-cultural influences such as Japanese/Indian cuisines. In addition, how utensils and tableware influence eating behaviour, and how they change perceptions of food and eating. This session was less detailed but gave rise to some informed discussion and whereas other sessions revealed differences, this was about shared experiences and observations.

Workshop 3 – Sensory Deprivation (May 2005)
Session facilitators: Prof. Farida Fortune and Dr Charles Spence;
Venue: The Design Laboratory

The third workshop examined how we live in a world preoccupied by sight, which is considered to be the primary sense, how this prevalence affects the balance of the other four major senses, the role of Sensory Design and its effect on well-being for those who wish to be more receptive to food through their senses. Dr Ranjit Sondhi, who suffers from degenerative tunnel vision, provided specific insight into the context for sensory deprivation. Also discussed was the predominance of foods based on visual attractiveness, how perception offers possibilities for new paradigms of behaviour, social relations and food rituals, the ability of Sensory Design to potentially redress the digital/visually orientated world around us, the significance of women's visual orientation and the psychological aspects of sensory deprivation.

This session was initially problematic in finding someone to join the workshop group who could articulate their sense of loss and use of the senses. However, with Dr Sondhi this was successfully overcome and it led to a fascinating and unusual discussion, which incorporated many new tangents and considerations in relation to Sensory Design.

Workshop 4 – Smart Technologies/New Materials (June 2005)
Session facilitator: Dr Peter Barham; Venue: Innovation Centre,
Central Saint Martins

The fourth workshop investigated the role of sensuality and how various
materials affects us psychologically and physiologically, how food
technologies can influence food texture, surface and consistency. The
workshop also explored new trends in food technologies, the manufacture
and design of smart technologies, the role of smart technologies in
activating and stimulating the senses and the selection of materials and
properties for the future application in Sensory Design in relation to
nutrition, dietary needs and well-being.

The session was complex in that food production and food process were
mixed with food technology. The former gave rise to techniques for
enhancing and controlling food, whilst the potential for a more informed
exploration as to how smart technology could assist in Sensory Design
was inhibited by the lack of available examples. (In hindsight the session
would have benefited from being conducted in two parts.)

Workshop 5 – Nostalgia and Sensory Alchemy (October 2005)
Session facilitators: Heston Blumenthal/Dr Marianne Moore;
Venue: The Fat Duck Restaurant, Bray, Berkshire

This was a very popular workshop, [Figure 4] which was restricted in size
due to the need to have Heston Blumenthal available to cook the meal and
for comment at the table. Nevertheless, for those that attended it was a
unique opportunity to have a food experience that explored all five senses
and appreciate the role of Molecular Gastronomy in food delivery. It was
a complex participatory session, where taste and flavour could be tested
and views exchanged first hand, during the act of tasting [Figure 5]. The
difficulty was to remain objective, to detach the analysis of the session
from the enjoyment of the food and the surroundings of the restaurant.
The outcome was a total seduction and a well received sensorial delight
that successfully built sensory awareness. It constructed a narrative,
through which food could engage with memory and nostalgia and the
definition of the landscape of the table could be considered [Figure 6].

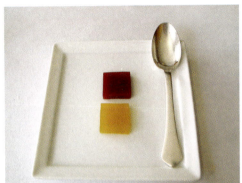

Figures 4 to 6,
left to right, top to bottom

Figure 4, Fat Duck Workshop, photo by Design
Laboratory team
Figure 5, Sensory Deception, photo by Vicky Hale
Figure 6, Science of Deliciousness, photo by Vicky Hale

Symposium – Sensory Design/'The Table Landscape' (Dec 2005)
Facilitators: Brent Richards (Chair) and Dr Marianne Moore;
Venue: The Lethaby Building, Central Saint Martins

The Symposium involved the presentation of papers by cluster members, based on each of the five workshops. This was organised as a vehicle for focusing the cluster into areas for future research, as a first step in evolving the case for establishing a new design discipline. The Symposium began with a sensorial overview – a series of cinematic examples were viewed, extracts from various contemporary European films such as 'Satyricon' (German) 'The Cook, his Wife, the Thief and her Lover' (UK), 'Jamón Jamón' (Spanish) 'Babette's Feast' (Danish), and 'Huveos de Oro' (Spanish), all depicting the 'landscape of the table 'ranging from food preparation, food etiquette, social intercourse, food preparation and taste. Thereafter, findings were presented in three parts, all followed by discussions, with video recording throughout. The Symposium was intended to simplify the scope of the cluster and enable the Team to seek a clear route towards a future research application. Whilst the insights proved fascinating, the day was a compact session and the number of presentations posed logistic difficulties. In hindsight, the Symposium could have been lengthened and made more specific.

Themes explored included:

- *The Landscape of the Table*
  Speaker Brent Richards (Architect and designer, Director of the Design Laboratory)
- *History, Anthropology and Psychology of Food*
  Speakers Dr Caterina Albano (Cultural historian/curator), Dr Hamish Park (Anthropologist), Dr Charles Spence (Psychologist)
- *Architecture, Social Design and History*
  Giuliana Salmaso (Salmaso Silvestrin Architects), Johnny Grey (Kitchen Designer), Philippa Glanville (V&A Historian)
- *Cuisine, Tableware and Performance Art*
  Andrew Benjamin (Molecular Gastronomy Chef, Bratislava), Prof. Rob Kessler (Ceramicist and NESTA Fellow), Prof. Francis McGlone (Neuroscientist Unilever and Liverpool University), Lucy Orta* (Artist/ Fashion Designer)

(*NB in Lucy Orta's absence there was a presentation of the film 'Late Lunch with Lucy' introduced by participant artist Lucy Stockton-Smith.)

Insights

The aim of the cluster was to provide a rich cross-disciplinary platform
whereby academics; practitioners, artists, designers and scientists could
engage in discussion and share insights. We found building a programme
for interdisciplinary discourse was a complex task when done within a
short time frame. In the process many issues had to be addressed including
varied use of nomenclature and scientific pragmatism over artistic
abstraction.

We found that the key issue when defining a new field of enquiry such as
'Sensory Design' is what strategy do you use for achieving focus? Should
focus be imposed at the outset in the form of a theoretical construct that
is then examined, explored and tested? Or should it be a longer process of
generating a landscape of possibilities pieced together step by step with no
ready conclusions or predetermined outcome?

It was not the cluster's aim to undertake detailed research in 1 year, rather
it was to enable an interested group of diverse specialists to cluster and
engage in dialogue and discourse. This built on the Design Laboratory's
previous interdisciplinary work. Due to the novelty of the subject and the
short period of time, it proved difficult to maintain consistency of the
cluster team and momentum in each topic.

Our discourse did reveal a very rich subject area and we realised the need
to encourage serendipity, allowing new guests to join the workshops
resisting imposing a focus too soon. The cluster activities have led to a
phase two project proposal entitled '*The Future Table Landscape*.'⁶ The
cluster process has led to new areas of consultancy with the London
Development Agency (LDA) Inspire programme, a Unilever workshop
in Brazil, involvement in the London Food Festival and inclusion in Prof.
John Krebs Christmas Lectures at the Royal Institution.

We would sincerely like to thank all those involved with the cluster and the
AHRC/EPSRC and those administering this process, for giving us this
opportunity to test the future and explore its potential in the field of
Sensory Design and its relationship to food.

Additional Reading

PALLASMAA, J., 2005. *The Eyes of the Skin: Architecture and the Senses.* Chichester: Wiley Academy.

ZARDINI, M., (ed.), 2006. *Sense of the City – An Alternative Approach to Urbanism.* Montréal : Canadian Centre for Architecture.

MCGEE, H., 2004. *Food & Cooking – An Encyclopaedia of Kitchen Science, History and Culture.* London: Hodder & Stoughton.

SNORRADOTTIR, A. and BJORGVINSDOTTIR, K., 2002. *About Fish.* Reykjavik: Lupina.

VILGIS, T. and ZIMMERMANN, A., 2007. *Wissenschaft al Dente.* Herder Freiberg.

THIS, H. & GAGNAIRE, P., 2006. *La Cuisine C'est de l'Amour, de l'Art, de la Technique.* Paris: Odile Jacob.

THIS, H., 2005. *Molecular Gastronomy: Exploring the Science of Flavour.* New York: Columbia University Press.

MCGEE, H., 2004. *On Food and Cooking – The Science and Lore of the Kitchen.* New York: Scribner Book Company.

LISTER, T. & BLUMENTHAL, H., 2005. *Kitchen Chemistry.* Royal Society of Chemistry.

BARHAM, P., 2001. *The Science of Cooking.* New York: Springer.

SCHWARCZ, J., 2005. *Let Them Eat Flax: 70 All-New Commentaries on the Science of Everyday Food & Life.* Toronto: Ecw Press.

BOURDAIN, A., 2006. *Decoding Ferran Adria* [DVD]. New York: Ecco Release data.

ADRIA, F. & SOLER. J., 2006. *El Bulli IV: 2003-2004.* New York: Ecco.

MERLEAU-PONTY, M., 2000. *The Primary of Perception.* Northwestern University Press.

The Emotional Wardrobe

Dr Sharon Baurley and Lisa Stead, (University of the Arts)

Overview

The central idea of the cluster is 'The Emotional Wardrobe' (EW), in which the conventions and cultures of fashion, as an expressive, emotional and communicative medium, are extended by integrating computer intelligence and digital communications. Similarly, digitally-augmented clothing is a paradigmatic goal of ubiquitous computing (ubicomp), the approach to computer design that takes advantage of mobile technology, wireless networks and personalisation. The EW is a fashion tool to explore and express the human condition, and it reveals and addresses emergent social, environmental, personal and technological concerns. It creates new challenges for design thinking in fashion and in computing. Our aim was to establish an interdisciplinary community centred on these themes, willing and able to advance design research by combining conceptual work with practical design examples and working prototypes.

In our vision of ubiquitous computing, digital systems will extend to clothing (and other everyday objects) via smart textiles and materials, which means that fashion will become a mediator of technology. To date much 'wearable technology' has been developed by the electronics and computing science sectors and has utilised clothing as a carrier of entertainment and communication systems. Less research has focused on the exploitation of technology for aesthetic, communicative and expressive purposes. 'What we are talking about here is a revolution, one which will require the electronics industry to think emotionally. . . we can not expect the fashion industry to adapt itself to technology. Rather the technology industry will have to learn how to deal with fashion.'[1] The fashion industry is not exploiting the potential that mobile and computational technology could offer, although notable exceptions include Elise Dee Co., MIT, USA, Cute Circuit and David Agnelli from the Interaction Design Institute, Ivrea, Italy, 5050 Studio Ltd., New York. To address

[1] MARZANO, S., (ed.), 2000. *New Nomads: An Exploration of Wearable Electronics by Philips*. Rotterdam: 010 Publishers.

the emotional application of technology to the body, a union of the two
industries is required. The integration of smart functionality into clothing
and other textile products will fundamentally change cultures of clothing,
peoples' relationships with them, and the way clothing is designed. The
development process will necessitate information and communication
technology (ICT) cultures to be synthesised with established cultures
of clothing and clothing design. This will require a multidisciplinary
approach, transcending the current boundaries, languages and processes
of the industries involved.

This cluster brought together the disparate and largely unassimilated
disciplines of fashion, technology and user research, and asked and
assessed whether such a merger could bring added value to the consumer
and the industries involved, and what this will mean to the process of
research, creation and production of an EW. The project was initiated and
hosted by Central Saint Martins College of Art and Design, University of
the Arts London. In the Wardrobe was Sharon Baurley, Martin Woolley
and Lisa Stead of the School of Fashion and Textile Design at Central
Saint Martins College of Art and Design, Erik Geelhoed of Hewlett-
Packard Labs, Phil Gosset of Vodafone Future Studies, Matthew Chalmers
of the Department of Computing Science at University of Glasgow,
Peter Excell of the School of Informatics at University of Bradford, Joan
Farrer of the School of Fashion and Textile Design at Royal College of
Art, Jeremy Pitt and Petar Goulev of the Department of Electronic and
Electrical Engineering at Imperial College London, and Christian Heath
of the Management Centre at King's College London.

The main themes that we set out to investigate throughout the year were:

Emotional connection

This is about gaining an understanding of how we create meaning through
what we consume, by enabling individuals to build their own stories
using personally relevant information including moods, interests, history,
geography and ethical concerns.

[2] CHRISTIE, I. and
WARBURTON, D., 2001. *From
Here to sustainability: Politics
in the Real World*. Earthscan
Publications.

Research[2] has highlighted consumers' deep dissatisfaction with the
'stress and spend' culture of millennium Britain. Increased affluence and
enhanced standard of living has not resulted in an increased sense of
well-being, and people are looking beyond consumerism for things that
give life meaning, enhance experience, and provide emotional connection
between people and things, people and places. Additionally, they are

[3] RHEINGOLD, H., 2002. *Smart Mobs: The Next Social Revolution*. Cambridge, MA: Basic Books.

[4] KYFFIN, S., 2002. *The Question of Design*. In: E. AARTS & S. MARZANO, (eds.) The new everyday. Rotterdam: 010 Publishers.

increasingly worried about the connected problems of waste, globalisation and sustainability. Clothing is an emotional medium. There is awareness in the ICT sector that computer system design needs to broaden to address social interaction and emotive expression. Issues might include:

- How will this impact on the traditional place and role these products have in our everyday lives?
- Will changing consumer requirements, fulfilled by smart textile technology, contribute to more sustainable production and consumption through creating stronger emotional connections between consumers, makers and products?
- Could the merger of fashion/clothing and digital technology contribute to the endeavour to make computer design more human-centric, individual and emotive?

Human connectedness

This is about broadening the range of expressive communication channels of clothing.

Advances in communication technology have provided new forms of messaging, such as email and text messaging, which aid personal and business communication. 'The killer applications of tomorrow's mobile information communication industry won't be hardware devices or software programmes, but social practices.'[3] Clothing is a communicative medium. The marriage of design and technology in the 21st century will require designers to design interactions, 'Not only are we designing the new material aspects of objects, but we are also creating new levels of relationships, between ourselves and the things we make, and between individual people and between groups of people mediated by those things.'[4] By bringing sensor and network technology to the body, new forms of communication could be enabled. Issues might include:

- Can the use of cutting-edge ICT in personal everyday products such as clothes help ubicomp achieve its goal of facilitating new rich forms of interaction while staying in the background of our lives?
- Could emotional aesthetics promote face-to-face and more personally expressive communication?
- Could personal 'emotional' communication provide therapeutic benefits for the wearer?

Customisation and creativity

This is about enhancing people's expressive and creative possibilities.

It has been suggested that in the future creativity will no longer be the preserve of the 'creative class'. People have always been creative within the boundaries of their lives, but by enlarging and dissolving those boundaries, people's creativity might well be enhanced. It will be imperative to educate and develop people who think in lateral and creative ways. Clothing is an expressive medium; it facilitates individualistic expression, allowing individuals to differentiate themselves and to declare their uniqueness. The success of Issey Miyake's APOC range, which allows low-tech customisation of garments through material technology, demonstrates that consumers welcome the chance to become part of the process of creation. Clothing aesthetics that can be dynamically personalised could encourage new ways of creative thinking through aesthetic, informative, cultural and gaming explorations. Issues might include:

- Could embedded intelligence satisfy intangible consumer requirements that are experiential, creative and sensory?
- Could active and interactive customisation lead to new forms of 'creative thinking'?
- Will the designer's role be more one of a facilitator, enabling users to 'co-create' and appropriate the technology? What would such a shift towards a democracy of design mean for the fashion industry in terms of the role of the designer, the manufacture of garments, and the fashion cycle of seasonal trends?
- How can wide-scale design of infrastructure for computation, communication and collaboration contribute to 'design for appropriation'?

Aim

Our aim was to explore how the value of clothing and fashion can be extended through its synthesis with information and communication functions, informed by and informing new technological developments, and building on the traditional concepts of clothing and associated cultures as expressive and communicative media that connect the body with our social world.

Objectives

Our objectives included:

- Forging a holistic, innovative and interdisciplinary research community through advisory group meetings, open workshops and collaborative development of concepts and prototypes.
- Exploring the implications for clothing in society and for the fashion industry, focusing on research and development in design processes and manufacturing (LCA), and how to design for personalisation, co-creation and appropriation by wearers.
- Contributing to research in ubiquitous computing by advancing design that is personal, adaptive and communicative.
- Determining ways to rationalise the cultures and timescales of different industries, in particular the in-built obsolescence of fashion and the development timelines of technology.
- Establishing a common forum for eliciting 21st century priorities and issues for further research, and to prepare and submit research funding proposals for new product development and design research.
- Highlighting future imperatives and directions for the relevant industries, namely high-specification products and more sustainable production and consumption [Figure 1].

Emotional communication & support

Net: used to maintain one-to-one, group, local and global relationships through emails, chat rooms, etc

Mob comms: nearly always used to maintain one-to-one, close relationships over distance – often ad-hoc comms, which can seem valueless. Used to maintain social relationships – group preening and status

Fashion: used to maintain one to others and one-to-one relationships through face-to-face communication. Can support close relationships or initiate communication with strangers. Used to maintain social status and group allegiance

Social impact

Net: less face-to-face communication – can assume a false identity

Mob comms: allow mobile behaviours that would normally appear rude, often a barrier to use when social rules conflict. – less face-to-face communication

Fashion: encourages face-to-face communication but can be used to construct a false identity. The 'messages' that are communicated are sometimes ambiguous and misunderstood

Self display

Net: expression of self identity through authoring tools – webpages, blogs, podcasts etc

Mob comms: phone as fashion statement: customisation of look, sound and function – conspicuous display of identity.

Fashion: expression of self-identity through aesthetics and meaning. Can be real or constructed self. Can be customised

Figure 1, Shared attributes between fashion, mobile communications and wireless communications

Activities

One of the main issues that arose from day one, was that of taking a 'thinking through doing' approach. We were conscious not to become bogged down in rhetoric, but to 'do' and 'make' things as a valid form of investigation and understanding. We took a cyclical divergent and concretisation approach, not to solve anything, but to elaborate the territory.

Workshop 1: 09.03.05 – 'Open Forum', Central Saint Martins College of Art and Design

The 'Open Forum' Workshop was a facilitated event to formulate 'what' and 'how' we would explore in the forthcoming workshops. We began with warm-up exercises to focus the members' thoughts on their own experience of clothing and fashion.

Methods of enquiry

'Bring and tell'

Cluster members brought in a favourite or disliked garment to discuss issues around: Does it evoke any particular emotions or memories? Does it have a story? Does it communicate your identity? When do you wear it? How does it make you feel?

'Scrapbox Challenge'

During the 'Scrapbox Challenge' we selected a garment that we disliked from a selection of second-hand clothes and evaluated its negative features in terms of its mis-match to our identity or interests. We then used parts of other garments, fabrics and fastenings to remodel the garment to make it acceptable. In small groups we discussed the changes we made and why we made them [Figure 2].

Figure 2,
'Scrapbox' challenge, fashion studios, Central Saint Martins, Charing Cross Road

'Brain Drawing'

We engaged in some facilitated 'daydreaming', thinking up 'wouldn't it be nice if…' scenarios/ideas, based around the three themes. Using 'Brain Drawing' techniques we condensed the 'wouldn't it be nice if' scenarios into problem statements and issues to be explored in workshop 2. This was facilitated by Remko van der Lugt of the Technical University of Delft, Netherlands [Figure 3].

Workshop 2: 06.04.05 – 'Explore', Department of Electrical and Electronic Engineering, Imperial College London

Definition of problem statements

The aim of the 'Explore' workshop was to identify a meaningful time and place for technological intervention within the problem statements, and uncover the interesting questions and issues that it posed. The problem statements for the thematic groups were:

Emotional connection

- How to reveal and respond to emotions?
- When would we want to reveal or respond to emotions, what might the emotions be and how could the wearer/user adapt and control this information?

Human connectedness

- How could real life become a game (a sub-culture), or a game become real life?
- What would define the game, how and when could the information be used to reveal/conceal allegiance and how could the wearer/user adapt and control this information?

Customisation and creativity

- How to collect and build up traces of history? What you saw, where you have been and so on.
- What they are, when would we would want to collect/share and exchange information, and how could the wearer/user adapt and control this information?

Appropriation of given designs,
images, logos, messages, symbols

Wouldn't it be nice if . . .

Steal and Mutate Corporate, Logos – to display on me
Could 'play' with your garment, move around aesthetics
I could change what a garment (I think) says
We could download patterns/colours to clothing
Garments had variable dynamics to 'dance' with us
We had computing systems, which are as expressive as clothing
Read images could be taken straight out of the brain
New forms of communication

Games performance

Wouldn't if be nice if . . .

If there was a reward. . . contained motivation surprise
Be part of a real life game-virtual world
Transform identities
I could play the chameleon game
Customise your clothing like an avatar in games
Wouldn't it be nice to display game state/identity in a public
environment

Showing history of places,
encounters, ideas

Wouldn't if be nice if . . .

Echoes of city history ripple across my sleeve
My garment helped me to reflect on the way. . .
My garment revealed what I value or think matters
Collected experience like memory
Your garment picked up and kept pictures of the 'everyday'
Memento sensory as aesthetics
Garment as a blog, and share blogs

Sub-culture

Wouldn't if be nice if . . .

My garments told me about a sub-culture I don't understand
My garments gave me a sense of belonging
We could discover subcultures and their nuggets, and share them
Re. Conscience – if sub-cultures could be defined by emotions
We explored/developed a new one
To share secrets

Figure 3, 'Brain drawing' – 'wouldn't it be nice if' garment scenarios

Methods of enquiry

We explored the problem statements through mapping scenarios. 'Role-play' was used to expand the scenarios and consider the context, and reactions and needs of multiple people within the scenarios. Each group documented their role-play with photographs, which were composed into a 'storyboard'. Key moments in the interaction were annotated. The role of the garments was considered, for example, whether they could be enhanced to aid social interaction, how they might 'behave' on command instinctively, or be triggered to react and what would be the key questions or issues were identified to take forward into the next workshop:

Emotional connection scenario – 'Shopping'

• Is it possible to use garments to disguise unconscious emotional display in order to support conscious display?

Human connectedness scenarios – 'On the Tube'/'In the Classroom'

• How could a garment be used to facilitate social interaction?
• How does clothing communication fit naturally into conversational threads?
• Is there any value in realising the knowledge of individuals as collective intelligence?
• How subtle do these codes need to be?

Customisation and creativity scenarios – 'Trading and Warping Logos'/ 'At the Castle'

• Could tools be designed to facilitate intuitive 'image picking' from others, which could then be personally modified?
• Different users might want to collect personalised information from the same source to make an 'experience' relevant and more enjoyable.

Workshop 3: 25.05.05 – 'Create', School of Informatics, University of Bradford

During the 'Create' workshop we used visualisation techniques to elaborate and concretise some of the scenarios from the previous workshop. The aim was to use different media to 'tell the stories' to a user group in the final workshop [Figure 4].

Figure 4,
'Play acting' – Multi-layered
conversational threads, 'Create'
workshop

Methods of enquiry

Initial ideas discussed were sketched by animation students to promote
shared understanding. These sketches were used as a basis for mocking-
up garment prototypes for the final workshop. The scenarios were then
'role-played' by actors as a way of concretising the stories, and filmed and
photographed. A Vicon motion-capture suite was used to isolate gestures
and postures involved in acting-out the scenarios. Working with the actors
was especially helpful as they were able to input their natural reactions
and gestures. The principle of the system is that the motion-capture
stick people can be reclothed with entirely different garments and body
appearances. This would be a powerful way of visualising the scenarios in
quite a complete form, because it would be possible to create 'futuristic'
garments in the computer animation in a way that was reasonably
realistic. This technology is readily available, having been developed for
fantasy movies and computer games [Figure 5].

Workshop 4: 06–07.09.05 – 'Observe', Hewlett-Packard labs, Bristol

The 'Observe' workshop was about eliciting feedback from a teen user
study group on the scenarios and stories of the past year, and also to test
out ideas around how we might design appropriable things using
'co-design' techniques.

Methods of enquiry

Co-Design is a method to elicit people's dreams and desires, as well as
preferences and priorities about a particular thing or place. The workshop
was facilitated by Stijn Ossevoort of ETHZurich, who has worked
extensively with this method. We asked study subjects to generate stories

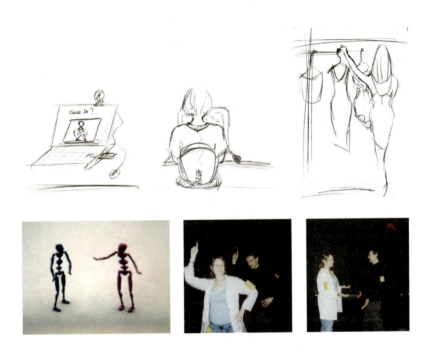

Figure 5, Generative techniques used in the 'Create' workshop. Sketches by F. Katherine You

by expressing the relationships they have with their clothing, for example, their favourite outfit. The user group created collages from images, text and colour to communicate their ideas. The idea is that these stories provide inspiration for product design, not solutions [Figure 6].

In a simple user study, we employed the prototype mock-ups as 'research probes' to communicate our ideas. The prototypes comprised simple touch and gesture textile sensors and light-emitting fabric display actuators. Study subjects were asked to provide responses to questions around the three thematic areas.

The Emotional Connection questions were:

- If your garment could tell you things about itself, what would you like it to tell you? Messages, its history, who made it, who else is wearing the garment (that is, a celebrity) How would wearing it make you feel, would you like it to communicate with another garment in the same brand?
- Would you like clothing to show your body signals or emotions?

 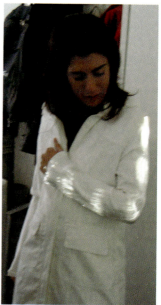

Figure 6, Co-Design techniques used in the 'Observe' workshop
Figure 7, Garment prototype as 'probe' for the user study, 'Observe' workshop

These are some of the responses:
'If your garment communicated with garments of the same brand you would know who else is wearing what.'
'If you displayed your heartbeat on your clothing then people will know if you are, for example, unconfident, and maybe people will be more sympathetic.'
'If you are wearing something that you are not actually happy about and your garment showed it, then you will not feel so confident.' [Figure 7]

The Human Connectedness group wondered:

• At the moment I can talk to someone face-to-face, on a landline, use a mobile to talk or text, send a letter, pass a note, stick a message on the fridge and so on. What if I could also send and receive messages through what I was wearing?
• What would I want to say with what I am wearing, rather than any of the above ways?
• What would I want to see or know from other people?
• Would I use it with people who are strangers?

These are some of the responses:
'You could say, "I'm hung over today, please don't talk to me" with your clothing.'
'Will encourage people to talk, which is a positive thing.'
'You could send out an SOS when you are lost.'
'It would be good if you could walk around with almost a kind of an advert explaining, for example, what you would like to buy or find and someone else could help you if they knew where to find that.'

The Customisation and Creativity questions were:

• What if you could adapt your clothing, and use others' clothing to do that? If you saw a pattern or logo on another's shirt, would you like to take it and put it on to yours?
• How about images off the web, or from your camera – would you put them on to your jacket for others to see? What for? What would you be saying about you and your relationship to others?

These are some of their responses:
'I would not like something that was just given to me, but would like an image from a friend who made or customised it.'
'Some images could stir discrimination, if someone is against some band that you were into, you would be judged.'

'If people had on their t-shirts a list of things they were interested in, it would be interesting; you may see that you do judge people. You could look at someone and say. . . what is that hat all about, but find out that you are very similar to that person.'
'An image might make you curious to talk to that person.'

In terms of meeting our aims and objectives we were able to foster an holistic, innovative and interdisciplinary research community through our experimental 'thinking through doing' approach which utilised the different skills of the group to formulate and explore near future scenarios for wearable technology. Design was seen as a shared activity across cluster membership and disciplines. A central concern for the EW was to position cluster members as facilitators of experiences for the wearer rather than dictators of use. Through our co-design and user study design experiments we have experimented with a method of designing for personalisation and appropriation by the consumer. This is a new way of working and thinking for the fashion industry, which could have major implications for the education and role of future designers. Through our co-design and user study design experiments to investigate user-centred scenarios, we have made a contribution to research in ubiquitous computing. The practice determined a method of designing for personalisation and appropriation by the consumer, which merged the ubiquity of computing with fashion culture and practices. Industrial solutions that rationalise the cultures and timescales of different industries would require further investigation. However, the cluster focus on 'design for appropriation' and customisation might offer a solution to counteract the disposable nature of fashion by making a single garment or system adaptable to changes in trends, and developments in technology. Through our experimental workshop techniques, we have established a method with which to try to determine catalysts and drivers for a wearable/ fashion tech market, a 21st century research priority, around which a new funding proposal is being written. Future imperatives for computing were highlighted by greater engagement with material culture, its drivers and consumers; also crucial was a design and development methodology, that is, using design or creative tools to facilitate multidisciplinary collaboration which promoted knowledge sharing and shared understanding. The imperative of sustainability was also highlighted in terms of consumer wearable technology being less about the materiality of the product and more about the intangible benefits it bestows.

We adopted an experimental approach to the methods of enquiry we used. Most of the 'thinking through doing' methods worked well as a means to focus everyone's mind on the topic or scenarios, as they were a means to make them tangible, rather than discussing something in the abstract. This methodology is also a good way of mobilising each other's tacit knowledge. We were experimental in that we took risks, as no one had experience of using the techniques for our particular purpose, and hence we didn't know where the processes would take us. This was effective in that we often had surprising results, but problematic as this process was not always 'comfortable', and some problems reflected normal negotiating situations.

Being comfortable with exploring unknown territory and new design spaces with unknown people from unfamiliar fields, using untried methods, is a major challenge associated with multi-disciplinary collaboration. It is also challenging to keep an open mind when the direction or outcome of an activity is not clear. However, the results or thematic priorities and topics that arise from multidisciplinary collaboration tend to be more robust and have greater integrity, as all related disciplines are present in the equation.

Insights

At the end of the year we had established a user-inclusive way of thinking about clothing/fashion that generated new research and design methods and revealed a series of critical issues and questions. The cluster year gave us space to think and question without the need to solve any technical problems. This resulted in a range of pertinent and interesting research questions to be explored in further research projects, a collection of generative research methods on which to build, and a group of key insights.

Key questions

Interaction: when, how and why we interact? How could technology facilitate and enhance these interactions?

Appropriation: how can we design for appropriation? How do users/ wearers take what has been designed and make it their own? How will user-appropriation affect the role of the designer, and the ways in which clothing is manufactured, sold and consumed?

Adaptive behaviour: technology changes the meaning of language; what kind of impact on human interactions and social norms might the EW have?

Sustainability: the EW is about consuming something intangible, beyond the materiality of clothing. Could clothing deliver messages about sustainability, and the ethical/unethical manufacture of garments? Could we build-in product longevity by understanding more about how people respond emotionally to them?

Privacy: would people be willing to relinquish some degree of perceived privacy in exchange for enhanced benefits?

Gender: female fashion design choices are very wide and flexible; would technical/smart clothing extend the boundaries of male fashion?

Key insights

Scoping the unknown: EW sectors and markets don't exist; defining territory is difficult, but exciting! Therefore, the process of eliciting desires is very important to determine catalysts and drivers for this new genre of fashion/clothing, for which we need to engage users from the start.

Design for appropriation: new design tools that enable people to create their own stories and meanings for an age of mass-customisation.

Participative design: is a new paradigm for fashion design. Users become co-designers. New generative tools are required for user participation. The prototype becomes a social probe. Participative design is an iterative process where the user provides insights, inspiration and feedback; the user creates and innovates!

Multidisciplinarity: knowledge flows need to be managed between people to facilitate knowledge creation and sharing. This process can be assisted by 'thinking through doing', using a broad range of generative techniques that help the thought process, and promotes a shared understanding.

Issues for design

It is clear that 'smart' clothing/fashion requires a rethink of the design process, not only in terms of the materiality of the product, but also of the 'intangible benefits' it can bestow via ubiquitous computing and mobile communications. In the face of technological shifts, the notion of a designer having a core skill is even more imperative, but added to that will be a transdisciplinary design skill of designing interactions and sensorial experiences. Design of smart clothing is complex, involving an array of specialists, as well as users for ideation and evaluation, meaning that design will become a collaborative activity rather than a singular one. We feel that design, through 'thinking through doing' techniques, could be pivotal as a means to facilitate teamwork working in a multidisciplinary group, becoming a translator or mediator. Such design is also complex as this sector doesn't exist. Design could also be pivotal in determining what the 'intangible benefits' might be, by engaging users in the design process to provide inspiration. Actively involving users in the exploration and design of garments using co-design or participative design techniques, are radically new ways of thinking and working for the fashion and textiles industry. These methods also have implications for the education and the role of the fashion designer, where the designer could become a facilitator of 'experiences' rather than an individual dictator of look and use. Design for appropriation, where people are empowered to create their own stories and meanings for an age of personalisation and a participative culture, will enable them to be proactive rather than reactive to technological change. The sustainable design agenda might be enhanced if 'intangible benefits' (communication, socialisation and expression) become more important than the materiality of the product itself, delivered through wireless dynamically-changeable clothing.

The mechanism of clusters or networks is very effective in defining or scoping new territory and design spaces, in that they allow risky and experimental exploration. Thematic work in new territories is often difficult to get funded without some kind of track record; a workshop project is a good precursor to larger scale research.

The Future for the Wardrobe

Future plans for the EW include a future international conference at HP Labs. It will aim to bring together like-minded people interested in wearable technology, interaction design, co-creation and emotion. The conference will feature papers, workshops and interactive technology demonstrations and contextualise the work of the group in an international setting of peers. We aim to be at the forefront of fostering a transdisciplinary community that merges its collective knowledge into a new research space with its own priorities, methodologies and visions of the future. In terms of further study, an integrated research programme is being written that will seek to determine what the catalysts and drivers of future consumer wearable technology that permits communication and expression might be, and by extension, the market. We propose to locate potential teenage user groups at the centre of the development of fashion/clothing design prototypes by engaging them as co-developers and evaluators. We're also planning to publish a book, which would encapsulate our vision of the future for this thematic area.

www.emotionalwardrobe.com

Additional Reading

Fashion theory

ASH, J. and WILSON, E., (eds.), 1992. *Chic Thrills: A Fashion Reader*. London: Pandora Press.

BARNARD, M., 1996. *Fashion as Communication*. London and New York: Routledge.

DAVIS, F., 1994. *Fashion, Culture and Identity*. Chicago: The University of Chicago Press.

ENTWISTLE, J., 2000. *The Fashioned Body: Fashion, Dress and Modern Social Theory*. Cambridge: Polity Press.

EVANS, C. et al., 2005. *Hussein Chalayan*. Rotterdam: NAi Publishers.

FINKLESTEIN, J., 1991. *The Fashioned Self*. Cambridge: Polity Press.

HOLLANDER, A., 1980. *Seeing Through Clothes*. New York: Avon.

KAISER, S., 1990. *The Social Psychology of Clothing*. USA: Macmillan Publishing Company.

LURIE, A., 1981. *The Language of Clothes*. London: Heinneman.

WILSON, E., 2003. *Adorned in Dreams: Fashion and Modernity*. 2ⁿᵈ ed. London, New York: I.B.Tauris.

Fashion and Technology

BOLTON, A., 2002. *The Supermodern Wardrobe*. London: V&A Publications.

LEE, S., 2005. *Fashioning the Future: Tomorrow's Wardrobe*. London: Thames & Hudson.

QUINN, B., 2002. *Techno Fashion*. Oxford, New York: Berg.

Computational Aesthetics / Interaction Design

ARK, W. S., 1999. A look at human interaction with pervasive computing. *IBM Systems Journal*, 38(4).

ETTER, R., 2005. *Aware Fashion* [online]. Available at: http://www.richardetter.net/awarefashion.php (Accessed 28 June 2005).

BAURLEY, S., 2005. Interaction Design in Smart Textiles Clothing and Applications. *In*: X. TAO, (ed.) *Wearable Electronics and Photonics*. Cambridge: Woodhead.

BAURLEY, S., 2004. Interactive and experiential design in smart textile products and applications. *Personal and Ubiquitous Computing*, 8(1), pp. 274-281.

CO, E. D., 2000. *Computation and Technology as Expressive Elements of Fashion*. Master's thesis, Massachusetts Institute of Technology.

CONSTAS, I. and PAPADOPOULOS, D., 2001. Interface-Me: Pursuing Sociability Through Personal Devices. *Personal and Ubiquitous Computing*, 5, pp. 1-6.

Cute Circuit. Available at: http://www.cutecircuit.com.

Fashion Victims. Available at: http://www.fashionvictims.org

Studio 50:50. Available at: http://www.5050ltd.com/

France Telecom's Studio-creatif. Available at: http://www.studio-creatif.com

FUSAKUL, S. M., 2002. *Interactive Ornaments*. Master's thesis, Royal College of Art.

GALBRAITH, M. L., 2003. *Embedded Systems for Computational Garment Design*. Master's thesis, Massachusetts Institute of Technology.

GALLOWAY, A., 2004. Fashion Sensing/Fashion Sense. *HorizonZero*, 16(August) [online]. Available at: http://www.horizonzero.ca/textsite/

International Fashion Machines. Available at: http://www.ifmachines.com

Interaction Design Institute in Ivrea. Available at: http://interaction-ivrea.it

MORIWAKI, K., 2004. Between the Skin and the Garden. *HorizonZero*, 16(August) [online]. Available at: http://www.horizonzero.ca/textsite/

MORIWAKI, K., 2005. From silk to microcontrollers. *Rhizome*, 4 June [online]. Available at: http://rhizome.org/discuss/view/16921

PAPADOPOULOS, D., 2004. *Fashion of the Times*. 50:50Ltd [online]. Available at: http://www.5050ltd.com/articles/Fashions_ofthe_Times.pdf

WEI, S. X. et al., 2003. Demonstrations of Expressive Software and Ambient Media. *In: Proceedings of the 5ᵗʰ International Conference on Ubiquitous Computing, UBICOMP2003, Seattle, 12-15 October 2003*. ACM Press, pp. 131-136. Available at: http://www.ubicomp.org/ ubicomp2003/program.html?show=demos

WHITTAKER, S., 2003. Things to talk about when talking about things. *Human-Computer Interaction*, 18, pp. 149-70.

SELKER, T. & BURLESON, W., 2000. Context-aware design and interaction in computer systems. *IBM Systems Journal*, 39(3/4).

Urban chameleon. Available at: http://www.kakirine.com/chameleon/

XS Labs. Available at: http://www.xslabs.net/theory.html

Smart or Electronic Textiles

PARADISO, R., LORIGA, G. and TACCINI, N., 2004. Wearable Health-Care System for Vital Signs Monitoring. *In: IFMBE Proceedings of MEDICON and Health Telematics 2004, Mediterranean Conference on Medical and Biological Engineering, Medicon 2004, Naples, 31ˢᵗ July- 5ᵗʰ August 2004* [CD-ROM], Volume 6.

RANDELL, C., BAURLEY, S., ANDERSON, I., MULLER, H. and BROCK, P., 2005. Sensor Sleeve: Sensing Affective Gestures. *In: Proceedings of the 9ᵗʰ International Symposium on Wearable Computers (ISWC), Osaka, 18-21 November 2005*. California: Institute of Electrical and Electronic Engineers.

RANDELL, C., BAURLEY, S., CHALMERS, M. and MULLERM, H., 2004. Textile tools for wearable computing. *In: Proceedings of the 1ˢᵗ International Forum on Applied Wearable Computing, Bremen, March 2004*. pp. 63-74.

VENTURE DEVELOPMENT CORPORATION, 2003. *Smart fabrics and interactive textiles: a global market opportunity assessment*. USA: VDC.

Design and Emotion

DESMET, P., 2002. *Designing Emotions*. Delft: Delft University of Technology.

DUNNE, A. & RABY, F., 2001. *Design Noir: The Secret Life of Electronic Objects*. Basel: Birkhausel.

NORMAN, D. A., 2004. *Emotional Design: Why We Love (or Hate) Everyday Things*. New York: Basic Books.

MATTELMÄKI, T. & KEINONEN, T., 2001. Design for Brawling – Exploring Emotional Issues for Concept Design. *In: Proceedings of The International Conference on Affective Human Factors Design, London, 26-29th June 2001*. Asean Academic Press.

Ubiquitous Computing

AARTS, E. and MARZANO, S., (eds.), 2003. *The New Everyday: Views on Ambient Intelligence*. Rotterdam: 010 Publishers.

ARK, W., DRYER, D. and LU, D., 1999. The Emotion Mouse. *In*: H. J. BULLINGER & J. ZIEGLER, (eds.) *Human-Computer Interaction: Ergonomics and User Interfaces*. Lawrence Erlbaum Associates, pp. 818-823.

BARKHUUS, L. et al., 2005. Picking Pockets on the Lawn: The Development of Tactics and Strategies in a Mobile Game. *In: Proceedings of the Ubiquitous Computing Conference, Ubicomp 2005, Tokyo, 11-14th September 2005*. LNCS 3660, pp. 358-374.

BICKMORE, T. W. and PICARD, R. W., 2005. Establishing and maintaining long-term human-computer relationships. *ACM Transactions on Computer-Human Interaction*, 12(2), pp. 293-327.

GERSHENFIELD, N., 1999. *When Things Start to Think*. London, Hodder and Stoughton.

GOULEV, P. and MAMDANI, E., 2003. Investigation of Human Affect During Electronic Commerce Activities. *In: Proceedings of Eurowearable 2003*. Birmingham: IEE Press, pp. 41-46.

GOULEV, P. and MAMDANI, E., 2003. Utilizing Real-time Affectivesensors to Incorporate Emotions into Human Computer Interactions. *In: Proceedings of the International Workshop on Wearable and Implantable Body Sensor Networks, London, 6-7th April 2004*.

GOULEV, P., STEAD, L., MAMDANI, E. and EVANS, C., 2004. Computer aided emotional fashion. *Computers & Graphics*, 28(5), pp. 657-666.

BELL, M. et al., 2006. Interweaving Mobile Games with Everyday Life. *In: Proceedings of the Human Factors in Computing Systems Conference, ACM CHI 2006, Montreal, 22-27th April 2006*. ACM Press, pp. 417-426.

KIRSCH, D., PICARD, R.W., RICHARDS, W. A. and HEIN, A.V., 1997. *The Sentic Mouse: Developing a Tool for Measuring Emotional Valence* [online]. Available at: http://vismod.media.mit.edu/tech-reports/TR-495/

MANDANI, E. H. and GAINES, B. R., (eds.), 1981. *Fuzzy Reasoning and its Applications.* London: Academic Press.

PICARD, R., 1997. *Affective Computing.* Cambridge, MA: MIT Press.

PICARD, R. W., 2000. Toward computers that recognize and respond to user emotion. *IBM System Journal*, 39(3/4), pp. 705-710.

PICARD, R. & HEALEY, J., 1997. Affective Wearables. *In: Proceedings of the First International Symposium on Wearable Computers, Cambridge, MA, 13-14ᵗʰ October 1997.* IEEE.

PICARD, R.W. and KLEIN, J., 2002. Computers that recognize and respond to user emotion: Theoretical and practical implications. *Interacting with Computers*, 14, pp. 141-169.

PIACRD, R.W., VYZAS, E. and HEALEY, J., 2001. Towards machine emotional intelligence: Analysis of affective physiological state. *IEEE Transactions on Pattern Analysis and Machine Intelligence*, 23, pp. 1175 - 1191.

PITT, J.V., MAMDANI, A. and STATHIS, K., 1998. A Cooperative Information System for the Connected Community. In: F. DARSES and P. ZARATE, (eds.) *Proceedings of the Third International Conference on the Design of Cooperative Systems, COOP'98, Cannes, 26-29ᵗʰ May 1998.* Rocquencourt: INRIA Press, Volume 2, pp. 72-76. .

PITT, J. V., and MAMDANI, A., 1999. Communication Protocols in Multi-Agent Systems. *In*: M. GREAVES and J. BRADSHAW, (eds.) *Specifying and Implementing Conversation Policies. Workshop Proceedings of Autonomous Agents Conference, AA99, Seattle, 1 May 1999.* ACM Press.

MARZANO, S. & ARTS, E., 2003. *The New Everyday, Views on Ambient Intelligence.* Rotterdam: 010 Press.

STEAD, L., GOULEV, P., EVANS, C. and MAMDANI, E., 2004. The Emotional Wardrobe. *In: 2AD: Proceedings of the Second International Conference on Appliance Design 2004, Bristol, 11-13ᵗʰ May 2004.* The Appliance Design Network.

WEISER, M., 1996. *Ubiquitous Computing* [online]. Available at: www.ubiq.com/hypertext/weiser/UbiHome.html

Mobile Communications

BERG, S. et al., 2003. *Mobile phones for the next generation: device designs for teenagers* [online]. Available at: http://research.microsoft.com/~ast/files/CHI_2003.pdf

ISHII, H. et al., 2002. ComTouch: Design of a Vibrotactile Communication Device. *In: Proceedings of the Symposium on Designing Interactive Systems, London, 25-28ᵗʰ June 2002*. ACM Press.

CRISLER, K. et al., 2004. A User-Centred Approach to the Wireless World. *In*: R. TAFAZOLLI, (ed.) *Technologies for the Wireless Future: Wireless World Research Forum*. New York: Wiley, pp. 15-74.

KIPÖZ, S. *Design Since the Mobile Phone Become a Fashion Item* [online]. Available at: http://www.ub.es/5ead/PDF/3/Kipoz.pdf

LASEN, A., 2002. A comparative study of mobile phone use in public places in London, Madrid and Paris [online]. Vodafone. Available at: http://www.dwrc.surrey.ac.uk/Publications/tabid/56/Default.aspx

EXCELL, P. S., 2002. The Future of Convergent Computer and Telecommunications Technology. *In*: R. EARNSHAW and J. Vince, (eds.) *Intelligent Agents for Mobile and Virtual Media*. London: Springer, pp. 47-54.

EXCELL., P. S., 2002. Future Usage Scenarios for Personal Communications Devices and Their Relationship to Safety Compliance. *In: Proceedings of the EMC Europe Conference, Sorrento, 9-13ᵗʰ September 2002*. IEEE, pp. 515-519.

EXCELL, P. S. & ROBISON, D., 2004. From a Constrained Present to a Ubiquitous Future: Envisioning the Evolution Path for Mobile Graphical Communications. *In: Proceedings of the Electronic Imaging and the Visual Arts Conference, Florence*, pp. 212-216.

ALLEN, P., ROBISON, D. and EXCELL, P. S., 2003. The Interaction of Cultural and Technological Processes: The Lessons of Mobile Media. *In: Proceedings of the Electronic Imaging and the Visual Arts Conference, London*, pp. 51-59.

SCAFFOLRD, P. EXCELL, P., 2004. Aesthetics-Driven Mobile Product Design as an Educational Vehicle. *In: Proceedings of the Electronic Imaging and the Visual Arts Conference, Florence, April 2004*, pp. 294-299.

User Research

BAURLEY, S., GELHOED, E. & MOORE, A., 2006. Communication-Wear: user evaluation of two prototypes. *In: Proceedings of the International Symposium on Wearable Computers, Montreux, 11-14th October 2006*. IEEE Press.

BLYTHE, M., REID, J., WRIGHT, P. and GEELHOED, E., 2006. Interdisciplinary criticism: analysing the experience of riot! A location sensitive digital narrative. *Behaviour & Information Technology*, 25(2), pp. 127-139.

DE BRUINE, A., JEFFRIES, H., GEELHOED, E., HULL, R. & PIGGOTT, N., 2005. Augmenting Digital Audio Broadcast with Rich Data. Paper presented at the *ACM SIGCHI International Conference on Advances in Computer Entertainment Technology, ACE 2005, Valemcia, 15-17th June 2005*.

GEELHOED, E. et al., 2005. Augmented Digital Audio Broadcast Home Trial [online]. Available at: http://www.hpl.hp.com/techreports/2005/HPL-2005-203.html

GEELHOED, E., BAURLEY, S., REID, J. & HULL, R., Probing Experiences: Logs, Traces, Self-report and a Sense of Wonder. Paper presented at *Probing Experience: Real-time interpretation and feedback of Psychophysiological and Behavioural events, Eindhoven, 8-9th June 2006*.

GEELHOED, E., 2003. *The Sound of Music and Word of Mouth: Hearing Music and Hearing about Music*. External HP labs report, HPL-2001-97. Hewlett-Packard.

REID, J., GEELHOED, E., HULL, R., CATER, K. and CLAYTON, B., 2005. Parallel worlds: Immersion in location-based experiences. *In*: G. VAN DER VEER, (ed.) *Proceedings of CHI2005, Conference on Human Factors In Computing Systems, Oregon, 2-7th April 2005*. ACM Press.

RANGANATHAN, P., GEELHOED, E., MANAHAN, M. and NICHOLAS, K., 2006. Energy-aware user interfaces and energy-adaptive displays. *Computer*, 39(3), pp. 31-38.

VOGIAZOU, Y., RAIJMAKERS, B., GEELHOED, E., REID, J. and EISENSTADT, M., 2003. Design for emergence: experiments with a mixed reality urban playground game. *Personal and Ubiquitous Computing*, 9/10.

WRIGHT, P., 2003. A framework for analysing user experience. *Usability News*, 2 April 2003.

Social Science

GAVER, B., DUNN, T. and PACENTI, E., 1999. Cultural probes. *Interactions*, 6(1), pp. 21- 29.

Psychology and Psychophysiology

ARGYLE, M., 1988. *Bodily Communication*. London: Routledge.

ARNOLD, M. B., 1960. *Emotion and personality*. New York: Columbia University Press.

BOURCSEIN, W., 1992. *Electrodermal Activity*. New York: Plenum Press.

CACIOPPO, J. T. and TASSINARY, L. G., 1990. Inferring Psychological Significance From Physiological Signals. *American Psychologist*, 45, pp. 16-28.

DAWSON, M. E., SCELL, A. M. & FILION, D. L., 2000. The Electrodermal System. *In*: J. T. CACIOPPO & L. G. TASSINARY, (eds.) *Principles of Psychophysiology: Physical, Social and Inferential Elements*. New York: Cambridge University Press, pp. 200-223.

DARWIN, C., 1965. *The Expression of the Emotions in Man and Animals*. London, Chicago: University of Chicago Press.

EKMAN, P. and DAVISON, R. J., (eds.), 1994. *The Nature of Emotion*. New York: Oxford University Press.

EKMAN, P., FRIESEN, W., 1969. The repertoire of non-verbal behaviour: categories, origins, usage, and coding. *Semiotica, 1*.

FRIDJA, N., 1987. *The Emotions*. New York: Cambridge University Press.

GIVENS, D. B., 2003. The Nonverbal Dictionary of Gestures, Signs and Body Language Cues [online]. Available at: http://members.aol.com/nonverbal2/diction1.htm

JAMES, W., 1984. What is an emotion? *Mind*, 9, pp. 188-205.

JONES, S. E., YARBOROUGH, A. E., 1985. A naturalistic study of the meanings of touch. *Communication Monographs*, 52.

MORIS, D., 1985. *Bodywatching: A Field Guide to The Human Species*. London: Jonathan Cape.

MORRIS, D., 1978. *Manwatching: A Field Guide to Human Behaviour*. London: Grafton.

PLUTCHIK, R., 1962. *The Emotions: Facts, Theories, and a New Model*. New York: Random House.

PROKASY, W. F. & RASKIN, D. C., 1973. *Electrodermal Activity in Psychological Research*. New York: Academic Press.

SCHLOSBERG, H., 1954. Three dimensions of emotion. *Psychological Review*, 61, pp. 81-88.

Neuroscience

CARTER, R., 2004. *Mapping the Mind*. London: Phoenix.

DAMASIO, A., 2003. *Looking for Spinoza: Joy, Sorrow and the Feeling Brain*. London: Heinemann.

LEDOUX, J., 1999. *The Emotional Brain: The Mysterious Underpinnings of Emotional Life*. London: Phoenix.

Co-Design

SLEESWICK, VISSER, F., STAPPERS, P. J., VAN DER LUGT, R. & SANDERS, E. B-N., 2005. Contextmapping: Experiences from practice. *CoDesign*, 1(2), pp. 119-149.

SANDERS, E. B-N., 2000. Generative Tools for Co-designing. In: BALL & WOODCOCK, (eds.) *Collaborative Design*. London: Springer-Verlag.

Sustainability

PAPANEK, V., 1995. *The Green Imperative*. London: Thames and Hudson.

PAPANEK, V., 1971. *Design for the Real World: Human Ecology and Social Change*. New York: Pantheon Books.

Demi. Available at: http://www.demi.org/ (guidelines for sustainable design)

European Partners for the Environment. Available at: http://www.epe.be/ (European sustainable trade think tank working between developing and developed worlds)

Research Centre for Inclusive Design. Available at: http://www.hhrc.rca.ac.uk/

MCDONOUGH, W. & BRAUNGART, M., 2002. *Cradle to Cradle: Remaking the way we make things* [online]. Northpoint Press. Available at: http://www.mcdonough.com/cradle_to_cradle.htm (an investigation into product manufacture)

New Economics Foundation. Available at: http://www.neweconomics.org/

**Interrogating Fashion: Practice Process and Presentation.
New Paradigms for Fashion Design in the 21st Century**
Prof. Sandy Black, (University of the Arts)

Overview

Fashion and clothing are part of a universal experience, the textile
and clothing industries occupying a powerful global position both
economically and in socio-cultural terms. Individuals have a strong
personal relationship with clothes, one which is intimate and passionate,
bound up with personal expression and identity. Fashion is however a field
which is under-researched and under-represented academically. Fashion is
a fast-moving industry often condemned as frivolous and unimportant,
but represents one of the major economic players on the global stage.
Fashion is one of the few remaining craft-based industries, relying on
manual labour for manufacturing across its wide spectrum of levels from
couture to mass production. The continuing impact of digital technologies
for traditional skills and processes raises complex issues for the fashion
industry whilst also creating new opportunities. Textiles and clothing
are now the focus of increasing research as the carriers of ever-growing
functionalities, from odour eating and moisture management to self-
cleaning and therapeutic properties.

The 'Interrogating Fashion' research cluster therefore took a
comprehensive view of fashion in its broadest sense and established
a much-needed forum for discussion of issues surrounding fashion,
considering new paradigms for its practice, processes and presentation.
The cluster aimed to identify key issues and questions from which
to develop research projects which will have genuine impact on both
academia and the manufacturing sector, creating new opportunities and
products which will, by design, be inherently more sustainable. Specific
objectives were:

- to develop innovative research in fashion design and presentation;
- to debate the ethical and environmental issues in the design, production and consumption of fashion, and develop concepts to address these issues;
- to examine the potential of materials, processes and technologies to create new and more sustainable paradigms for fashion production;
- to explore the relationship of the individual with future fashion.

The cluster created synergies across a range of perspectives by bringing together diverse practitioners and disciplines (design, manufacturing and retail, marketing, cultural theory, art practice and curation, technology, materials science. . .) to interrogate and challenge the practices and processes of fashion, deliberately integrating the traditional divisions of production, consumption and representation. Three overarching and interrelated themes were established for the cluster framework:

- *Digital Fashion*: from craft to mass customisation.
- *The Fashion Paradox*: transience and sustainability.
- *Fashion in Context*: presentation and display, audience and engagement.

Although setting an ambitious agenda, this breadth and scope was essential in creating an overview of the key issues faced by this major global industry, whose pervasive influence impacts many aspects of design, cultural and technological production. The cluster aimed particularly to interface with the fashion industry and included involvement and representation from retailers, consumer goods and communication sectors.

Digital Fashion encompasses research into innovative fashion products – clothing, footwear and accessories – through materials, design and manufacturing processes. It focuses on the interface between traditional craftsmanship and emerging technologies such as 3D design for fashion using body and foot scanning data, leading to a new paradigm of customised clothing on demand. It explores the new fashion design environment and its human/computer interactions. *The Fashion Paradox* examines the complex contradictions between fashion's economic importance and its inbuilt obsolescence and wastefulness. It addresses the major need to reconcile ethical, environmental, social and personal agendas through future design and manufacturing cycles, and discusses the influence of consumer behaviour, changing trends and the importance of the role of the designer in making choices. *Fashion in Context* debates the theme of fashion presentation and the recent blurring of functions between museum and retail display. It focuses on the power of fashion as an innovative medium of communication, and the relationship between body and clothing, theory and practice. The three themes naturally overlap, but created an effective practical focus for workshops, debates and symposia.

Fashion itself may not be too different in the future but higher performance will be expected from clothing and fabrics in a range of ways such as 'self cleaning' through protective nano-scale coatings, or 'smart' fabrics which can monitor environmental conditions and respond to needs by delivering therapies or even raising the alarm.

Activities

The 38 cluster members comprised a wide-ranging group of fashion and textile practitioners, artists, product designers, computer and material scientists, cultural, design and marketing theorists, fashion historians, curators, musicians and industrialists. These were drawn from within the London College of Fashion, University of the Arts London, from eight other institutions including international members from Holland, Australia and the United States and from industry.[1] The majority already had a previous working relationship with the Principal Investigator, Sandy Black, which facilitated the convening of such an intensive programme of activities for the year. During the first 6 months, three 1.5-day workshops, one on each theme, were held to 'seed' concepts and to fuel debate, continued in the symposium. Presentations of work were given by cluster members and invited speakers, then small groups debated prepared questions as a springboard for further discussion, to identify key themes and issues. The workshops generated really positive energy through knowledge sharing and focused discussion, and consolidated the cluster itself. Interdisciplinary groupings have been crucial to the cluster development and its emerging themes, none of which are completely discrete. The Digital Fashion strand generated a joint press briefing with BT and resulting press coverage, and the Fashion Paradox debate brought together opposing views and led to further targeted industrial involvement of retailers, raised awareness and established an agenda for further internal and external conferences. The website facilitated involvement from overseas and remote members and became an increasingly important communication and development tool for exchange of ideas for the final event which took place at the end of November.

[1] Interrogating Fashion. Available at: www.interrogatingfashion.org for a full listing.

Concluding events and symposium

A 2-day event was mounted as the culmination of the year's activities. This comprised a public debate and performance demonstrations of Digital Fashion concepts at the Institute of Contemporary Arts (ICA) London, and a symposium at London College of Fashion (LCF) addressing the emerging issues, with a participative 'fashion exchange' moneyless auction and an experimental artist's performance by Caroline Broadhead providing a complement to the traditional academic activities. Bringing issues alive in performative ways was highly effective in creating community and engaging everyone to participate and consider the practical embodiment of theory. At the ICA, five brief presentations set the scene and a panel of eight diverse cluster participants debated questions arising from the Digital Fashion workshops. This was followed by experimental demonstrations of concepts utilising emerging technologies in practice. To demonstrate the reality and scope of today's fashion business, projected above the panel was a simultaneous screening of actual retail activity in Top Shop, Oxford Circus, on a busy Saturday afternoon, contrasted with the more rarefied activity in the Savile Row shop of cool urban designers Oki-ni, transmitted live by webcam. The audience was able to observe shopping as anthropologists might study behaviour, to demonstrate the huge difference in pace relating to the different market levels representing both 'fast' and 'slow' fashion.

Performance demonstrations

These comprised four interactive demonstrations of research work-in-progress. Joanna Berzowska, co-founder of International Fashion Machines, now Director of Extra Soft Labs, Concordia University,

Figures 1a/b and 2,
left to right

Figure 1a/b, Urban Heart Angels outfits demonstration incorporating Nyx LED technology for public interaction. Photo by Akio
Figure 2, Miriorama demonstration by Laptop Jams: Jeremy Radvan and Stuart Smith. Photo byDuska Zagorac

2 Joanna Berzowska. Available
at: www.berzowska.com

Canada, showed her *Memory Rich Clothing* responding to intimate
interactions, such as touch or whispering, with light and colour changes;
the *Constellation* dresses which connect and light up, and the *Kukia*
dress using shape memory materials to slowly open and close flowers.[2]
Intermedia architect Thomas Kitazawa (Goldsmiths) presented *Urban
Angels* whose interactive outfits incorporating LED display, designed by
Georgie Ichikawa (LCF), would potentially connect the public to a massive
audio-visual urban installation, *Rhythmicity* [Figures 1a/b]. Sarah Kettley
(Napier University) demonstrated interactive electronic jewellery which
responded to physical proximity and by implication to social distance
when moving through space. *Miriorama* by Jeremy Radvan and Stuart
Smith of Laptop Jams showed the potential for movement of the body
and clothing to inspire drawing on the computer and in future for fashion
design [Figure 2].

Symposium

The final symposium at LCF included keynote lectures from practitioners
related to each of the themes: Joanna Berzowska for *Digital Fashion*,
raising issues by integrating electronic and responsive clothing with social
interaction, Lucy Orta for *Fashion in Context*, on her art practice
engaging with disadvantaged groups through clothing, and designer
Katharine Hamnett for *The Fashion Paradox* on the trials of developing an

Figure 3a/b, Menswear and womenswear outfits from Katharine E Hamnett collection,
in 100% organic cotton, ethically and environmentally sourced and manufactured.
Courtesy the designer

ethically and environmentally sound fashion collection [Figures 3a/b]. Each speaker provided clear focus for these themes based on the evidence and conviction of their own practice to stimulate discussion in the subsequent themed groups. These resulted in new ideas and proposed projects to continue the multidisciplinary work within the themes of the cluster.

Insights and Emerging Issues

Digital fashion: from craft to mass customisation

Craft and emerging technologies

The Digital Fashion workshop comprised speakers on a range of craft and technology applications for fashion including 3D bodyscanning (Jeni Bougourd LCF [Figure 4], electronic woven textiles (Stan Swallow, Intelligent Textiles [Figure 5], digital printing (Hitoshi Ujiie, Philadelphia University; Lee Nicoll), rapid prototyping for products (Janne Kyttanen, Freedom of Creation, Holland [Figure 6], and future possibilities of digital technologies for fashion including 'active skin' and digital personas (Ian Pearson, futurologist for BT). Kenji Toki (Japan) presented his artworks integrating traditional *urushi* lacquering with forms developed in CAD and rapid prototyped; Sarah Kettley presented her interactive jewellery, and Claudia Eckert (Cambridge) spoke on design theory across disciplines. The group questioned the impact of emerging technology on design and manufacturing processes and how craft and technology can be joined in successful marriage. A notion of the hybrid was looked at, in terms of materials, processes and language. Designers are developing new competences: learning about new materials and processes, or collaborating to make products through different disciplines working together.

New design and manufacturing processes

Utilising new materials and methods, or existing materials in new processes, or new materials with traditional processes can deliver benefits of more sustainable production by creating innovative products with less waste, and moving towards the new paradigm of 'fashion on demand'. The convergence of digital technologies across many platforms is having profound effects on lifestyle and breaking down divisions between previously separate areas. The integration of different technologies to produce finished products, for example rapid prototyping and 3D printing or 3D knitting, allied to digital 2D printing and image making, digital communications and 3D scanning technologies, points towards more

Figures 4 to 6,
top to bottom, left to right

Figure 4, Point cloud data image from 3D body scan

Figure 5, Prototype one piece keyboard, electronic
woven textile, by Intelligent Textiles Ltd. Courtesy the
designers

Figure 6, Punchbag rapid manufactured in one piece, by
Freedom of Creation. Courtesy the designers

[3] For example: Brooks Brothers and TC2 technology in New York, Bodymetrics virtual try-on for jeans in Selfridges, London and Bon Marche in Paris.

[4] *Proceedings of the 2005 Interdisciplinary World Congress on Mass Customization and Personalization, MCPC 2005, Hong Kong, 18-21st September 2005. Proceedings of the International Textile and Apparel Association Conference, ITAA 205, Washington, November 2005.*

[5] TAO, X. M., (ed.), 2005. *Wearable Electronics and Photonics.* Cambridge: Woodhead Publishing. TAO, X. M., (ed.), 2001. *Smart Fibres, Fabrics and Clothing.* Cambridge: Woodhead Publishing. STYLIOS, G. K., 2004. Interactive Smart Textiles: Innovation and Collaboration in Japan and South Korea. London: Global Watch. *Proceedings of the Avantex symposium and Techtextil trade fair.* Available at: www.techtextil.com. *Proceedings of the Nanotechnologies and Smart Textiles for Industry and Commerce Conferences 2004 and 2006.* London: Institute of Nanotechnology. Available at: www.nano.org.uk

[6] KRANS, M., 2005. Photonic fibres. *In: Proceedings of the 2nd International Plastic Electronics Conference & Showcase,* Frankfurt, 24-25th September 2005.

[7] An experimental research partnership founded by Maggie Orth and Joanna Berzowska, out of MIT Media Lab, investigating electronic functionality in textiles and clothing. Available at: www.ifmachines.com

customised and personalised products in the future [Figure 7]. Presenting on topics from applications in printed products and jeans to new bespoke tailoring were Philipa Ashton (LCF), David Tyler (Manchester Metropolitan University), Andrew Crawford (Bodymetrics, UK), Frances Ross (LCF) and Suzette Worden (Curtin University, Australia).

Enhanced global communications, coupled with the increasing pace of technological and scientific advances, has resulted in western lifestyles speeding up. With globalised markets, manufacturing and supply chains, location is in theory less important, but providing customised products and services close to the consumer opens up new niche markets in declining manufacturing sectors such as the UK. There is an opportunity to address the needs of markets related to disability, ageing or much larger consumer segments seeking an individual rather than a trend look (comfort and good fit being key). Creative design thinking must underpin these developments, by offering innovation and flexibility, tailored to personal requirements, as a quasi-bespoke service. This provides for individual needs (for example, fit) and desires (for example, colour preference) with an updated service based on technology, whilst still benefiting from a cost-effective production processes. There will, in consequence, be a different role for designers, negotiating choices in dialogue with consumers. Retail systems for 3D virtual fit and custom clothing manufacture are emerging in the US and in Europe,[3] and 3D fashion design is in development.[4] How long before we have true 'fashion on demand' and can walk into a bureau with our body measurements on a card and come away with a new bespoke outfit in a matter of hours?

Wearable technologies

There is a rapidly growing volume of research into 'smart' fabrics and 'intelligent' clothing, accessories and interiors which will enable the integration of electronic functionalities into fabrics via new technologies, materials and processes.[5] This will render clothing more responsive to our needs for protection, care and wellbeing, in addition to its aesthetic qualities, and will change our relationship with what we wear in the near future. The surface of our clothes has the potential to become a constantly changing interface, when current research on flexible displays by technology companies such as Philips (Holland)[6] and Cambridge Display Technologies (UK) is fully realised [Figure 1]. Research is also underway in several countries into responsive colour and pattern changes in fabrics, for example the *Electric Plaid* from International Fashion Machines.[7]

[8] BLACK, S., 2007. Trends in Smart Textiles. In: L. F. VAN LANGENHOVE, (ed.) *Smart Textiles for Medicine and Healthcare: materials, systems and applications.* Cambridge: Woodhead Publishing. See also: www.numetrex.com & www.warmX.de

[9] Proceedings of Interrogating Fashion Research Cluster, 2007. Available at: www.interrogatingfashion.org.

[10] FINKENZELLER, K., 2003. *The RFID-handbook,* 2nd ed. Wiley & Sons.

[11] O'CONNOR, M., 2005. *RFID and the media revolution* [online]. Available at: http://www.rfidjournal.com/article/articleview/1508/1/1/

Many issues were raised in discussions as to the future nature of fashion and textiles in this wider context. Will we expect more help from our clothing in conducting our lives, to combat increasing fears, to sense hostile or polluted environments or to monitor changes in our physical condition? If we look to embedding into clothing more technological functions such as music and communications how can these be as flexible as current fashions? Why would we want wearable technology, when we don't yet know the long term effects of the gadgets we are currently using? If our intimate and emotional states can more easily be revealed through electronic textiles and functionalities, will our clothes know more about us than we do? What are the opportunities created?

Wearable computing has been under development for over 20 years, but commercially successful fashion products are proving elusive, until the various elements, such as robust conductive textile technology, power sources, performance reliability, washability, and importantly design are sufficiently synchronised – estimates range from 5 to 15 years. However, the sportswear and healthcare sectors have launched niche products incorporating technologies onto the commercial market, such as snowboarding jackets with mp3 players, and recently, the Numetrex heart monitoring sports bra, and the WarmX heated vest.[8]

Pervasive computing in society

As more and more functionalities are routed through mobile devices, and ubiquitous computing becomes the norm, could we choose whether to be 'connected' – to interact with sensors, chips and tags embedded throughout the physical environment? Will we retreat into a 'digital bubble' as our own avatar, creating our own virtual reality as proposed by futurologist Ian Pearson?[9] Could the body become the computer interface, the skin activated with implanted technology for uses from aesthetic appearance and drug delivery to surveillance? The merging of the private and public spheres, the dissolution of clear boundaries between common knowledge and personal information is already very evident. The implications of satellite tracking and GPS are by turns threatening (Big Brother controlling mechanisms) or reassuring (monitoring the whereabouts and safety of children, or the health and wellbeing of the elderly and infirm). Like nanotechnology, RFID tagging – of products and people from clubbers to prisoners – has raised major issues and has both its champions and detractors.[10,11] Often artists are the first to highlight

¹² MEDIAMATIC, 2006.
Internet of Things. Workshop,
Amsterdam, May 2006.

issues through experimentation with emerging technologies as demonstrated at the ICA event by Joanna Berzowska's work. With the pervasive potential of a new 'Internet of Things',[12] who will be in control of our identity and social interactions? With a 'smart second skin', could we be buying identities on eBay?

Fashion incontext: presentation and display, audience and engagement

Fashion offers a means for other subjects to engage new audiences. Fashion, textiles and costume attract some of the largest audiences in museum and gallery exhibitions. This readiness to engage with something as universal as textiles and clothing can be used to advantage for innovative projects of educational or social nature in addition to celebration and communication of fashion designs and concepts, as demonstrated by the work of Helen and Kate Storey (see below). Industry cluster member, Unilever, represented by Phil Sams, deals with fast-moving consumer goods, and has, over the past 5 years engaged with fashion through involvement with London College of Fashion, and others, to communicate future concepts to scientists. By holding a 'fashion mirror' to science and a 'science mirror' to fashion, a mutual dialogue and exchange has taken place, to inform our new, and evolving, relationships with clothes, demonstrating the communicative power of fashion.

The discussion workshops speakers ranged from curators, artists and makers to research and development in the consumer goods industry, and included designer/researcher Helen Storey (London College of Fashion), artist Caroline Broadhead (Middlesex), researcher/maker Dai Rees (London College of Fashion), fashion curator Judith Clark (London College of Fashion), fashion historian Christopher Breward (V&A Museum), digital researcher Jane Harris (Central Saint Martins), cultural theorist Joanne Entwistle (London College of Fashion) and designer/ researcher Jessica Bugg (London College of Fashion). The purpose was to raise questions around the presentation and display of fashion from museum to gallery and retail, looking at how these contexts for fashion have started to overlap. Nicky Ryan, (London College of Communication) lecturer and researcher, outlined the tensions between museum and retail visual cultures, and their commercial and cultural intersections. The emergence of hybrid spaces highlights dualities: the commodification of the museum and aestheticisation of the store; minimalisation and mutability; rationalisation and enchantment; corporate appropriation

of the arts; luxury and waste and the anti-brand.[9] Questions which were
addressed in the small group discussions included: Why is fashion curation
so relevant now? How can new audiences who do not normally visit
museums be engaged? What can museums and retail stores learn from
each other? How can virtual display enhance the experience of clothing in
museum collections?

Fashion curation: audience and engagement

The multiplicity of fashion and the breadth of its definitions and
meanings to different audiences requires a focused approach to
exhibitions. Contemporary and innovative fashion curation offers the
potential to look at fashion in new ways in a fast-moving environment,
and consider what curation means as boundaries between traditional
formats blur, creating new hybrid spaces. Problems with traditional
fashion curation are static display, conservatism and elitism – exhibitions
may be too conceptualised for a non-traditional audience. How can the
significance of 'low end' or high street and 'value' fashion be addressed
and a critical distance achieved? Technology may be a vehicle to engage
new audiences, or previously hostile, disinterested or 'difficult' audiences
with fashion histories, cultures and practices, through new channels. Soon
we may engage with the virtual more effectively than the real in museum
contexts as digitisation reaches the three-dimensional object. Do new
experiences only have to be dependent on technology?

Some areas of fashion/clothing are not well represented in museum
collections therefore simply not curated in this context, including social
biography of clothing and everyday fashion. The dominance of the
fashion catwalk presentation was challenged. In the digital age, has
catwalk as theatre and high drama had its day, or will it endure and
evolve?

Blurring of museum and retail functions

The blurring of functions of shop, museum and gallery has been
accelerating; galleries and museums in particular are staging events which
bring more diverse activities and audiences into the arena: live music,
fashion promenades, performances, fetes, late night openings with cafes,
bars and other cultural events, and every exhibition has its merchandising
and related publications. Starting at high end fashion and now at all levels,
many stores have sought to align themselves with the cultural values of
museums and created a more spaciously designed presentation where the
clothes (for sale) are made to look as precious as exhibits. The question

[13] ERHMAN, E., BREWARD, C. & EVANS, C., curators, 29th October 2004 - 25th July 2005. *The London Look Exhibition*, Museum of London.

[14] A 1997 Wellcome Trust Sci-Art project by fashion designer Helen Storey and developmental biologist Dr Kate Storey, Primitive Streak is a collection of dresses illustrating the development of the first 1000 hours of human life. Available at: www.helenstoreyfoundation. org

[15] ORTA, L., 2003. Lucy Orta: Body Architecture. Verlag. ISBN 3-88960-066-2. See www.studio-orta.com

[16] Katherine Hamnett. Available at: www.katherinehamnett.com

[17] Kate Fletcher. Available at: www.katefletcher.com

arises whether retail sometimes 'curates' fashion better than museums – retail has less constraints and can be much more flexible, whereas museum curators provide expertise and overview. Further analysis of audience response to fashion related exhibitions is necessary, why they work, why they are popular and how they relate to other forms of fashion communication. The power of fashion is evident, and also the enduring influence of the fashion image as an object itself – one of its most potent legacies.

Fashion as a catalyst for raising social issues

Exhibitions such as *The London Look*[13] show how fashion is a superb vehicle for illustrating social and cultural change. The diverse practices and work of artist/designers Lucy Orta, Helen Storey and Caroline Broadhead, all participants in the cluster, demonstrate how fashion and clothing can be used as a catalyst to raise and communicate social and cultural issues and concepts, and engage non-traditional audiences through clothing and fashion. Helen and Kate Storey's 1997 *Primitive Streak*[14] collection of dresses toured the world and now has an educational life communicating biological science to both adults and children and in schools and other communities. The use of site-specific or unconventional locations for artworks and interventions re-contextualises the work and finds new audiences by taking the work to them, instead of waiting for them to engage with museums and galleries. This methodology is evident in the performative and site-specific work of artist Caroline Broadhead who uses clothing as metaphor, and Lucy Orta, Rootstein Hopkins Chair of Fashion at LCF. Orta was previously a fashion designer, and has developed an art practice which combines aspects of clothing, sculpture, architecture and industrial design to stage events which engage participation, increase social interaction, and raise awareness of social and humanitarian issues in contemporary society.[15]

The fashion paradox: transience and sustainability

The eternal cycles of fashion were the concern of this thematic area – its production, consumption, obsolescence and importance to global economics. Speakers included artist Lucy Orta, ethical and ecological fashion designer Katharine Hamnett,[16] sustainability theorist Kate Fletcher,[17] textile designer Rebecca Earley (Chelsea) and eco-fashion designer Sarah Ratty (Ciel), designer Susannah Dowse (TRAID Remade), dye technologist Derek McKelvey (ex M&S) and Unilever scientist Philip McKeown.

This theme was particularly successful in debating fundamental issues which must be addressed by the fashion industry with respect to ecological, ethical and sustainable considerations within its practices. The broad context covers the paradox of fashion consumption and evolution sustaining major economic infrastructures and employment worldwide; fashion cycles and the desire for fashion engendering change, obsolescence and consumption; the mechanics of the design and manufacturing processes within the fashion industry's supply chain; ethical considerations and environmental impact of textile and fashion design and production; consumer behaviour and humanitarian and social issues influencing emerging trends. The Fashion Paradox is also an ideological opposition between environmentalists, who usually ignore fashion and treat it as an irrelevance, but neglect to acknowledge its power and influence, and the fashion industry which until recently has not addressed ecological issues, its focus being on the market and production. The remit of this cluster however, in the face of these enormous issues, was to focus on the role of design in fashion product development, and evolve new solutions and methodologies which would, through intelligent and considerate design be more sustainable.

Key questions raised were: What difference could the fashion industry make if it changed to ethical and environmentally sustainable practices? How can we meet both our symbolic and fashion needs and transform our relationship with clothes? How can slow fashion become a new paradigm? Why is ecological or ethical clothing usually outside mainstream fashion? Can a new eco-philosophy fashion paradigm be created through design?

The sustainability agenda and considerate design

The issues of environmental impact, sustainability, clothing lifecycles and eco-philosophy design solutions for clothing need to be tackled at all levels of the fashion industry in a manner which encourages positive change. The role of design in decision making within the fashion industry is a key focus for the Interrogating Fashion cluster. It is important to tackle the major problems at the outset of design, and not apply poor 'retro-fit' solutions near the end of the development and production process. There is a necessity for a new intelligence about design and ways of reframing, defining and approaching problems to generate solutions with the wider social, ecological and sustainability contexts in mind. Considerate Design is a more approachable construct which is now being developed and tested by cluster members.

Shades of green and the role of the designer

The role of the designer carries with it crucial responsibilities for
choices in materials and processes, which inherently have ethical and
environmental implications. Small changes towards more eco-friendly
materials and processes within a large company can have a real impact.
The concept 'Shades of Green' identifies a product's eco-credentials and
incremental levels of changes in manufacturing or operational processes.
The issue to be examined here: Is a little change at a time in the direction
of eco-design enough ? Where does a fashion company draw the line
in responsibility? Is it better to get a 'light green' product out on the
market than to wait for a 'dark green' one which may take very much
longer? Could this be turned into a marketing labelling system for easy
recognition by consumers?

Can better design seduce more consumers into buying ethically and
environmentally sound products? Can ethical and environmentally sound
clothing and fashion be reconciled with the economic realities of the
mainstream fashion business [Figure 3], or is it destined to be only a niche
market, itself subject to whims of fashionability?

The slow fashion paradigm

The current 'fast fashion' ethos of cheaper and faster clothes is inherently
unsustainable and cannot continue indefinitely. As a direct contrast
to faster, cheaper disposable fashion, slow fashion comprises less
obsolescence through Considerate Design possibilities, design for long-
term use and wear (as in certain 'luxury' goods), intelligent and innovative
choice of materials, minimal waste and concern for the entire lifecycle
of the product. Longer lasting and 'low maintenance' clothing could be
viable, fostering a new relationship with clothes.

In order to create new fashion paradigms to address the Fashion
Paradox, the sustainability agenda must now be completely integrated
into fashion and textiles education and into industry – perhaps as a
form of 'sustainability literacy' to underpin design thinking and impact
production processes at all levels. The cluster identified the need for a two-
pronged attack on the status quo of fashion to persuade both the retailers
and the manufacturers of the importance of the sustainability agenda, and
the necessity of a contribution to society beyond the profit margin – to
consider the 'triple bottom line' of economy, society and ecology.

Conclusion

Interrogating Fashion has resulted in the setting of an agenda for both
short- and long-term research projects in the design, production and
presentation of fashion. The awareness raising of its activities has begun
to impact a much wider sphere of professional and academic debate
and practice, and highlighted the importance of the role of the designer
to influence future manufacturing and business. Design thinking is
at last becoming more central to the business agenda. The impact of
Interrogating Fashion within the academic community is evident through
a number of initiatives both inside and outside the London College
of Fashion. For example, The Institute of Nanotechnology adopted
the theme of The Fashion Paradox for a conference, and a new MA
programme named Digital Fashion has been developed at LCF to reflect
this research agenda.

Several key concepts have been consolidated which unite disparate
areas and provide an underpinning to the development of new research
projects. These include The Fashion Paradox, Considerate Design, Low
Maintenance Clothes, Slow Fashion, Personalised Fashion, Digital Fashion
and Fashion on Demand. The potential for emerging technologies and
digital fashion to contribute to a more sustainable future is an emerging
theme for innovation. Could Digital Fashion help solve the Fashion
Paradox?

Unless we harness the digital landscape to create less but smarter
fashion more sustainably so our clothes perhaps last longer than one or
two seasons, don't need washing so often, can have multiple formats,
or change their shape, pattern or colour in response to changing
requirements, then the mountains of fashion waste will never be reduced.
To counter the environmental impact of clothes care, low maintenance
clothing needs to become a reality.

With design at the core, new ways of thinking about clothes, applications
of new technologies, materials and processes can lead to new products
which reconcile the economic imperatives of fashion with sustainability,
at the same time meeting our personal and symbolic needs. Companies
who have been part of the problem in unsustainable production are
now becoming part of the solution in ethical and environmental terms.
Whatever the outcomes of current research, we will undoubtedly develop
a fundamentally different relationship with our clothes and with fashion

itself. The Fashion Paradox agenda will be fundamental in fashion education and practice, and must now underpin all future approaches to fashion design disciplines. With such a large agenda to tackle, the work of the cluster has only just begun.

Additional Reading

UJIIE, H., 2006. *Digital Printing of Fabrics*. Cambridge: Woodhead.

WANG, Y., 2006. *Recycling of Textiles*. Cambridge: Woodhead.

Design Performance
Dr Jillian MacBryde and Dr James Moultrie, (University of Strathclyde and University of Cambridge)

Overview

[1] GREAT BRITAIN. Treasury, 2005. *Cox Review of Creativity in Business: Building on the UK's Strengths*. London: The Stationery Office.

[2] GREAT BRITAIN. Department of Trade and Industry, 2005. *The 2005 R&D Scoreboard: The Top 750 UK and 1000 Global Companies by R&D Investment* [online]. Available at: http://www.innovation.gov. uk/rd_scoreboard/

[3] DESIGN COUNCIL, 2005. *Design in Britain*. The Good News Press Ltd.

The importance of design to the UK economy and to the performance of UK companies has recently been the subject of much discussion. The Cox Review,[1] commissioned by the UK Treasury, highlights the need for increased awareness of the role design and creativity can play in the growth of companies. The report shows the immediate need for UK companies to compete with foreign rivals through increased design activity. In a parallel report[2] the positive relationship between design and business performance is established. This is backed up by research at the Design Council,[3] whose annual 'Design in Britain' report found, 'Companies that see design as integral to their work find it positively affects business performance.'

Even with the growing recognition of the importance of design and design performance, there has been very little attention given to managing design performance. Certainly there is not a shared vision of design performance across the different communities associated with design.

The authors identified the Designing for the 21st Century Initiative as an opportunity for UK academics from different disciplines to come together to investigate this important, but fragmented area of research. It was recognised that cross-fertilisation of ideas, concepts, approaches, methods and processes could be a key source of competitive advantage for the UK. The authors therefore set about writing a proposal for funding for a 'Design Performance' cluster, and at the same time set about recruiting core members to the cluster.

As suspected the authors found that research into Design Performance was very fragmented, with researchers from design, management, performance measurement, building design, finance, social sciences and so on. all working in different areas and with different views. Probably the clearest split was between those focused on process performance and those focused on product performance. It was clear at the outset that the UK plays a key role in the international performance measurement (PM) community, with a number of internationally recognised groups (for example, Cambridge, Cranfield, Strathclyde and Warwick). A number of researchers from the PM community were focusing on design performance, although much of this work is focused on measurement of the design process (for example, Cranfield, Nottingham, Strathclyde).

Researchers from the building design community were also found to be looking at design performance. Much of this work focuses on performance from a 'product' perspective. For example there was work being carried out with an environmental perspective (for example, Cranfield, Nottingham), technical/structural performance (for example, Glasgow Caledonian) and facilities management (for example, Napier). There was also work related to value management, some of which relates to aesthetic performance (for example, Cambridge).

The researchers found considerable activity within the design community looking at optimisation (for example, Cambridge, Loughborough, Strathclyde). There was little work looking at design performance from a financial perspective (for example, Dundee) and from a work organisation perspective (for example, Sheffield). Research relating to outsourcing of design (for example, Warwick) also has a clear performance link as has collaborative design (for example, Brunel, Cranfield, Strathclyde).

Aims and Objectives of the Cluster

Having gathered together an interdisciplinary grouping interested in Design Performance, the authors and their newly formed group agreed that the overall aim of the cluster should be to provide a platform to facilitate the sharing, consolidation and promotion of activities in design performance research and practice. Specific objectives were to:

• Bring together researchers from diverse communities who can really lead the field in design performance at an international level.
• Develop a research agenda, along with priorities and groupings to take the key research issues forward.

- Start groupings of collaborative activity to tackle key research issues and form innovative research partnerships that go beyond the design disciplines.
- Work towards a common language and reference framework.
- Support leading edge research that is both socially aware and economically enterprising.
- Create a dialogue between designers, artists, engineers, architects, social scientists and so on.
- Involve industry in these key discussions.
- Encourage cross-fertilisation of ideas, concepts, frameworks and approaches.
- Disseminate information to the wider community.

Activity

During the first quarter of 2005, the cluster held their first meeting at Strathclyde University. This meeting took the form of a mini-conference/ workshop and was chaired by the Principal Investigator, Dr Jill MacBryde. Initially each participant gave a short presentation of ongoing work connected to design performance. The group then held workshop discussions on current activity and research challenges. Following the first workshop the website went live. Notes from each of the cluster events are available on the cluster website.[4]

[4] Design Performance. Available at: www.dmem.strath.ac.uk/ desperf

During the second quarter the cluster held their second meeting, this time hosted by Steve Evans, Fiona Lettice and Palie Smart at Cranfield University [Figures 1 – 4]. The Designing for the 21st Century Initiative Director, Tom Inns attended this workshop and provided valuable input. The focus and deliverable of the workshop was a SWOT (strengths, weaknesses, opportunities and threats) analysis of UK design performance research, and included a review of the current literature and identification of opportunities for future research.

The third workshop took place in Cambridge University in August, this time hosted by James Moultrie and Finbarr Livesey. This meeting took the results from the previous workshop forward by identifying and rationalising key themes and potential research projects. The outcome was a list of prioritised research challenges and groupings of members to move forward with research initiatives such as project proposals, future collaboration, publications and joint ventures. These groups held meetings between August and December to develop research proposals.

Figure 1, Mapping exercise to agree scope of Design Performance cluster
Figure 2, Hard at work at Cranfield University workshop
Figure 3, Mapping exercise
Figure 4, SWOT analysis

The fourth and final workshop took place at Strathclyde University. Here, the cluster members discussed the draft research proposals and further developed research plans, including plans for joint publications. The cluster also discussed two track streams they had secured for the PMA 2006 and Euroma 2006 conferences.

The cluster was deemed to be a success by its members. It achieved its goal of bringing together a diverse community to look at the important issue of managing the performance of the design process. The cluster has resulted in a cohesive, multidisciplinary research team who have a shared research vision and a research plan. The team believe that, together, they are well positioned to contribute internationally leading research. The deliverables of the Design Performance cluster can be summarised as follows:

- identified current activity in design performance;
- SWOT analysis of UK design performance research;
- review of current literature;
- identification of opportunities for future research;
- development of key themes and research projects;
- rationalisation of research challenges;
- identification of groupings to move forward with proposals.

The funding received from the Designing for the 21st Century Initiative allowed the Design Performance researchers to review research activity in the area of design performance and to identify gaps in knowledge.

The remainder of this chapter will present some of the insights that came out of the cluster activities. The current state-of-the-art in terms of design performance measurement at both the level of the firm and at a national level will be presented. The chapter will close by highlighting gaps in knowledge and discussing the Design Performance cluster's future research agenda.

Insights

Design performance at the level of the firm

⁵ BLACK, C. D. & BAKER, M. J., 1987. Success Through Design. *Design Studies*, 8(4), pp. 207-216.

There is much evidence, both statistical and anecdotal, of how design can increase the performance of companies.

⁶ WALSH, V., ROY, R., BRUCE, M. & POTTER, S., 1992. *Winning by Design: Technology, Product Design and International Competitiveness.* Oxford: Blackwell Business.

⁷ ROY, R. & POTTER, S., 1993. The commercial impacts of investment in design. *Design Studies*, 14(2).

⁸ ROY, R., 1999. The long term benefits of investing in NPD by SMEs. *New Product Development & Innovation Management*, December, 281.

Since the 1980s, there have been a number of studies that have aimed to determine the benefits of investing in design. Without exception, these studies have found a positive relationship between a firm's design orientation and commercial success. However, there are clear challenges of attributing success to a single factor (design), and especially one that is difficult to define. Black & Baker[5] examined the 'design orientation' of around 60 small engineering firms, using 'company growth rate' as a measure of success. They discovered that 95 per cent of the companies with a negative growth rate made no use of professional design skills. In contrast, high growth companies made significant use of industrial design throughout the NPD process. Following a similar approach, Walsh et al[6] compared the performance of eight 'design conscious' firms with a selection of 41 non-design-conscious competing firms. They identified a generally positive relationship between design consciousness and success. The same group of researchers (The Design Innovation Group – DIG) completed two further studies exploring the value of design. In 1992, the outputs of structured interviews with 42 British and 9 overseas 'design conscious' firms confirmed the positive relationship between performance and average profit margin.[6] In the early 1990s, the UK Government provided funding for small companies to utilise professional (external) design expertise under the 'Support for Design Scheme'. Using 221 firms who benefited from this scheme as a data source, the DIG conducted a study titled 'Markets that Reward Investment in Design' (MADRID). They demonstrated that 89 per cent of the projects resulted in profits and the average payback period was 15 months after launch. They also identified several indirect benefits, such as reduced costs, reduced stock, increased margins and improved company image, ultimately concluding that 'design' was considered the main influence on commercial success in 88 per cent of the cases.[7] In 1999, the DIG revisited the data collected from their earlier studies and conducted some follow-up interviews to explore the longer-term benefits of design investment.[8] They concluded that the growing firms tended to design more innovative products, using external expertise where appropriate. More generally, these firms were viewed to be using more modern management practices and had a positive attitude towards product design.

[9] HERTENSTEIN, J. H., PLATT, M. B. & BROWN, D. R., 2001. Valuing design: enhancing corporate performance through design effectiveness. *Design Management Journal*, 12(3).

[10] VON STAMM, B., 2004. Innovation: what's design got to do with it? *Design Management Review*, 15(1).

[11] GEMSER, G. & LEENDERS, M., 2001. How integrating ID into the NPD process impacts on company performance. *Journal of Product Innovation Management*, 18(1), pp. 28-38.

[12] JUILHET, G. B., 1995. *French SMEs and Design*. Paris: Ministère de l'industrie.

[13] ZENTNER, P., 1989. Design for staying alive. *Director*, November, 149.

[14] LORENZ, C., 1994. Harnessing design as a strategic resource. *Long Range Planning*, 27(5), pp. 73-84.

[15] BORJA DE MOZOTA, B., 2002. Design and Competitive Edge: A model for management excellence in European SMEs. *Design Management Journal*, 2(1).

Hertenstein et al[9] also set out to establish the 'value of design' in a 5-year study of 51 companies across four sectors. A panel of experts (from the Design Management Institute) ranked the companies to distinguish those which exhibit good design through their products; using their own definitions of good design. The results indicated that the 'design-led' firms outperformed their competitors at a statistically significant level for 12 measures of financial performance (including growth rate, return on sales, return on assets and so on). A common difficulty with these studies is the ambiguity of the definition of design. In 2004, Von Stamm[10] noted that despite much debate over the last 2 decades, there is still confusion about the boundaries between design, design management and new product development.

Both Gemser[11] and Juilhet[12] set out to specifically explore the value of investment in 'industrial design' through carefully designed research studies. Julhiet concluded that one third of company respondents (from a sample of 565 firms) invested in industrial design and 40 per cent of these did so regularly. Investment was typically around 10 – 15 per cent of the total development budget and was found to have a favourable impact on the company image, product appearance and customer satisfaction. Gemser studied the role of industrial design in 20 SMEs and identified a positive relationship between industrial design involvement and company performance. However, she noted that this magnitude of relationship is dynamic, depending upon the industry environment and the pervading competitive strategies. So, industrial design investment may progress from being an 'order winning' differentiator to an 'order qualifying' price of entry over time. In addition to empirical studies, there are many articles from well-respected commentators and academics, which provide further evidence of the importance of design. Zentner,[13] in a popular press article for example, claims that clear product differentiation through effective design can provide significant commercial advantage. Lorenz[14] supports this view, adding that conventional means of differentiation (cost and quality) are now 'entry tickets' – design is now the key to producing meaningful distinction; not just shape and appearance, but character.

Gaps in knowledge and areas for future research – at the level of the firm

A review of the literature demonstrates the importance of design on competitiveness. But for something so important, the literature reveals very little by way of guidance on measuring design performance within organisations. The research team believe that design is a 'valuable asset for company performance'[15] and therefore should be managed effectively to

[16] MILGROM, P. and ROBERTS, P., 1995. Complementarities and fit: strategy, structure, and organizational change in manufacturing. *Journal of Accounting and Economics*, 19, pp. 179-208.

[17] MILGROM, P. and ROBERTS, P., 1990. The economics of modern manufacturing technology, strategy and organization. *American Economic Review*, 80, pp. 511-528.

[18] PETTIGREW, A. M. and FENTON, E. M., 2000. *The Innovating Organization*. London: Sage Publications.

[19] NIXON, B., 1998. Research and development performance measurement: a case study. *Management Accounting Research*, 9(3), pp. 329-355.

[20] KERSSENS-VAN DRONGELEN, I., NIXON, B. and PEARSON, A., 2000. Performance measurement in industrial R&D. *International Journal of Management Reviews*, 2(2), pp. 111-143.

[21] O'DONNELL, F. J. & DUFFY, A. H. B., 2002. Modelling design development performance. *International Journal of Operations and Production Management*, 22(11), pp. 1198-1221.

[22] CRILLY, N., MOULTRIE, J. & CLARKSON, P. J., 2004. Seeing things: response to the visual domain in product design. *Design Studies*, 25(6), pp. 547-577.

[23] MACBRYDE, J. & MENDIBIL, K., 2006. Factors that affect the design and implementation of team-based performance measurement systems. *International Journal of Productivity and Performance Management*, 55(2), pp. 118-142.

ensure a company's success. Yet there is very little academic work, leading to practical understanding and tools, that enable firms to manage design performance as part of the constellation of mutually reinforcing elements that are prerequisites for sustainable corporate performance.[16,17,18]

Whilst design performance does not have a particularly large community of researchers, the UK has been internationally leading in the field. Research into design performance has been tackled from a number of perspectives. For example there has been work on R&D performance,[19,20] product development process,[21] aesthetic design,[22] design team performance[23] and design collaboration.[24,25]

When looking at the literature on design performance, new product development has had the greatest coverage. But even within the new product development literature, there is little consensus on what to measure.[26] Measuring the impact of knowledge management and the measurement of intangibles is also an area with little consensus.[27] Nevertheless, there are numerous widely dispersed and unorganised listings and publications suggesting NPD measures.[20, 26, 28, 29]

It is the view of the researchers within the Design Performance cluster that design is much more than just the product development activity. The problem is, existing research may help companies to manage particular projects, products, teams and activities – but there is relatively little that helps a firm to manage design in its widest context. Cooper and Kleinschmidt[30] also point out that the focus has tended to be on project level investigations, measuring the performance of individual projects or products.

The Design Performance cluster believe that research is needed which will define and synthesise the dimensions of design. Once the dimensions of design are clarified, this should allow for the development of a performance measurement system that supports design management in the 21st century – a Design Scorecard. Such research will help companies to understand how they can use design for competitive advantage in their particular setting. Further it will provide firms with a tool that will help them to integrate design performance measurement in order to achieve consistency and alignment, which we believe is so important to success. Specifically, the cluster believe that further work is needed to address the following gaps in knowledge:

[24] RIEDEL, J., PAWAR, K., CONTE, M. & SANTORO, R., 2005. The ARICON Virtual Enterprise Readiness Assessment Approach for New Product Development (NPD). *In: Proceedings of the International Product Development Management Conference, Copenhagen, 12-14th June 2005.* EIASM, pp. 1403-1415.

[25] ROGERS, H., GHAURI, P. & PAWAR, K. S., 2005. Measuring International NPD projects: an evaluation process. *Journal of Business & Industrial Marketing*, 20(2), pp. 79-87.

[26] GRIFFIN, A. & PAGE, A., 1996. PDMA Success measurement project: recommended measures for product development success and failure. *Journal of Product Innovation Management*, 13, pp. 478-496.

[27] MARR, B., SCHIUMA, G. & NEELY, A. D., 2004. The dynamics of value creation: mapping your intellectual performance drivers. *Journal of Intellectual Capital*, 5(2), pp. 312-322.

[28] LOCH, C., STEIN, L. & TERWIESCH, C., 1996. Measuring development performance in the electronics industry. *Journal of Product Innovation Management*, 13, pp. 3-20.

[29] BEAUMONT, L. R., 1996. Metrics: A Practical Example. In: M.D. ROSENAU JR, A. GRIFFEN, G. A. CASTELLION & N. F. ANSCHUETZ, (eds.) The PDMA *Handbook of New Product Development*. New York: John Wiley & Sons.

[30] COOPER, R. G. & KLEINSCHMIDT, E. J., 1986. An investigation into the new product process: steps, deficiencies, and impact. *Journal of Product Innovation Management*, 3, pp. 71-85.

- Although it is believed that the design may be able to help UK firms create sustainable competitive advantage, what exactly (in terms of activities and processes) companies should be managing is not explicitly understood. A more precise understanding of design activities within their organisational and competitive contexts is needed.
- Obscure links between the 'hard' and 'soft' dimensions of design and organisational processes; the interaction among the economic, ecological, ethical, emotional, technical and behavioural dimensions of design are largely unexplored. Moreover, existing mechanisms and processes do not support the identification, strategic evaluation and exploitation of existing design factors.
- Very little work links the strategy and performance measurement literatures with the design literature – certainly not work that recognises the multifaceted nature of design and the more emergent nature of strategy in knowledge intensive, dynamic environments.[31]
- The Balanced Scorecard[32] and the performance measurement 'industry'[33] has not addressed the complexity and rate of change in design techniques and management processes.

In addressing these gaps, it is hoped that further research will help companies to understand how they can use design for competitive advantage in their particular setting. Indeed a tool that will help firms to integrate design performance measurement in order to achieve consistency and alignment, which we believe is so important to success, is the ultimate goal of the cluster.

Design performance measurement at a national level

Recently, researchers have begun to focus on the value of design to a nation (or region). However, there have been comparatively few studies taking a regional or national perspective. Sentence[34] surveyed 800 British manufacturing companies to establish the relationship between design activity and economic performance; specifically the impact on profitability, growth and exports.[35] In this case, design was defined as 'all activities required to bring a product to market'. The study demonstrated a positive relationship between business performance and the rate of design expenditure.

The UK Design Council annually collects data on the creative and design industries to provide a snapshot of how design is being used.[3] The Danish Design Centre[36] conducted the first empirical analysis to understand the macro-economic effects of design (that is, firms employing professional designers). Both of these studies concluded that design is economically

[31] NIXON, B., 2006. *Strategic Choice and Management Control Systems: A Review of Theories and Challenges for Development. In:* Z. HOQUE, (ed.) *Methodological Issues in Accounting Research: Theories and Methods.* London: Spiramus Publishing.

[32] KAPLAN, R. S. and NORTON, D. P., 1996. *Translating Strategy Into Action - The Balanced Scorecard.* Boston: Harvard Business School Press.

[33] NEELY, A., KENNERLY, M. and WALTERS, A., (eds.), 2004. Performance Measurement and Management: Public and Private. Papars from the *Fourth International Conference on Performance Measurement and Management, PMA 2004, Edinburgh, 28-30ᵗʰ July 2004.* Bedfordshire: Centre for Business Performance, Cranfield School of Management.

[34] SENTENCE, A. & WALTERS, C., 1997. *Design, Competitiveness and UK Manufacturing Performance.* London: Centre for Economic Forecasting, London Business School.

[35] SENTENCE, A. and Clark, 1997. *Contribution of Design to the UK Economy.* London: Design Council.

[36] DENMARK. National Agency for Enterprise and Housing, 2003. *Economic effects of Design.* Danish Design Centre.

[37] WALTON, M. & DUNCAN, I., 2003. Building a Case for Added Value Through Design. Auckland: Industry New Zealand, NZ Institute of Economic Research.

important. However, many of the conclusions are still aimed at the firm rather than national level. In 2003, The New Zealand Institute for Economic Research[37] compared the competitiveness ranking of nations (from the World Economic forum 2002) against a 'design-index' derived from the Global Competitiveness Report (extent of branding, capacity for innovation, uniqueness of product designs, production process sophistication and extent of marketing). They identified an almost linear relationship between this compound design index and national competitiveness. The top 25 competitive nations also scored highest on the design index. However, the results need a health warning, as there is some concern over circularity in results.

Gaps in knowledge and areas for future research – at a national level

The Design Performance cluster believes that despite strong evidence on the importance of design, there is little ongoing data to enable the true position of the UK to be established. The focus on innovation performance and R&D investment has raised the profile and investment in these areas. However, design plays a key role in the effective exploitation of new technology and its impact at a national level is not sufficiently understood. Thus, there is a need for stronger evidence on the national impact of investment in design.

There is a need for further work to effectively understand the value of design for both a firm and also a region or nation. The landmark studies carried out in the UK are now over 10 years old and perceptions of design have changed in that time.

None of the reported works have investigated the role of design in supporting the exploitation of technological innovation or in entrepreneurship. Beyond case-based evidence, there is little reliable data in this area, which is of key importance in the development of new industries.

The perceived gaps in knowledge and thus opportunities for research include:

- It is difficult to establish the success of initiatives targeted at improving national design performance, as there is currently no way of evaluating design in firms.
- Current perceptions on the migration of design activity overseas is also difficult to establish reliably, as there are no existing mechanisms to enable ongoing comparison.

[38] DESIGN COUNCIL, 2005. Design Index: The Impact of Design on Stock Market Performance [online]. Available at: http://www.design-council. org.uk/en/About-Design/ Research/Design-Index/

[39] SAJEVA, M., GATELLI, D., TARANTOLA, S. & HOLLANDERS, H., 2005. *Methodology Report on European Innovation Scoreboard 2005, European Trend Chart on Innovation*. EU Commission.

- Whilst there is much evidence supporting the importance of design, this is only available in small snap shots. A more comprehensive approach to understanding design activity at a national level is needed.
- By collecting data at a national level, it should be possible to make stronger connections between design and performance at an individual firm or sector level.

In addition to empirical studies of the benefits of design, there have been other attempts to investigate the importance of design, R&D and innovation on company and national performance. An investigation by the Design Council[38] found that a 'Design Index' of companies which had been recognised in awards for their achievements in design, were more financially successful than their rivals. The study revealed that the share price of these 'design aware' companies grew at a much higher rate than the FTSE 100 group of firms. However, although the results look conclusive, there are methodological uncertainties in the selection and sector of the companies in each group.

In a similar way, it is possible to draw some conclusions on national innovation performance from the R&D scoreboard, which demonstrates a positive link between R&D investment and company share price. Both of these studies are cited by the Design Council's[3] 'Design in Britain' report as evidence that design improves business performance. The links between these and reasons behind the phenomena have not, however, been explored in any great detail. The R&D scoreboard typically uses the 'Frascati' definitions of design, innovation and R&D. The Frascati Manual is a publication of the Organisation for Economic Co-Operation and Development (OECD) which provides the international standard practice for compiling and analysing research and development statistics and provide guidelines for the measurement and interpretation of data on innovation activities in industry. Thus the R&D tax credits and scoreboard focus explicitly on investment which seeks to increase the stock of knowledge to devise new products and processes. Use of design consultancies and design itself is generally viewed as falling outside of this definition. Further detail on innovation expenditure can be found in the EU 'Community Innovation Survey', which provides measures of 'innovation related expenditure, rates of innovation and factors which have encouraged or hindered innovation'. This is an EU wide survey, following a standard methodology, to enable comparison between nations. Again however, explicit measures of design performance are not included.[39] Measurement of performance in R&D has become

⁴⁰ GRUPP, H. and MOGEE, M.
E., 2004. Indicators for National
Science and Technology Policy:
How Robust are Composite
Indicators? Research Policy, 33,
pp. 1373-1384.

increasingly popular over the last 5 years.[20] Grupp & Mogee[40] provide a comprehensive analysis of such science and technology indicators and suggest that the use of 'scoreboards' leaves room for manipulation in the policy system.

The 'value added' scoreboard may also provide insight into design performance. This scoreboard provides a key benchmarking tool for companies to compare their 'wealth creating' characteristics against their EU competitors. This scoreboard enables a comparison of the top 800 UK firms and 600 EU firms. Measures of value added are extracted from company reports.[2]

Other potential sources of information can be gained from international design awards. There are over 25 such awards, with around six internationally recognised awards. Data from awards such as IF and Red Dot in Germany, IDEA in the USA and G-Mark in Japan might inform an analysis of region, investment and success in design. Indeed, in the most recent Red Dot awards, it was noted that entries by Asian firms have quadrupled over the last 2 years and 98 Asian designs received 'distinctions' this year compared with 33 in 2004.

A further insight into national design performance might come from an analysis of major brands in each region. Currently, Business Week in association with Interbrand publishes an annual review of the global 'top 100' brands.

Collectively, these sources highlight the potential value of a 'scoreboard' for design and also indicate the clear gap in current measurement systems to address this opportunity. The Design Performance cluster are advocating further research with the aim of developing a performance measurement system that enables a more complete understanding of design's contribution to the national economy. Specifically, the researchers wish to conduct further research to allow the development of a 'Design Scoreboard', based around a model of national design performance. Thus, the key questions to be addressed include:

• What are the elements of a model of national design performance?
• Using this model, what type of data is available to present a complete picture of design performance at a national level?
• How could these measures of design performance be instrumented to enable viable ongoing collection, analysis and communication of design performance at a national level.

Discussion on the Success of the Design Performance Cluster

The Designing for the 21st Century Initiative has provided this group of researchers with an invaluable opportunity. One of the most important outcomes, for the Design Performance cluster members, is the fact that we have gathered together a strong and enthusiastic multidisciplinary team with a shared research vision. The team is truly multidisciplinary, MacBryde, Martinez and Evans are best known for their work in performance measurement, whilst Moultrie and Demian come from a design and design management background. Pawar and Riedel principally work in the area of design management; Nixon is a chartered accountant with academic and industrial experience and a track record in financial management of new product design and development. Duffy is perhaps best known for his work in the area of computer aided engineering design, design optimisation and process optimisation. Livesey has a background that links the economic context of manufacturing with policy decisions.

The Designing in the 21st Century Initiative provided us with the opportunity to bring together researchers who, under normal circumstances, would be unlikely to have met, let alone form such a strong coalition. Having worked together on the Design Performance cluster during 2005 this team are confident that together they form a very strong group, capable of internationally leading research in the area of design performance.

The group has now developed a good working relationship, and has developed a long-term vision for collaboration. This vision includes the following aims:

- To improve the competitive position of the UK at a national and firm level through better application and utilisation of design.
- To develop a robust approach to understanding the comparative design performance of firms (cf. balanced scorecard for design).
- To develop a generic performance measurement approach for use in firms, networks and extended enterprises that will highlight the strategic and operational significance of the design activity and enable improvement in their competitive position through design.
- To develop a detailed understanding of the competitive position of the UK in comparison to other nations in terms of design performance. To develop indicators of design performance in relation to design clusters

and regional distribution as well as at a national level. To monitor the trends and developments in design activity at a firm and regional/national level (cf. the R&D scoreboard) to inform government policy and firm strategy.

• To develop a pioneering position for understanding design in knowledge intensive sectors that will have implications for international competitiveness.

Cluster members would be happy to hear from like-minded researchers who might be interested in collaboration.

Additional Reading

DESIGN COUNCIL, 2005. *Design in Britain*. The Good News Press Ltd.

EUROPEAN COMMISSION, 2004. *Monitoring Industrial Research: The 2004 Industrial R&D Investment Scoreboard.*

GRIFFIN, A., PAGE, A., 1996. PDMA Success measurement project: recommended measures for product development success and failure. *Journal of Product Innovation Management*, 13, pp. 478-496.

NIXON, W., 1998. Research and development performance measurement: A case study. *Management Accounting Research*, 9(3), pp. 329-355.

OECD, 1994. *The measurement of scientific and technical activities: standard practice for surveys of research and experimental development – Frascati Manual*. OECD Publishing.

O'DONNELL, F. J. & DUFFY, A. H. B., 2002. Modelling design development performance. *International Journal of Operations and Production Management*, 22(11), pp. 1198-1221.

Index